ABSTRACTION UNBOUND

SUE DAVIS

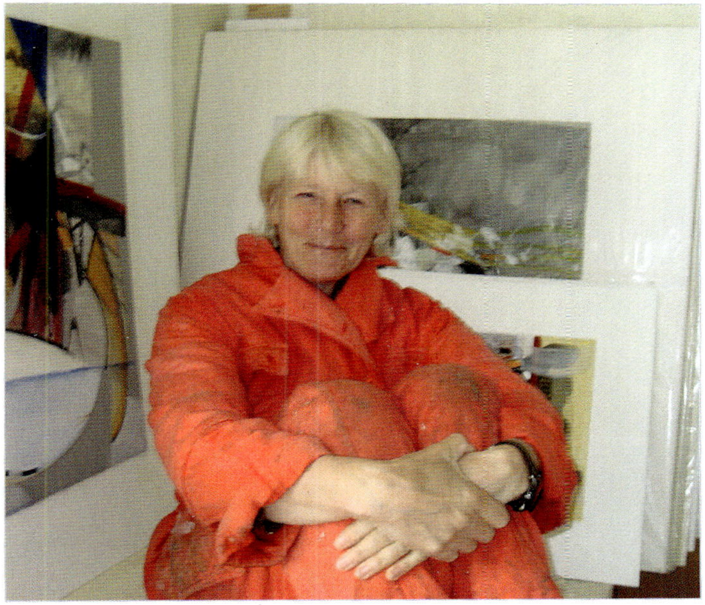

Abstraction Unbound

First Edition published 2015

Front Cover: *Drumroll* (detail)

ISBN 978-0-948385-77-3

Printed & Published by:
The St Ives Printing & Publishing Company, High Street,
St Ives, Cornwall TR26 1RS UK

www.stivesnews.co.uk

FOREWORD – PETER DAVIES

This book is a glorified expliqué, a mega statement, by an accomplished abstract painter. It poses as many questions as it answers and leaves the reader a potential wealth of speculative or interpretive responses. This is apt because good art is invariably open-ended and as spectators of her never-less-than mysterious pictures we are required to use our imaginations to 'finish' the work in hand.

Since she moved from Hertfordshire to Cornwall in 2000, Sue Davis finds herself, however unwittingly, allied to a 'tradition' of west country modernist painting centred on St Ives. Her cultured background ensures, however, that she has introduced something entirely her own to the contemporary Cornish scene. Like her father, a 'tachist' painter of kind, Davis has had to teach. This has imparted an articulate zeal adding definition and educational elucidation to her work. Her passages here are eminently quotable and steer a sensible course between the high brow and the common sense. We are told how observational drawing, that ABC of visual art, is "the difference between a flash on google and reading a book". We are also introduced to a self-declared "intuitive, childhood approach" in her artistic quest for authenticity, significance and permanence. Inherent here is what the New York School painter and polemicist Robert Motherwell termed abstract expressionism's winning combinations of psychic and plastic automatism, and to the extent that open-ended and unfettered process is central to that Davis gives good account of the materials, processes, colour and visual sources that inspire the art.

Aspects of the artist's biography help unravel the mysteries of her style, particularly that to do with her origins as a painter. A 40-year friendship with a German Expressionist sculptor Hedy Hoffman opened her eyes to the grand possibilities of modern art. The emigre studied at the Slade during the 1930s where she befriended the future Cornish-based neo-romantic-turned tachist painter Bryan Wynter. Though Davis never met Wynter she became attracted to his free association randomness and crypto surreal stream-of-conciousness strategies. The Zennor-based

Wynter established a legendary status and became a later almost obligatory source of inspiration for younger artists like Davis. Another harbinger of Davis' future development was her specialisation on ceramics at first St Albans School of Art then at Central School, London where the pursuit of academic drawing was nicely complemented by the challenging ceramic practise of tutor Gordon Baldwin who, as Davis says, "pushed the boundaries." During many post-student years Davis both taught in schools and ran a ceramic and mural business. The millennial move to Cornwall, however, signalled an intention to at last pursue 'purer' fine art expressions.

Making a living fostered an intimate awareness of commercial and vocational compromises to artistic creativity. She has again neatly explained how "the triumph of commercial rationalisation leads to the need to rehabilitate the soul of the modern world." The challenge of the corrosive high tech media age has thrown down the gauntlet of gratuitous glint. The answer is to go within, be oneself and remain true to the essence of the plastic arts. For this she has entertained interdisciplinary osmosis. Complex ceramic process has encouraged Zen-like chance or accident in terms of chromatic or textural randomness. The firing processes of the kiln have had real implications for abstract painting which has appropriated such effects as fumage or 'raku' distortion. In this vein she speaks of a liberational "release from formality into intuition".

Teaching has also been a cathartic experience where ideas and issues, be they psychological or plastic, are externalised in a therapeutic way leading in turn to further possibility. The common assault of dumbing down, celeb culture, a dismantling of state fine art educations and a YBA-led iconoclasm are sidestepped by Davis. In its place she posits her hopeful notion of 'Abstraction Unbound'; a clarion call for the ongoing and open-ended exploration of plastic expression in the face of an infinite void. American abstract expressionism and Parisian Orphism are her foremost role models. Also relevant to 'Abstraction Unbound' is Kandinsky's notion of 'inner necessity' with its sense of the spiritual in art. While the visual flux of her paintings "does not hold any recognisable images" from the concrete observed world the undeniable effect is of a magical and perpetual state of becoming, like life itself, within the four-sided boundaries of the pictorial object.

ABSTRACTION UNBOUND

'Abstraction Unbound' is an invented term that separates my approach to abstraction from that employed by others, and best expresses the activity I am engaged in. As an experimental artist I choose not to use any reference to a known scene or any tricks or hidden meanings for people to discover. This doesn't mean the images are shallow and thoughtless, more that they seek to mine the deeper recesses of self and make unconscious statements about the inexpressible. The quality of it is the freedom of thought that it offers to both the artist and the viewer.

INTRODUCTION

In this writing I do not wish to imply that other forms of art, which use recognisable images dealing with myth, politics or scientific ideas, are less valuable than mine. There are many strong and worthy artists tackling their ideas in other ways. My thoughts about the value of it and my commitment to it have been formed over a long period of working in many different ways including figuratively, objectively and with fantasy.

Pure abstraction has been around for at least a century but still it is considered by many to

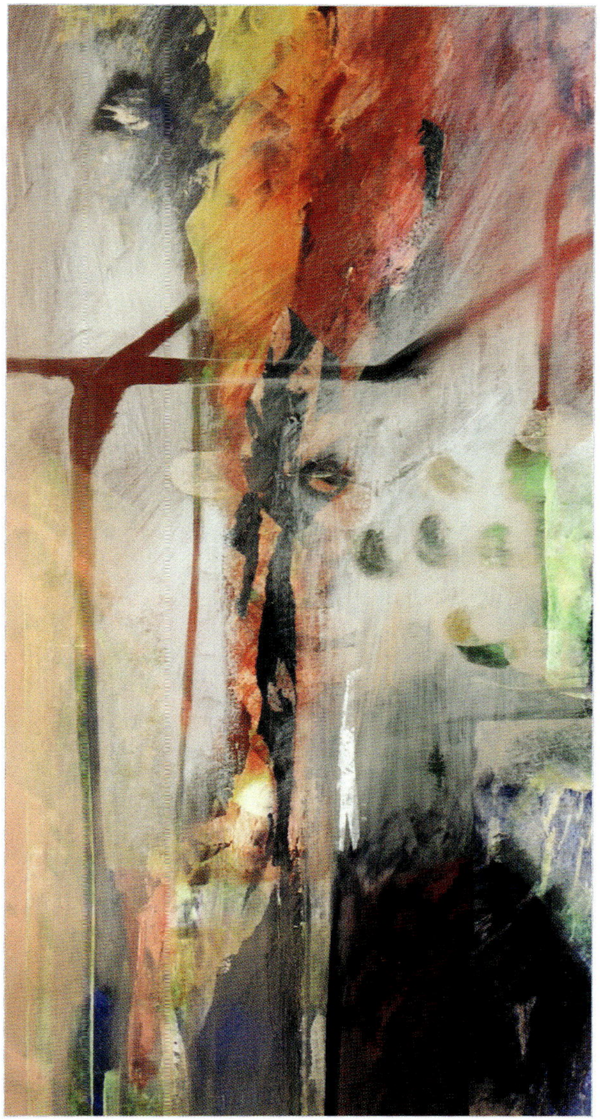

blush creek *acrylic on paper* *70 x 35cm*

be new and difficult to fathom. It sometimes appears intellectual and out of reach, but at other times it can look so simple that it can be perceived as an 'easy option'. This book, then, is mainly a showcase for my work, and the various avenues explored so far, but also an attempt to explain that there is a depth of thought involved in creating my work. Because through my life I have concentrated on visual aspects, rather than allowing more time for development in writing and the attainment of knowledge that would be required for a wider view, this account is a personal view. Although many books and philosophies have been dipped into they have not always remained in the forefront of my mind, and my opinions have changed and varied at different times.

This is not intended to imply that my approach to abstraction is the only way. It is merely a telling of the journey towards a single outcome, hoping to give the reader insight into my process and the decisions made. With luck, showing my work and sharing the journey towards that outcome will lead the reader to a position whereby the mind can be released, so that looking at a piece of art will be a pure unadulterated relationship between the viewer and the picture.

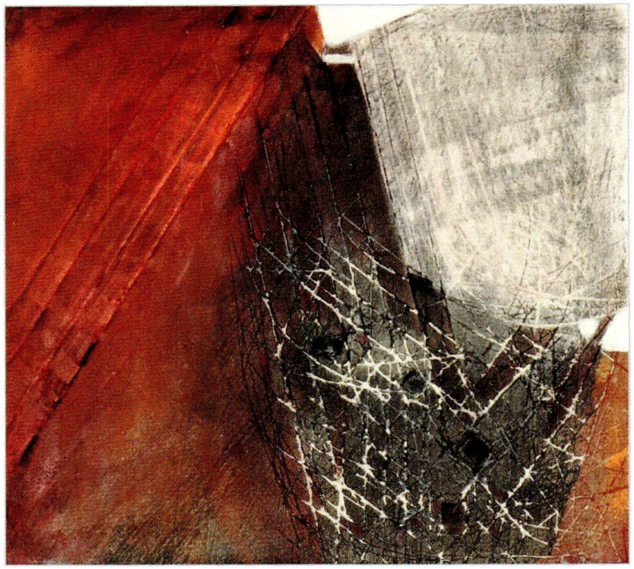

madder char
acrylic on plaster
25 x 25cm

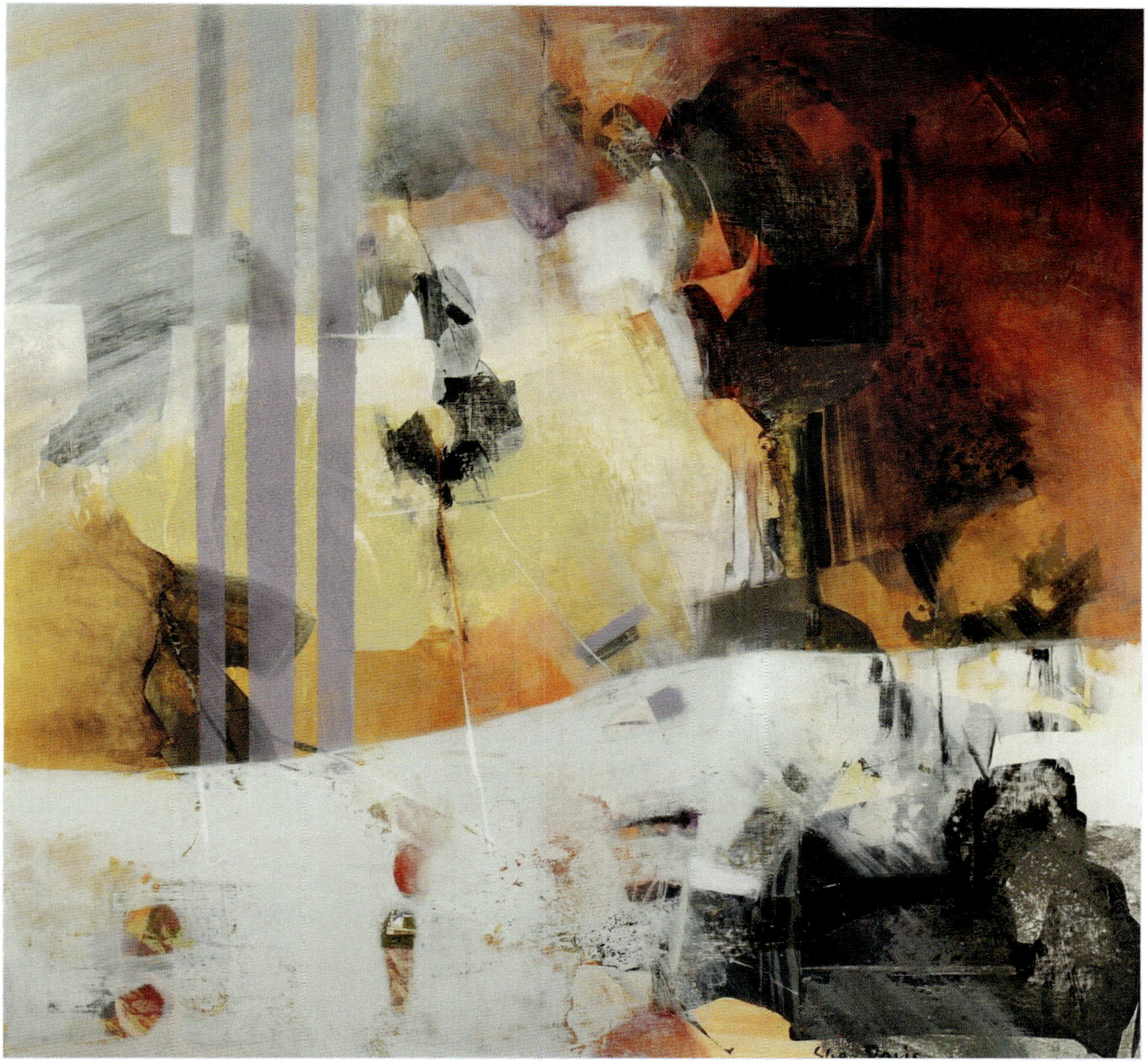

ochre stride *mixed media on board* *94 x 94cm*

EARLY EXPERIENCES

From the moment the birth film lifts from our eyes and after we have found essential succour to sustain our bodies the choices are ours, and these decisions form our lives. Which sense to follow? Are we able to follow many senses or just one? For the visual artist it is often observation that is the preferred choice. Watching is one way to learn, and the way people move shows us as much about what they are saying as the words themselves and how they are said. Observing the growth and decline of our surroundings and the movement of wind and water reveals information about our environment.

The tool often used to aid this visual awareness is observational drawing. It helps us take in a lot more information that we may miss on a quick glance. It is the difference between a flash on google and reading a book. Whilst the academic approach is extremely important as an aid to observation and thinking there is however another point of view – the intuitive childlike approach, which can bring freshness, freedom and spiritual insight. That is not to say that insight does not occur in academic drawing but there can be a stagnation in over-emphasising technique and accuracy. The former emphasises the importance of acquiring and absorbing information whilst concentrating intently, and the other opens up a fearless experimental approach, often found in children. It is the freedom of children's minds before they have learnt the rules of society that often captures a simple essence of some thing or thought. Whichever way is chosen there are always decisions followed by more questions. How much risk to take? How much will to impose?

Thankfully this rich debate about drawing and the meaning of art will go on forever and is sustained by our own encounters and experiences.

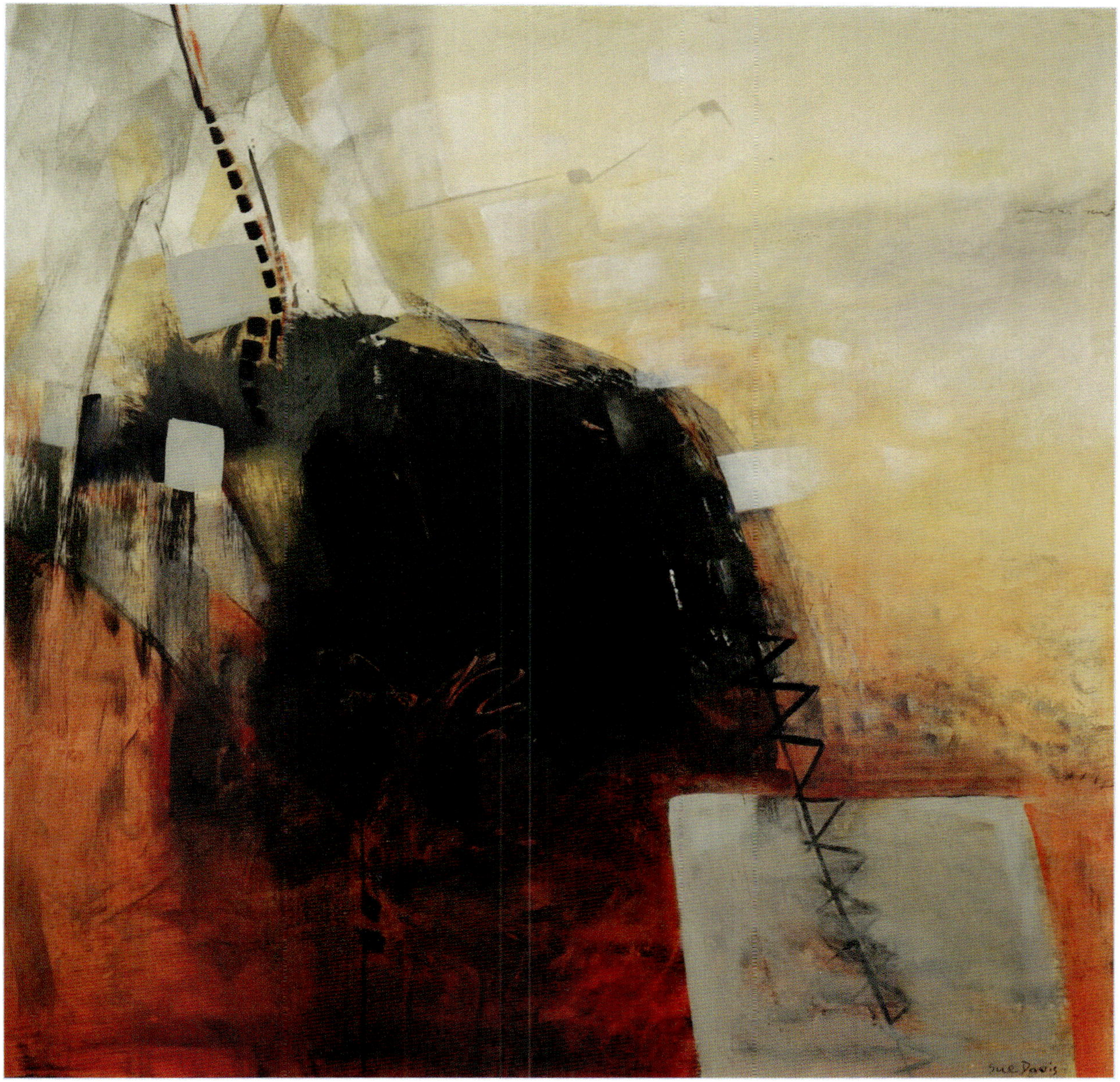

how can that be *mixed media on board* *100 x 100cm*

ENCOUNTERS

One important encounter which influenced my thinking was my forty year friendship with Hedy Hoffman, a fine draughtswoman who grew up amongst the intelligentsia in Dresden where her father Eugen Hoffman, a German Expressionist sculptor, taught at the Hochschule fur Bildende Kunste. His work appeared in Hitler's notorious Degenerate Art exhibition. Hedy was helped out of Germany by Oskar Kokoschka, a friend of her father. She arrived in England on her own at the age of sixteen and eventually attended the Slade where she met Bryan Wynter, who remained her friend and correspondent for many years until his death. To speak with her about her upbringing and experiences was enlightening and stimulating and opened up many fields of interest for me. Together Hedy and I visited exhibitions and I was shown the work of artists such as Kurt Schwitters and Odilon Redon that I might not otherwise have discovered without her friendship. She believed strongly that drawing was the most important aspect of creating and her admiration for the skills of artists such as Lucian Freud invoked many verbal skirmishes between us.

In contrast to the formality of this academic approach, my father, who had in his youth been a member of the Camden Society of Arts and enjoyed the pictures of Graham Sutherland, Mark Tobey, Paul Klee and Kandinsky, was keen on a less structured approach. After much experimentation he finally arrived at Tachiste painting, a wet-in-wet technique that allows the colours to flow and be guided, as he believed this gave him access to the spiritual or the subconscious without the constraints of subject. His desire was to paint for a living but, having a family to support, he became a teacher and eventually a headmaster. With his passion for the arts and his belief that he should nurture imagination he produced many creative activities with the children in his care. Throughout our childhood we were always making things, attending myriad musical and theatrical events, like the Black Theatre of Prague, the mime artist Marcel Marceau and many visits to Sadlers Wells, exhibitions and churches. We had many frenetic discussions about drawing and where genuine art stems from, which have probably led to my current point of view. I now feel it is possible to

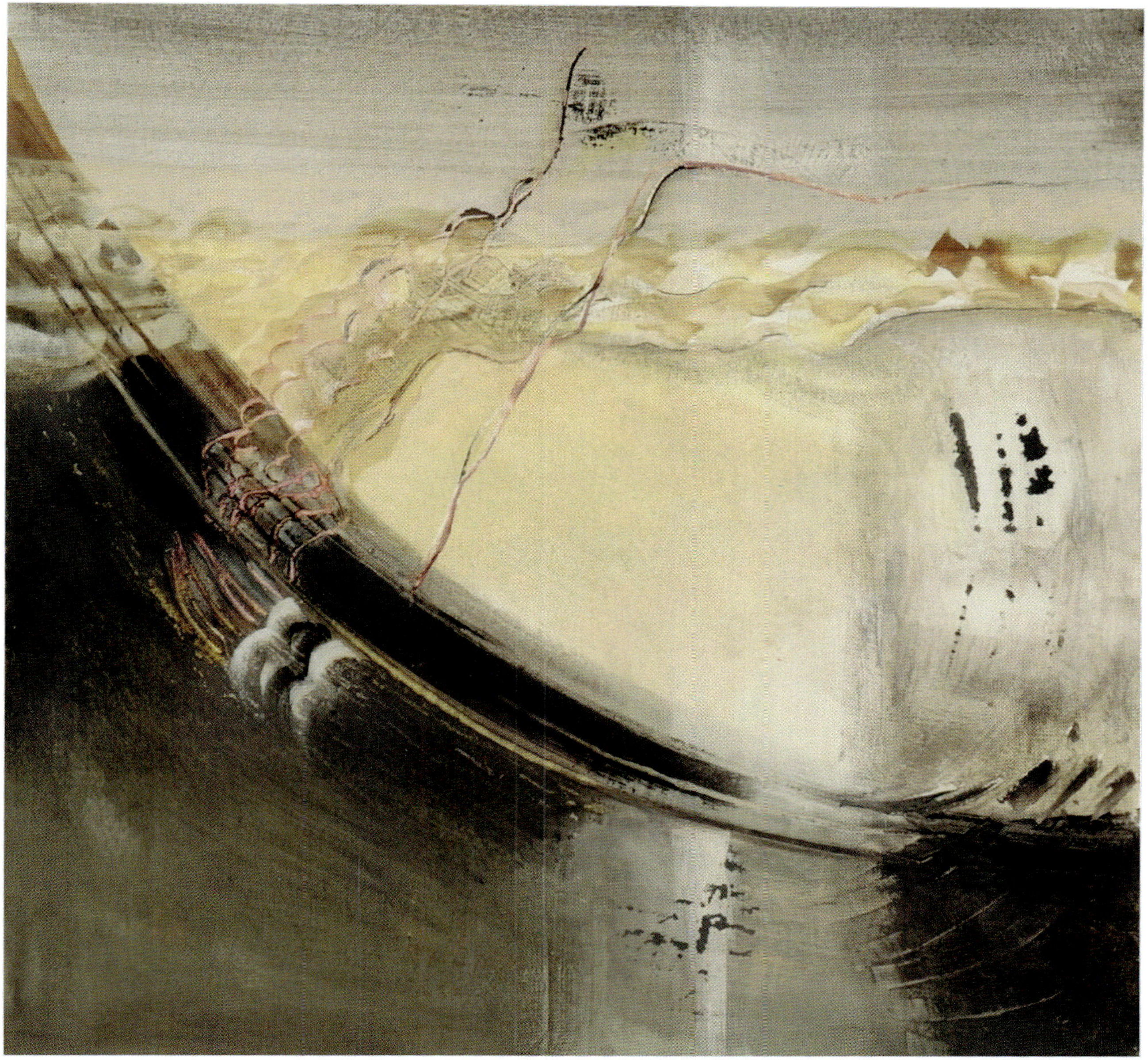

scarp wave *mixed media on plaster* *52 x 52cm*

embrace both the academic and intuitive approach. My argument, after many hours invested, is that one should first be able to draw academically, in order to be free to put it aside. With my two kinds of experience in mark making, both with observational drawing and freely expressed marks that are not attached to objects, I can use one approach to sustain the other.

I had taken my GCEs at Hitchin College of Further Education, where Quentin Crisp had been one of the life models. He was also a model at St Albans School of Art, where I completed my foundation year. Having the opportunity to try various disciplines there I settled for ceramics, partially because my father was concerned about the ability to make a living from fine art.

Attending the Central School of Art in Southampton Row, London was a rich experience that confirmed the work ethic I had been brought up with. We were expected to be active five days a week and at least three nights until 8.30 in the evening and in addition to produce, in our spare time, four drawings a month for a scathing crit, plus all the usual essays. I loved the manipulation of clay but found the lack of colour worrying - colour can be achieved by chemical wizardry and industrial techniques but, it has to be admitted, brown has a very large place in ceramics! The deferred gratification and potential for mishaps until the final firing were rather sad - I'm obviously a restless, impatient person.

Central's emphasis on academic drawing, which I continued for many years, sustained me through the various moves I have made. The different approaches to the vast amount of practical skills to acquire were challenging and, coupled with a variety of philosophical approaches, totally absorbing. Each lecturer had his unique emphasis. Dan Arbied used to talk about magic dust making his pots special whilst HG (Harding Green), our leader, was passionate about Italy and its art: Mick Casson, a consummate craftsman, was talented, earthy and promoted a highly skilled craft tradition, while Gordon Baldwin pushed the boundaries both technically and creatively. The ever-present ideals of Bernard Leach and Shoji Hamada, who attended our degree show, rubbed uncomfortably against the demands of industrial processes.

As it turned out, I was able to earn my living with this education in various ways. As many artists do, I spent time teaching in secondary and tertiary education, latterly as Head of Art

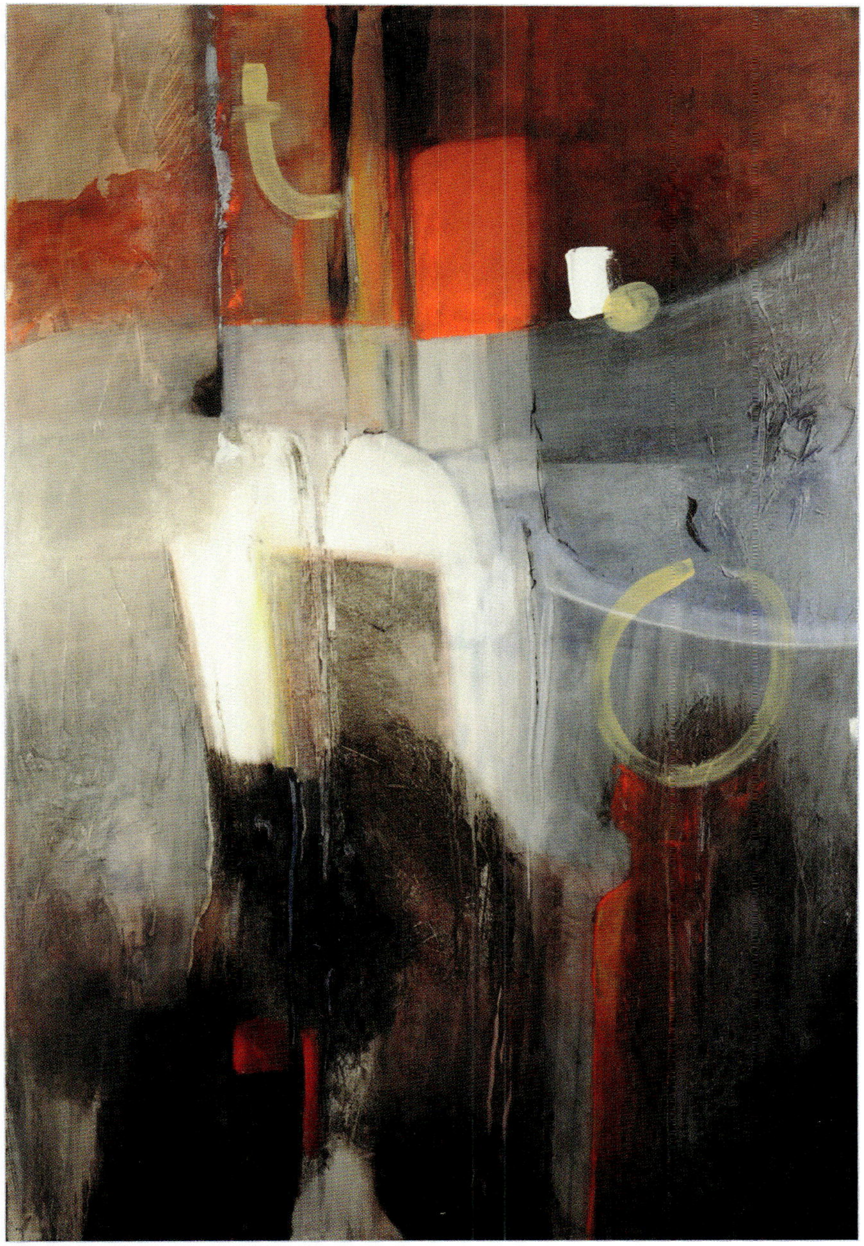

to be or not
acrylic on board
150 x 100cm

in a Harrow school which eventually I left to visit and stay in the USA for a few months. To supplement my wages and keep my hand in whilst teaching I also ran a co-operative pottery, and on my return to England I started a ceramic and mural painting business which combined drawing with ceramics. This left me time for personal exploration, and the strong division between the art work that earned my living and my individual work was an important part of my development. Before this separation the need for an income forced me to make compromises. The division of these activities allowed me to concentrate on the clients' wishes, whilst at the same time I was able to explore freely other avenues. This personal work I exhibited through mixed and solo shows in London, Hertfordshire, Cambridgeshire and Tokyo. I completed over 1300 commissions with this business which kept me for fifteen years until I sold it to move to Cornwall in 2000, since when, thankfully, I have been able to concentrate on my own artistic development.

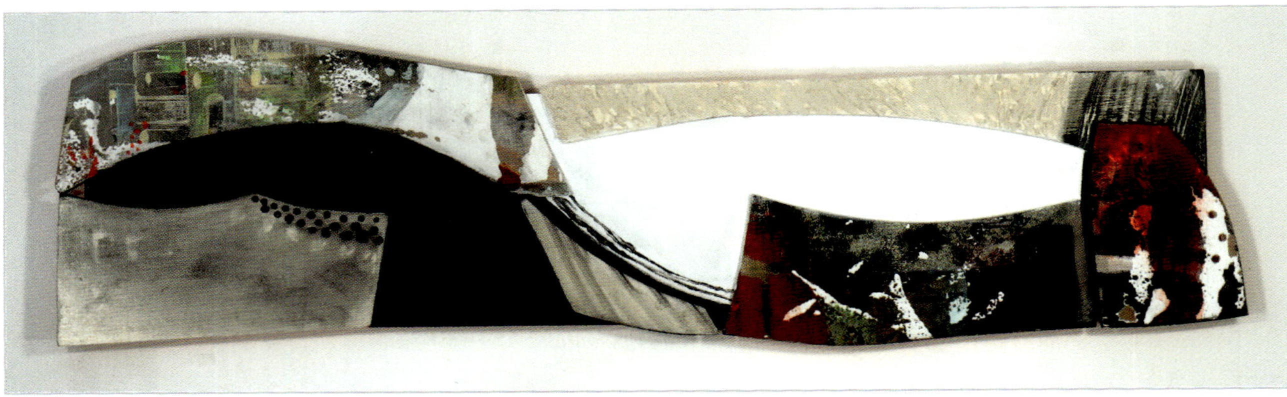

Slice *mixed media construction* *100 x 28cm*

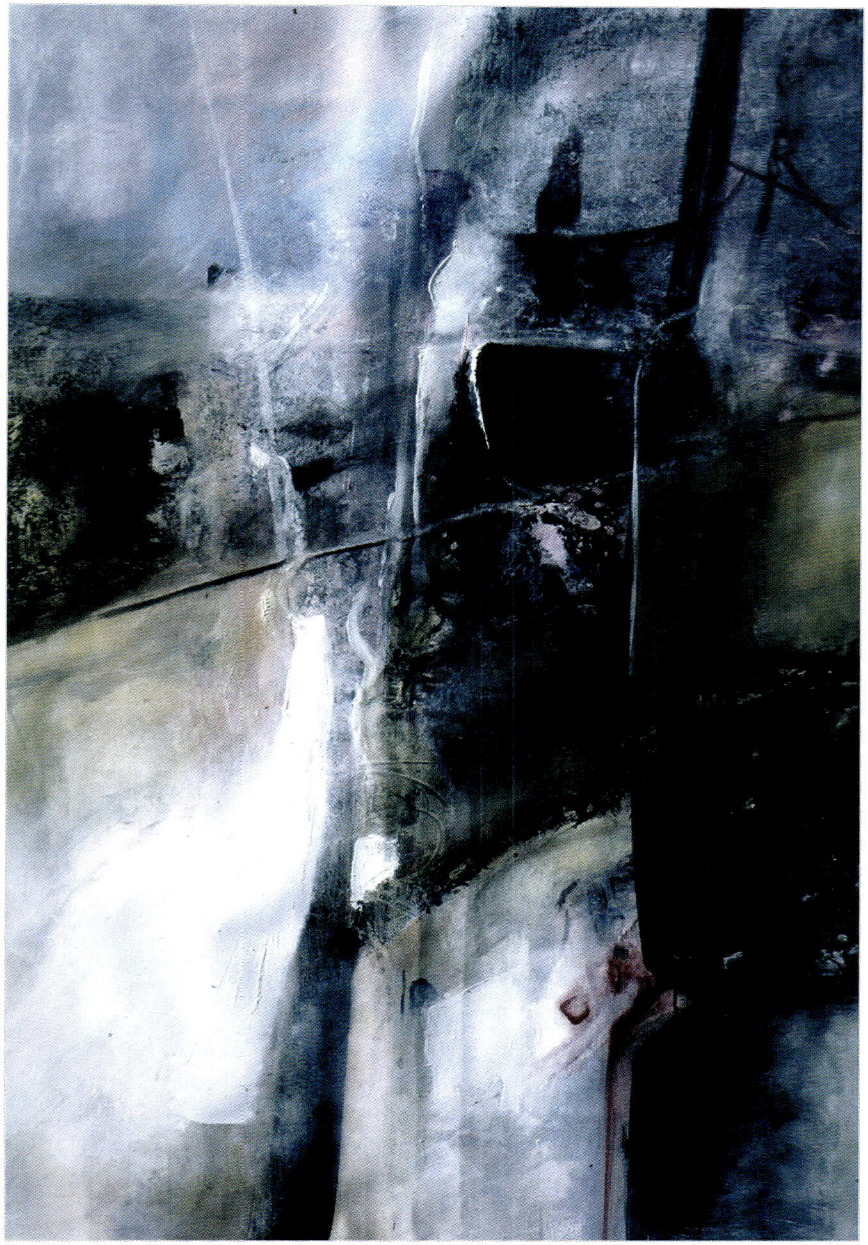

graphite tracks
acrylic on paper
97 x 68cm

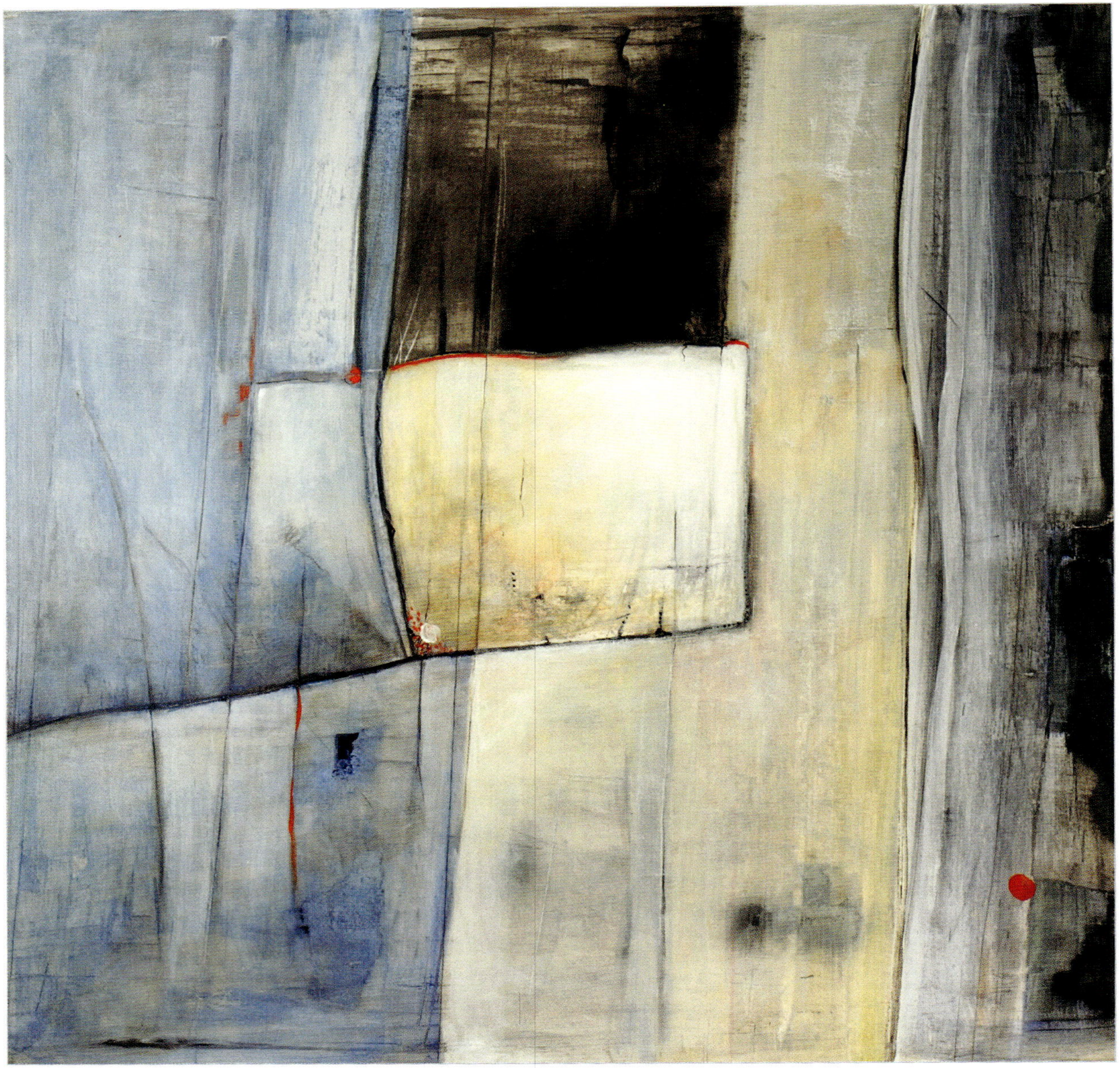

fragile face *mixed media on plaster* *60 x 60cm*

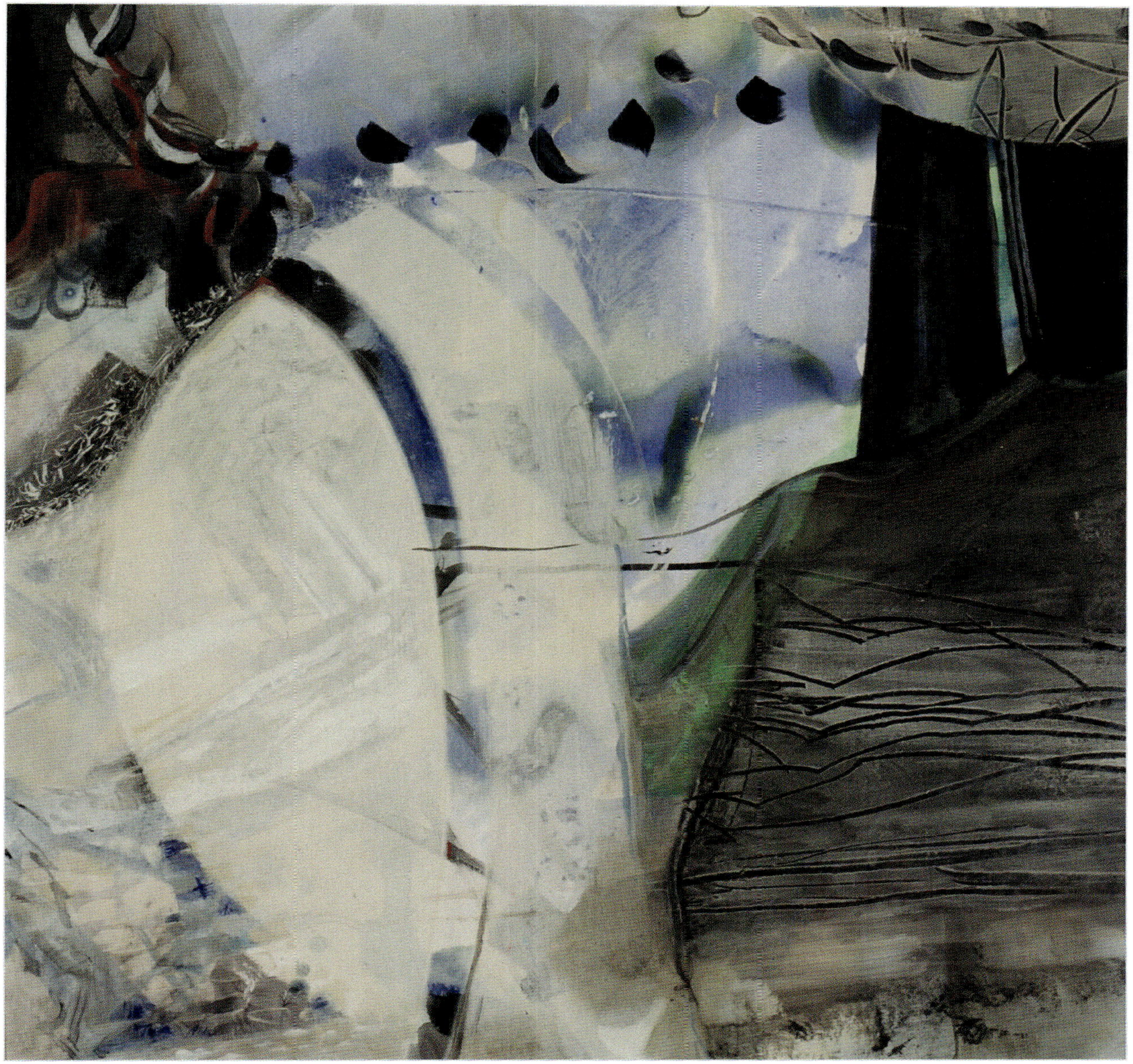

blutch *mixed media on paper* *83 x 83cm*

REASONS WHY ARTISTS WORK

The initial training for artists is at least four years. This training usually continues throughout an artist's life as they are always looking for fresh ways to express themselves and are keen on gaining new skills. However it appears that many people see little value in the arts as it is not clear that it has any economic place. The desire to create art in the first place entails an awareness that there is something else to being human other than making money. I have only to think of the cave painters who felt the need to produce art images even though it may have had little practical function.

Today art has been pushed into the realms of luxury and it is no longer thought of as an essential tool for society. In the light of this perceived redundancy there must be a personal drive and passion involved within artists to give them the strength to continue. It is not necessarily a turbulent passion – more a quiet determination that what they are doing is of value to them and the wider society. Today every minute detail of life is examined and documented, validated and linked to finance, consequently it seems utter madness to pursue art. Yet it is this 'useless' quality that gives us another dimension. We all have a place that we know exists but find hard to identify, but we know it is very important. Call it 'soul' – but disengage the word from the heavy load it carries. For practising artists it is unquestionable that they are engaged in something valuable which must be pursued. It is those that are tenacious, no matter what field they are working in, that bring something extra to the world. Nelson Mandela expressed the same passion for life when he said "There is no passion to be found playing small – in settling for a life that is less than the one you are capable of living".

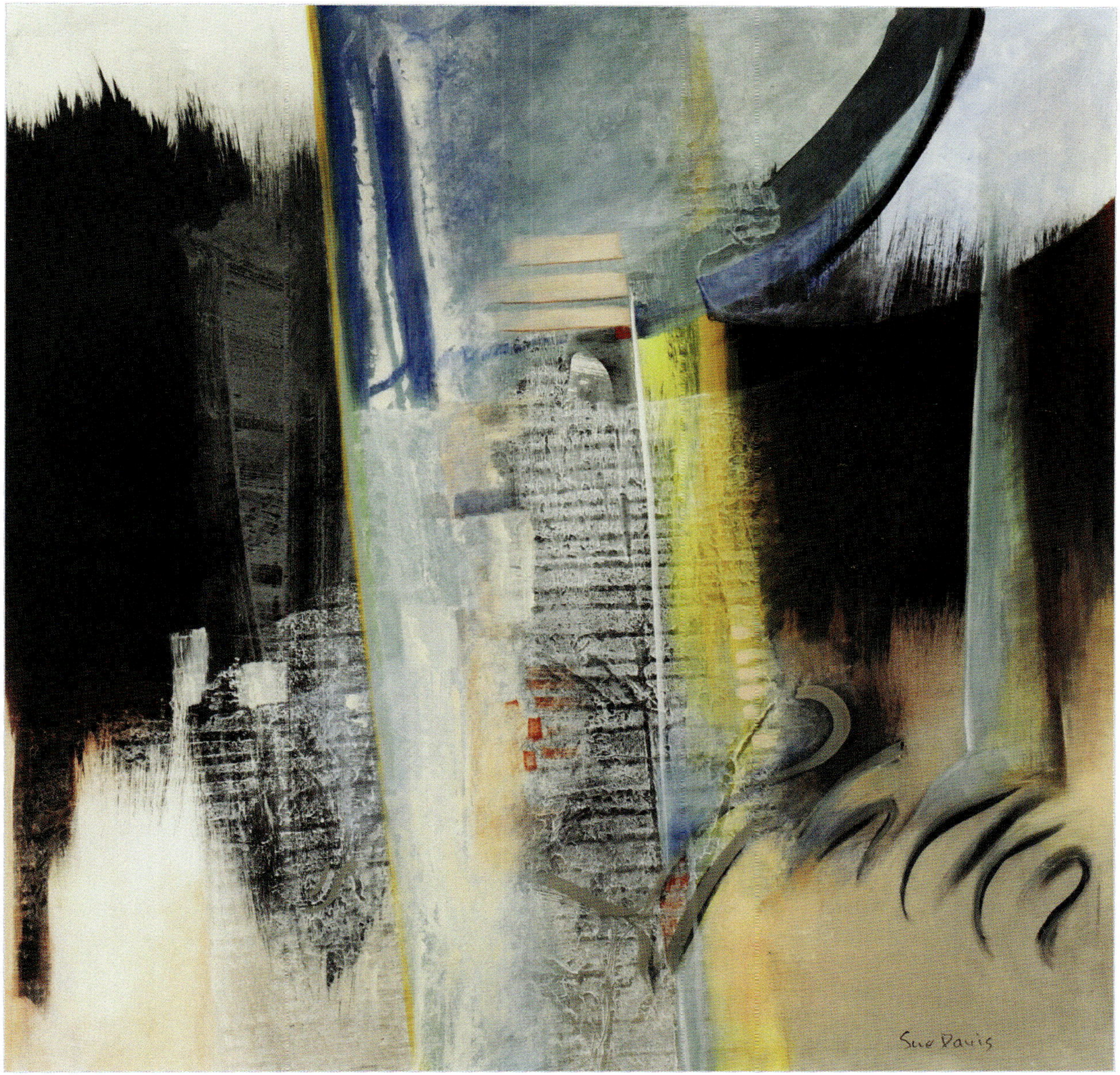

candle *acrylic on board* *106 x 106cm*

SOCIETY AND ART

It is often expressed that art should be relevant to society. Now that it has escaped from religion always reminding us of our duties, and the fact that these days we have a mass of images telling us what to think (albeit connected to product), it is not surprising that artists have turned to shock and grunge. The 'Young British Artists' come to mind. Most people will know of the dirty bed of Tracy Emin and the blood head of Marc Quinn. Many artists have successfully followed that path but my attempts were poor, and tended to ape the obvious repetition of horror shown in the media. The fashion for grunge and the use of degrading images holds facile solutions, but how important is it to remind us of the slummy aspects of life? Should art not try to lift us away from the mundane, raise our thoughts above the commonplace, like the leap of a fish, especially as the media are doing a fine job of lowering them? My choice is joy and the celebration of colour, life and curiosity – hopefully not to be confused with sentimentality which is so much used at Christmas to open our purses. The arts can be a valuable platform for the expression of raw life, a vehicle to help rebalance life – but sometimes there is just too much reality. This part of a poem written by my friend Carol Parnell illustrates why I pulled away from that approach:

My friend the artist
is painting masked faces,
and the imprisoned souls
stare out in fixed horror
through acrylic eyes.
No motion no breath
touches their death-in-life.
That which must be changeable
is now immutable.

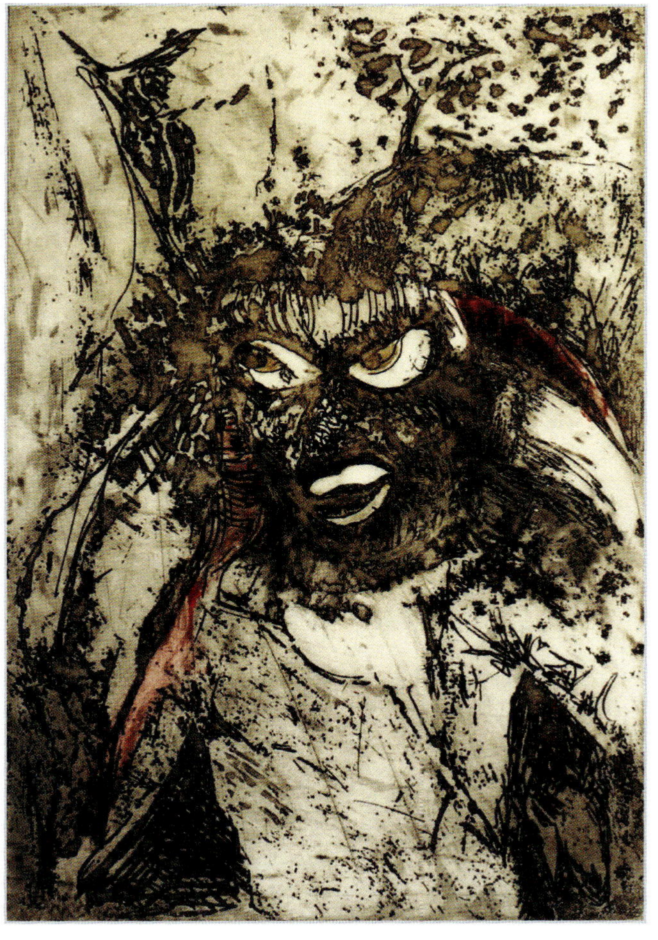

hunter

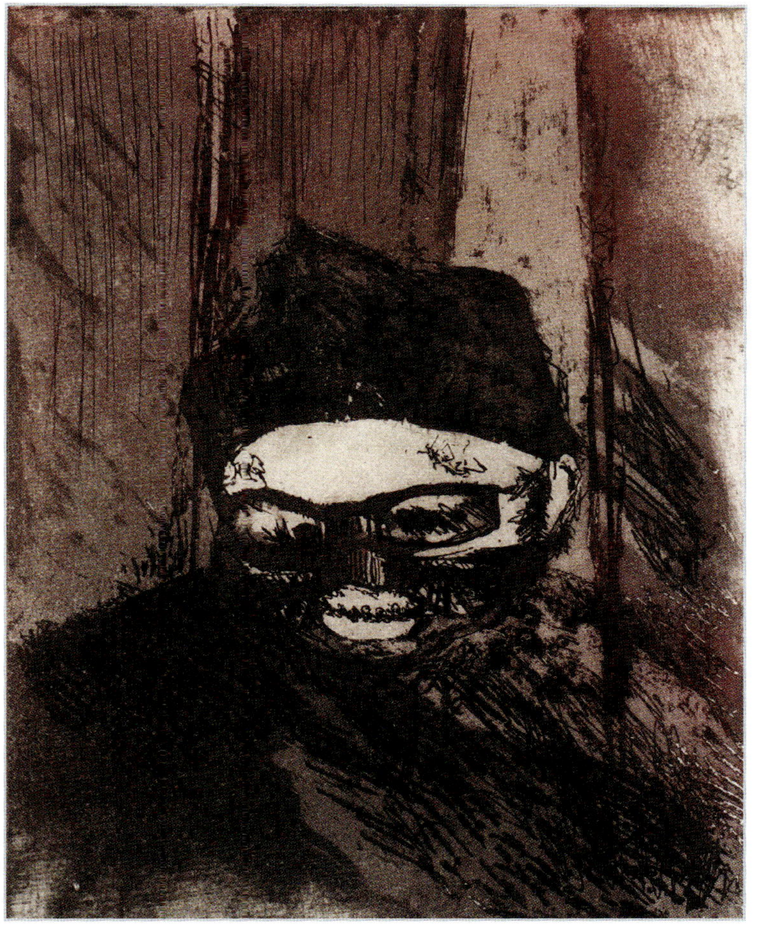

IRA

Etchings

In choosing beauty I feel it is very important not to wander into sentimentality which is so often unwittingly indulged in, producing easy-feeling images on the cheap. This comfort of clichés leads to fake emotion which allows the artist and audience to fantasise about themselves and their feelings. Abstraction for me is a way to acquire beauty with form, with enchantment of the unknown without sentimentality, hopefully making me look more at the world than at myself.

It would be desirable for art to be carried out communally, as in the process of rug making where the whole family or village would have each had their role – sheep farming, dying wool, designing and making as a joint effort. Today artists function mainly as individuals and, because of automation, it is hard to see where communal creation has a place. In some ways artists are bridging that gap when they exhibit and share.

The process of making is a way of understanding and communicating with oneself and others, but with abstraction it is hard to understand how it communicates with others. It does require a certain openness of attitude, nicely expressed by Gertrude Stein (the American writer and brave collector of modern art who moved to Paris in 1903): "It looks strange and it looks strange and it looks very strange; and then suddenly it doesn't look strange at all and you can't understand what made it look strange in the first place." To me this implies she has given the art time, as we do with music. We are prepared to listen to music for a length of time, and repeatedly. Not everything will connect with all people but, as with music, it may speak to someone and address (or allow them to escape) the day to day problems, polemic structures and philosophies they are juggling with.

In this very packaged, sorted, rule-bound world with so much modern technology and graphic reproduction, images are no longer rare. Artists have to take care that they maintain their individual stance as well as communicating with society, as it is only then that they can bring new thoughts to share. There is a danger that the repetition of success becomes a habit. Artists who avoid regurgitating what has gone before, and are aware of the danger of making 'product', give a fresh point of view to the world using free association, that in turn frees imagination.

An imaginative mind takes in many ideas, juggles and sorts them and then applies reason to help make personal decisions. The nurture of imagination is important as it broadens one's horizons and aids the understanding of other people and cultures. In some ways it could help dispel the fear that makes people intolerant. When one arrives at personal

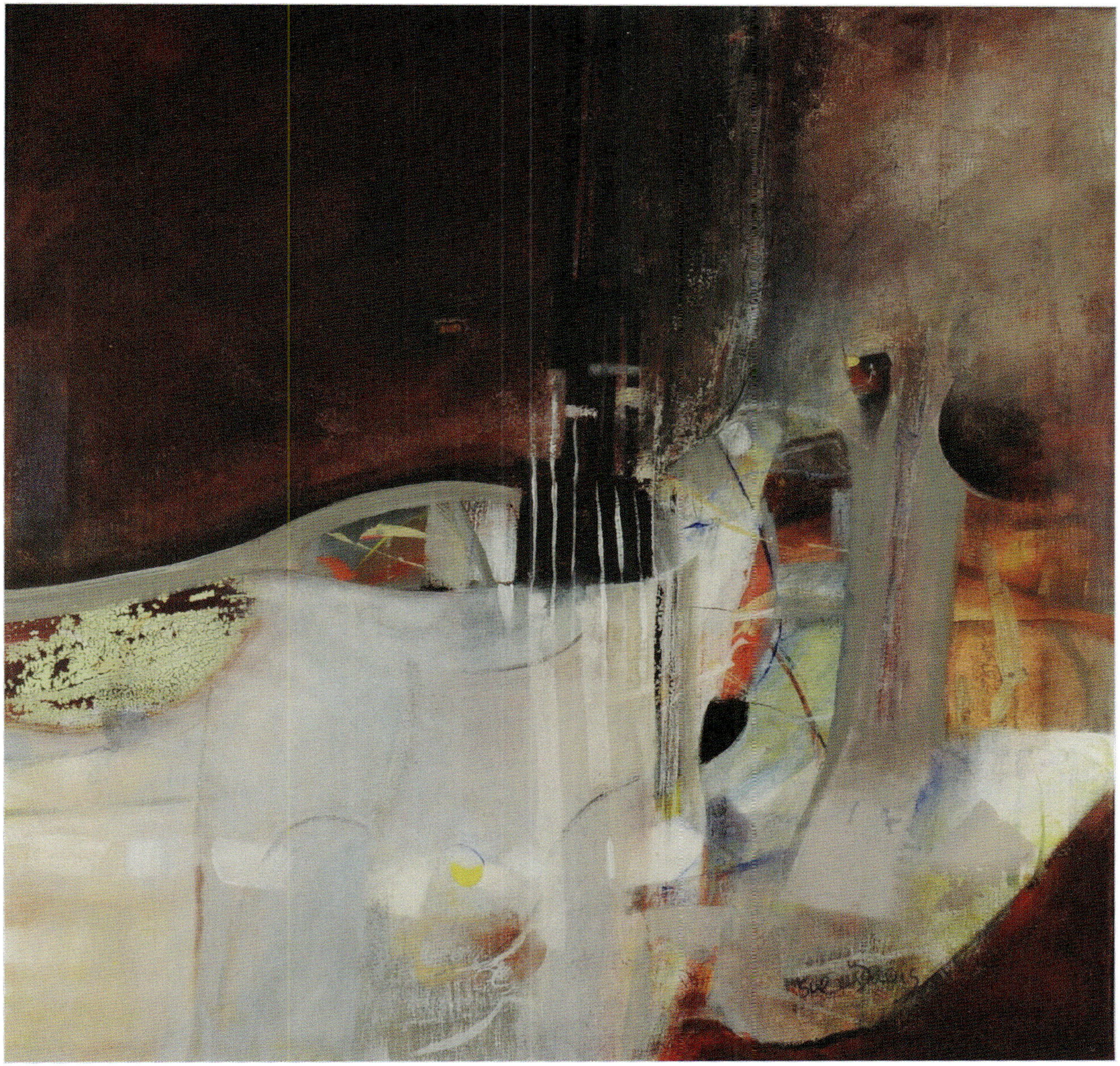

frit limit *acrylic on canvas* *76 x 76cm*

conclusions they are more likely to be untainted and may lead to a more inclusive attitude. On a more commercial theme, imagination feeds innovation in many fields, not only the visual. All areas can benefit from these ideas including manufacturing, science, management and society as a whole. It is a tool to access different parts of the brain which, placed together alongside accepted reasoning, can bring thoughts and solutions that integrate with contrasting thoughts. The apparent triumph of commercial rationalisation certainly leads to the need to rehabilitate the soul in the modern world.

Like any organic process art must continually change, always in a state of flux, slow or fast but definitely moving. Wilhelmina Barns-Graham, an artist who lived for a while in St Ives without the recognition I feel she deserved, certainly exemplified this spirit of exploration.

Abstraction has been around for a long time. Recently abstract paintings done 40,000 years ago have been found in a Spanish cave at El Castillo.

The approach to any art work is the same as it is with music, go to it freely with no preconception, let it come to you, give it time and involve your own experiences. In some sense you are the maker and hopefully it will stimulate different thoughts at different times to different people.

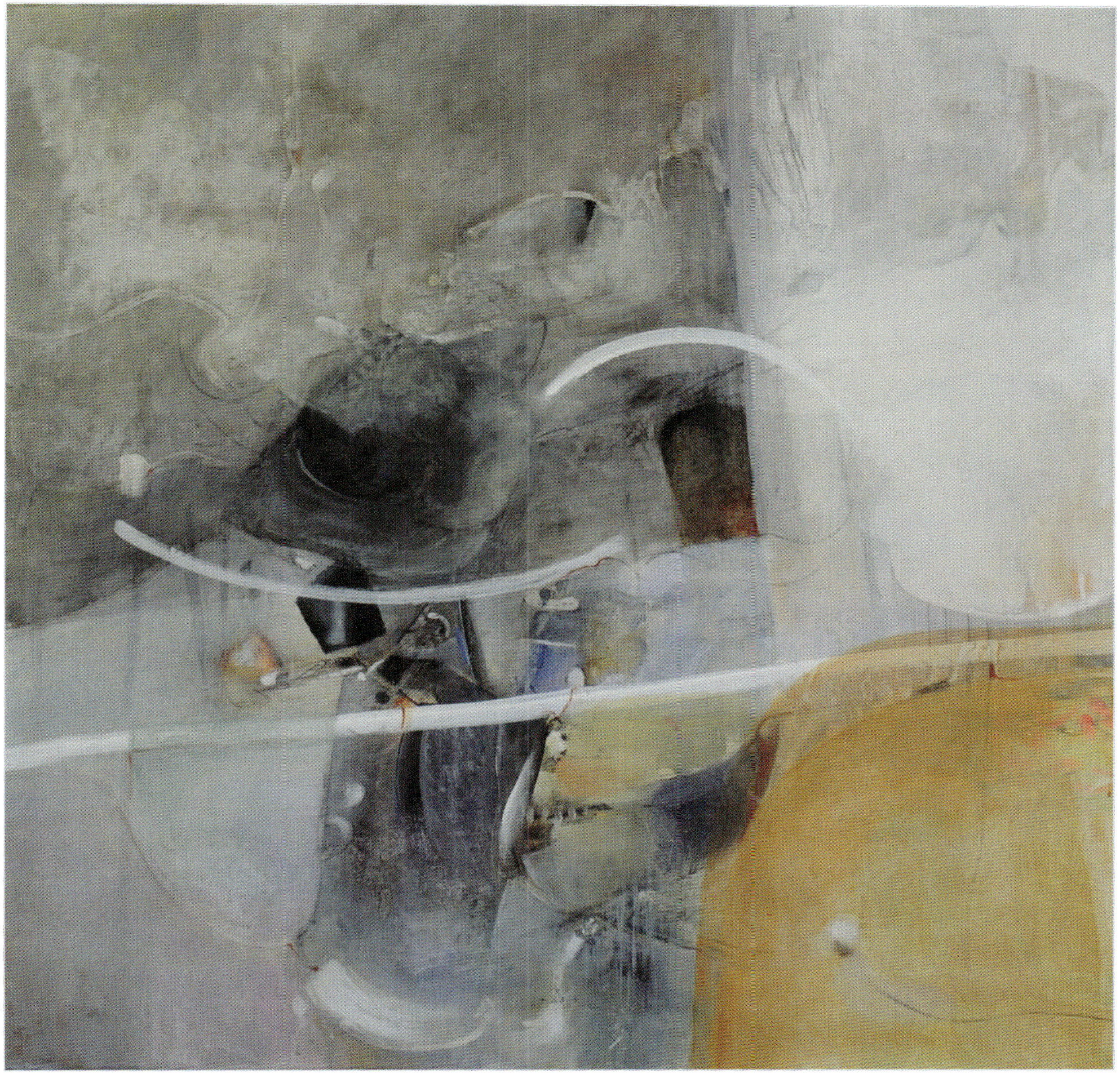

cord *acrylic on canvas* *73 x 73cm*

MARKETS

There are of course many ways of using the skills of an artist and it is the job of commercial artists to enhance the desirability of the things they are employed to promote. This is not very different from patronage in medieval times, where the patron would decide the subject and the artist was limited to solving technical difficulties. Somewhere along the line 'fine art' got separated from commercial art, which is anyway a term I am very uncomfortable with as it immediately suggests that fine art is of more value than other disciplines. I wish there was a better way to distinguish those artists that are solving a client brief from those that are working as individuals. Advertisements have great power harnessing our emotions and feeding dreams, and when dealing with the mass market it is probably wise to repeat well-known images. Impressionism, which has been around since the mid-1800s, is frequently used commercially as it is easily recognised, and still regarded by many as new. When fine art was left to individuals, and was no longer commissioned by patrons of the church and the aristocracy, artists were given freedom but left them with the problem of earning a living, unless they had private means. It has become the job of fine artists to produce and make something unique which communicates to individuals rather than the mass market. Because of this pressure, there is a tendency to look at images by other artists who are commercially successful and think 'I can do that'. This can lead to a proliferation of fake second-class images which maybe sell as they are recognisable and probably cheaper than the original. I think Robert Delaunay, who was interested in orphism (which concentrated on form and colour rather than objects), was expressing this dilemma when he said "most painters are really peeping-toms, whereas what they really should aspire to is to be seers". It is very important to look at others' work but there must be an awareness of the risk of being derivative. In wanting to make a unique, honest statement for oneself there is a huge number of things to consider, as one is sorting out how to operate and what one is trying to do – but the personal journey and the depth of that journey are both important to the individual artist and why she creates.

In this time of 'sensational art' many consider that art is about the politics of attention and this may be so for those that are able to create a celebrity status, but in contrast there are many artists who produce quietly with little time for what, to them, is the alien commercial world. Early educational ideas were that art was valuable for many aspects of society and should be part of that society for everyone.

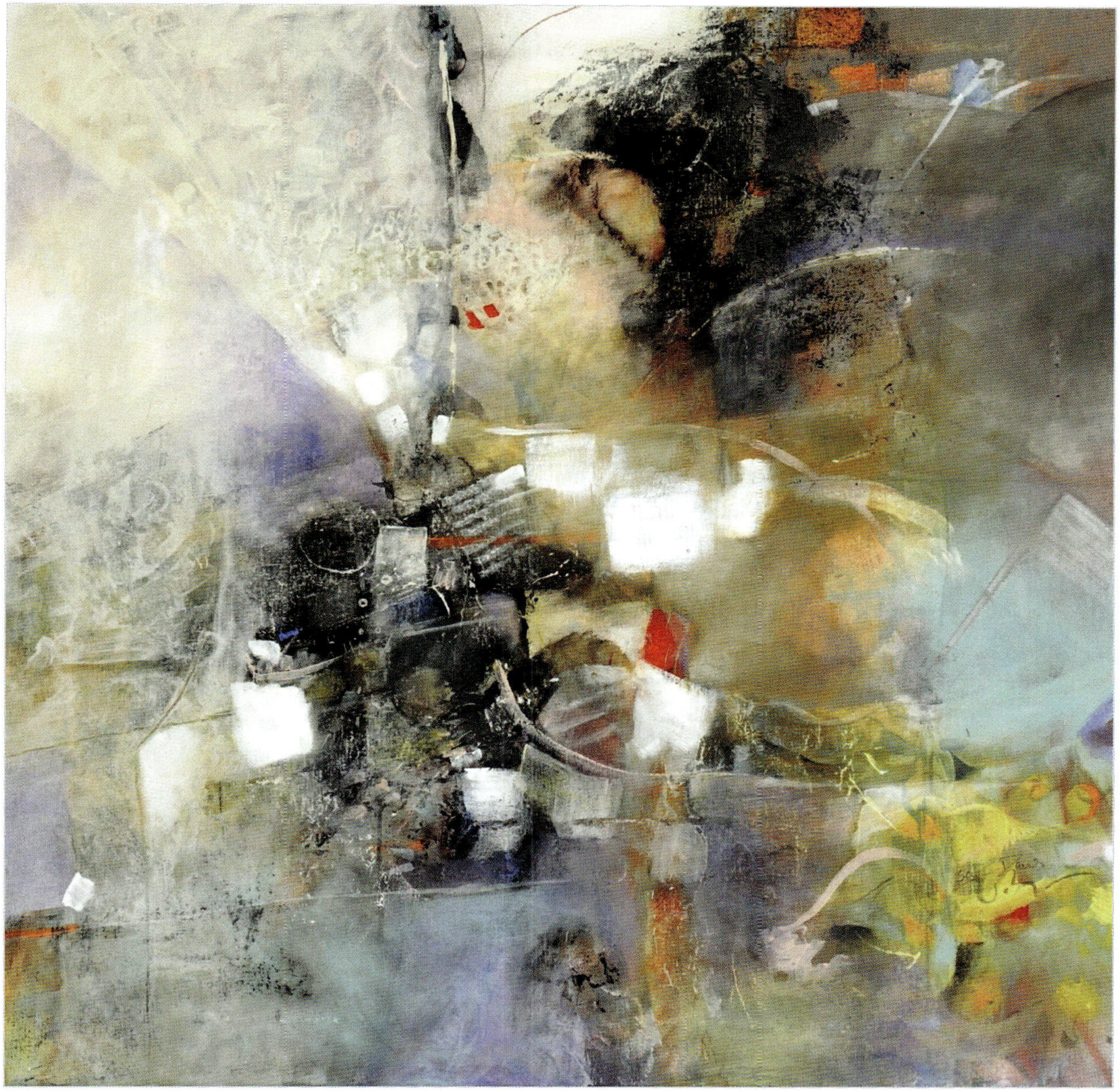

clouden *mixed media on canvas* *76 x 76cm*

However it now appears to be a luxury for the rich and not needed by the rest of society but, strangely, the capitalists have seen value in it and have captured and monopolised the art world with false claims and inflated prices.

Many galleries dissuade the general public from entry as they appear too precious and make people feel they are expected to know about the things displayed – consequently most of the time spent in them is spent reading the labels. The pressure all this puts on artists is not conducive to creativity as it curtails experimentation and good artists are often forced to be formulaic, producing the same as they have done in the past. Maybe this is where 'Abstraction Unbound' enters the arena as it is for you to decide what it is about, without duty or knowledge attached, a huge relief in this cling-wrapped world.

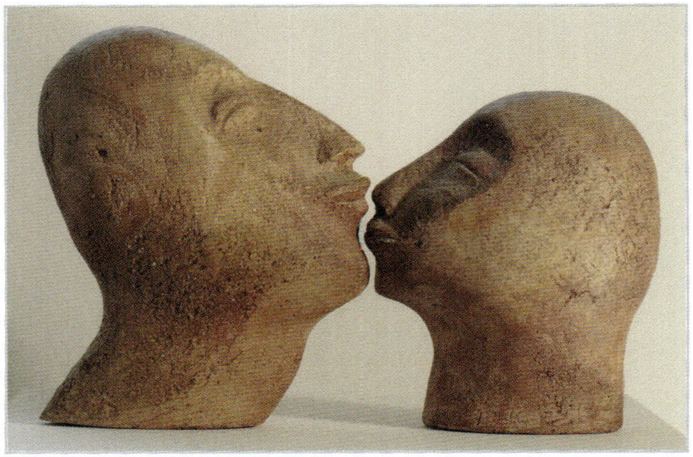

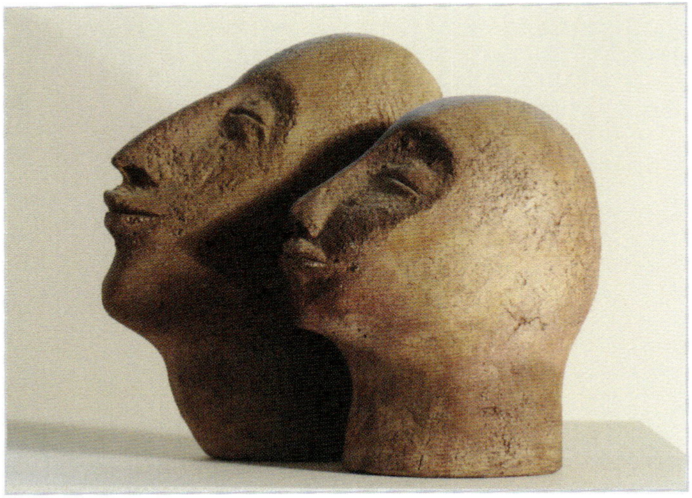

The economic pressure on galleries, who have to maintain their premises and cover advertising and running costs to gain their livelihood from sales, makes them seek the security of known artists, that is to say someone the public have confidence in because they have seen them before. An early personal experience comes to mind. On rising every Sunday at 6am to attend the Covent Garden craft market with my ceramics (the stall being fairly hard to acquire), time and time again the view was that my ceramics were 'wonderful' and 'so unusual'. Those same passers-by then went to the next booth only to purchase what must have been the millionth pinch pot, very much the fashion at the time, which probably had been copied and faked from the originals many times over. Purchasers seem to need the comfort and reassurance of knowing that others considered their purchase valuable, and often what

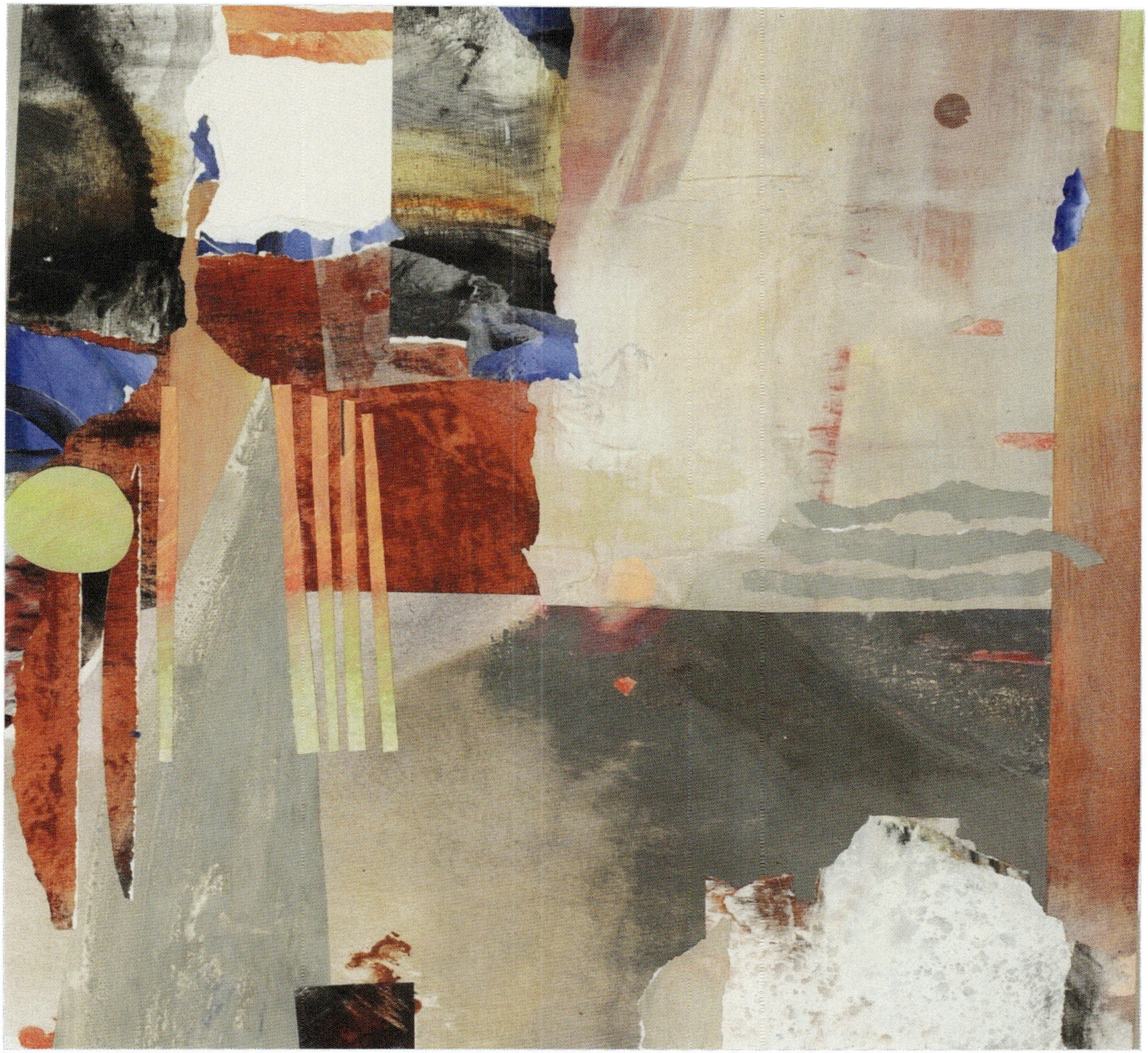

skin cast *mixed media collage* *38 x 38cm*

starts out as being genuine art becomes a commodity and denies the very reason why art is important. Galleries looking for this reassurance end up being indistinguishable from each other. Fashion takes hold and proliferation of the same ideas floods the so-called art world. Artists are just as guilty of this as the commercial outlets, and the Arts Council (perhaps the one hope for discernment and opportunity), seems to chase sensational art that has little connection to humanity. State art galleries seem to feel they should bow to the common denominator and purchase from populist artists. Those artists have often spent more time gaining their notoriety than actually working on their art. I have realised in the course of writing this book how much time and effort goes into achieving this notoriety. All this rather suggests that even the Arts Council and the people who have the power to patronise do not really have the expertise or confidence to pick for themselves.

The English seem particularly bad at striking out with their own opinions about art – it is said that in mainland Europe 40% of people buy real art whereas only 10% of people in England purchase genuine art. I feel this may have something to do with the restrictions in our education system. I am told by Italian friends that in Italy all pupils are taught aesthetics and art history right through their schooling and it is regarded as part of everyone's make-up. This is very apparent when visiting Italy – the towns appear to be very cared-for and aesthetically considered, there are few large shop windows favouring business thus destroying the appearance of the historic towns. As we all know, appearances are extremely important to most Italians, and they are renowned for their innovative forward thinking in product design.

In the past it was believed in England that art was taught to further social, moral and economic aims but today the view is very narrowly exam- and fiscally-driven. The community art of today could be very educational for future generations of art appreciation, but it often degenerates into the sort of Blue Peter quick fixes which have tainted many educational projects. There is a duality about the teaching of art in our schools. On the one hand there is a sense of elitism, i.e. art thought of as a special subject and a place for the talented, but it is also thought of as a haven for those that are not academically minded. Neither of these acknowledges that it is one of the only places where students of all abilities are encouraged to think for themselves.

All this pre-selection of people and the narrowing of education affects how people function for themselves and in society and, for me, reinforces our detrimental class system, which in turn produces a divergent society. This class system, coupled with the celebrity culture we now embrace, defines a worthwhile person

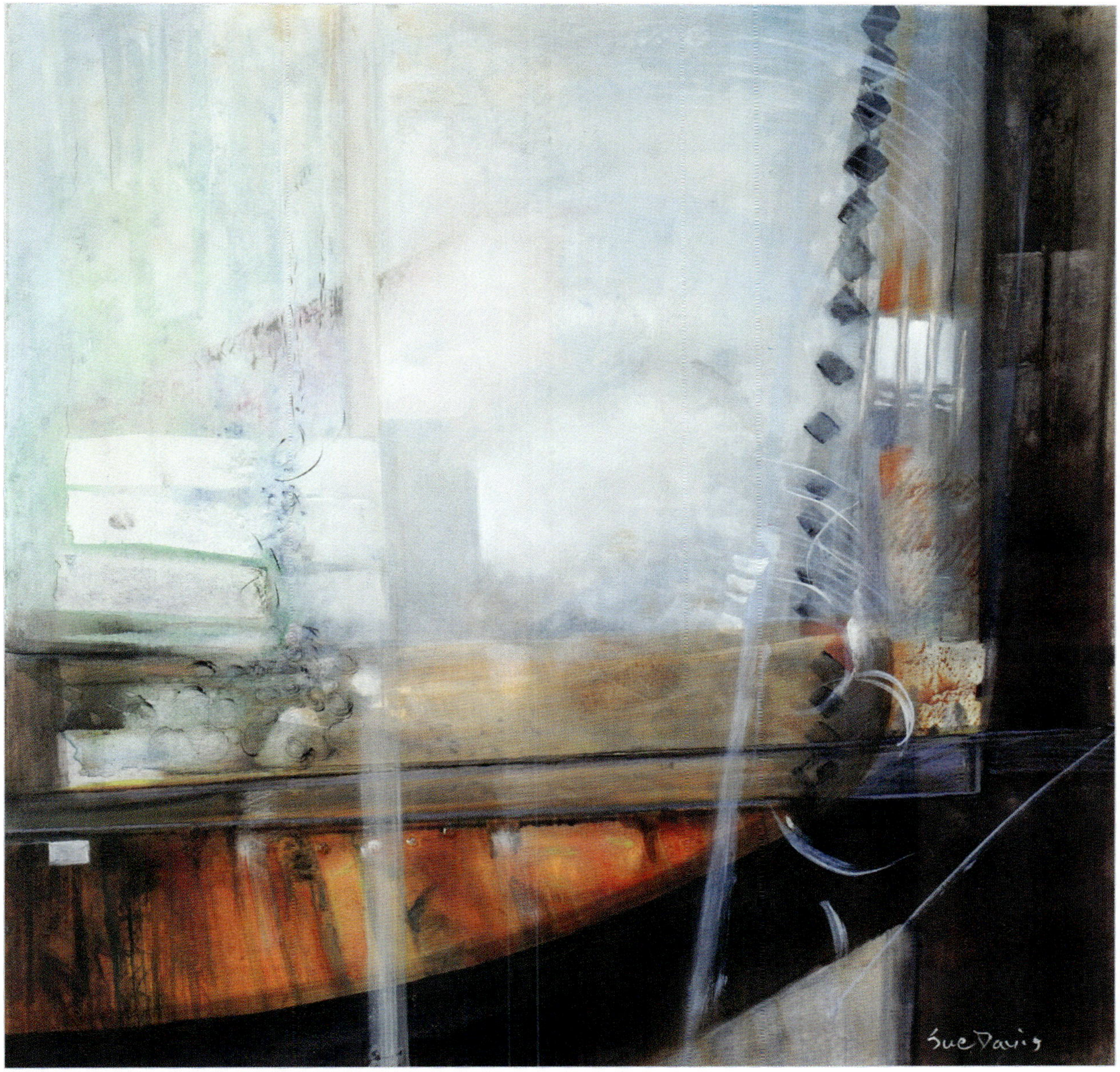

moist pane *acrylic on board* *60 x 60cm*

as one who has money rather than one who has achieved (how many artists' or scientists' names do we know when so many recognise the latest game show host). Most authentic creators reside in the realms of the unknown and they are aware their communication is not necessarily an understood communication. George Braque, the 20th century French artist noted as a pioneer of cubism alongside Pablo Picasso, said "In the end the problem with art is that you can explain everything about it except the bit that matters."

To avoid this commercial trap and create genuinely individual work, it is necessary for artists to recognise the problem and push hard to their own satisfaction, abandoning old moorings and becoming content to gain the luxury of knowing they remain true to themselves. Such artists pursue their own creativity and steer away from the common denominator, creating something that no one else can. They should step out with assurance without the need for back-up, look forward to the future, attempt different approaches to selling, confident that there are people who are weary of being told what is good, and can recognise something that has been made with integrity. The Dada movement in the early 20th century questioned the validity of art after Marcel Duchamp coined the term 'anti-art'.

The Dadaists, a movement that considered the reason and logic of a capitalist society had led people to war, expressed their rejection of that ideology with art that embraced chaos and irrationality. One of Duchamp's contributions was the 'ready-made' urinal, now famous and sadly repeated by many artists making it part of the establishment today. His most significant contribution to modern thought, for me, was the proposition that it is the viewer who creates, rather than the artist. He actually gave up art work completely.

flint wash

mixed media on paper

67 x 87cm

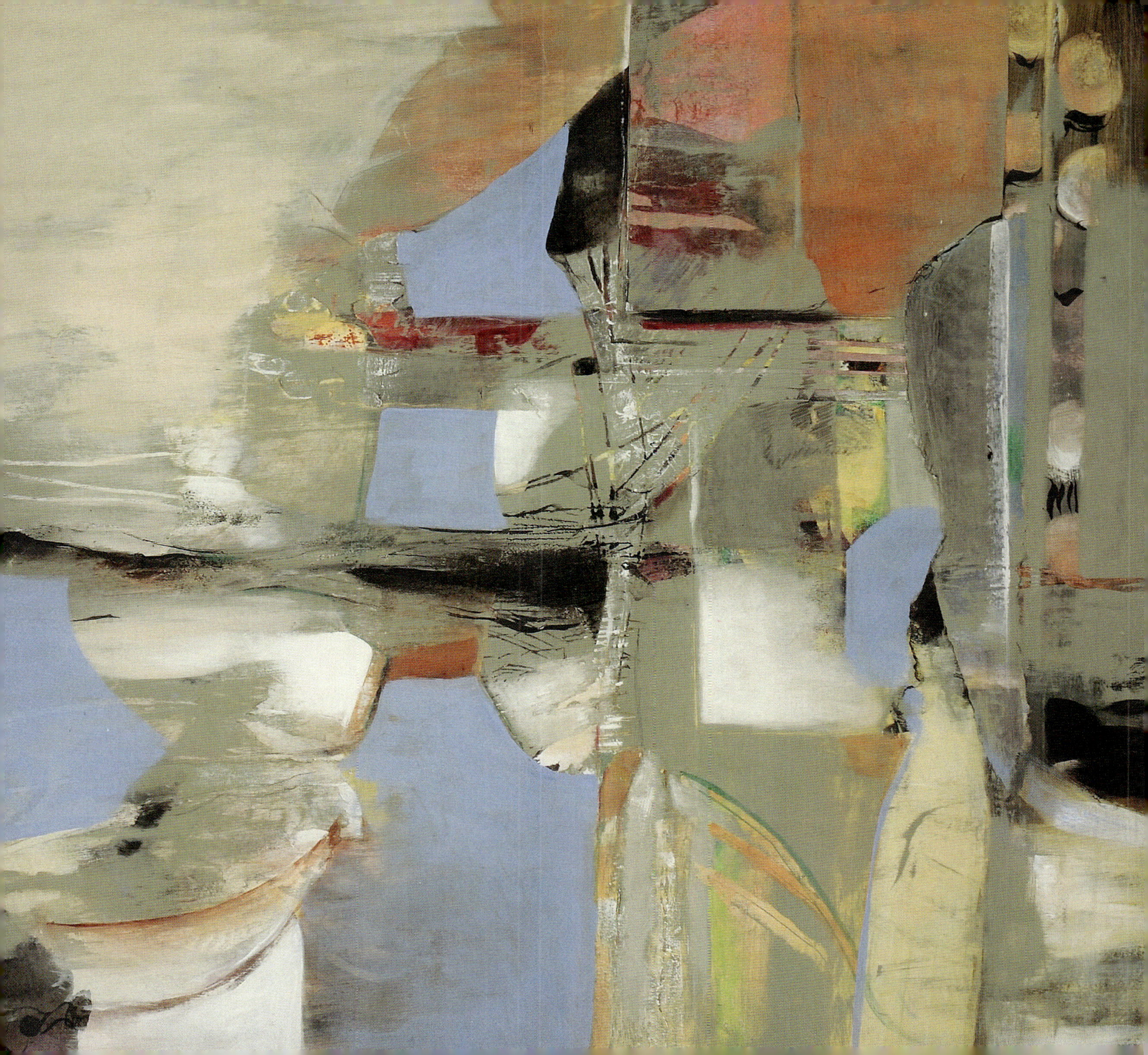

TOOLS

DRAWING

Drawing is one of the main tools towards creating a piece and it is often a long and hard journey to acquire the necessary skills. Many hours are spent processing the vast amount of information available in a chosen subject. Not only the shape, placement and viewpoint, but also relationships within the scene and the entanglement of light and shadow, have to be considered. Once through the initial pain barrier it is most absorbing and exciting. This intense observational process, and the decisions about what to include and what to leave out, engaged in whilst drawing, is the mainstay of a unique vision and this academic discipline, once instilled, is hard to break out from. For me, however, a preparatory sketch often shows too much and leaves less excitement for the main work. Also it constitutes a preliminary form of image, and implies the mind has an image to portray, which is not the case when working on 'Abstraction Unbound'.

I don't fully understand this, but art seems to have something to do with accessing depth, something to do with spirituality. Many people connect this with religion. I envy their ability to do this as it gives them a focus and a reason for the existence of their spirituality, but for me it is not connected with a deity. Today it could be thought of as 'the force'. I am reassured when I realise that others such as Kandinsky and Ruskin also connected art with spirituality, and there are some like Jeanette Winterson who believe the arts are the redemption of man. It is easier for me to connect with this thought when I put conventional drawing aside and work intuitively. The release from formality into intuition gives me freedom and the images created become looser and more fluid until the decision to completely abandon any hooks into reality and rely on myself is inevitable. Making this move into pure abstraction takes the shackles off and this freedom enables me to explore more. Occasionally I feel guilty about not using the academic approach and sometimes I feel the need for the anchor of subject and, who knows, I might return one day but for some time the excitement of experimenting and the rush of ideas bombarding me is almost overwhelming.

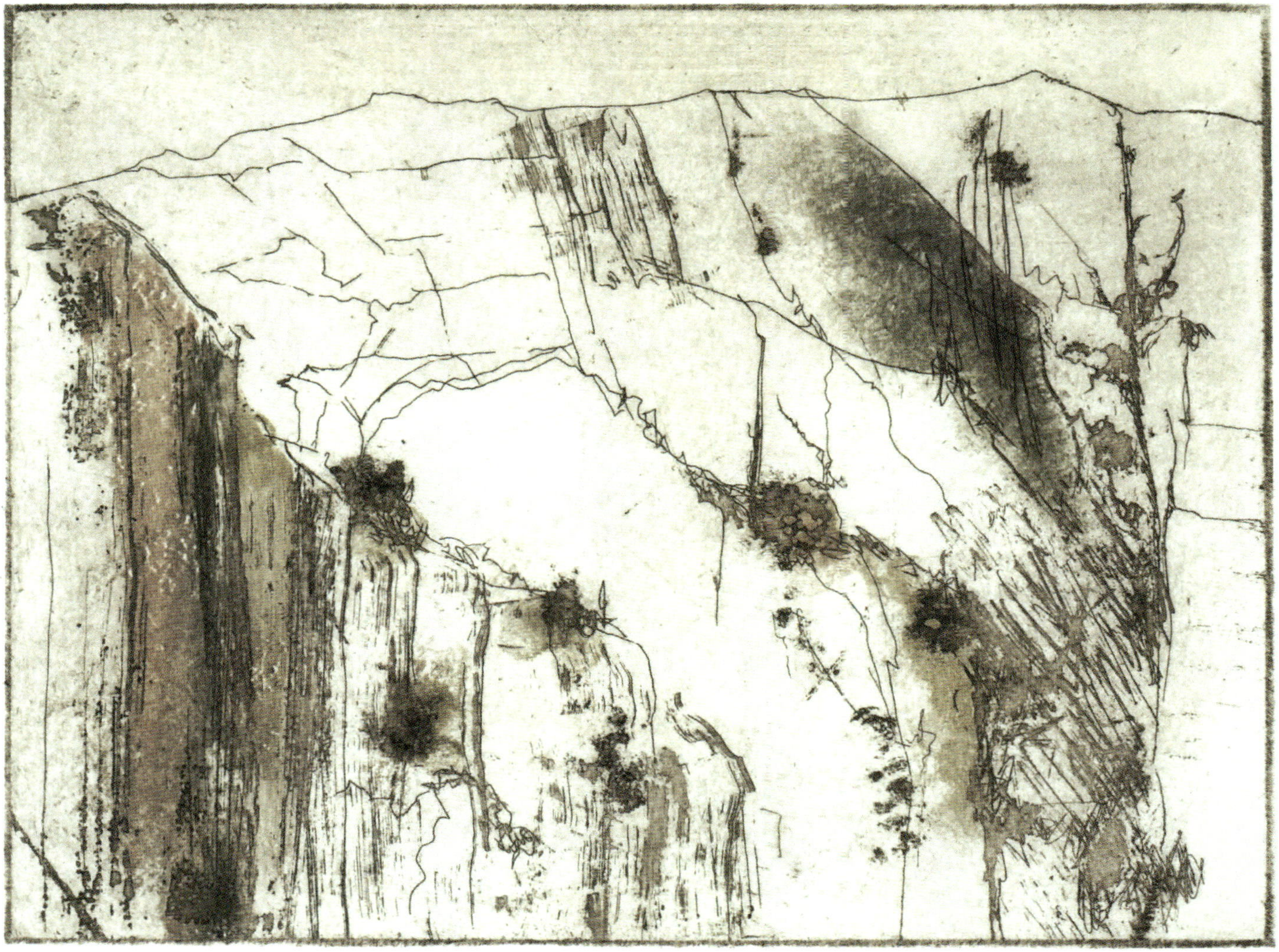

face *dry point* *20 x 30cm*

Artists and other cultural producers draw on all types of knowledge and cognitive processes to create. Just as the importance of drawing, mentioned above, is very valuable, to seek out and try different grounds and media is critical. When using different materials, it is the exploration of their properties and the gaining of skills to manipulate them that provides fresh associations and unpredictable results. The important aspect is to learn personal judgement and selection. Interaction between different ideas and skills opens doors of richness, just as different facets of life, locally or globally, could enrich ideas. There is a choice between travel or the recognition that there are avenues close by to explore.

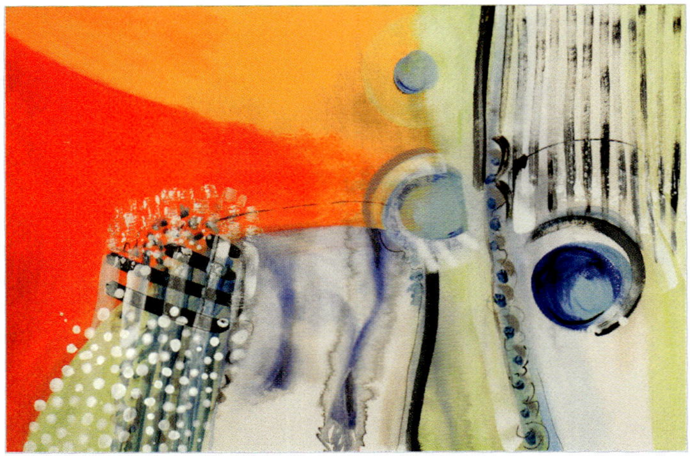

pitter patter

Remember William Blake talks about a world in a grain of sand –

"To see a World in a Grain of Sand
And a Heaven in a Wild Flower
Hold Infinity in the palm of your hand
And Eternity in a hour"

As there is no actual starting point to pure abstraction, and no image to gain – a piece begins with delightful expectancy, assumes direction only to get lost, moving out and away towards territories known or impossible. The manipulation of materials and colour is played and wrestled with until, with luck, it pushes towards clarification but leaves enough space for invention and curiosity. There is a balance and form to be discovered as the work is considered independently of associations and in this freedom the fear of doing something wrong is dissolved. The importance of being wrong plays a huge part in creativity and if you are not prepared to be wrong then you will never find anything unique.

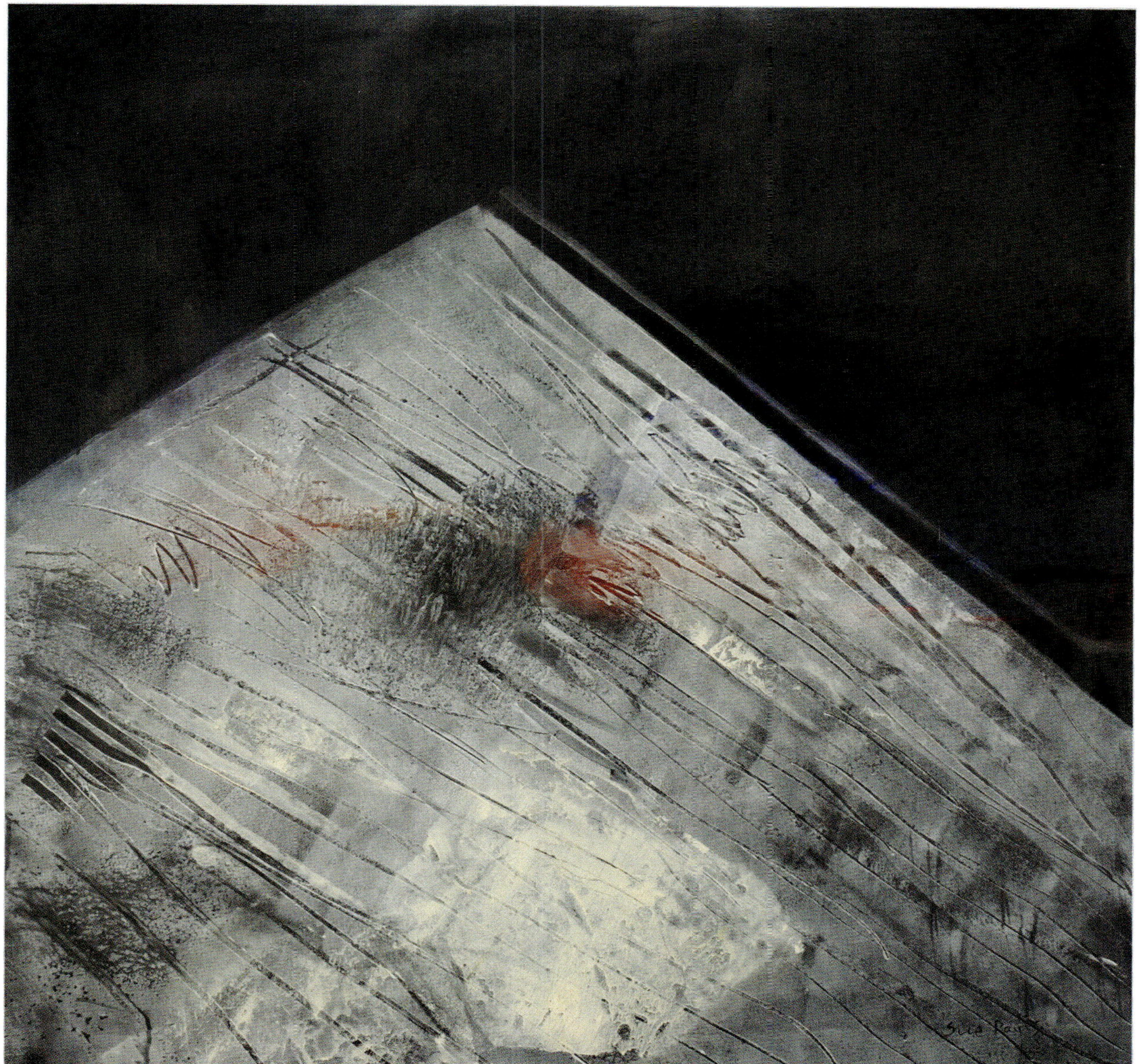

liquid layers *acrylic on board* *100 x 100cm*

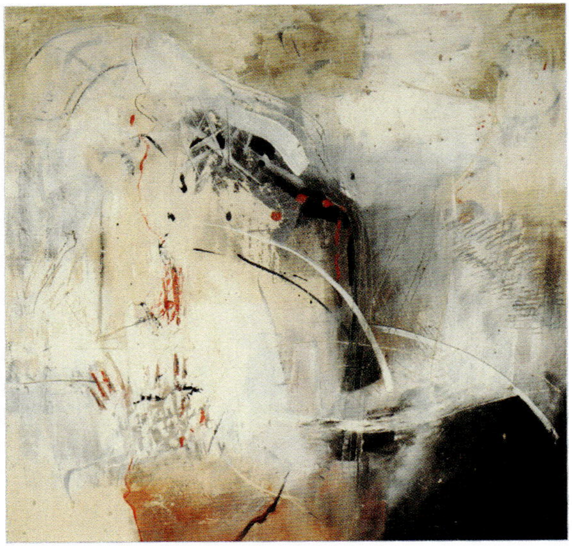

scarft *mixed media on plaster* *60 x 60cm*

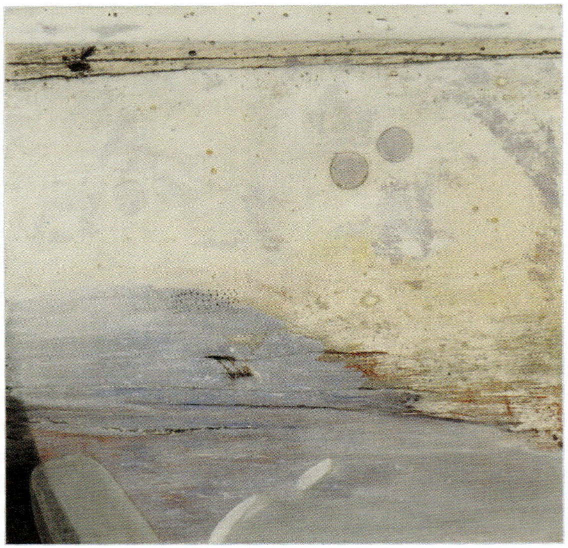

rock pooling *mixed media on plaster* *40 x 40cm*

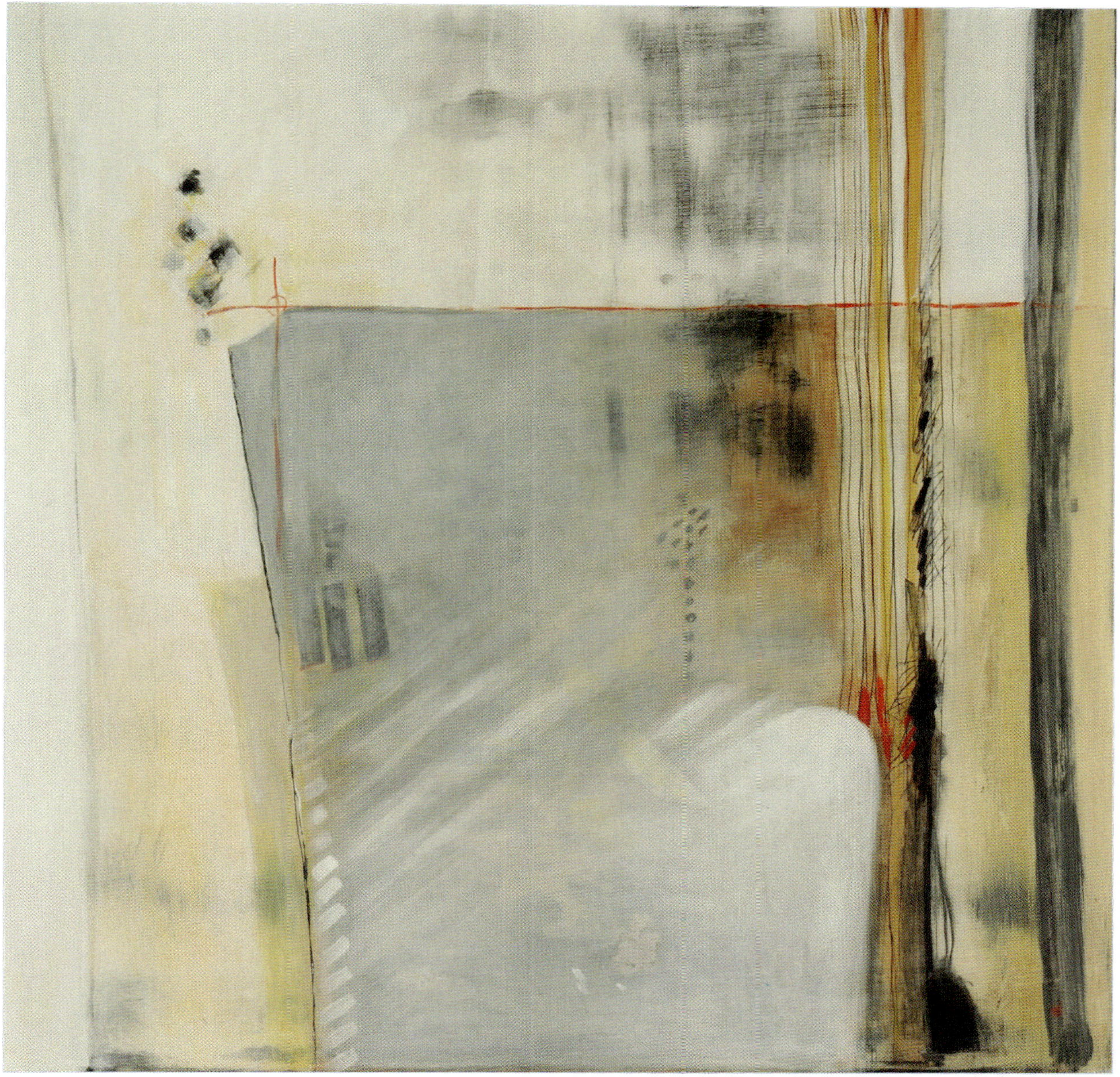

more than a trace *mixed media on plaster* *72 x 72cm*

There is a strange draw towards colour and its great capacity to create mood changes; some people dream in colour; some think colour has a feel and a smell. High contrast combinations of colour, such as black and white, have an attention-grabbing power, and bright colour in images can give joy but colour can also provide a soft, unctuous, calming feeling which in turn mixes and leaks, vibrating musically and descending into rich sombre darkness. It is how you choose to use colour that sets you apart and makes your statement personal.

Rothko's resonated reds glow
saturated, translucent
sunshine seeping at the edge
passing to oblivion
and back refreshed.
Goya's reds punctuate and stab
spilling over the surface
from the depths of the shadows
defining anguished lips
and flagging allegiance.

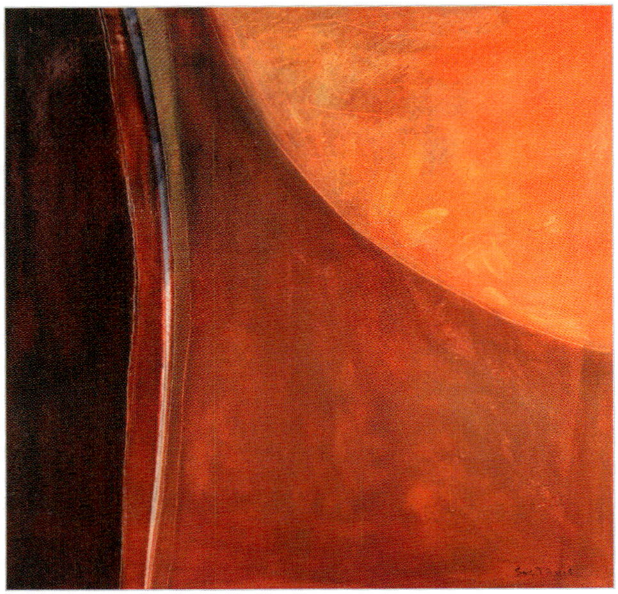

red earth *mixed media on board* *100 x 100cm*

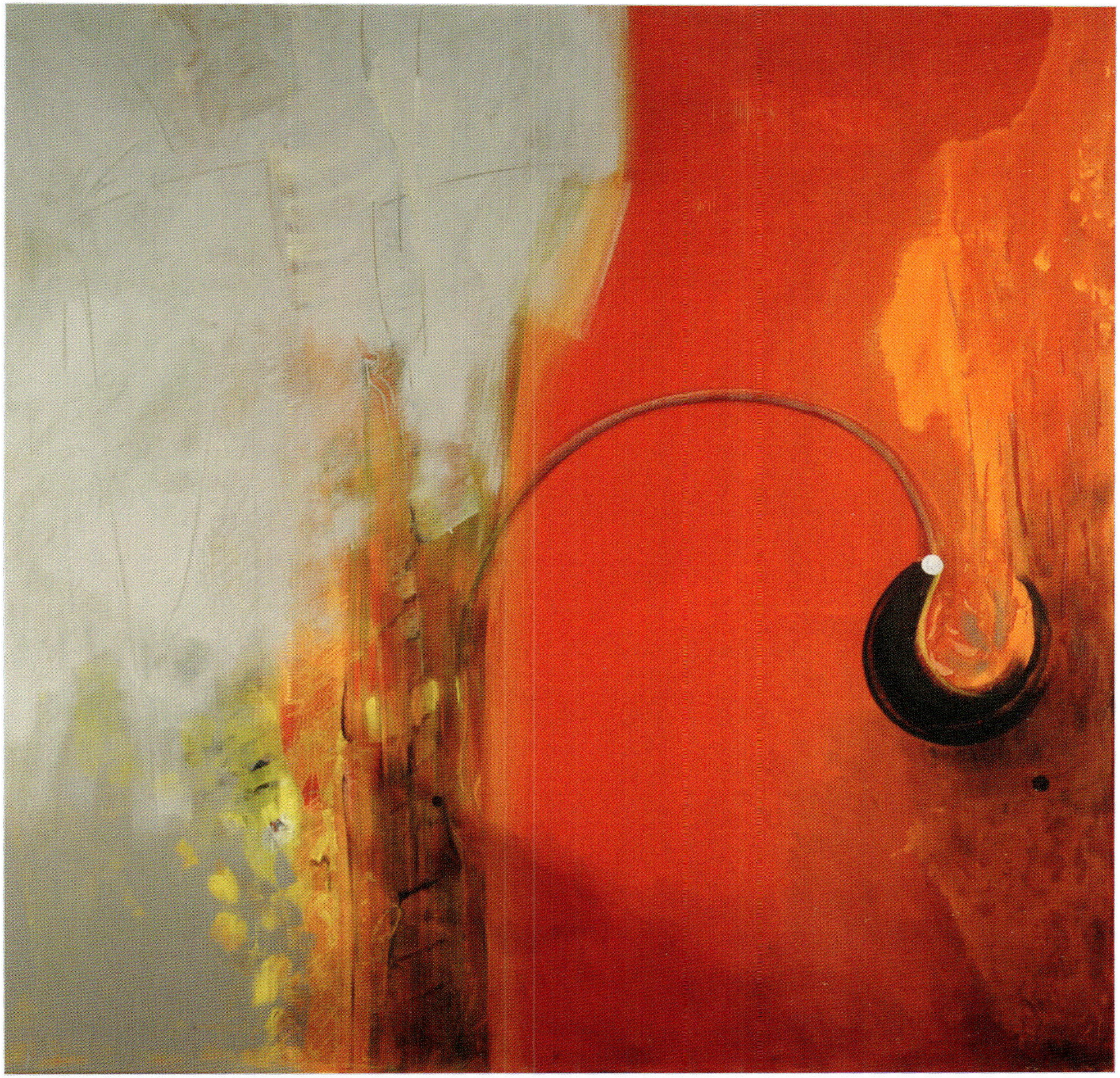

flush *mixed media on canvas* *100 x 100cm*

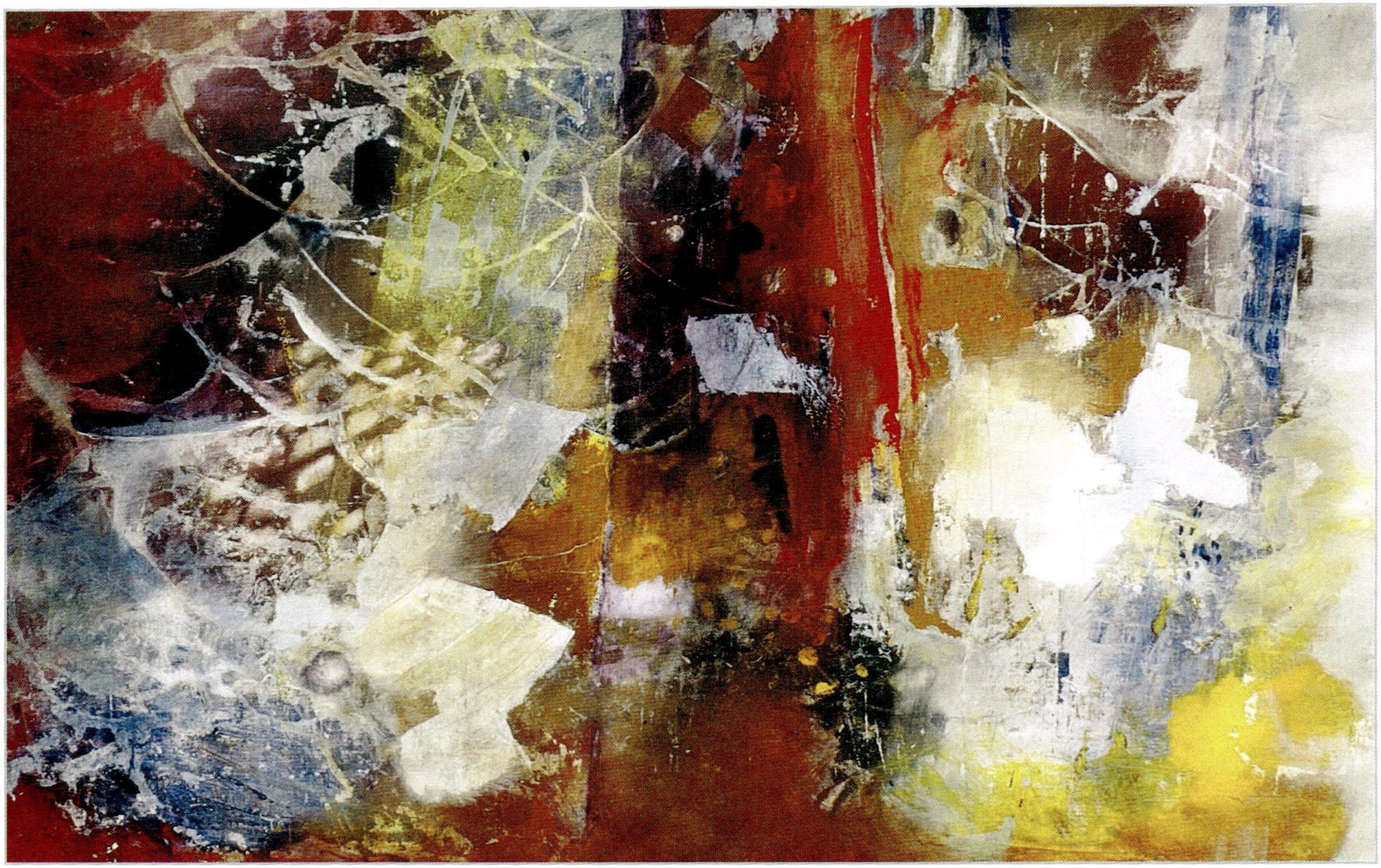

spritely tow *acrylic on canvas* *160 x 120cm*

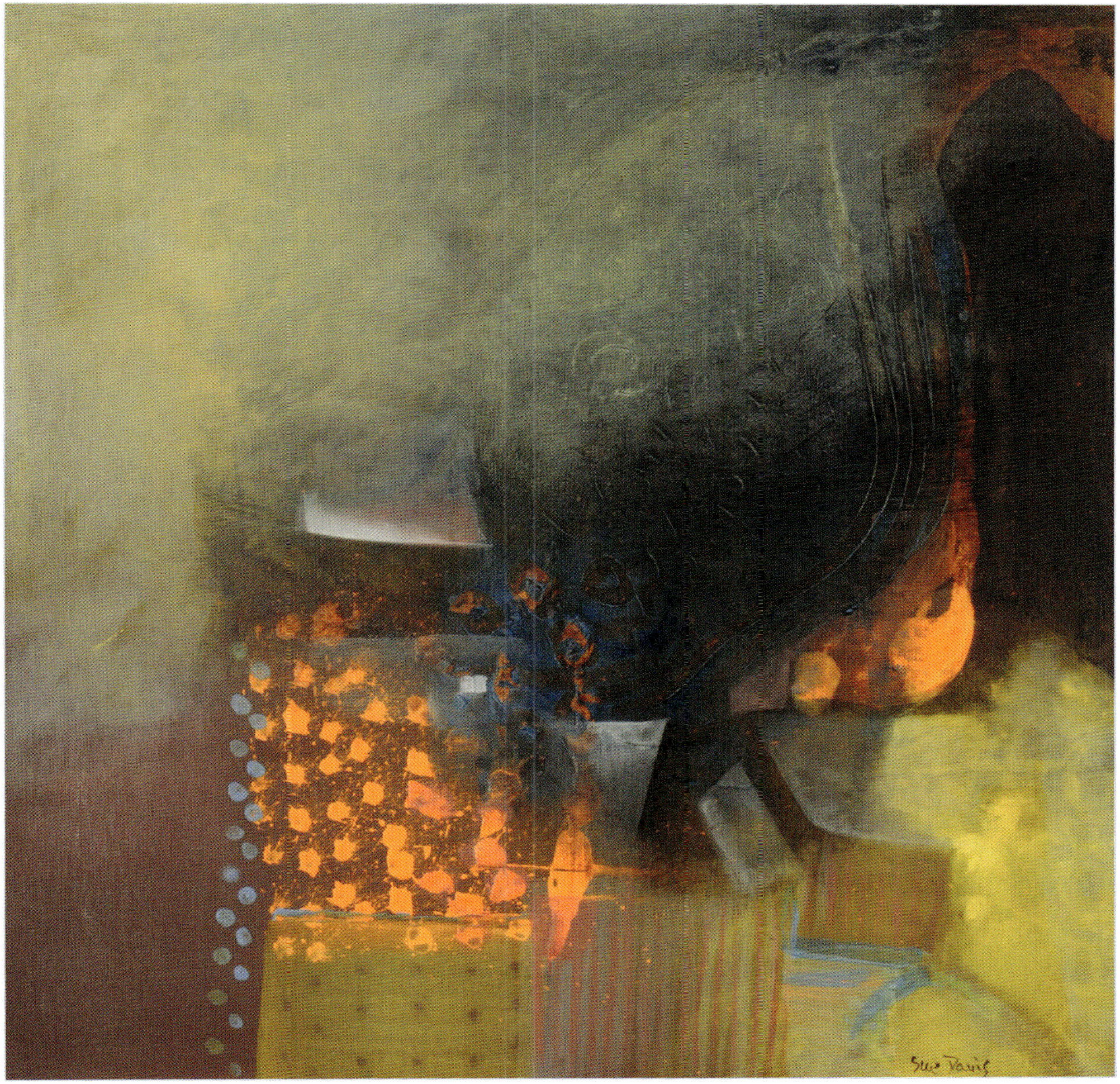

tumble *mixed media on board* *60 x 60cm*

The fact that the artist has to interpret his subject and make his own selections leads many people to say that all art is effectively abstract. To some extent I understand this position, but reference to reality is a hindrance for the pure abstractionist. If pure abstraction is subjective rather than objective, that is to say existing in the mind not linked with an object, then are there any visual influences? Novalis, a German Romantic poet, author and philosopher who was very concerned with education, has been quoted as saying "Painting is fundamentally a translation into a visual language of the invisible states of mind". I like to think he was talking of the freedom found when completely working from yourself with no reference points. Nothing is in the mind but that which comes to it through the senses.

Having acknowledged that abstraction is not about things, I nevertheless recognise there have to be influences. For me, the objects are not as important as the way the shadows and light become visible as they play on surroundings. It is not the boat I'm looking at but the 'wet fire' it throws onto the water and in turn the 'wet fire' reflected back on the hull as the ripples glint in the sun. Light in nature creates the movement of colours.

"The shafts of sunlight penetrating windows changing the solid forms the flicker of illuminated pathways passing through a wooded glade in a soft breeze the energetic patterns thrown on surfaces from the glass reflections. The dappled sound of water as it flows and ebbs catching the sunlight on its moving surface as the glints on the sea link up in chains to nowhere. The impenetrable strength of the rock strata as it crumbles on to the land. Flow of the shadows as the clouds creep over the land on their desperate journey and the soft washing of wind over grasses ending their day and reminding us of the gentle deep subtle movement as water flows and ebbs in its depths.

Dance today the light is brilliant, sparkling on the webs and dancing in the shadows as the breeze moves through the trees, everything shimmering and playing. Reflections everywhere light bouncing off glazed surfaces, it's a butterfly day.

Giant grass is waving in the breeze crossing and uncrossing intermingled with large grey leaves. Moving stiffly revealing their terracotta backs. All fragmented by the rain curtain that plops off the sill in large sloppy drops whose sound creeps into vision.

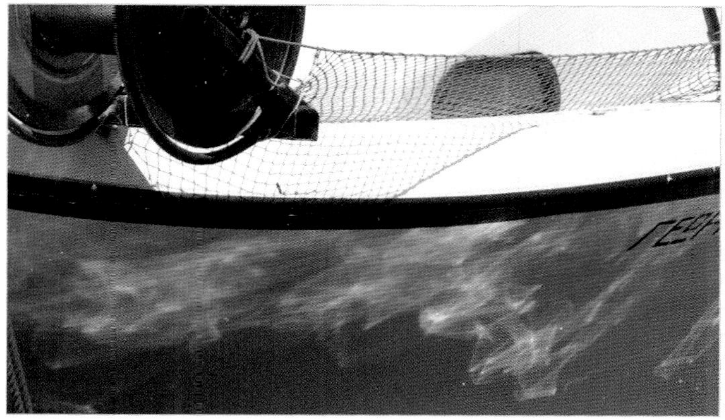

In the distance a grey horizon nestling under an electric sky, but giving way to the cool green fields. Sunlight shafts heading right up to the window reflecting the rooms' contents. Focus on the window and I see outer and inner fusing together. Focus again and I appear amongst those two worlds. Feel the breeze and stillness in tandem and yet there is a third element. My past and future flit through the present."

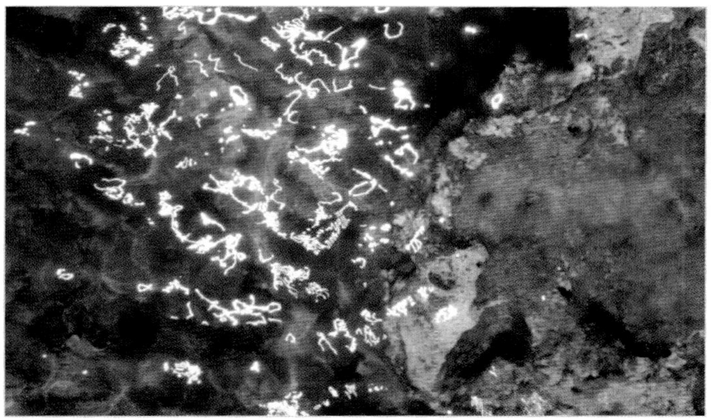

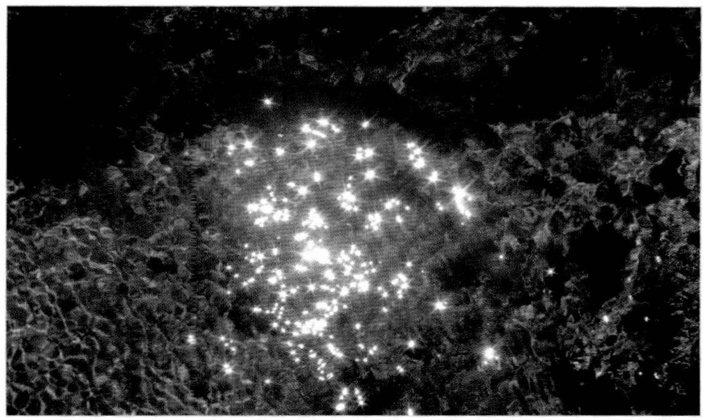

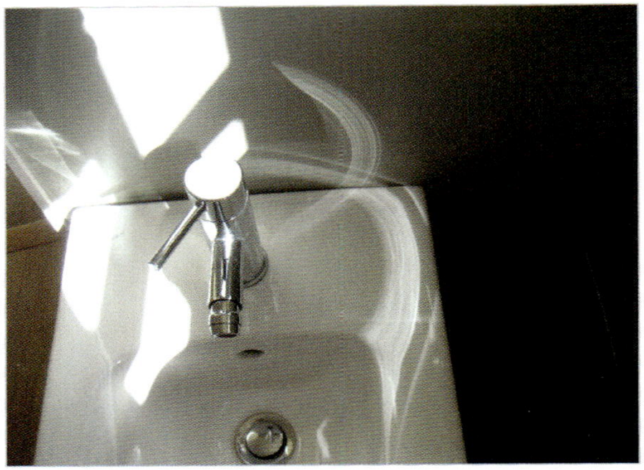

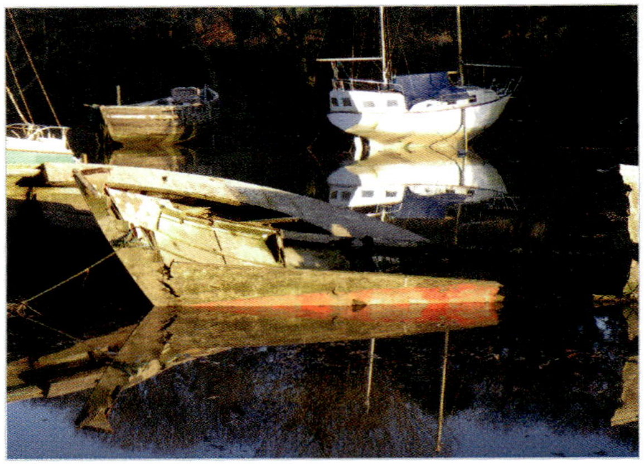

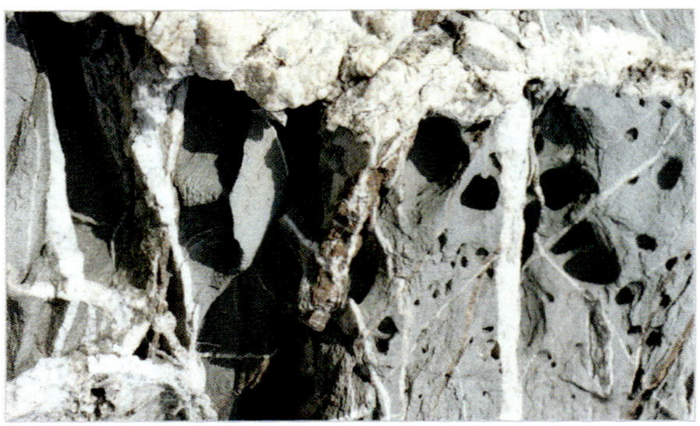

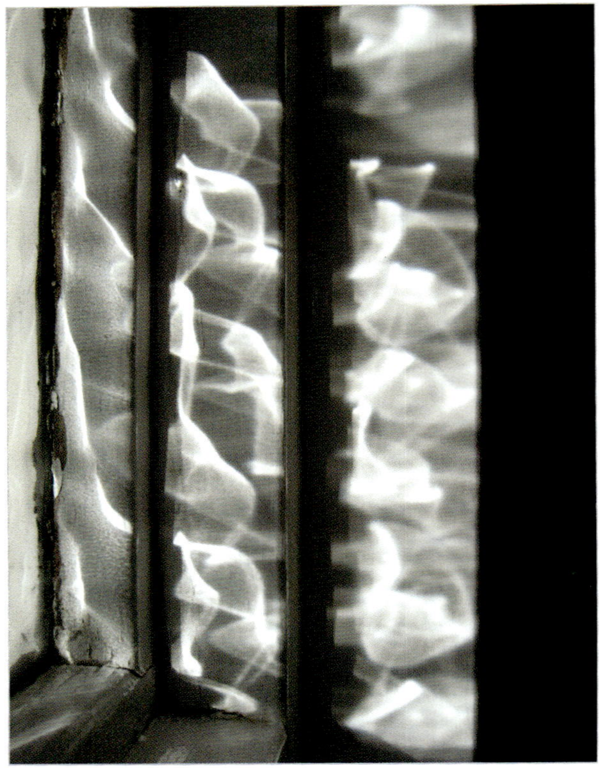

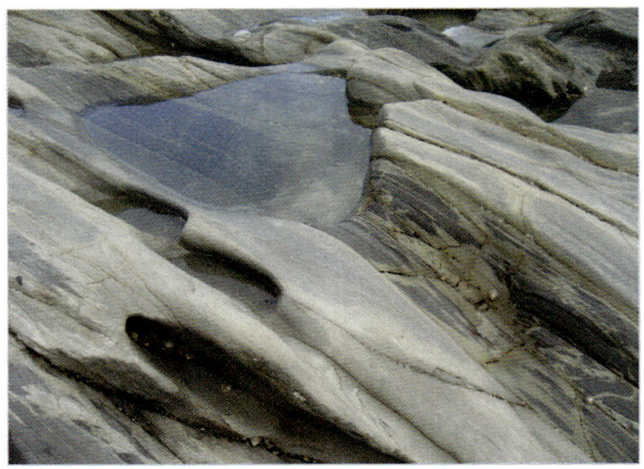

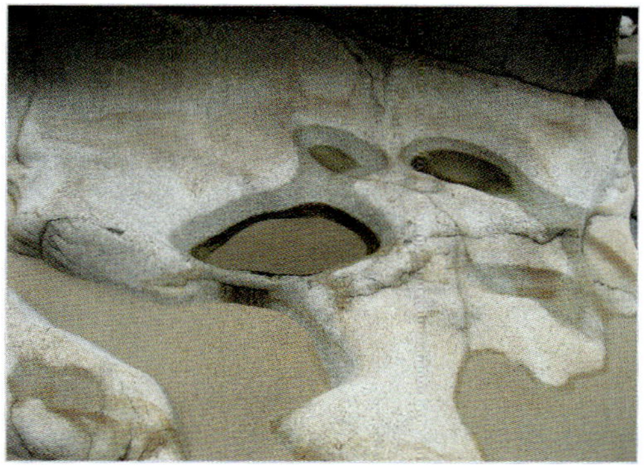
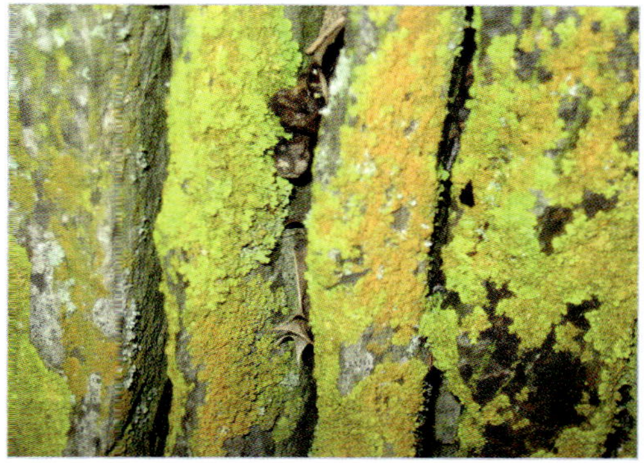
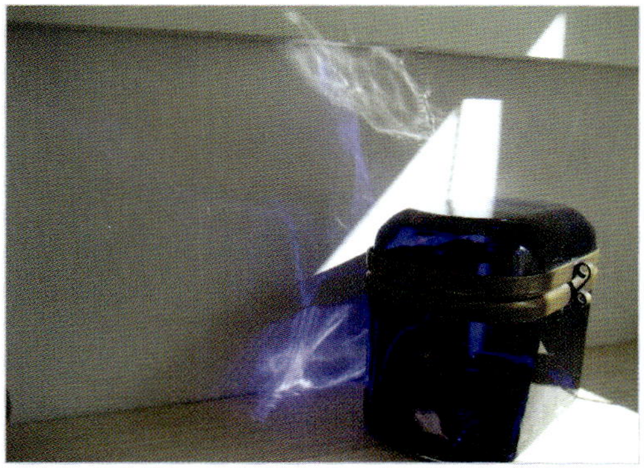
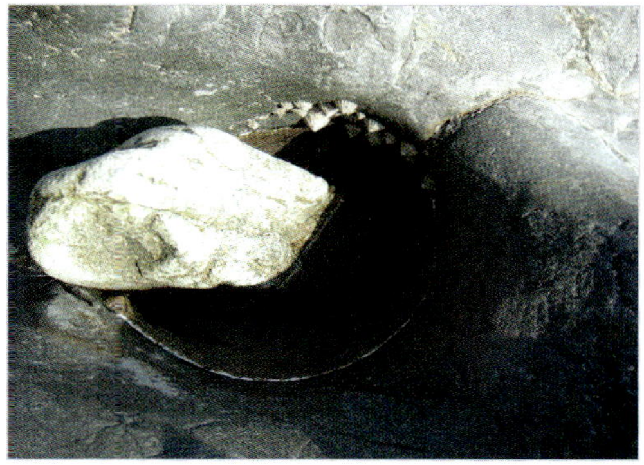
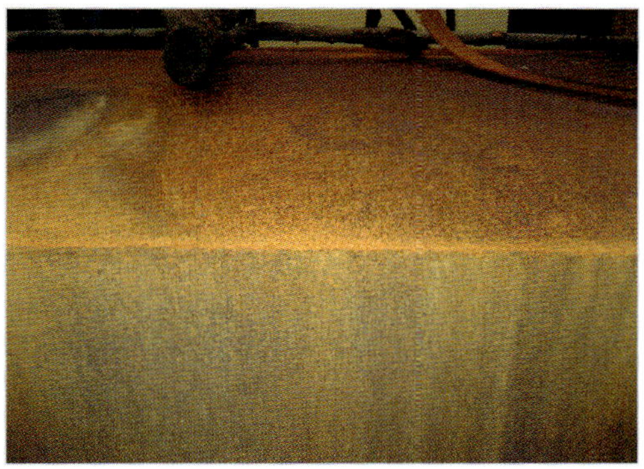
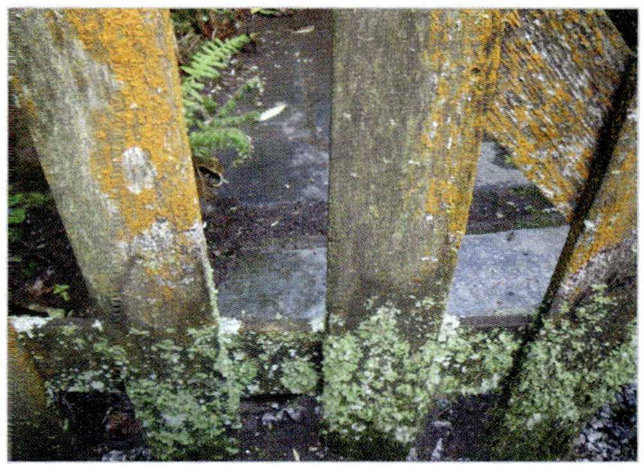

There is so much energy in the natural world – how can we fail to acknowledge it?

DECISIONS TOWARDS ABSTRACTION

Although representational pieces give a clue about the subject, the reference to the object or scene surely limits the imagination to that object or scene. An apple is an apple. It could be a very beautiful apple; but it is still an apple even when it has been painted in a semi-abstract, modernistic way. There is art of historical importance, telling a story, aided by knowledge of the event. This knowledge adds to the enjoyment for some people but it is still guiding the viewer into how to think. The need for hooks, historic clarity, structure and purpose has a great appeal in our busy world and much good art is objectively based on facts or things.

A white cup and saucer may have all sorts of light and shadow, colour casts, light spots and reflections but maybe the cup and saucer image closes the riddle and many people just see the object alone. Could those elements be better expressed without the object? Is it the cup and saucer which is interesting or is it the residue from it? There is a delicate, mobile balance between chance and intention, and intention alone can be predictable and cold whilst chance alone is sometimes irresponsible and vacuous. These elements together, under the eye of an active artist, are an immense resource and 'Abstraction Unbound' gives this freedom without tying thoughts down to place, time or things.

There are difficulties in working without reference but the main thing is to trust yourself and start, trust your own instincts without wandering into others' territory. Drawing is involved but not of things – however the intensity of looking, when trained to draw, has a lasting presence and this, along with the skills gained manipulating materials, and your life experiences, provides the information you need to produce your personal statement – in some ways abstract drawing is akin to doodling but it usually contains more space and depth. Experience often allows an artist to move faster and intuitively, giving excitement, flow and sensitive feeling to the pressure and placement of small marks, without having a verbal reason. The philosopher Montaigne identified the way he approached his writing: "I try to work without preconception or any marks which come to mind employing nothing but my own natural resources and judgement. Fumbling their way forward, swaying, stumbling and tripping over, rarely feeling satisfied for the troubled cloudy visions beyond." This is how it feels when embarking on a purely abstract piece. It is the inquisitiveness and exploration of the journey that is important, not the arrival.

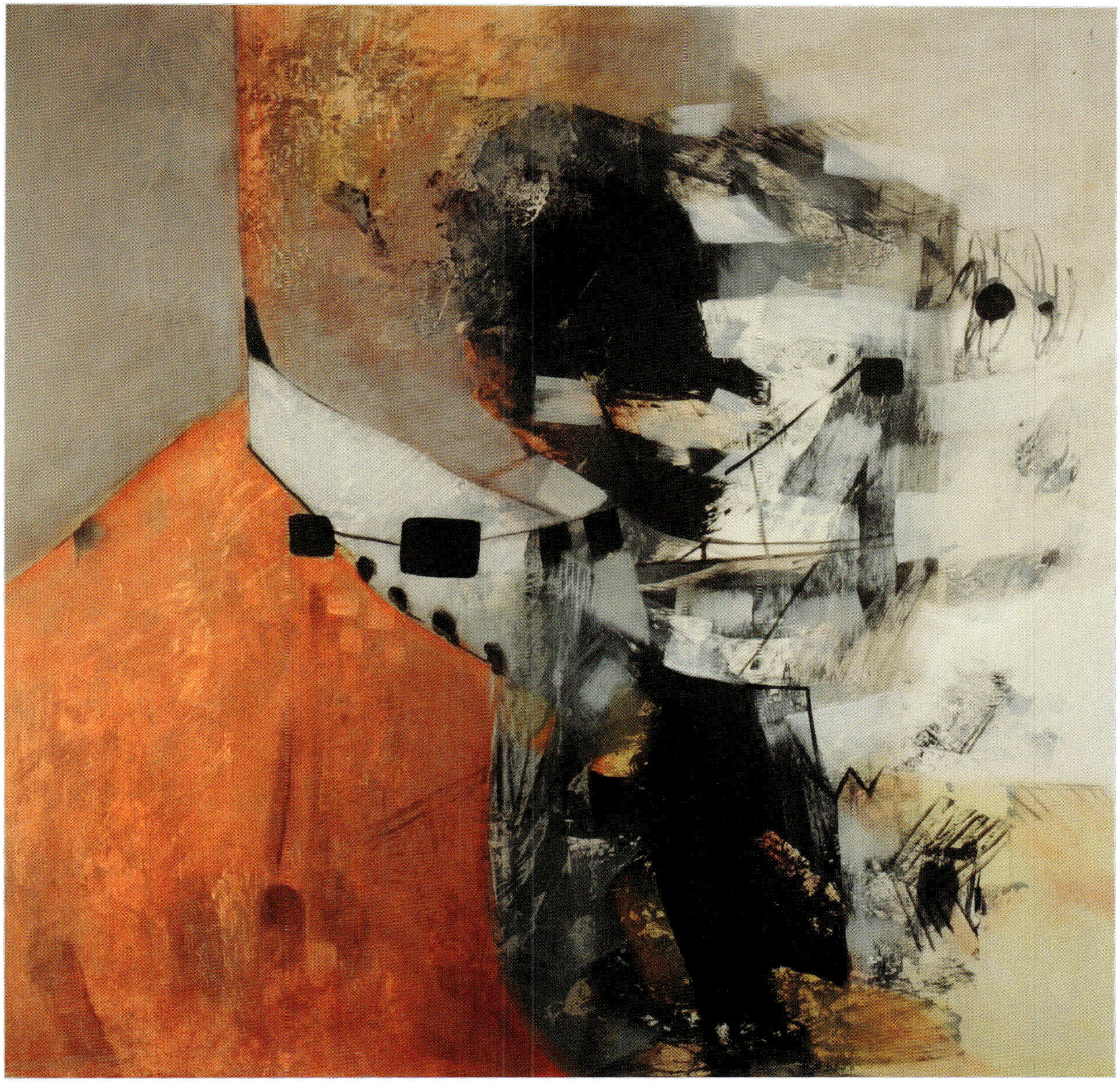

shaft not shimmer *mixed media on board* *100 x 100cm*

The function of education is to give the student abundant knowledge in various fields of human endeavour and yet at the same time free his mind from all tradition so that he is able to investigate, to find out, to discover – and the arts are very much part of this process. The intermingling of experiences in our unique daily lives could lead to unexpected pairing or grouping of thoughts and, together with our common sense and linear reasoning, and then coming to a new conclusion. The individualistic approach favoured in modern art, especially abstraction, pushes artists into their own carapaces and they are often creating out of their own space, but the process is about rebalancing of thought and the awareness of different possibilities. This comes from a quiet centre in you; whilst engaged in the work, and even through the struggles that are inevitable, you know that is what you are meant to do. The conversation one has with oneself examines the truth of the shapes produced and the placement needed to create a coherent image, or may lead to the acceptance that the part you have coveted throughout needs to be destroyed. When things go well there is a sense of completeness. A sense of harmony, space, proportion and strength all play their part. It is the creation of something with that force that gives a curious delight when I produce something that wasn't there before.

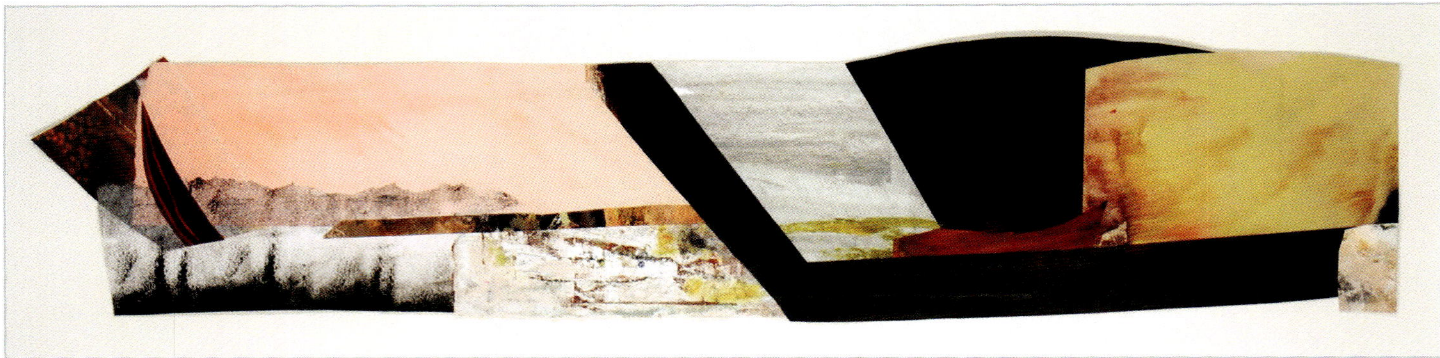

summers eve *mixed media collage* *125 x 45cm*

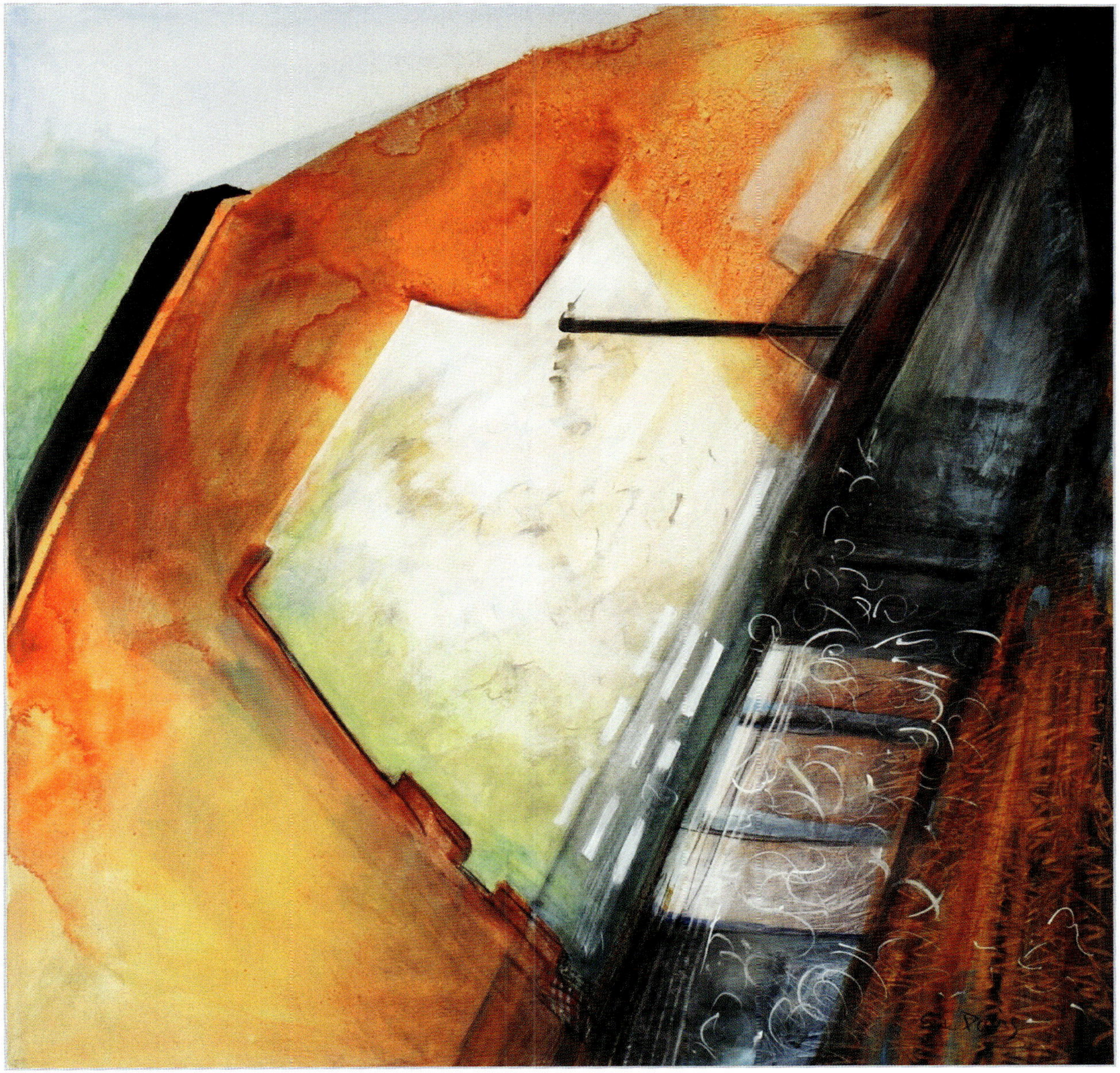

chance window *mixed media on board* *110 x 110cm*

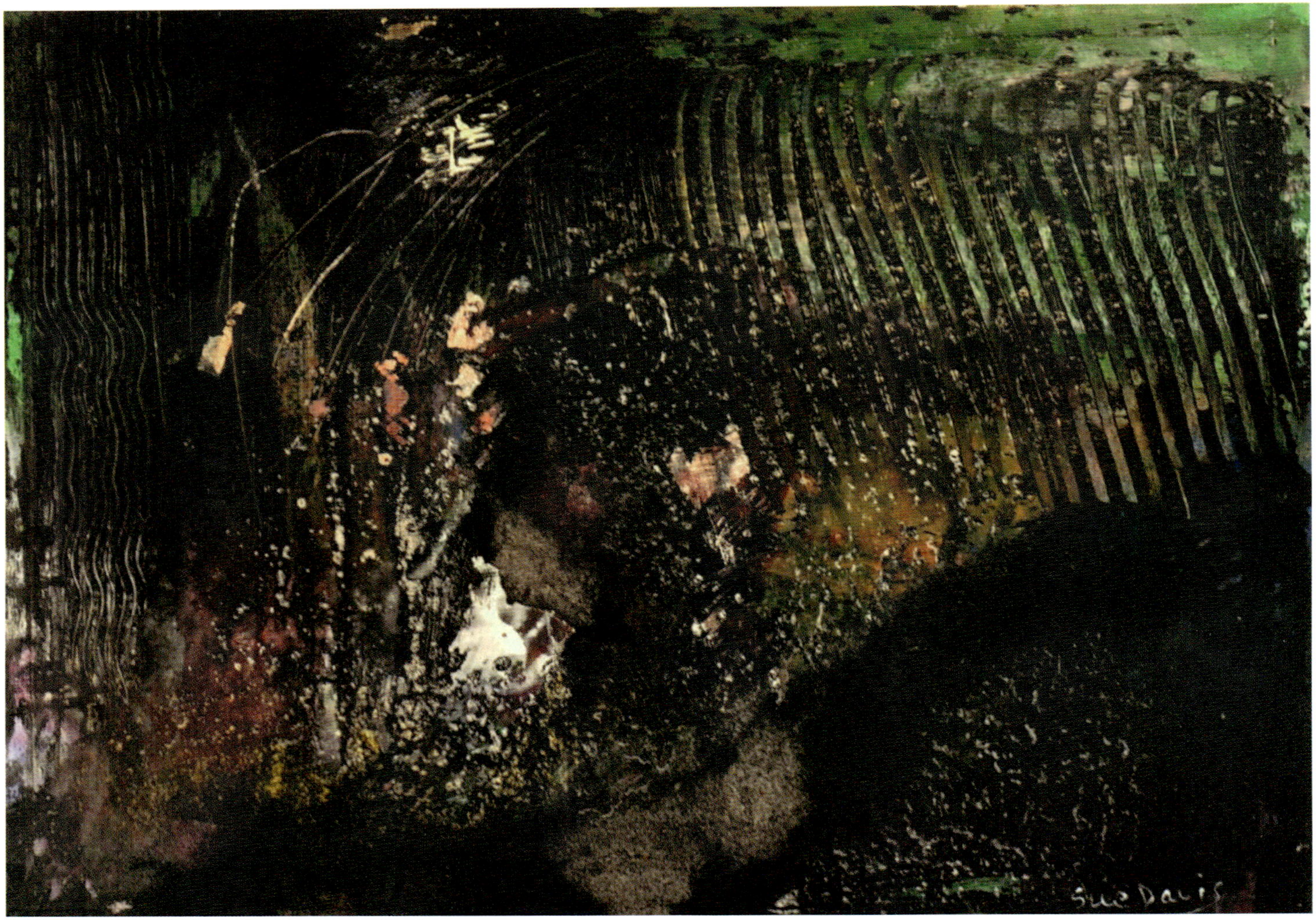

tracked embers *mixed media on board* *68 x 50cm*

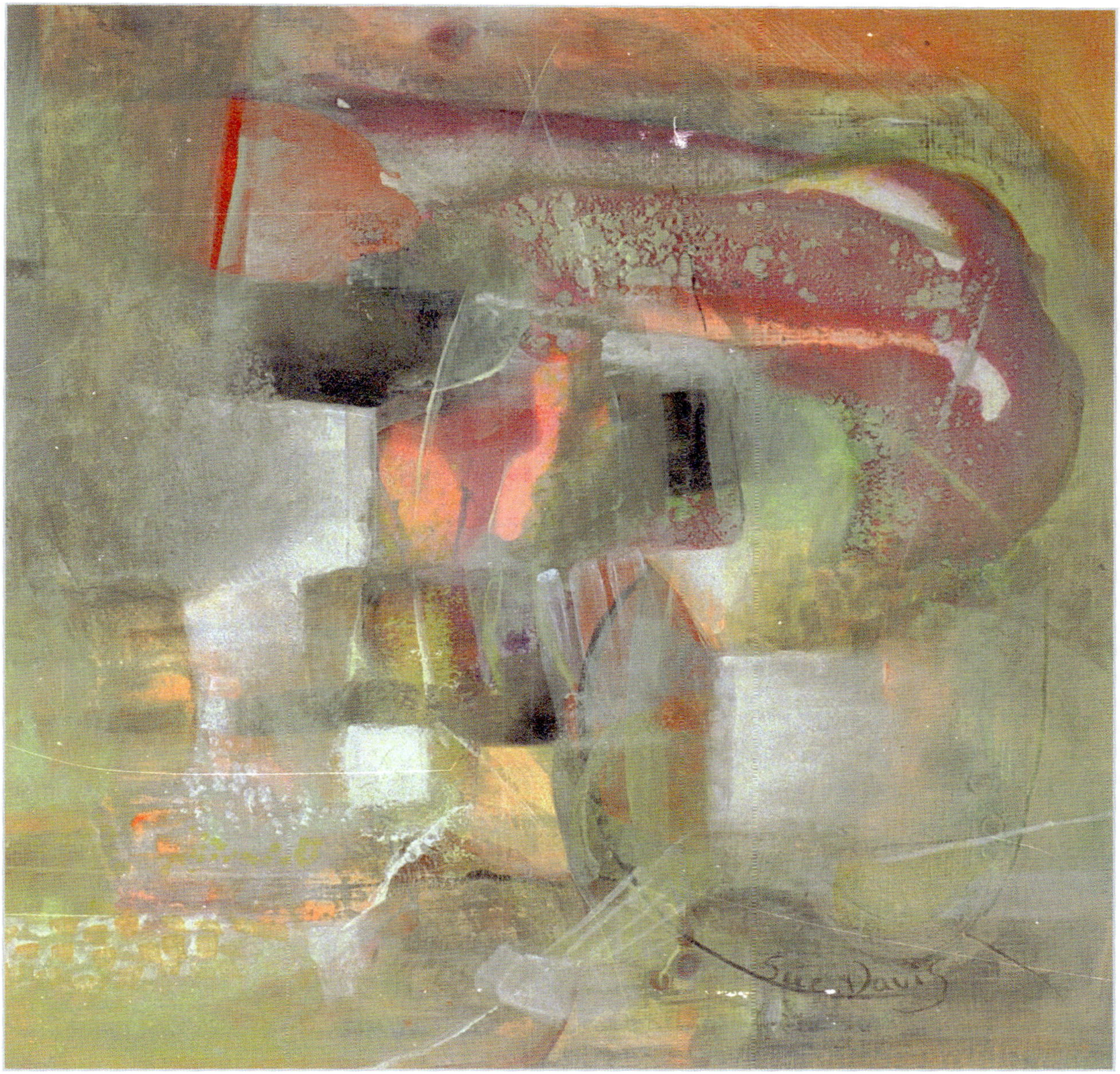

luminous lurch *acrylic on board* *35 x 35cm*

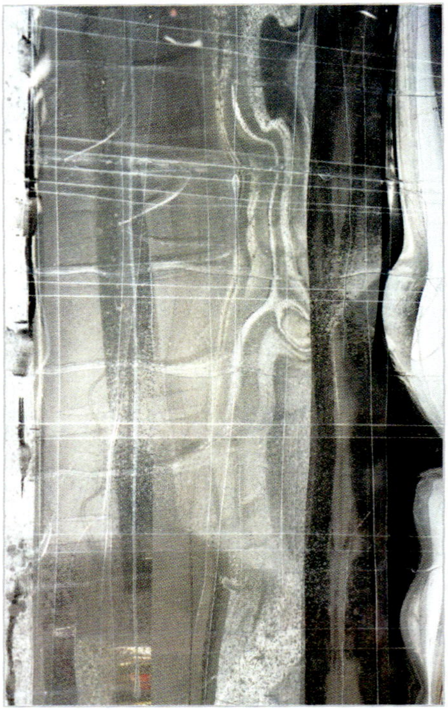

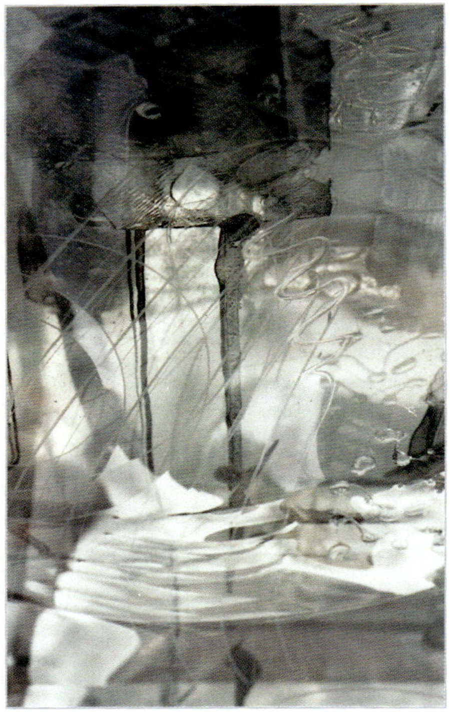

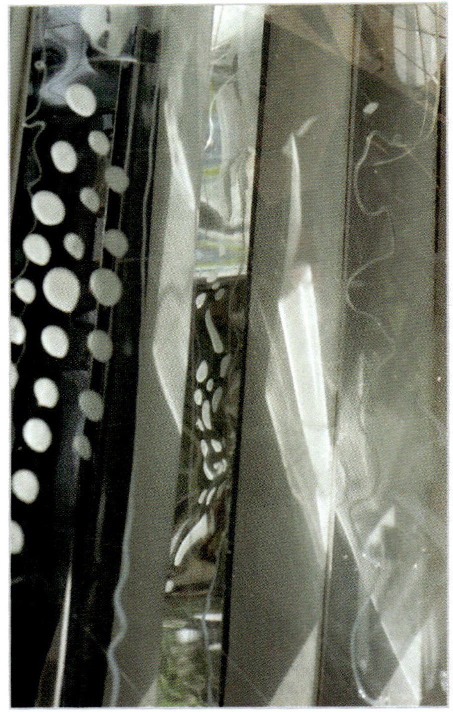

constructions

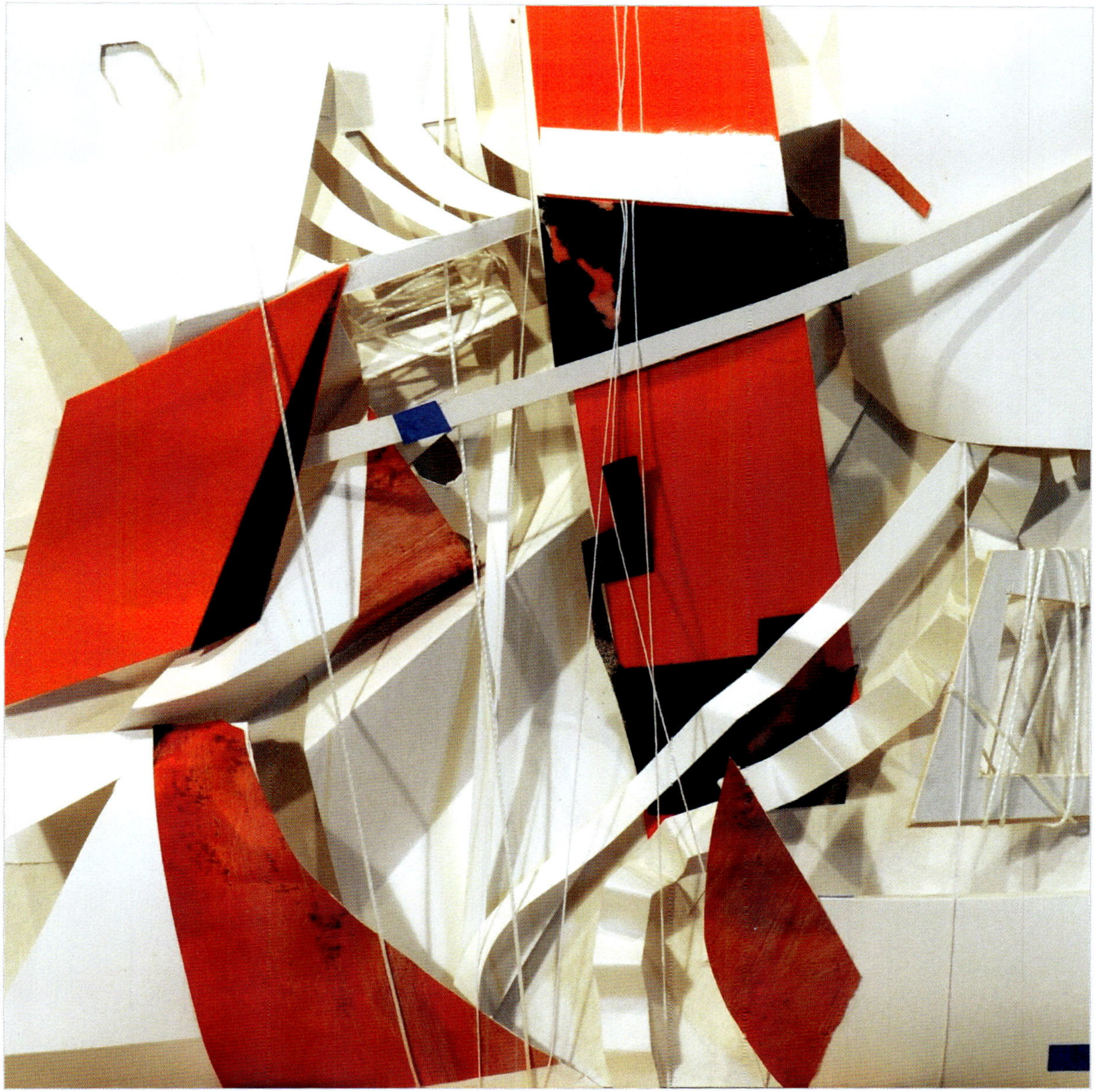

pasmore riot *construction* *31 x 31cm*

PERSONAL CONCLUSIONS

Although abstraction is thought of as a single style, there are many approaches to it and an equally large variety of solutions. Abstraction may stem from objects or landscape (such as the tradition in St Ives), philosophy or scientific schemes (like Bridget Riley's work) or material and process. The closest art movements to 'Abstraction Unbound' (this being the term I feel most comfortable with) are 'Abstract Expressionism' and 'Orphism', in that my approach essentially does not hold any recognisable images. As there is no actual starting point and no image to progress towards, it has to be an exploration and leap of faith coupled with a discerning sensibility.

The concept of 'Abstraction Unbound' derives from somewhere within. Somewhere we cannot grasp. It is a place that is on the edge of something – it is a questing to access something I know is there but do not wish to find. It is a place that is dark at times but has great joy. It is about regaining the spiritual for art. For those that believe it is connected to organised religion it is gained from outside. Putting those havens aside, spirituality comes from within and is available to everyone. Many artists believe in the redemptive power of artistic consciousness. I also believe the arts occupy a place which can force people to confront themselves face to face and provide a link between humanity and the unknown inner universe, possibly to achieve lost contact with the subconscious, but probably just a space for dreaming. Looking at art provides an encounter, and there is little point if you know in advance what it contains. Hopefully it talks back to you, opening up fresh ideas. Each artist will impose practices and rules that they think are important to a piece. One of my concerns is the need for the piece to stand the 'test of time'. That is to say I would like there still to be interest and new thoughts arising from them in years to come. With that in mind, probably due to my early experience with three dimensional work, some form of depth is desirable. This is often not the case with many abstractions such as those of Piet Mondrian, Terry Frost or Barnett Newman, who concentrated on the two dimensional qualities of an image, but it is present in the work of Lee Krasner and Bryan Wynter. Visual stimuli and ideas are involved but they are without any direct reference to known images, memory, nostalgia, legend, myth, or knowledge – it is just intuitive freedom.

As I have changed donkeys from ceramics to painting in mid-career I have not always been in 'the right place at the right time', which has to a degree left me on the edge of the fine art world. Coupled with the decision to pursue 'Abstraction Unbound' which is hard for people to tune into, I have to accept that I may never achieve critical acclaim. I would say there are hundreds of good artists producing good work. If you can decide what you like for yourself, Aladdin's caves await you. Leave behind what you see in the commercial galleries; ignore the critics and their words; choose your own freedom; rely on yourself. Let a work come to you and into your thoughts. It can be anything and it is owned by you.

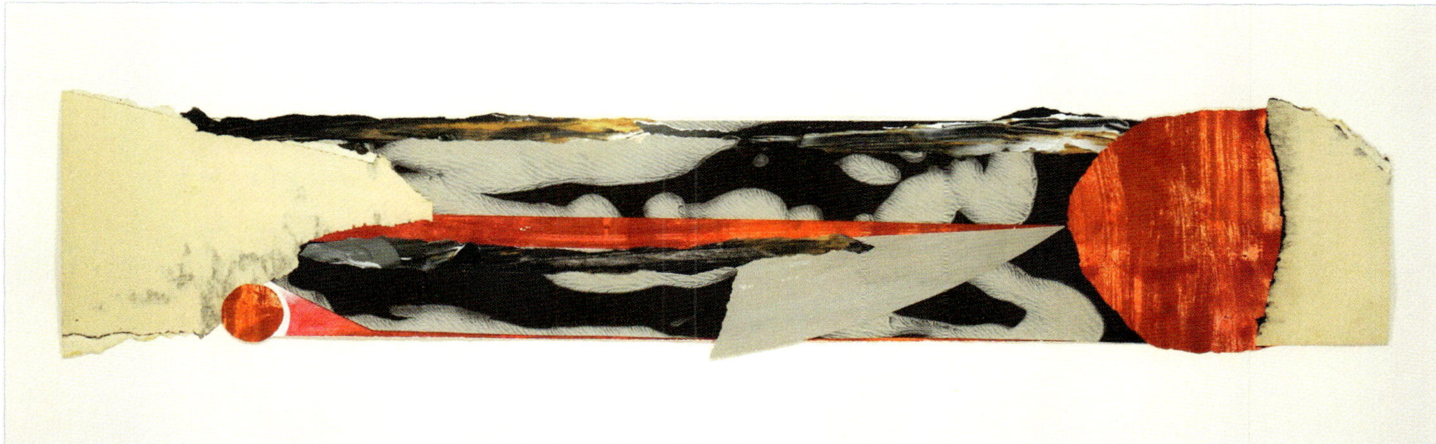

Midday *mixed media collage* *125 x 45cm*

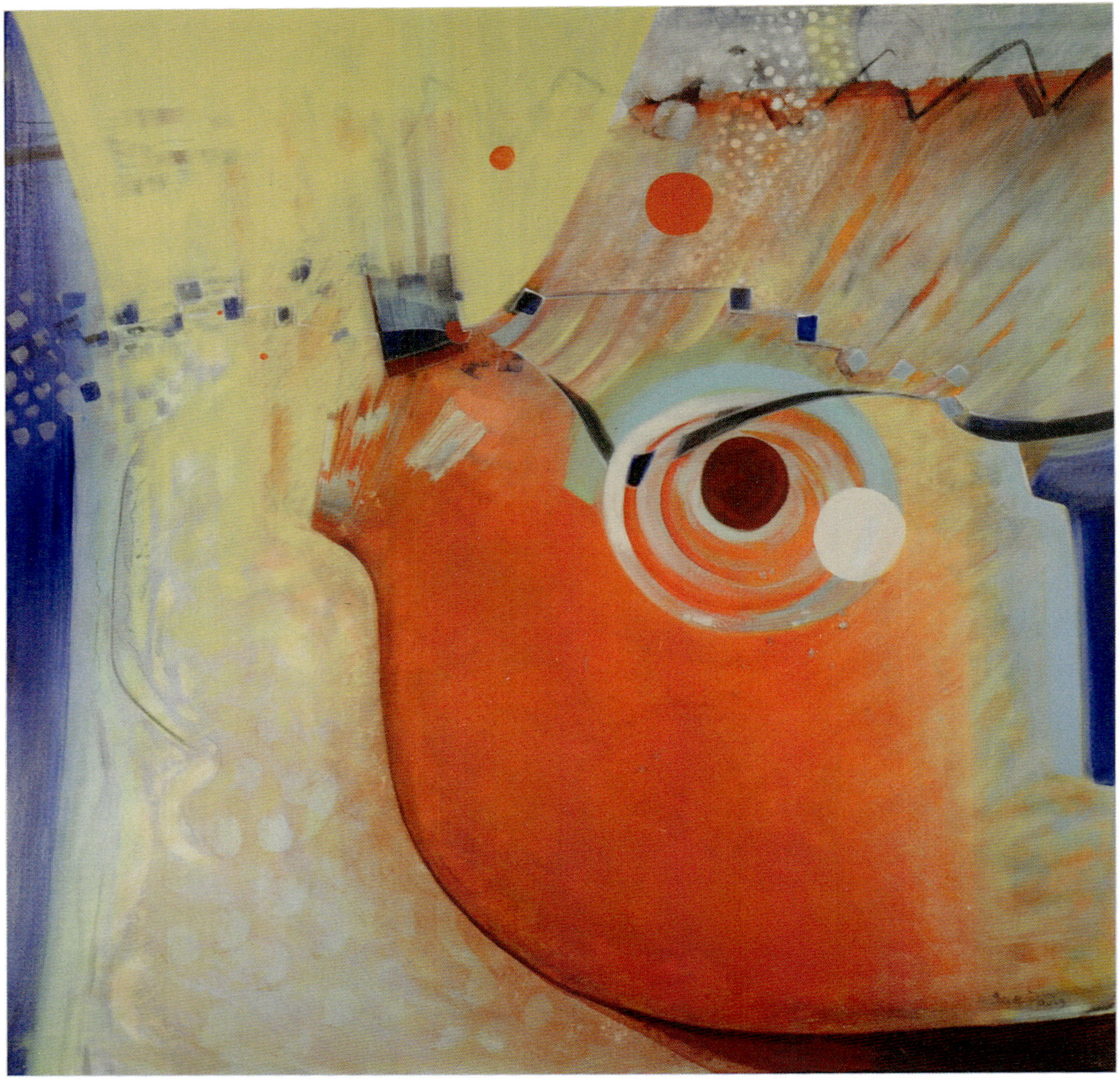

drum roll *mixed media on canvas* *100 x 100cm*

LIFE

Ca[...]nca

The Most Beloved Movie of All Time

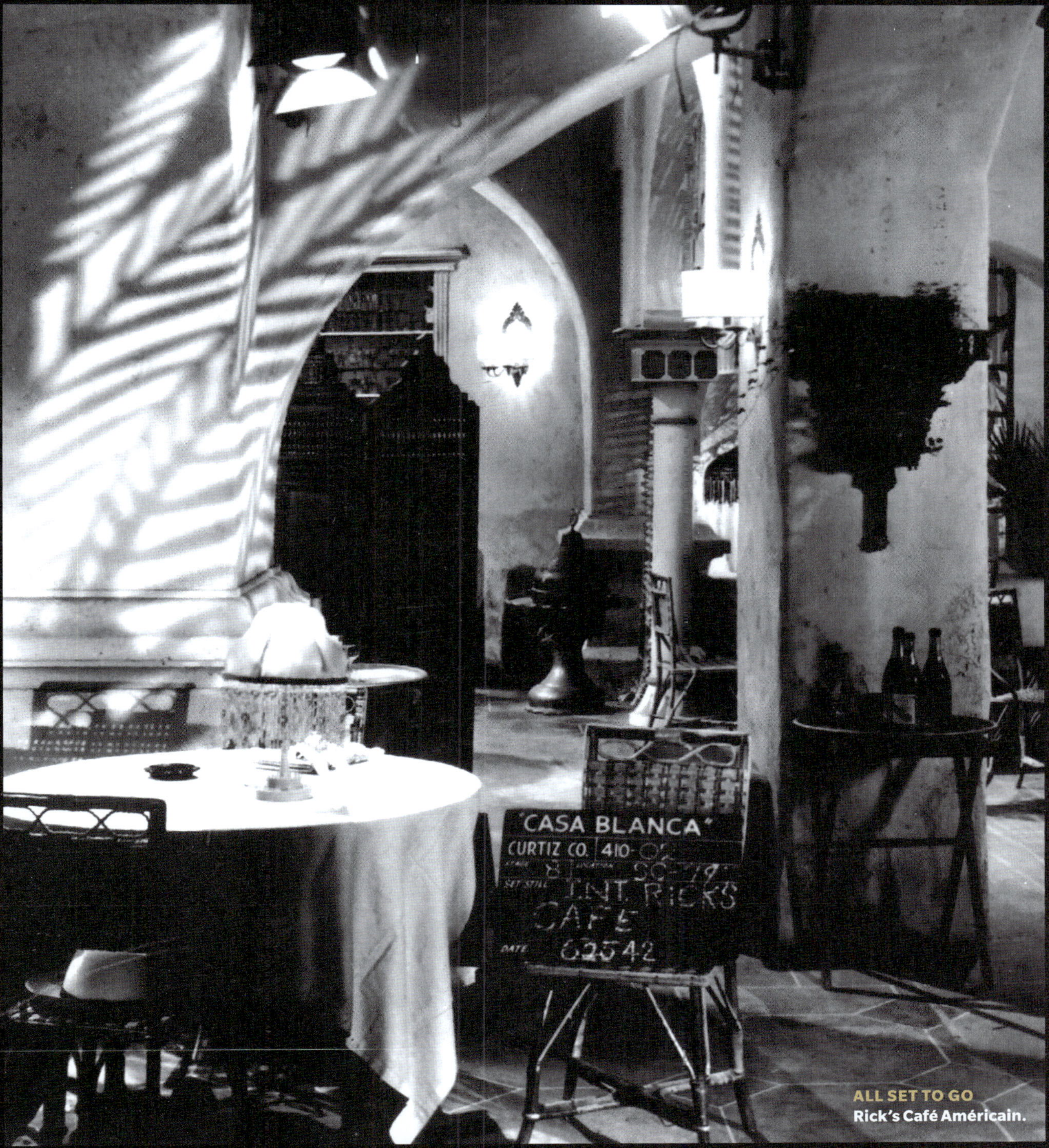

ALL SET TO GO Rick's Café Américain.

MARC WANAMAKER/BISON ARCHIVES

CONTENTS

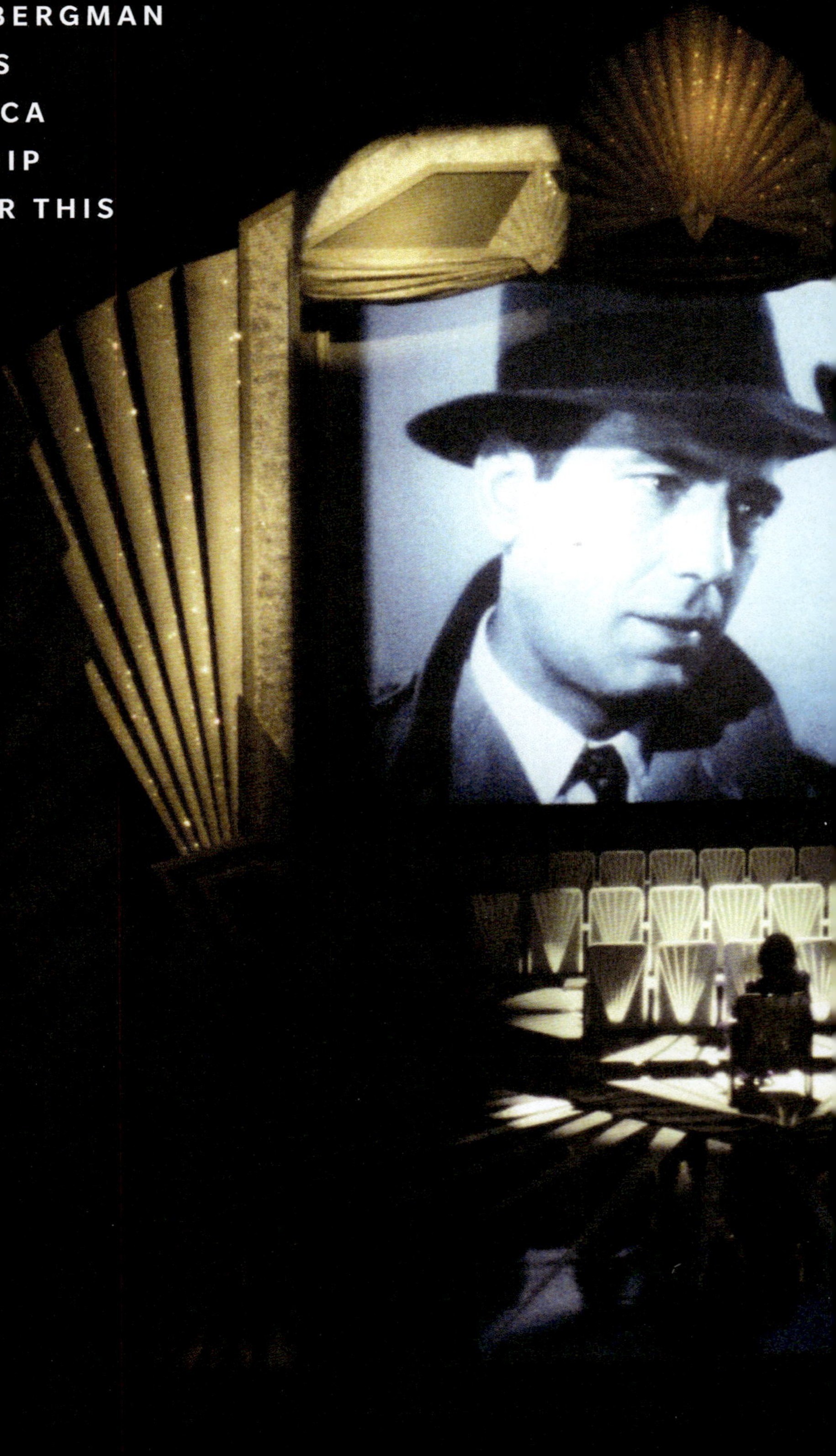

THAT'S ENTERTAINMENT
Actor Lucie Arnaz, who performed "Hooray for Hollywood" for the 53rd Academy Awards ceremony in 1981, watched a clip of *Casablanca*.

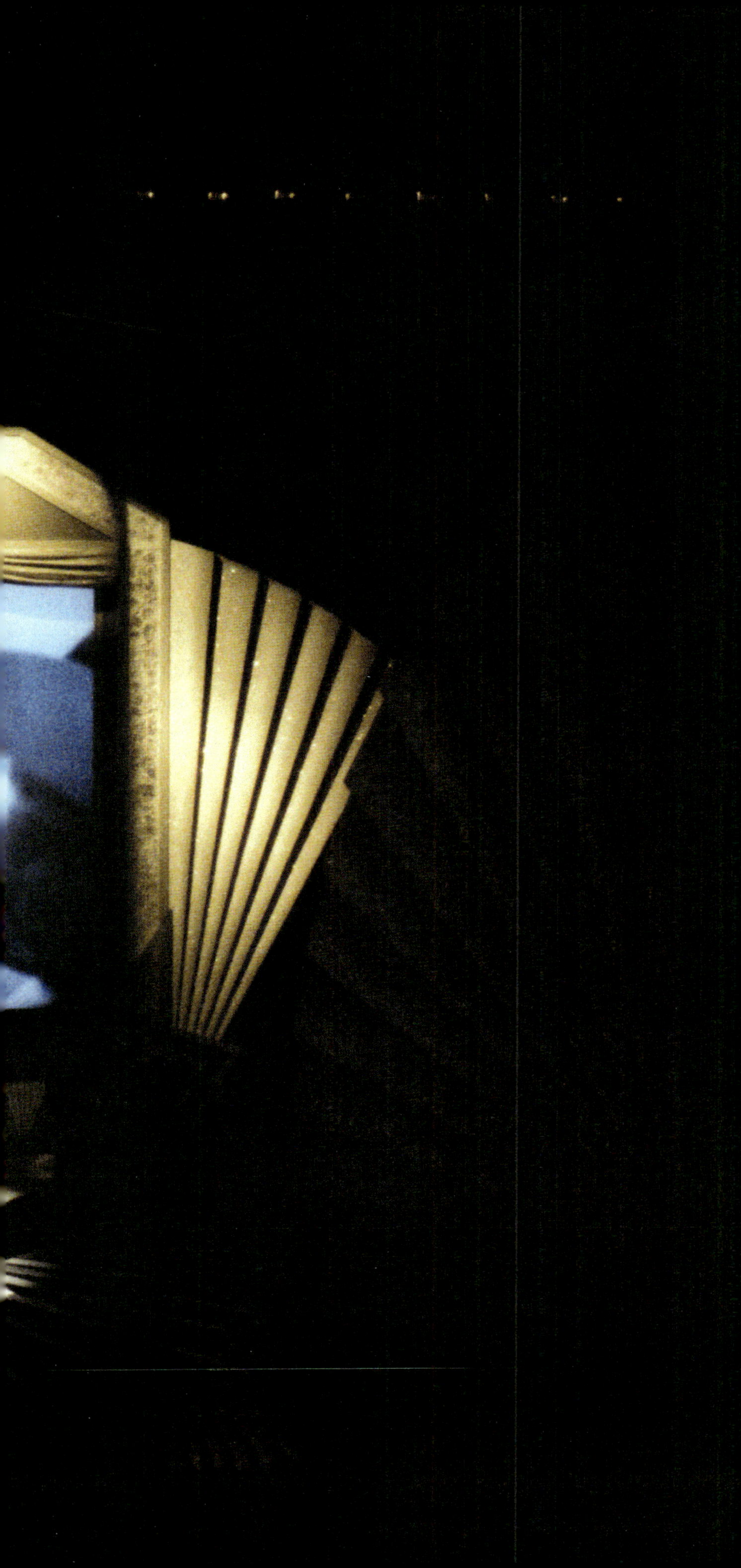

LIFE CASABLANCA
75TH ANNIVERSARY

EDITOR/WRITER Eileen Daspin
EDITORIAL DIRECTOR Kostya Kennedy
DIRECTOR OF PHOTOGRAPHY Christina Lieberman
ART DIRECTOR Mimi Park
COPY CHIEF Parlan McGaw
COPY EDITOR Joel Van Liew
PICTURE EDITOR Rachel Hatch
WRITER-REPORTER Daniel S. Levy
PHOTO ASSISTANT Alessandra Bianco

TIME INC. BOOKS
PUBLISHER Margot Schupf
SENIOR VICE PRESIDENT, FINANCE Anthony Palumbo
VICE PRESIDENT, MARKETING Jeremy Biloon
EXECUTIVE DIRECTOR, MARKETING SERVICES Carol Pittard
DIRECTOR, BRAND MARKETING Jean Kennedy
SALES DIRECTOR Christi Crowley
ASSOCIATE DIRECTOR, BRAND MARKETING Bryan Christian
ASSOCIATE DIRECTOR, FINANCE Jill Earyes
ASSISTANT GENERAL COUNSEL Andrew Goldberg
ASSISTANT DIRECTOR, PRODUCTION Susan Chodakiewicz
SENIOR MANAGER, FINANCE Ashley Petrasovic
SENIOR BRAND MANAGER Katherine Barnet
PREPRESS MANAGER Alex Voznesenskiy
ASSOCIATE PROJECT AND PRODUCTION MANAGER Anna Riego Muñiz

EDITORIAL DIRECTOR Kostya Kennedy
CREATIVE DIRECTOR Gary Stewart
DIRECTOR OF PHOTOGRAPHY Christina Lieberman
EDITORIAL OPERATIONS DIRECTOR Jamie Roth Major
SENIOR EDITORS Eileen Daspin, Alyssa Smith
MANAGER, EDITORIAL OPERATIONS Gina Scauzillo
ASSOCIATE ART DIRECTOR Allie Adams
COPY CHIEF Rina Bander
ASSISTANT EDITOR Courtney Mifsud

TIME INC. PREMEDIA
Richard K. Prue (Director), Richard Shaffer (Production), Keith Aurelio, Kevin Hart, Rosalie Khan, Patricia Koh, Marco Lau, Brian Mai, Rudi Papiri, Clara Renauro

SPECIAL THANKS Brad Beatson, Brett Finkelstein, Melissa Frankenberry, Kristina Jutzi, Simon Keeble, Seniqua Koger, Kate Roncinske

Published by LIFE Books, an imprint of Time Inc. Books, 225 Liberty Street, New York, NY 10281

Vol. 18, No. 3 • February 2, 2018

We welcome your comments and suggestions about LIFE Books. Please write to us at: LIFE Books, Attention: Book Editors, P.O. Box 62310, Tampa, FL 33662-2310

THIS PAGE ABC PHOTO ARCHIVES/GETTY
FRONT COVER EVERETT
BACK COVER EVERETT

INTRODUCTION

LOVE, ALWAYS

In the truest, most affecting love stories there are no happy endings. Romeo could not have Juliet. Scarlett could not end up with Rhett. Antony could not live with Cleopatra—nor Richard Burton with Elizabeth Taylor. Likewise, although *Casablanca's* screenwriters struggled with the details of the film's last moments, they ultimately knew that Rick and Ilsa would have to give each other up. The film at its core is about self-sacrifice and honor. Rick had to do the noble thing, the right thing. That is why audiences loved it in 1943 and why on its 75th anniversary, we continue to love it today. *Casablanca* represented and represents our best selves, our ideal world.

There are of course plenty of other contributing factors to *Casablanca's* popularity and endurance: murder, heroism, intrigue, spies, double crosses, and black-marketeers, all in an exotic locale. The acting was superb. Humphrey Bogart, in a role that turned him into an international sex symbol, mesmerized audiences as the emotionally wounded cynic who transforms into a self-sacrificing idealist. Ingrid Bergman as his true love, radiated purity and principles. Bit players and extras, many of them European immigrants who had escaped Hitler, infused the film with a verisimilitude that central casting could never have duplicated. The dialog sparkled, the moral code was clear.

"I feel about *Casablanca* that it has a life of its own," Bergman said toward the end of her life. "There is something mystical about it. It seems to have filled a need, a need that was there before the film."

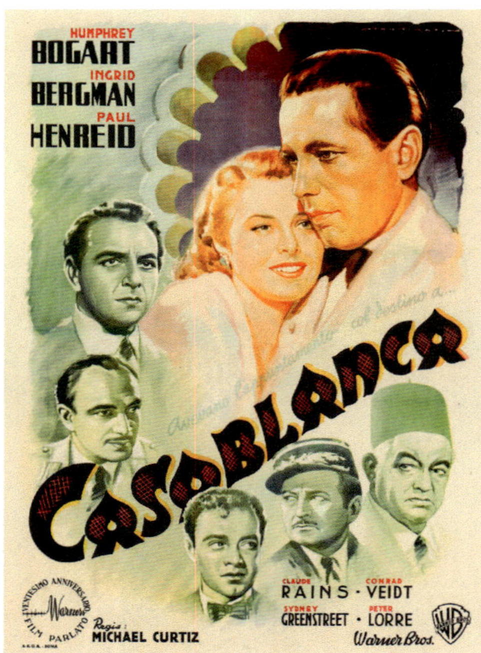

HERITAGE AUCTIONS

Yet from the beginning, the film's success defied reason. Some early readers at Warner Bros. discouraged producer Hal Wallis from acquiring the play that inspired the movie, *Everybody Comes to Rick's,* because it was melodramatic hokum. "This guy Rick is two-parts Hemingway, one-part Scott Fitzgerald, and a dash of café Christ," commented writer Robert Buckner. For all of Bogart and Bergman's on-screen chemistry, off-screen they never clicked. An early showing of the final cut, in Warner's Huntington Park theater, got a lukewarm reception. Even screenwriters Julius and Philip Epstein, who were responsible for most of the script, wrote to Wallis saying they thought the film was going to be a big flop. Wallis kept the note, Julius told Aljean Harmetz, author of *Round Up the Usual Suspects.* "Whenever we had an argument with him about anything, he would open his desk, take out the memo and give it to us."

Fate seemed to intervene in *Casablanca's* favor at each juncture. *Everybody Comes to Rick's* landed with Wallis five days after the bombing of Pearl Harbor and was rushed into production to take advantage of an expected demand for war films. Wallis wanted William Wyler to direct, but Warner's Michael Curtiz was available, so he got the job. In a deal to secure Cary Grant for *Arsenic and Old Lace,* Warner almost lent Bogart to Columbia, Grant's studio, but the swap got called off because of Columbia's scheduling issues. The biggest bit of luck for *Casablanca* was Operation Torch, the invasion of North Africa by Allied troops, many of whom came ashore at Casablanca, the port city in northern Morocco, prompting Warner to move up the release date by more than half a year.

Audiences connected immediately and *Casablanca* became

MARC WANAMAKER/BISON ARCHIVES

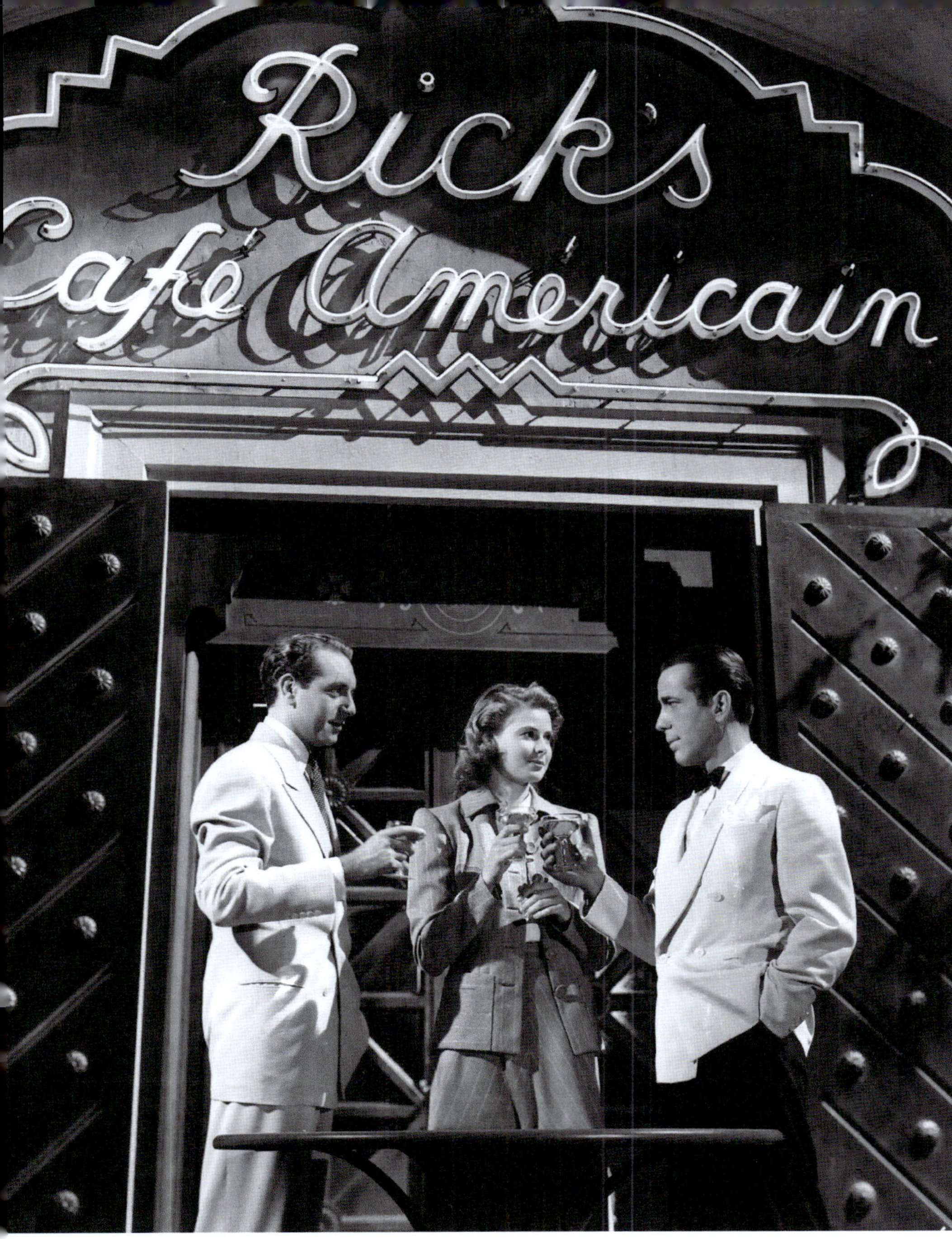

EXOTIC LOOK

The poster on the opposite page was produced in Italy in 1946, the year the film opened in that country, and sold for a record-breaking $478,000 in the United States in 2017. At left, Paul Henreid, Ingrid Bergman, and Humphrey Bogart toast on the Rick's Café set for a publicity still.

the sixth top-grossing movie for 1943 and, the following year, the winner of three Academy Awards—for Best Picture, Best Writing, and Best Direction. But it was really Bogart's death in January 1957 that resurrected the actor as a renegade hero, and with him, the reputation of *Casablanca*. An arts theater in Cambridge, Massachusetts, began screening *Casablanca* for Harvard students, who started showing up in snap-brim hats and trench coats, able to quote sections of the film by heart. Bogie fever spread. *To bogart* became a verb for the 1960s counterculture, meaning to hang on to a shared marijuana cigarette, after the actor's penchant for smoking. Bogart's ghost turned up in a Woody Allen play and movie, *Play It Again, Sam,* offering romantic advice to its nebbishy hero.

Today, there is hardly a list of best films of all time that doesn't include *Casablanca* in its top five. Some even have it at No. 1. The movie is densely plotted. There are no chase scenes or special effects (unless you count the spinning globe used just after the opening credits). Its characters are ambiguous, complex. The story is sentimental. It celebrates sacrifice and idealism. In short, *Casablanca* possesses none of the features of a 2018 box office hit. And yet the film is as beloved as ever, its themes and ideals serving as a lingua franca connecting disparate generations. As Senator Elizabeth Warren has written, "Each time I watch it, *Casablanca* gives me hope."

Here's looking at you, *Casablanca*. ■

DARK VICTORY
In March 1944, crowds arrived at Grauman's Chinese Theatre for the 16th Academy Awards, where *Casablanca* would win three Oscars. Due to wartime restrictions, only two searchlights were allowed to illuminate the theater.

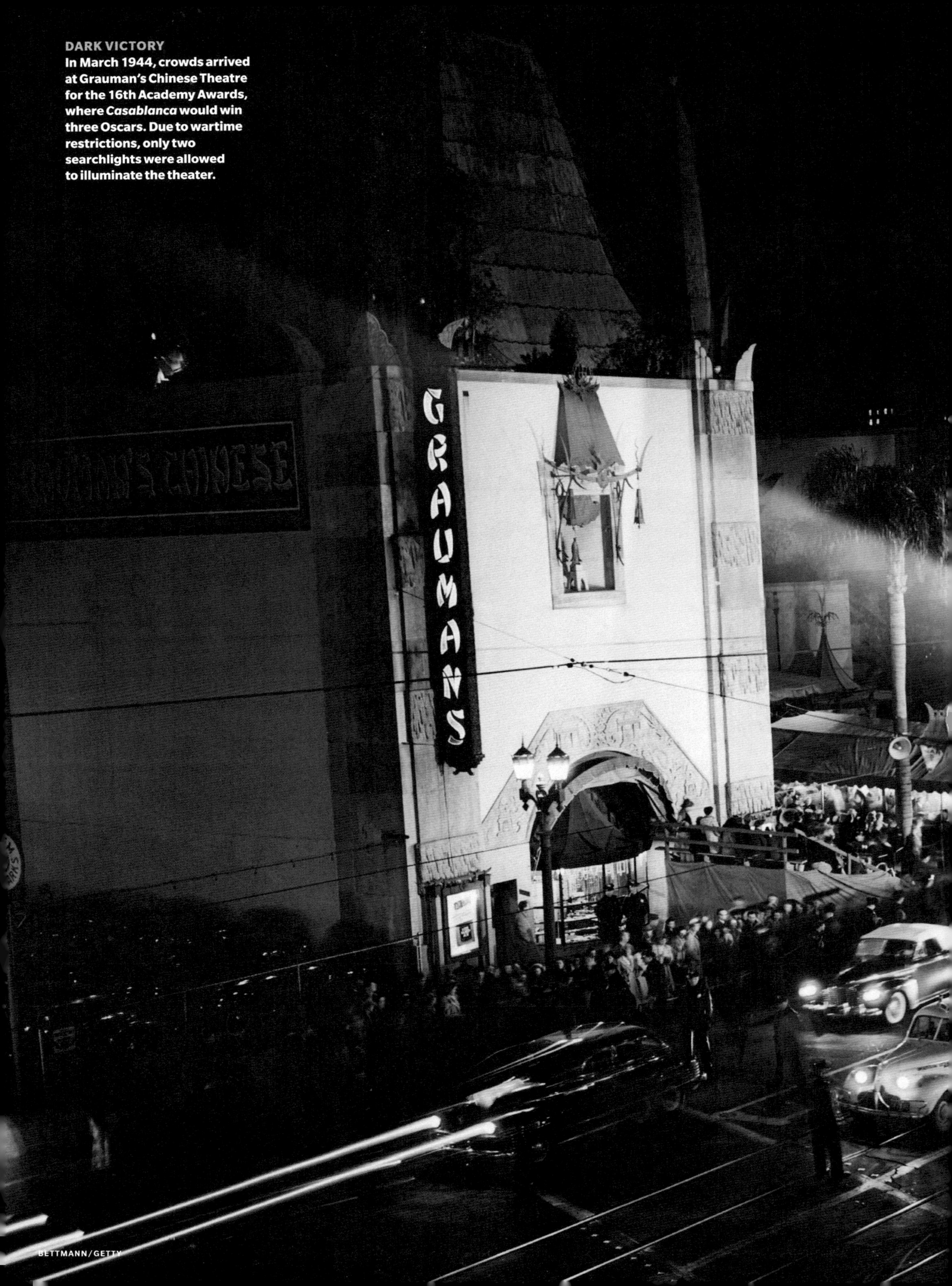

BETTMANN/GETTY

A HOLLYWOOD PRODUCTION

As the United States entered World War II, studios rushed to get films underway before talent shipped out for combat. One of the first to get the green light: *Casablanca*

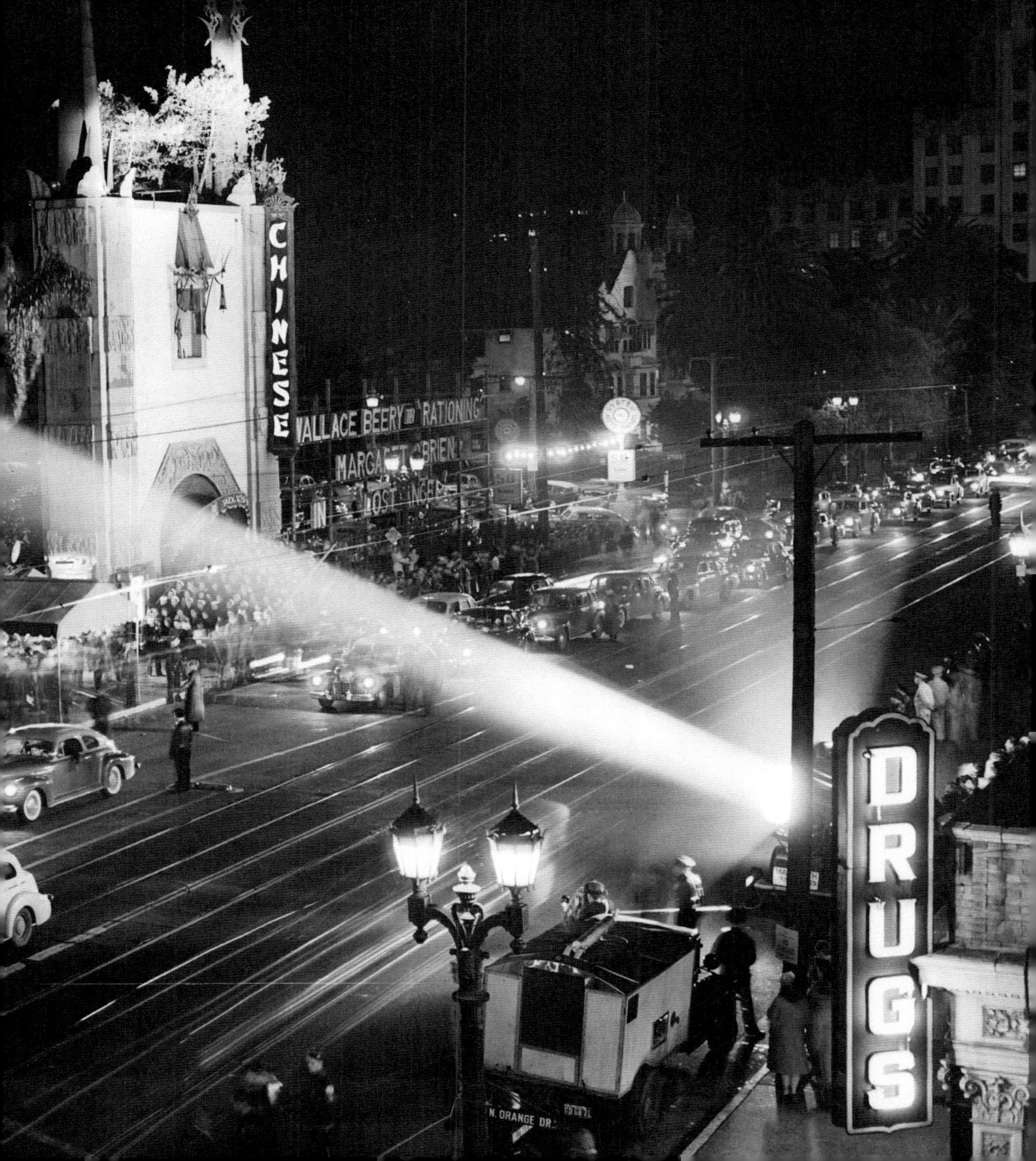

On December 12, 1941, with America reeling from the attack on Pearl Harbor, an unproduced stage play, *Everybody Comes to Rick's,* landed on the desk of Warner Bros. producer Hal Wallis. The melodrama centered on an American expat in Morocco and the plight of refugees seeking to escape Adolf Hitler; its characters were undeveloped, its dialog was hokey, and it had been rejected by studios throughout Hollywood.

But Wallis liked the play's romance and exotic locale, which echoed *Algiers,* a 1938 hit similarly set in North Africa. And the timing was, well, optimal. For U.S. audiences freshly committed to beating the Germans, what could be more appealing than "the story of a laconic American solving the problems of Europeans," Wallis wrote in his autobiography. He agreed to pay an unprecedented fee, $20,000—the combined annual salary of roughly half a dozen Warner employees—and within the month, had settled on an evocative, one-word title for the property, *Casablanca,* after the Vichy-controlled port where the action unfolded.

Of all the forces that propelled one of America's best-loved films to the silver screen, few were as important as World War II itself. The idea for the plot originated with Murray Burnett, an English teacher and aspiring playwright from New York who traveled to Austria in 1938 just after that nation was annexed into Nazi Germany. He witnessed terrified refugees fleeing the country and returned home to write about it. Jack Warner, the studio's head, was stubbornly anti-Nazi before many of his contemporaries and was determined to produce a film to expose Hitler. Filming began with only half a script because principal writers Philip and Julius Epstein, before setting pen to paper, had flown to Washington for a month to serve their country assisting Major Frank

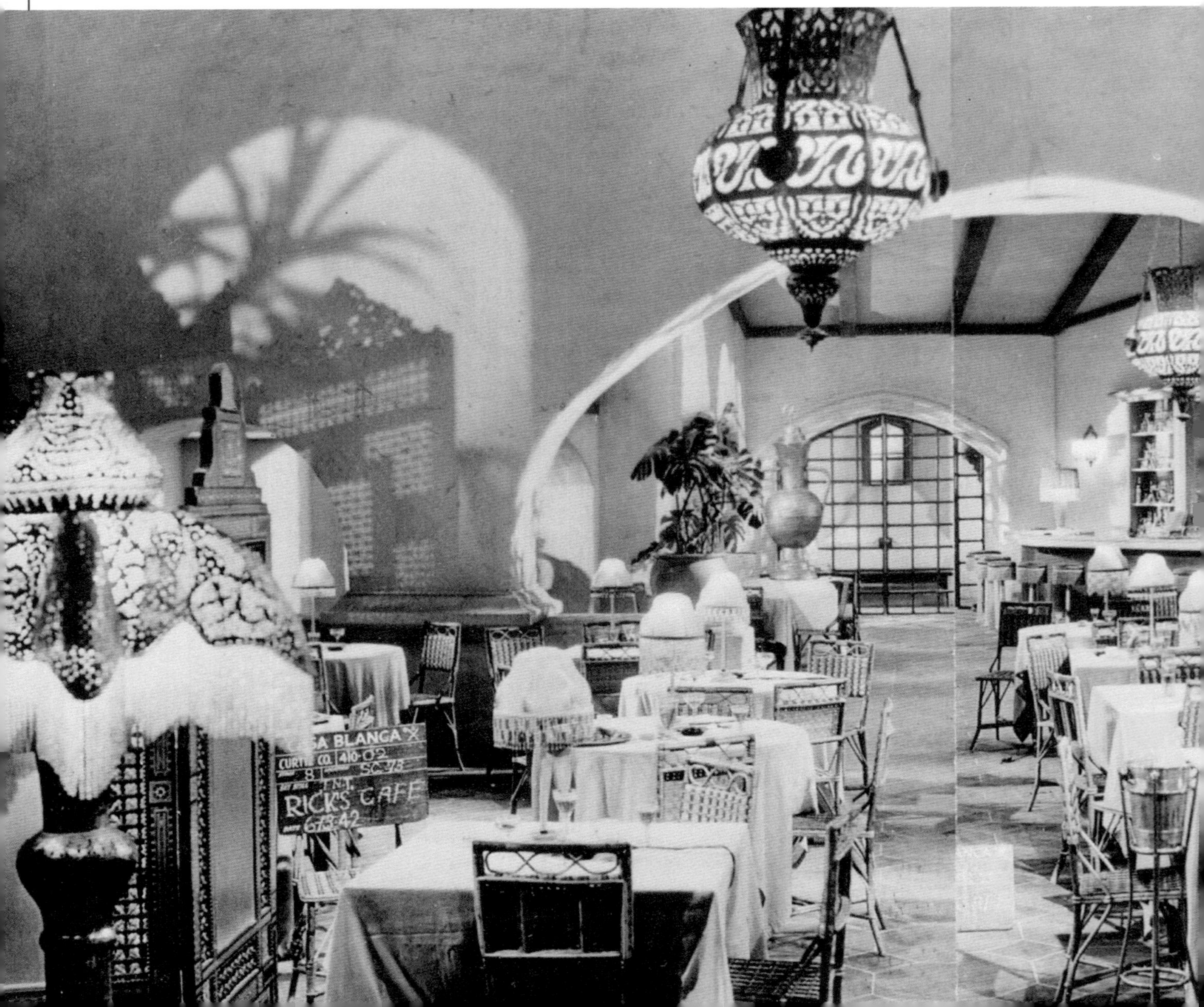

Capra prepare a propaganda film series for U.S. troops.

Even the federal government, seeking to inject films of the period with issues important to the military effort, played a role in shaping *Casablanca*'s narrative. All studios were instructed to ask themselves one question: Will this picture help win the war? More direct intervention came from Hollywood's own censors at the Production Code Administration (PCA), an industry morals watchdog. The PCA objected to explicit mentions of sex between the lead lovers, Rick and Ilsa; snipped at the plot thread involving Louis Renault, the womanizing police

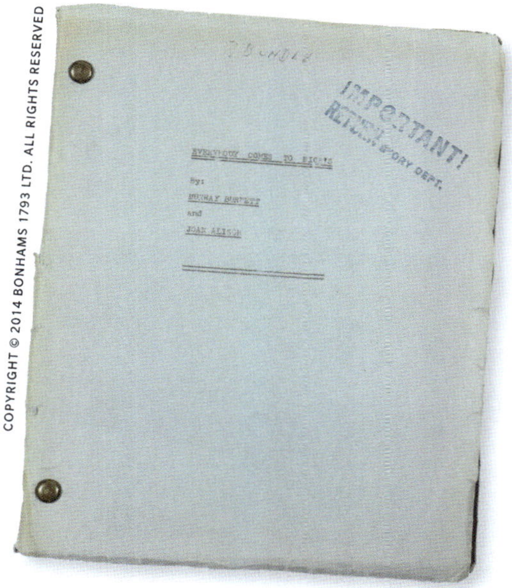

PAGE-TURNER
***Casablanca* was based on the unproduced play *Everybody Comes to Rick's*. The copy at left, with notes from Warner Bros. staff, sold at auction for a little more than $106,000 in 2014. Rick's Café Américain, seen below in a studio composite photo, was one of the few original sets built for the film. Most were recycled from other Warner Bros. productions because of wartime restrictions on building supplies.**

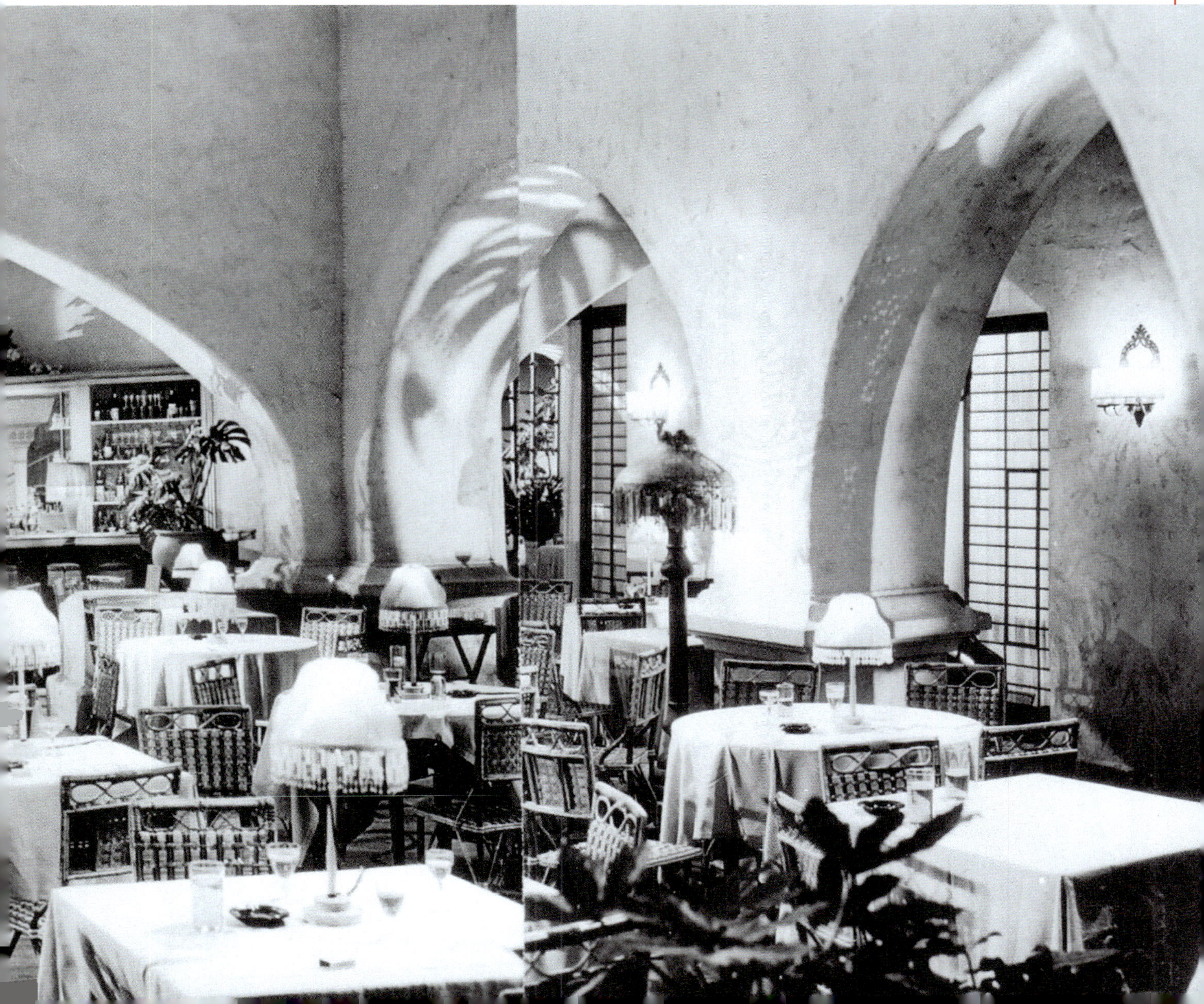

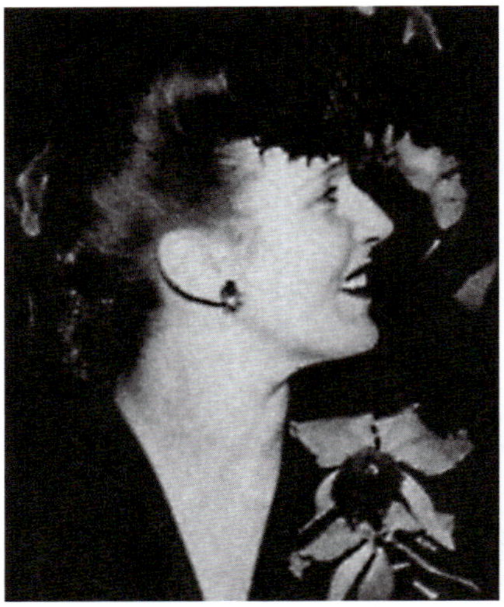

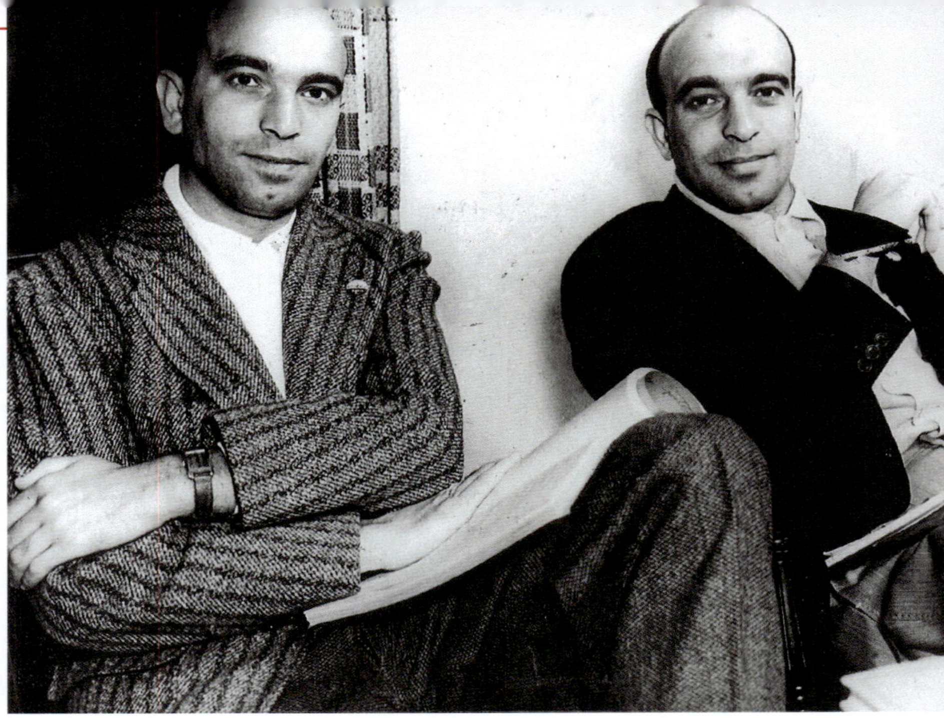

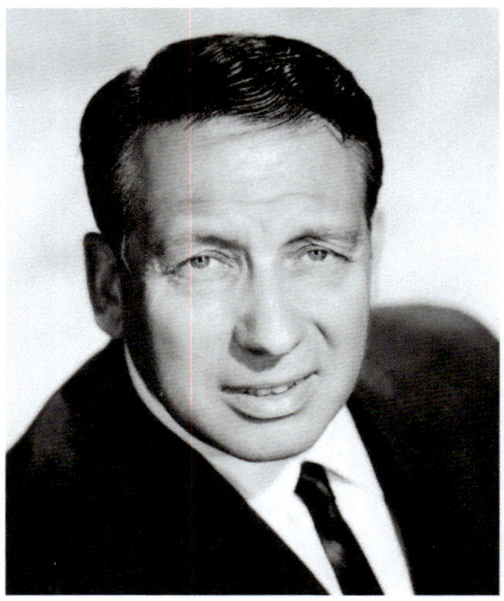

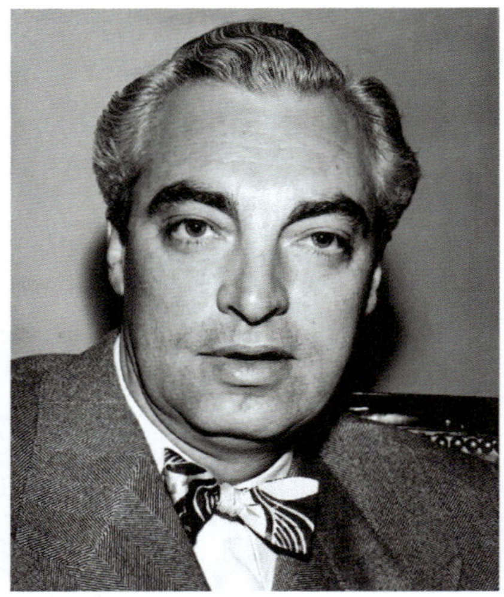

prefect; and objected to an early version of the ending, which had Rick shooting the Nazi villain, Major Strasser, in the back instead of the chest. The reasoning: The scene would reflect badly on the behavior of Allied troops.

Like most enduring films, *Casablanca* is a product of its era, an era that happened to be high-minded, prudish by today's mores, and deeply patriotic. But the movie's genius lay in its ability to fit not only the needs of wartime audiences but also of audiences who came many decades later, writes Aljean Harmetz in *Round Up the Usual Suspects,* a well-researched account of the making of the film. "There are better movies than *Casablanca,* but no other movie better demonstrates America's mythological vision of itself—tough on the outside and moral within, capable of sacrifice and romance without sacrificing the individualism that conquered a continent, sticking its neck out for everybody when circumstances demand heroism."

As with any Hollywood filmmaking enterprise, a myriad of ego, deadline, and financial pressures also came into play. Wallis had to hire some 75 actors and dozens of crew members and prepare a set in a matter of months. He was at odds with Jack Warner, his imperious boss, and his hands were tied by wartime restrictions on building and costume materials. Humphrey Bogart argued constantly with director Michael Curtiz, never got beyond polite with his costar, Ingrid Bergman, and spent most of his time in his trailer playing chess, hoping to avoid his jealous wife, Mayo Methot. Actors struggled with how to approach scenes because half of the script was written on the fly, with an ending decided only the day before the film wrapped. As Harmetz writes, "*Casablanca* was a mosaic of fortune—good and bad."

EVERYONE'S A CRITIC
Top left: Joan Alison, who co-wrote *Everybody Comes to Rick's*. Twins Julius and Philip Epstein (top right) were the primary writers on *Casablanca* but annoyed Jack Warner by regularly arriving at the studio in the afternoon. Other contributors were Howard Koch (above, left), who criticized the Epsteins' comic approach, and Casey Robinson (above, right), who found "the love story deficient." Opposite: The opening credits.

Everybody Comes to Rick's began with a trip that Burnett and his wife, Frances, took to Europe in 1938. Burnett had read about Hitler, but until he got to Vienna, where Frances had extended family, the Nazi threat meant little to him. Austria had just been annexed by Germany and the country's capital was "an indescribable horror, a city of marching feet," Burnett said. Though Jews were still permitted to leave, they were barred from taking money and valuables with them, and Frances's family implored the Burnetts to help some relations smuggle out prized possessions. The couple agreed, and in August they made their move, departing via train with Frances wearing a heavy fur coat and Murray's fingers laden with diamond rings. Soon after, in the south of France, the Burnetts stumbled upon a tableaux that movie lovers now know well. Walking into a café, they discovered a glamorous nightclub teeming with refugees from all over Europe, and a black man playing the piano. "What a setting for a play!" Murray supposedly whispered to his wife, according to the 2017 book *We'll Always Have Casablanca* by Noah Isenberg.

Inspired by these memories of Europe on the brink of war, Burnett in the summer of 1940 began work on the stage play with his writing partner Joan Alison. By the time they finished the 97-page, three-act script, they had settled on the title *Everybody Comes to Rick's,* after the bar in Casablanca where the action takes place. The story follows Rick, an American ex-lawyer who has cheated on his wife in Paris and moved to Morocco. Many of the drama's plot points, characters, and even chunks of dialog would survive the

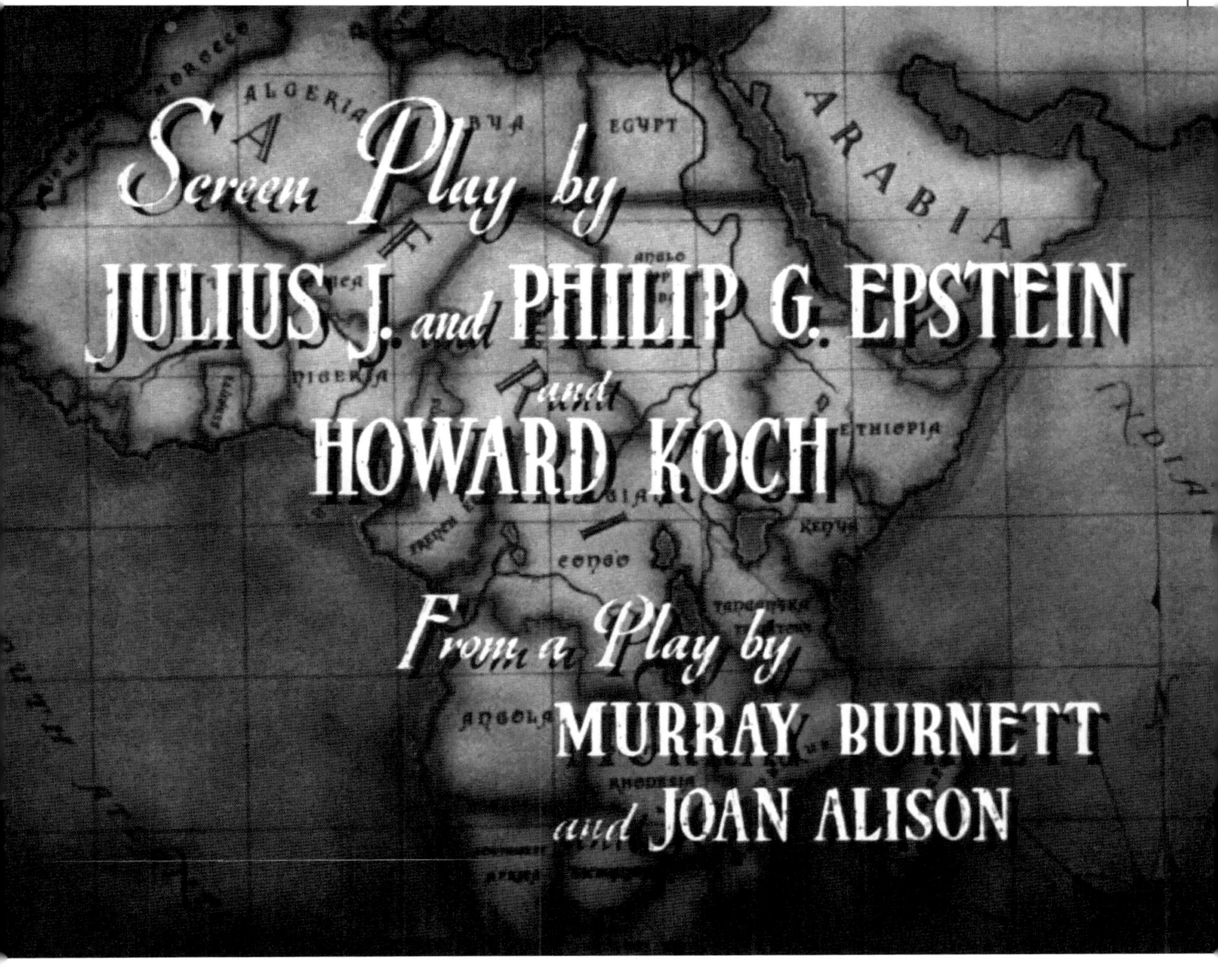

A COUPLA CHARACTERS
Below: Rick Blaine (Humphrey Bogart) talks to Captain Renault (Claude Rains). Bogart and Rains struck up a friendship during filming and occasionally went out for drinks together at the end of a day's shooting. Opposite: The set of Renault's office, where Major Strasser tells resistance hero Victor Laszlo that he will never leave Casablanca.

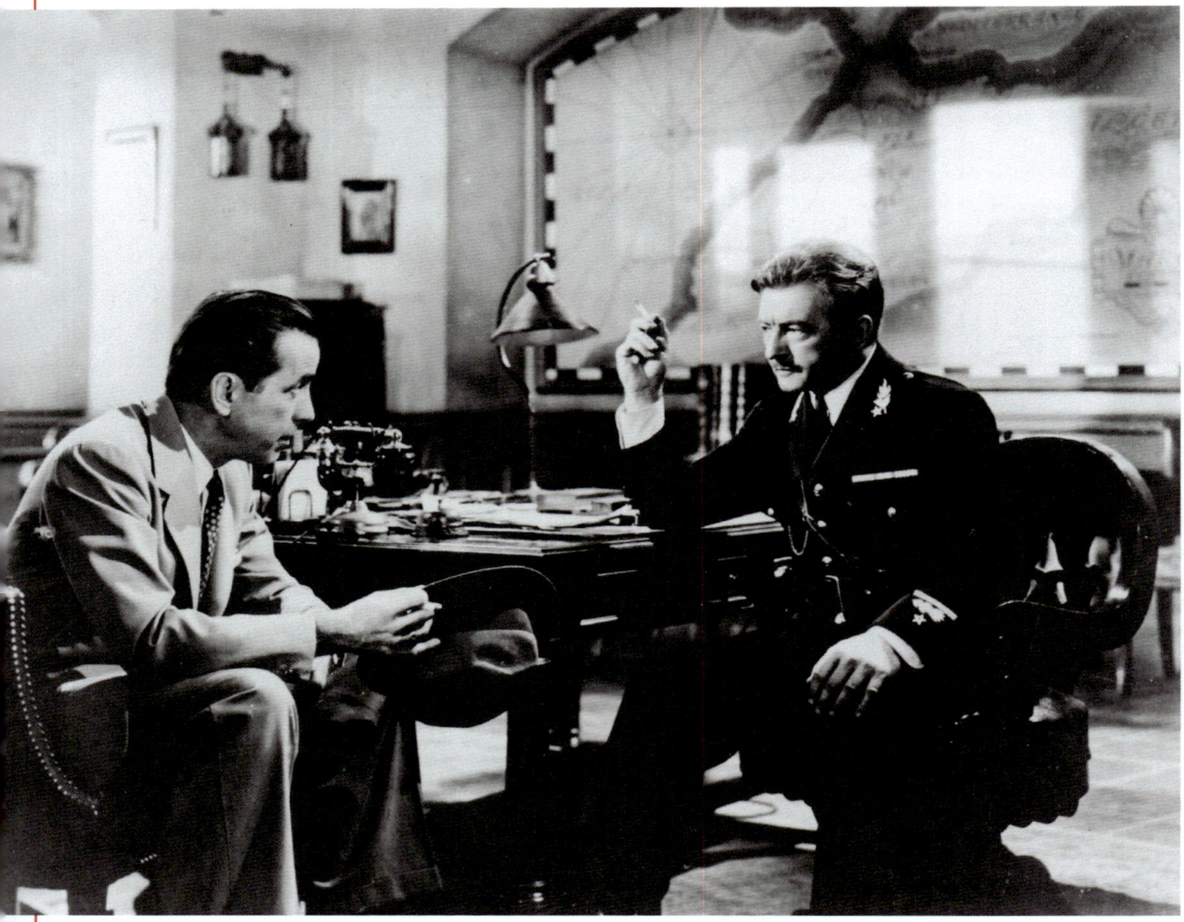

WARNER BROS./MOVIEPIX/GETTY

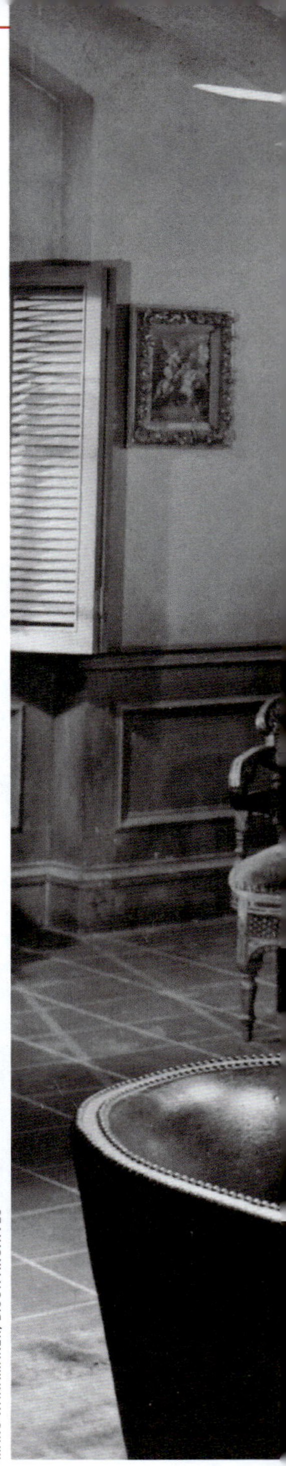

MARC WANAMAKER/BISON ARCHIVES

studio sausage-making process and make it to the big screen. There was the love story involving Rick, murky letters of transit, the black-marketeer Ugarte, and minor roles, too, like the pushy interloper who tries to force his way into Rick's café early on. In *Everybody Comes,* he's an upper crust Englishman, not from the Deutsche Bank, as in the film. But the dialog is almost verbatim. "Now, look here!" he tells Rick. "I've been in every gambling room between Honolulu and Calcutta, and if you think that I'm going to be kept out of a bloody dive like this without going to the authorities, you're very much mistaken, sir." To which Rick replies evenly, "Your money's good at the bar." And after a beat, "You're lucky the bar's still open to you."

Broadway producers optioned the play, but never moved forward with it, in part because of the taboo sexual relationship between Rick and his paramour, a brassy American named Lois Meredith (later to become Ilsa Lund). Hollywood appeared equally unenthusiastic. The drama made the rounds with the major studios for a year, with barely any interest, save a reported $5,000 lowball offer from MGM. Finally, the head of the

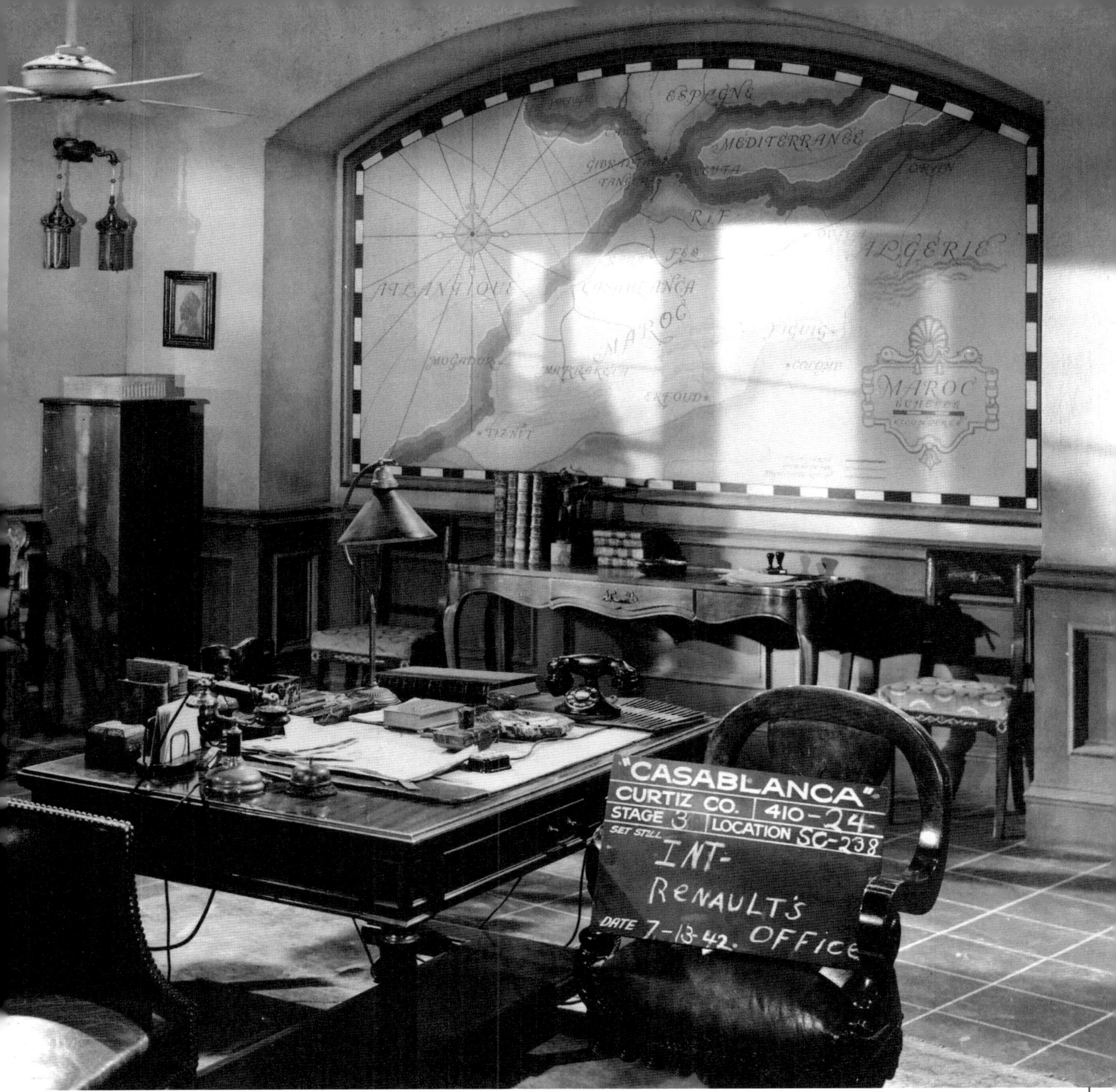

Warner Bros. story department flagged the script for Wallis, and at least one prescient reader gave the play a positive review, concluding, "Excellent melodrama. Colorful, timely background, tense mood, suspense, psychological and physical conflict, tight plotting, sophisticated hokum . . . A box office natural—for Bogart or [James] Cagney, or [George] Raft in out-of-the-usual roles and perhaps Mary Astor." After soliciting a few more opinions, Wallis authorized a formal offer two days after Christmas, 1941.

Everybody Comes to Rick's could not have landed at a more apt home than Warner Bros. Founded by four brothers—Jack, Harry, Albert, and Sam Warner—the studio scored its first hit in 1923 with *Where the North Begins,* starring Rin Tin Tin, a German shepherd who'd been found in a World War I trench. Over time, the siblings pieced together a scrappy, sprawling empire with a working-class ethic and vaguely ethnic stars—Bette Davis, James Cagney, Edward G. Robinson. While MGM was known for its homespun gloss, and Paramount for its European sophistication, Warner Bros. earned a reputation for

TRANSITIONAL STAGE
The Budapest-born S.Z. Sakall, below, at left, as Carl the waiter, and opposite. He had been a star in Europe and before the war had worked with *Casablanca* director Michael Curtiz, also from Hungary. Like many émigrés, Sakall had a slow adjustment to life in Hollywood.

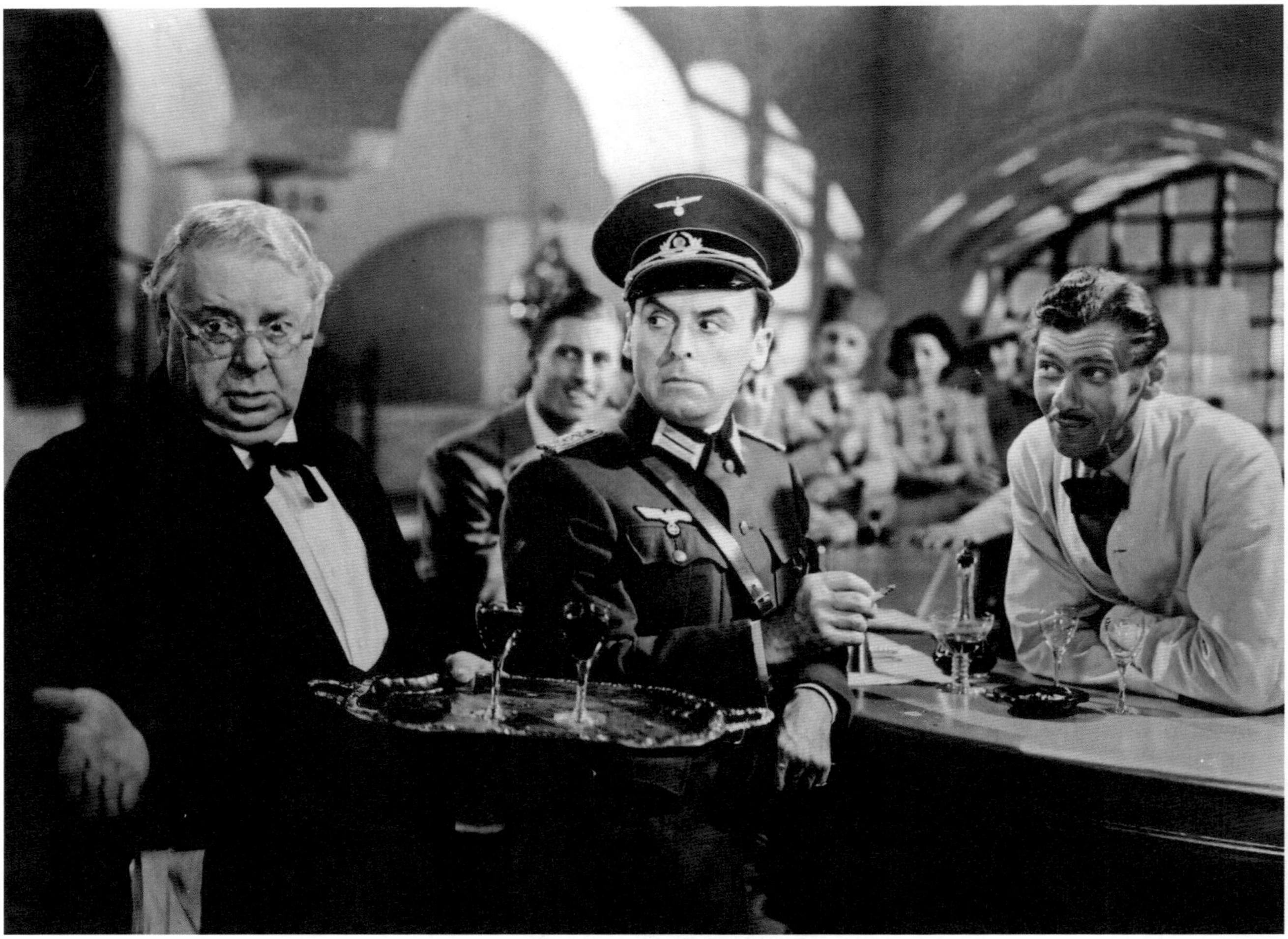

© WARNER BROS., COURTESY PHOTOFEST
MARC WANAMAKER/BISON ARCHIVES

penny-pinching and fast-paced, action-oriented films churned out at a breakneck pace, some 570 in the 1930s alone.

War as a historical subject was popular with most of the studios, yet throughout the 1930s they steered clear of Germany's aggression in Europe for fear of dampening foreign sales. Jack Warner, on the other hand, was an early and ardent Hitler hater, made more so when the head of the studio's office in Berlin was beaten by brownshirts. Jack was the first studio head, in 1933, to close operations in Germany, and as the Nazis invaded Austria, Poland, Czechoslovakia, and Denmark, he was almost always the first to withdraw from those countries as well. In 1938, Jack underscored his stance by hosting a fund-raising dinner in his home for the Hollywood Anti-Nazi League. (Groucho Marx called Warner Bros. "the only studio with any guts.") And Jack followed it up in 1939 with one of the first anti-Nazi films of the era, *Confessions of a Nazi Spy,* about an FBI agent who uncovers a band of Nazis in the United States. In *Round Up the Usual Suspects,* Harmetz compares Rick's neutrality in *Casablanca* to the other studios' willingness to look the other way. Paramount, MGM, and Fox, she points out, were still operating in Germany in 1939.

The United States' entry into World War II following the bombing of Pearl Harbor evaporated industry reluctance to go after Hitler, and all of the big studios, including Warner, geared up to capitalize on the moment. As Americans said goodbye to their sons, brothers, husbands, and fathers shipping off to war, producers readied slates of war-themed films. At Warner, that included not only *Casablanca,* but also *Watch on the Rhine, This Is the Army, Action in the North Atlantic,* and *Destination Tokyo.* Doing the right thing, it turned out, was also good for the bottom line. In 1941, Warner's drama *Sergeant York,* about a much-decorated World War I hero, was the industry's top moneymaker,

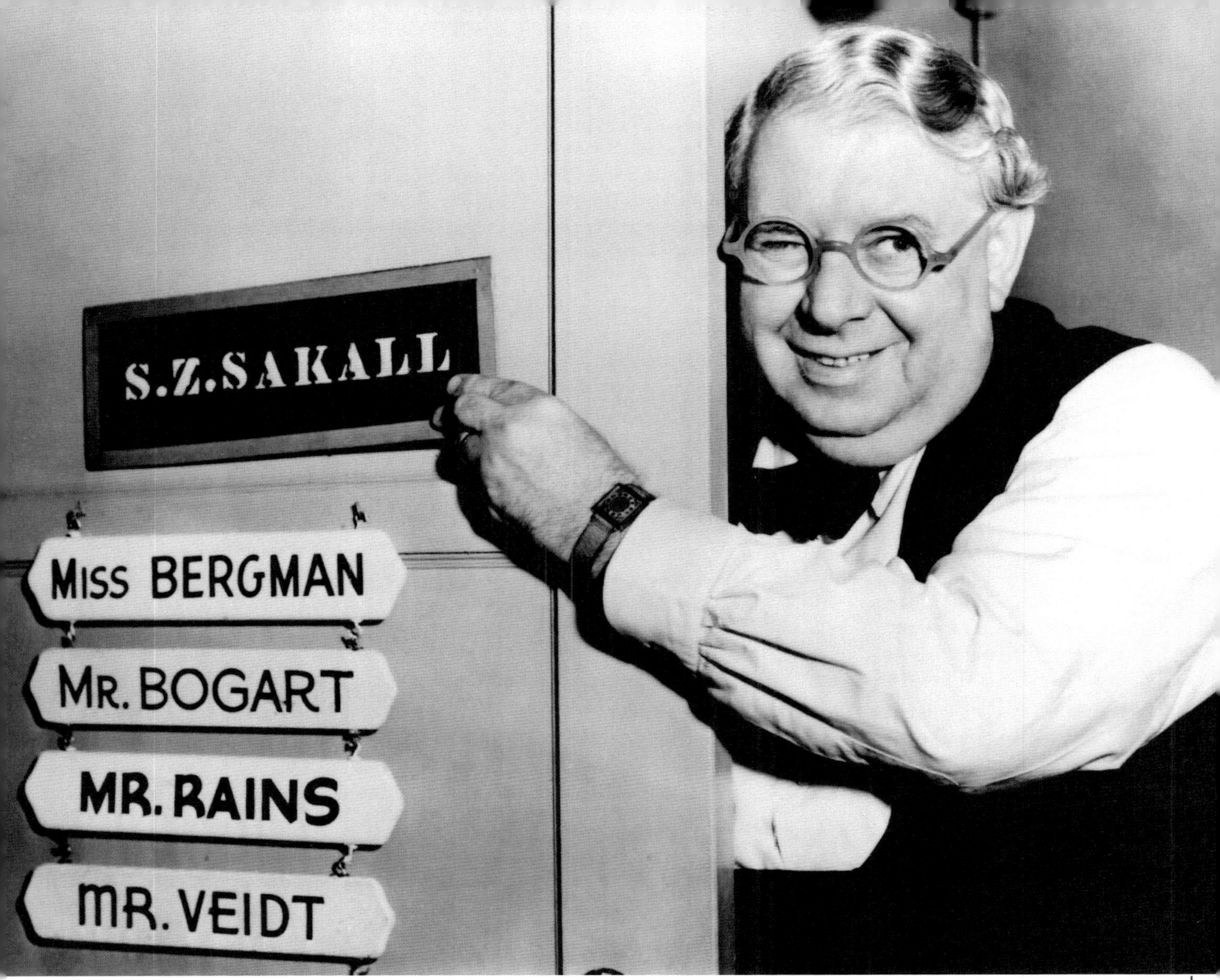

earning more than $6 million.

Following the Christmas holidays, Wallis began his search for a director for *Casablanca*. His first choice was William Wyler, fresh off of *Mrs. Miniver*, a wartime romance, and Wallis shipped a copy of *Everybody Comes to Rick's* to the director, who was vacationing in Sun Valley, Idaho, with producer Darryl Zanuck. Wyler never responded—he was said to be too busy at cards with Zanuck—and Wallis could not afford to wait. He reached out to a handful of other candidates, all on the Warner lot, and took a number of meetings. Most left him uninspired and in the end he chose Warner contract director Michael Curtiz, with whom he had worked well in the past.

By February, Wallis had lined up Bogart, providing the project with a marquee name, but casting other roles became an exercise in jujitsu, since he was also working on a second World War II movie, *Watch on the Rhine*. The search for Victor Laszlo, the hero on the run, was typical. Wallis first thought about newcomer Joseph Cotten, who had created a sensation as Jedediah Leland, the theater critic in *Citizen Kane*. But Cotten was unavailable and after screen testing a handful of unknowns, Wallis turned to Austrian-born Paul Henreid. Then the question became, would Henreid be better as the Czechoslovakian anti-Nazi in *Casablanca* or as the German anti-Nazi in *Watch*? Further complicating the calculations, Henreid had just come off shooting *Now, Voyager*, appearing as the romantic lead opposite Bette Davis. He was offended by the offer of the love triangle's third wheel, behind Bogart, and had to be convinced into accepting by his agent.

Finding the right Ilsa was just as complicated, and before signing Ingrid Bergman in April, Wallis considered a number of other actresses. And he looked at both women and men to tackle the role of Sam the piano player. With so many young people signing up for military duty, or just owing to competing obligations, even filling minor roles became a challenge. Wallis was three weeks into production when he signed his last actor, S.Z. Sakall, as Carl the waiter, who also works in the Casablanca underground.

Casting was a breeze compared with producing a script for *Casablanca,* as recounted in great detail by Harlan Lebo in *Casablanca: Behind the Scenes.* The studio system of the era was brilliantly efficient at marshaling the manpower, sets, and technology to crank out films quickly, but writing requires time, lots of it, which Wallis did not have. It took a combination of seven different writers to come up with the tone, characters, and plot he wanted. Half of the screenplay wasn't composed until after filming began, and an ending wasn't finalized until just before the movie wrapped.

Once Julius and Philip Epstein returned from their Washington assignment, however, things began to look up. Known around the Warners lot as the Brothers, Julie and Phil, or simply the Boys, the 32-year-old Epsteins were identical twins who often finished each other's sentences and were known for adding sparkle to scripts that needed it. They also had experience adapting stage plays and deserve much of the credit for *Casablanca*'s witty, rat-a-tat dialog, and some of the most famous lines, including "Round up the usual suspects," which they claimed they thought of simultaneously while driving along Sunset Boulevard one day. The high-octane exchanges between Rick and Renault, the corrupt police prefect, are pure Epsteinese:

DISTRESSING NEWS
Ingrid Bergman as Ilsa with Bogart in a flashback to the couple's time in Paris, when they learn of the imminent German invasion of the city. Opposite: Curtiz lined up the shot of Bergman and Bogart reading the news. Crews built the realistic set for this Montmartre café on a Warner back lot street.

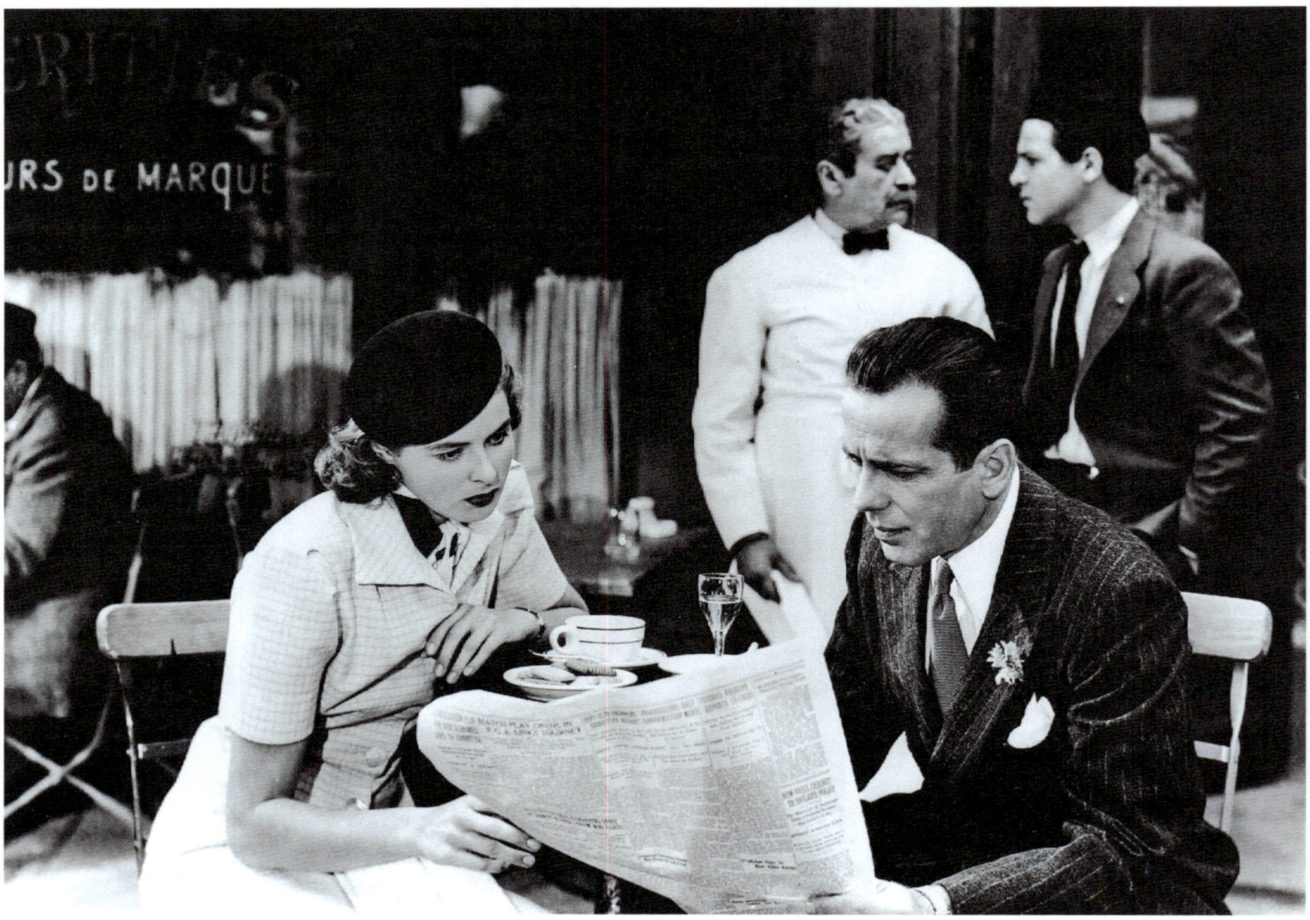

WARNER BROS./KOBAL/REX/SHUTTERSTOCK (2)

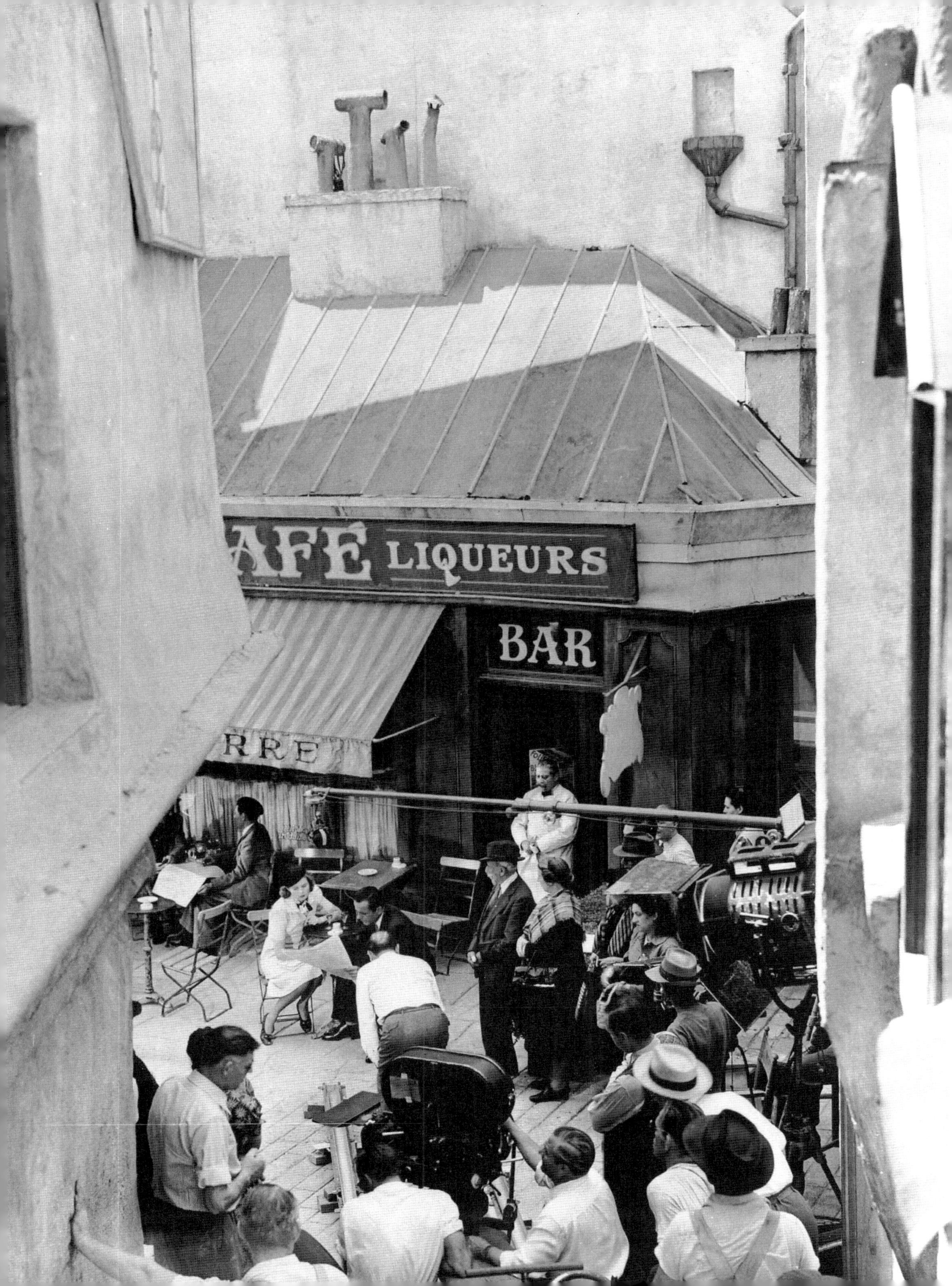
AFÉ LIQUEURS
BAR
RRE

Renault: And what in heaven's name brought you to Casablanca?

Rick: My health. I came to Casablanca for the waters.

Renault: Waters? What waters? We are in the desert.

Rick: I was misinformed.

Yet with deadlines looming, Wallis was anxious for a finished script and in early May brought in Howard Koch, the writer behind Orson Welles's *War of the Worlds* radio play, to help the Epsteins. Koch's task was to thicken the political plot, and he added touches like Rick's backstory of fighting for the Loyalists during the Spanish civil war and running arms to Ethiopia. The collaboration was not a blissful one. The Epsteins and Koch bristled at each other's contributions, and as they completed their assignments, rewrote what the other had done. Koch sought to interject weight and tone down the Epsteins' banter; the Boys in turn removed Koch's ponderousness.

Wallis began to worry that he would not make his start date. Soon, he would have cast and crew at the ready, with nothing for them to do. Without a working script, he would incur $30,000 a day in lost production costs and salaries, according to Lebo. Wallis was particularly worried about Rick and Ilsa's romance, which felt stilted and weighed down by clunky conversation. When the two were locked in an embrace in La Belle Aurore, with the Germans nearing, Ilsa's demand for a kiss was almost belligerent: "Hitler or no Hitler, kiss me." Lebo calls the line "the worst wartime come-on ever."

To breathe life into the romance, Wallis brought in yet another script doctor, Casey Robinson, one of the studio's top writers and an expert in sweet talk. (Under Robinson, the Hitler line was softened to the more urgent "Kiss me, kiss me as if it were the last time.") Robinson proposed several revisions, which slowed progress again, and when shooting

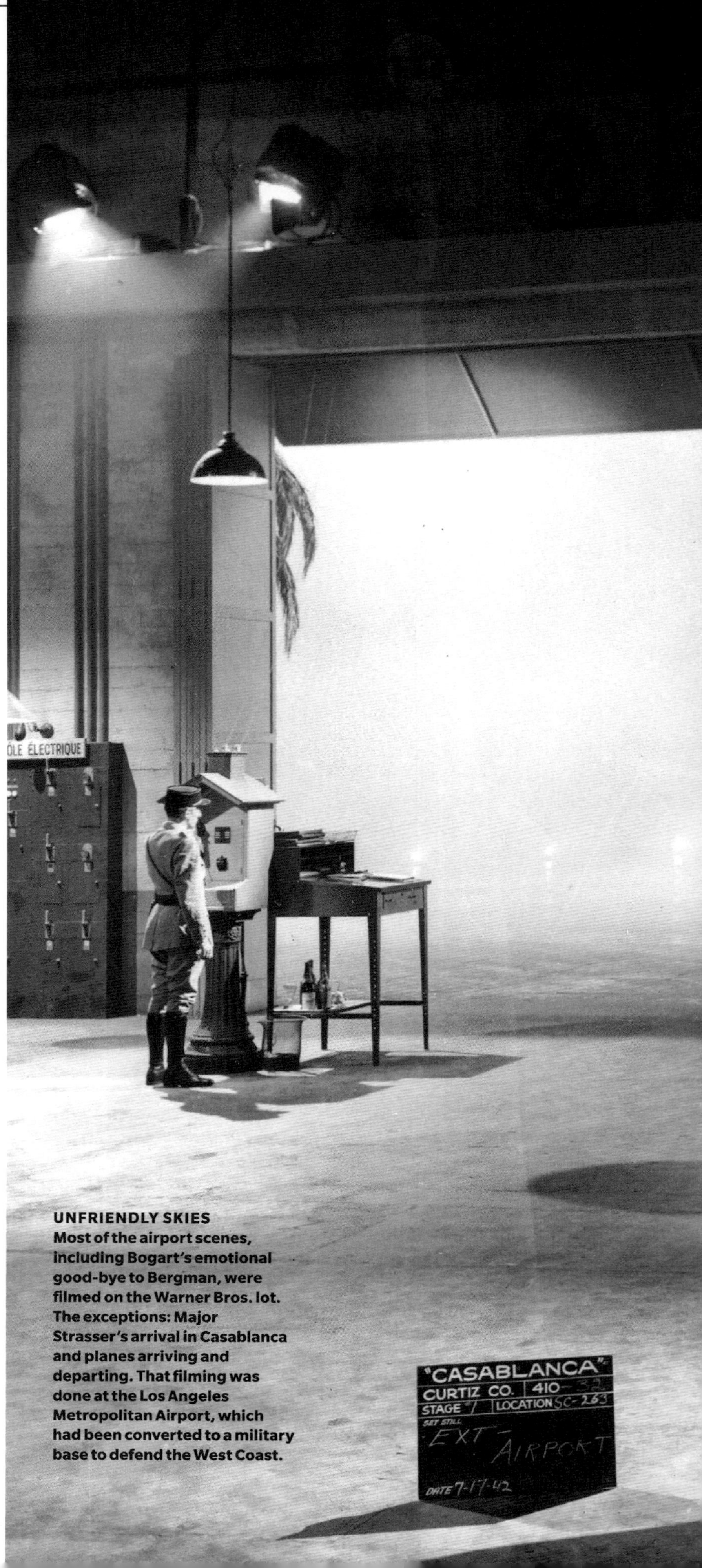

MARC WANAMAKER/BISON ARCHIVES

UNFRIENDLY SKIES
Most of the airport scenes, including Bogart's emotional good-bye to Bergman, were filmed on the Warner Bros. lot. The exceptions: Major Strasser's arrival in Casablanca and planes arriving and departing. That filming was done at the Los Angeles Metropolitan Airport, which had been converted to a military base to defend the West Coast.

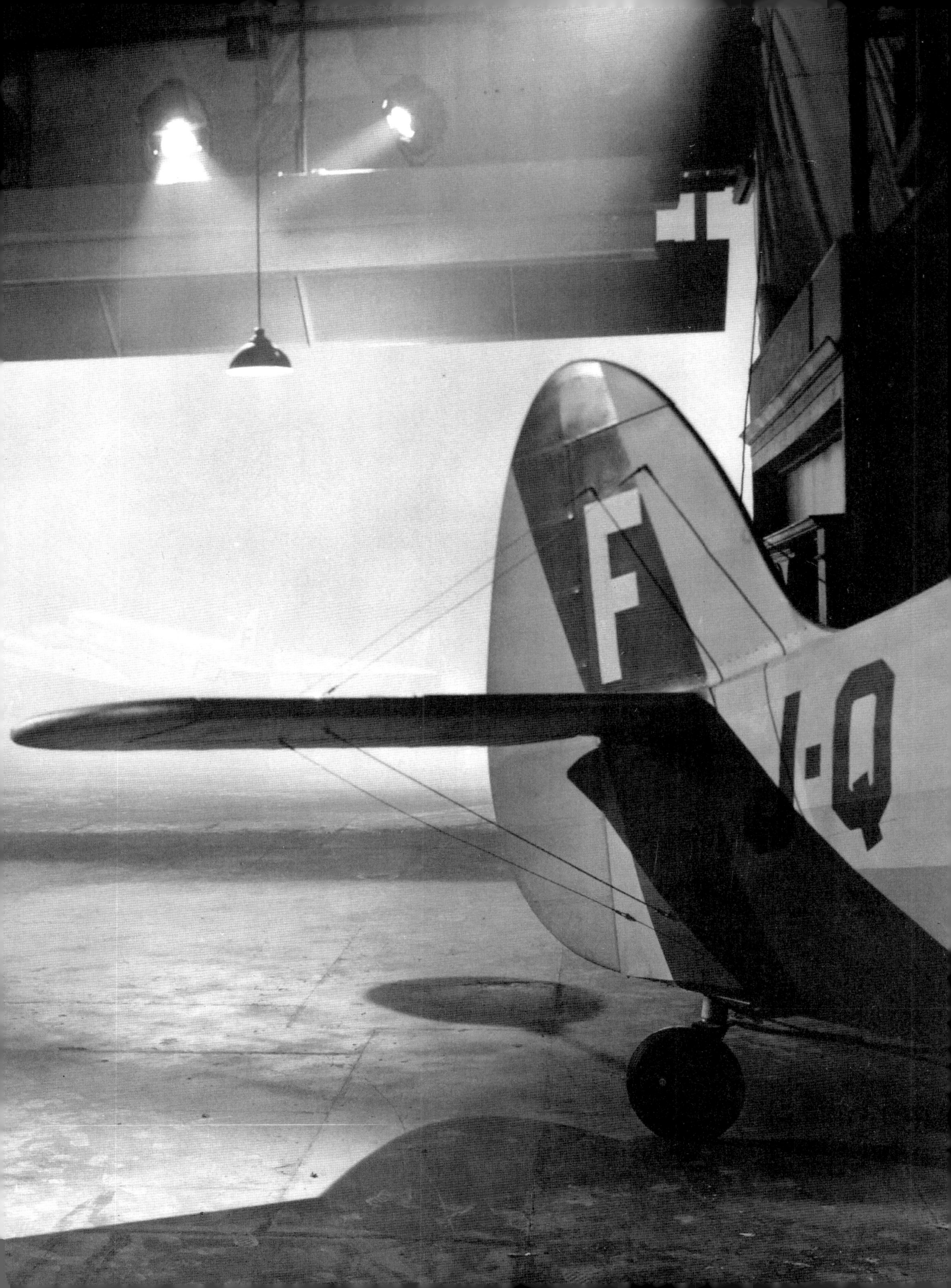
F
-Q

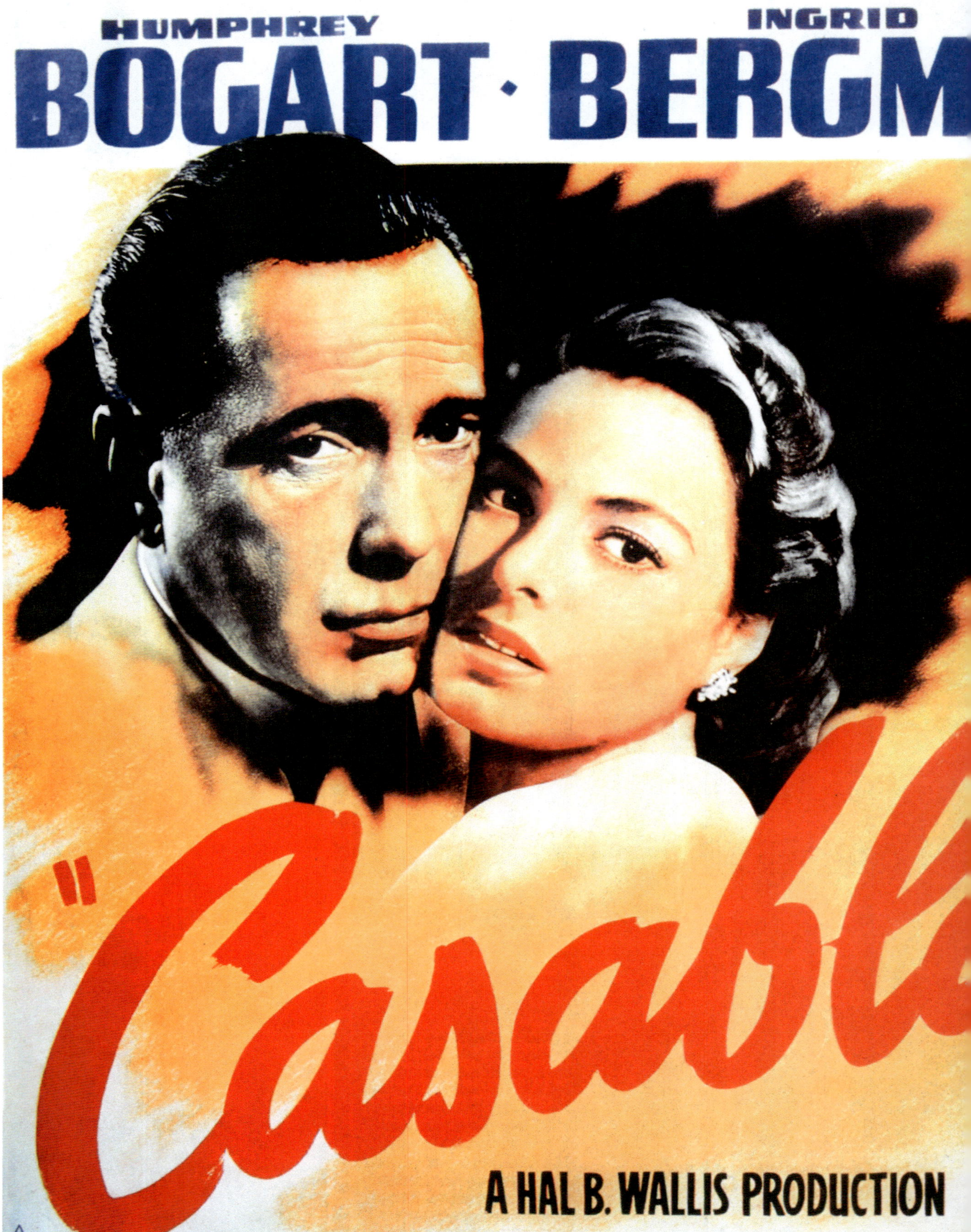

MOVIESTORE/REX/SHUTTERSTOCK

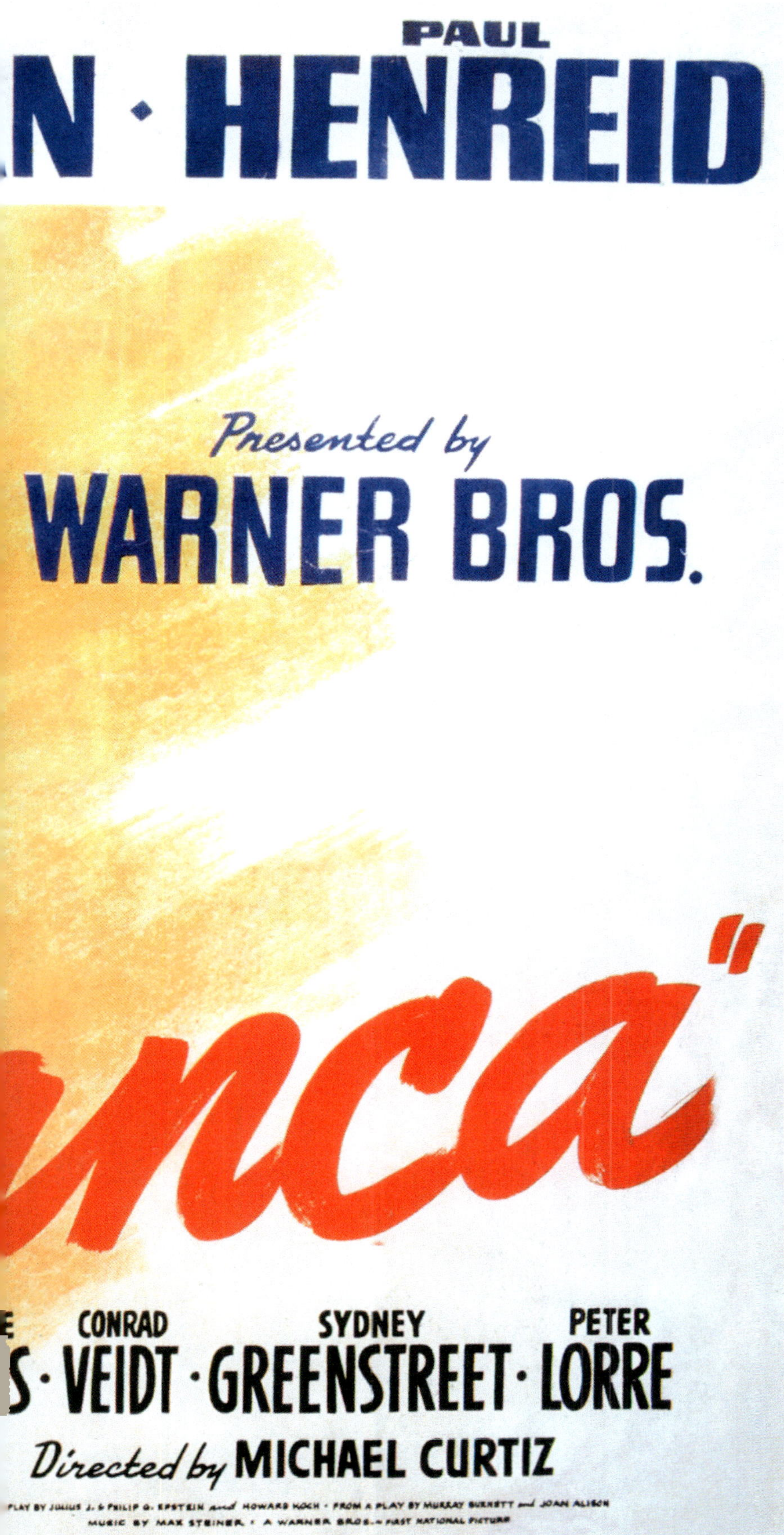

finally started on May 25 it was with just half a script completed. "Every day they were handing out dialog and we were trying to make some sense of it," Bergman remembered later. "Every morning we said, 'Well, who are we? What are we doing here?' And Michael Curtiz would say, 'We're not quite sure, but let's get through this scene today and we'll let you know tomorrow.'"

By the end of June, with just three scheduled weeks of filming left, the Epsteins, Koch, and Robinson still had not figured out a satisfactory ending. They knew that Ilsa would go with her husband. What they couldn't work out was how she could give up Rick forever and still give audiences an emotionally satisfying finale. At this point, almost all 75 of Warner's contract writers were helping out. Finally on July 16, hope emerged in the form of a memo, "The Changes for New Ending." In it, the writers proposed that Ilsa would realize that she was to go on the plane to Lisbon with her husband and leave Rick behind. Distraught, she would argue that she should stay, while Rick would remain collected and firm, even as he would tell her she belongs with Victor and that he has a job to do, too. "Ilsa, I'm no good at being noble," Rick would conclude, "but it doesn't take much to see that the problems of three little people don't amount to a hill of beans in this crazy world. Someday you'll understand that. Not now. Here's looking at you, kid."

Shooting was concluded by August 3, 11 days behind schedule, and by the end of the month, postproduction was completed, too. At this point, *Casablanca*'s rollout was

HIT PARADE
Of all the films that Warner Bros. made during the war years, only *Shine On Harvest Moon* and *This Is the Army* sold more tickets than *Casablanca*.

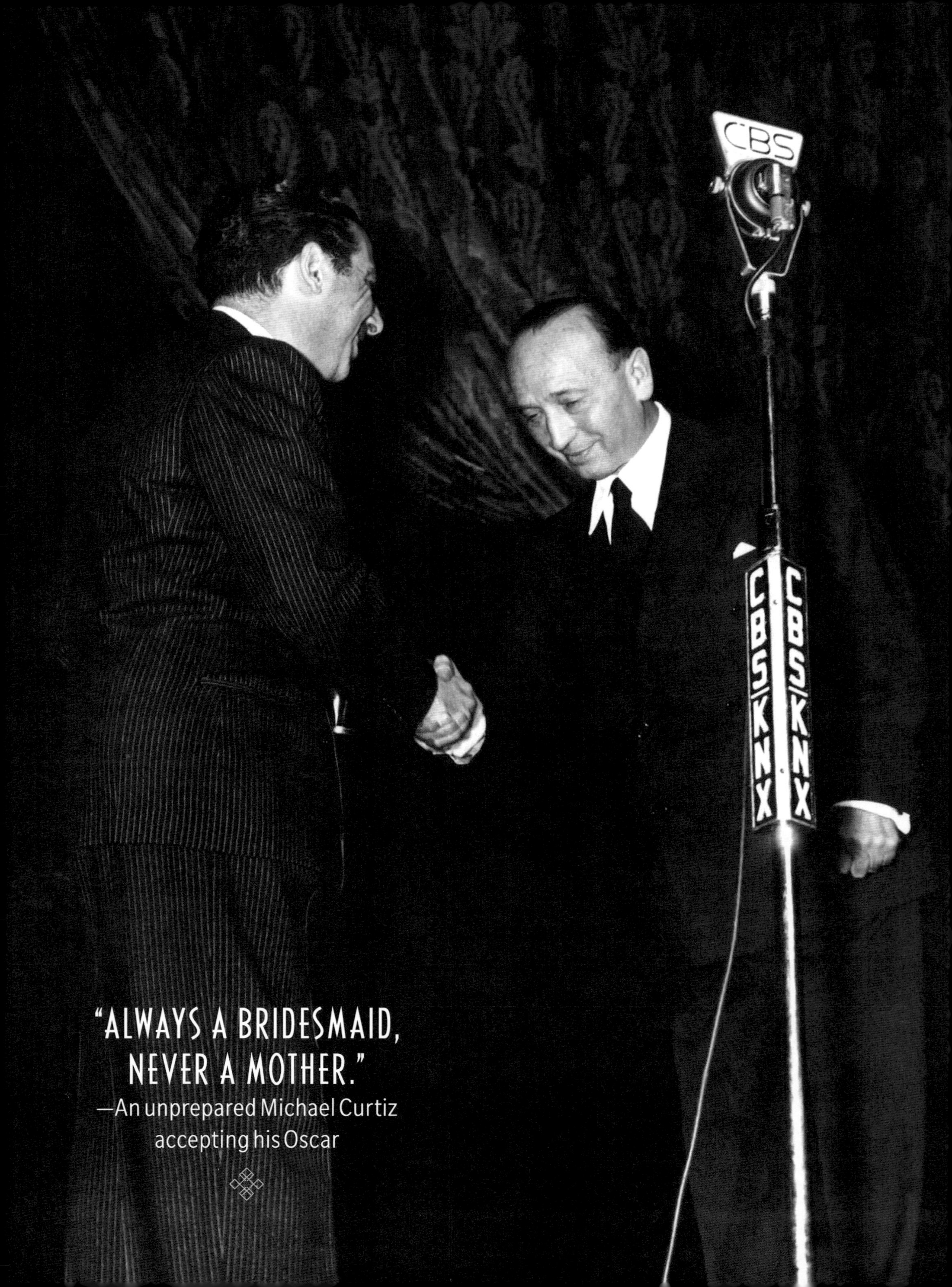

"ALWAYS A BRIDESMAID, NEVER A MOTHER."
—An unprepared Michael Curtiz accepting his Oscar

supposed to be pro forma. After edits and trims, the film was completed and a few previews were held. It was canned and scheduled for release 10 months later, in June 1943, with Warners hoping for a hit.

As events turned out, they didn't have to hope. When the Allies invaded North Africa in early November 1942, Warner was in the enviable position of having a film ready to release with a title that was in news stories around the globe. The studio pushed up the premier to the earliest date that made sense—November 26, Thanksgiving Day, at the Hollywood Theater in New York, just 18 days after the Allied landing. The New York run broke attendance records, and when *Casablanca* opened for general release in January 1943, ticket sales around the country were strong.

From there, it was a short trip to Oscar nominations. *Casablanca* received eight nods from the Academy of Motion Picture Art and Sciences and won in three categories: Best Screenplay, Best Director, and Best Picture. It was a roller coaster of a night. Accounts vary, but it has been reported that Hungarian-born Michael Curtiz drew laughs when he accepted the Best Director statuette in his humorously garbled English idiom. "So many times I have a speech ready, but no dice. Always a bridesmaid, never a mother."

More dramatically, when the Best Picture award was announced, Hal Wallis rose to accept, as the film had been his project almost completely, but Jack Warner elbowed him out of the way and rushed to the stage and the limelight. According to Wallis's autobiography, the audience audibly gasped at the maneuver. "Almost 40 years later, I still haven't recovered from the shock," he wrote. A month later, Wallis's contract was canceled. Wallis never won another Best Picture Oscar, and Warner Bros. would not take one home for more than two decades. ■

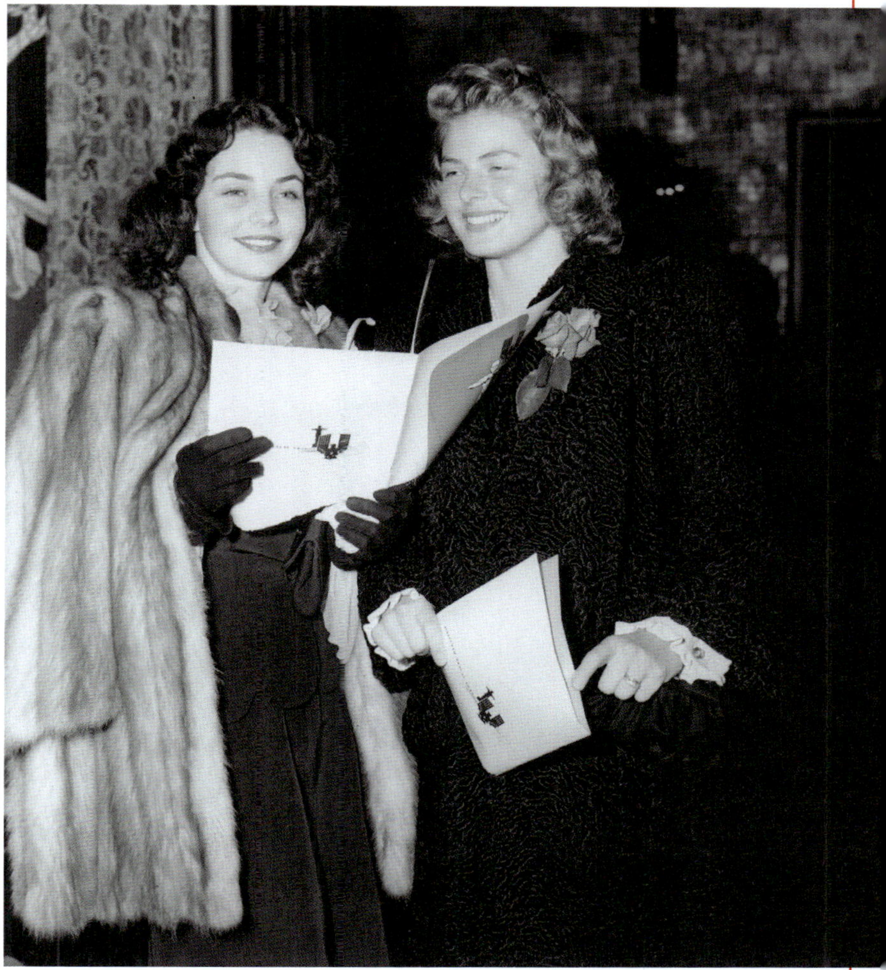

AP/REX/SHUTTERSTOCK

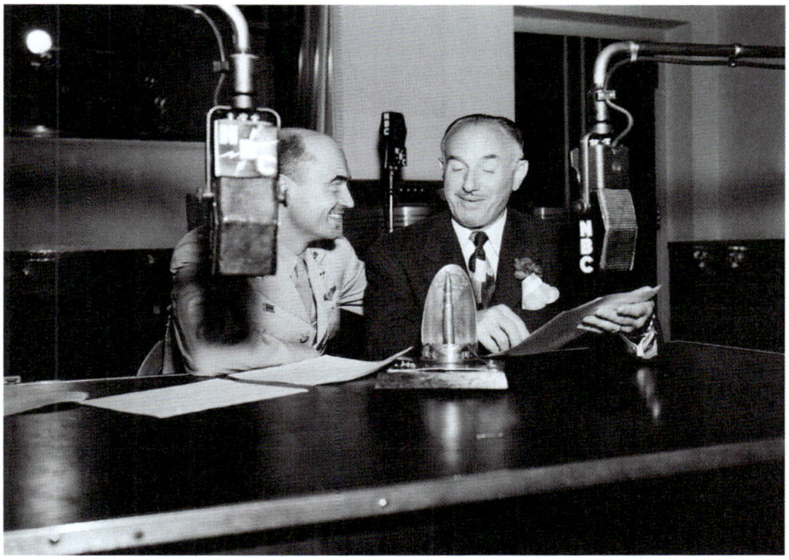

NBC/GETTY

OH WHAT A NIGHT
Opposite: Michael Curtiz accepting the Oscar for Best Director at the 16th Academy Awards in 1944. Top: Two Best Actress contenders that year were Jennifer Jones, left, who won for *The Song of Bernadette*, and Ingrid Bergman, nominated for *For Whom the Bell Tolls*. Above: Colonel Joseph McMicking, left, with Jack Warner, on an *Army Hour* broadcast following Warner's Oscar win for *Casablanca*.

EVERETT

WHEN BOGART MET BERGMAN

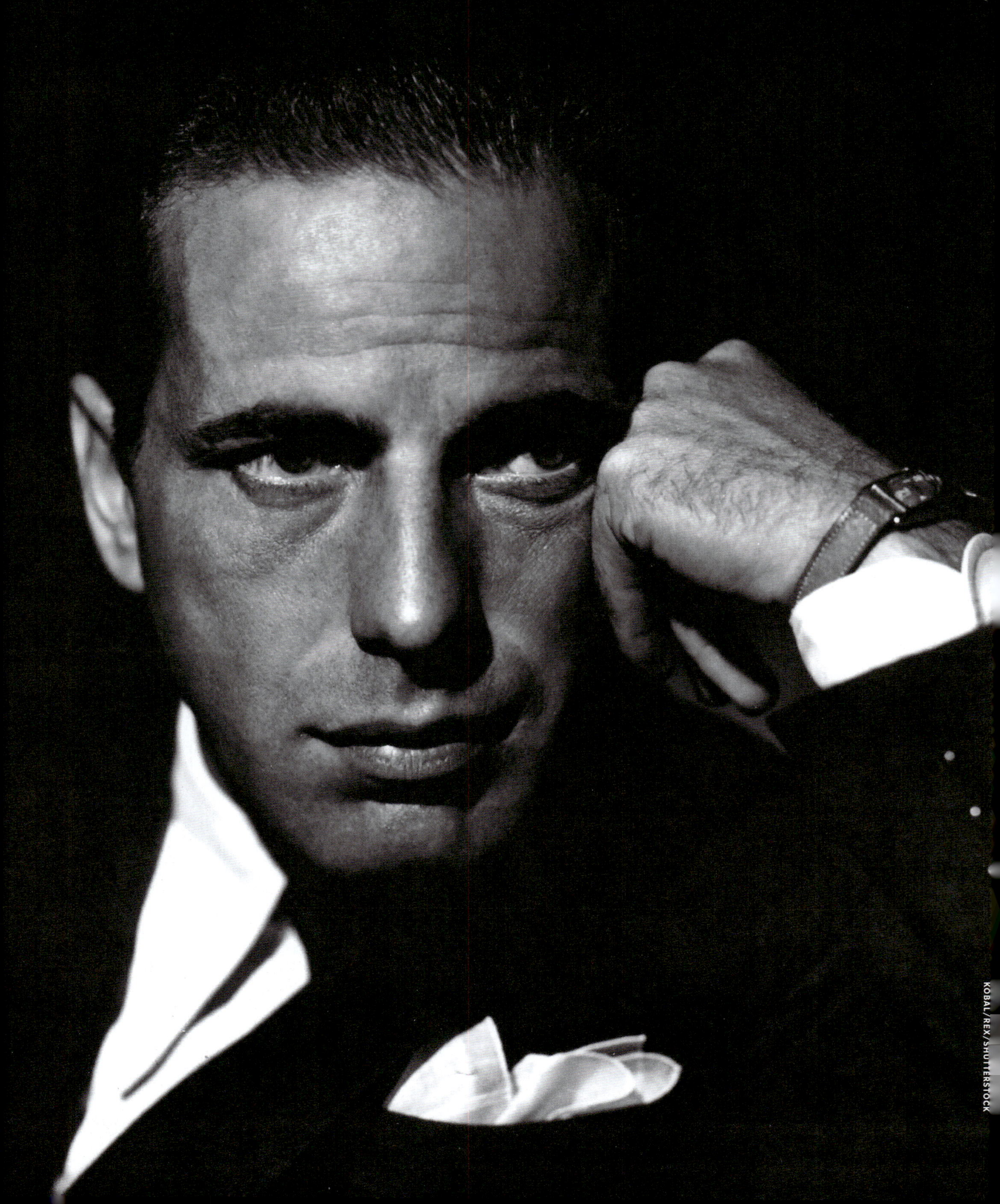

KOBAL/REX/SHUTTERSTOCK

He was a rich kid from New York who played tough guys. She was a Swedish ingenue with her eye on an Oscar. Their on-screen romance became Hollywood legend

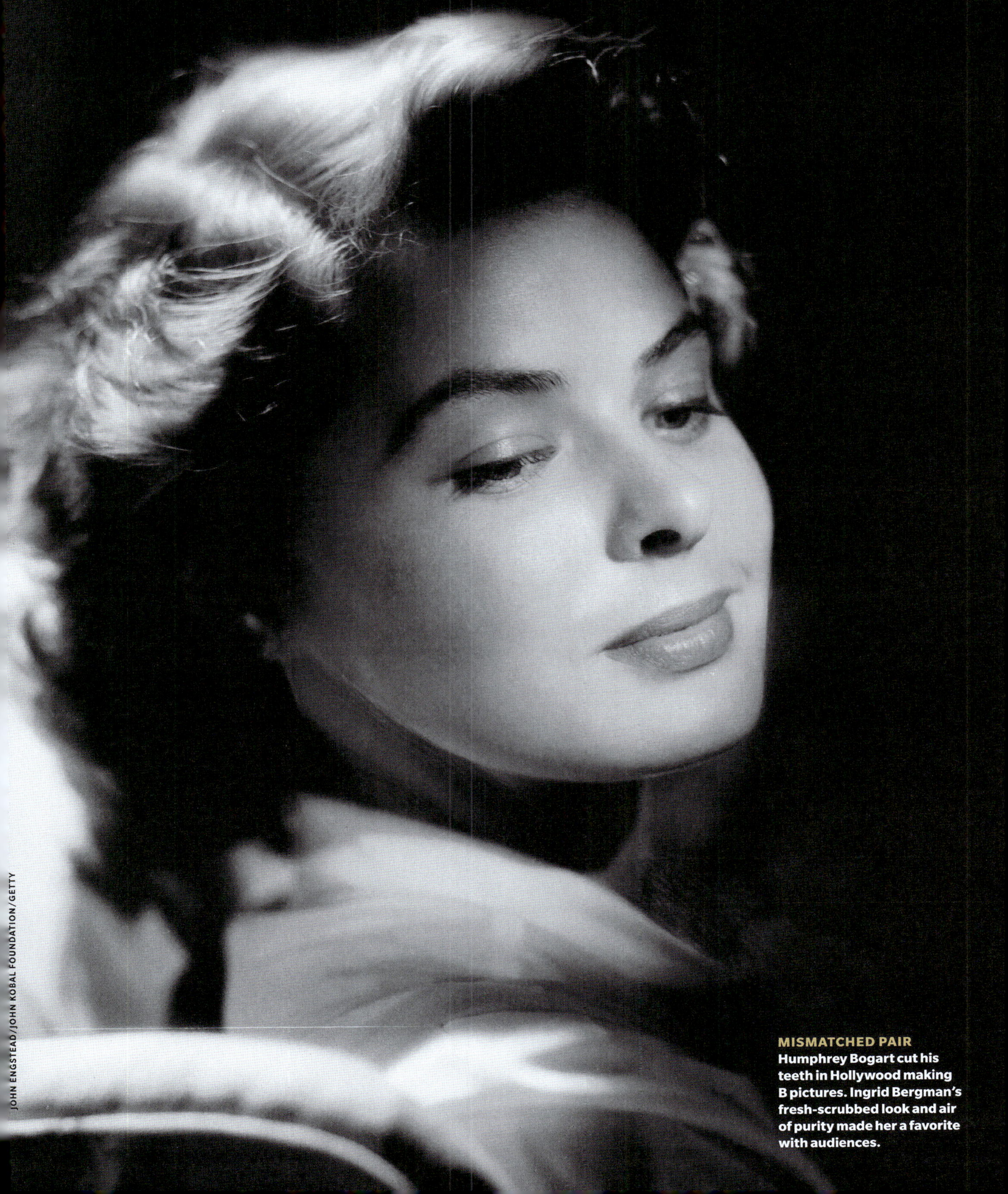

JOHN ENGSTEAD/JOHN KOBAL FOUNDATION/GETTY

MISMATCHED PAIR
Humphrey Bogart cut his teeth in Hollywood making B pictures. Ingrid Bergman's fresh-scrubbed look and air of purity made her a favorite with audiences.

When filming for *Casablanca* kicked off on May 25, 1942, Humphrey Bogart, cast as romantic lead Rick Blaine, was one of Hollywood's go-to toughs. Square-jawed and narrow-chested, Bogart had a five o'clock shadow and a mood to match. He was rarely the guy to get the girl in a film and was filled with anxiety that he would not be able to pull off *Casablanca*'s "love stuff," as he called it. Ingrid Bergman, as Bogart's former flame Ilsa Lund, was equally conflicted. The statuesque Swede wanted to make her mark as a serious actress, not as another ingenue. She had hoped to be cast in a different film altogether and dismissed *Casablanca* as fluff. Sixteen years Bogart's junior, Bergman would lament later that she kissed her costar but never got to know him.

Yet once director Michael Curtiz trained his lens on the pair, their smoldering on-screen magic was unmistakable. Bergman, shot with gauze filters and her eyes sparkling with catchlights, glows under Bogart's gaze. Bogart's face shows itself as a map of hurt, hardness, and devotion. The café-owning cynic who early in the film declares, "I stick my neck out for nobody," becomes transformed into a patriot who sacrifices his love to help protect Europe from the Nazis.

"The Warners here have a picture which makes the spine tingle and the heart take a leap," raved *New York Times* critic Bosley Crowther in his November 27, 1942, review. "Mr. Bogart is, as usual, the cool, cynical, efficient and super-wise guy who operates his business strictly for profit but has a core of sentiment and idealism inside... Miss Bergman is surpassingly lovely, crisp and natural as the girl and lights the romantic passages with a warm and genuine glow."

How Bogart and Bergman came to be regarded as the most romantic on-screen couple ever is almost as

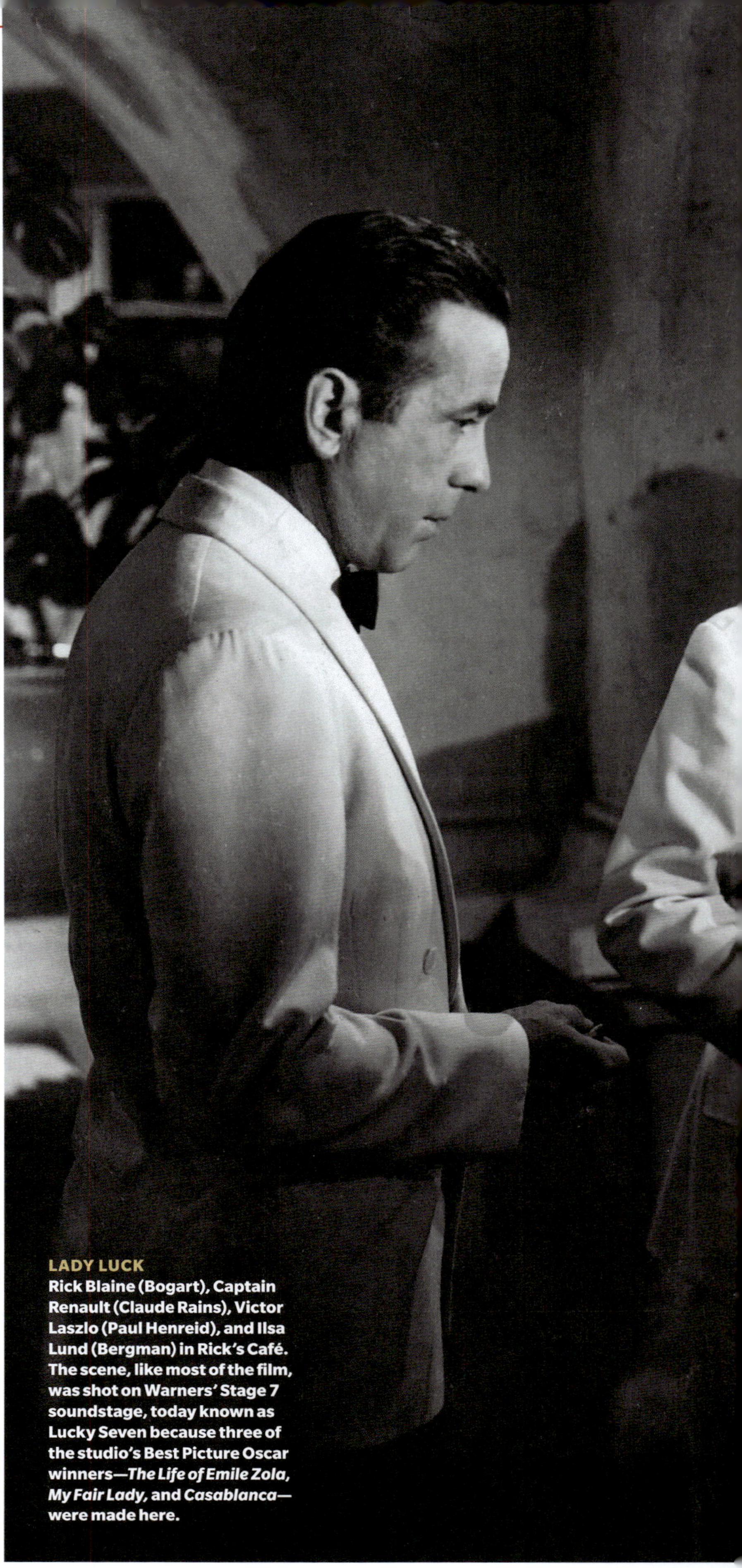

LADY LUCK
Rick Blaine (Bogart), Captain Renault (Claude Rains), Victor Laszlo (Paul Henreid), and Ilsa Lund (Bergman) in Rick's Café. The scene, like most of the film, was shot on Warners' Stage 7 soundstage, today known as Lucky Seven because three of the studio's Best Picture Oscar winners—*The Life of Emile Zola*, *My Fair Lady*, and *Casablanca*—were made here.

JACK WOODS/WARNER BROS./KOBAL/REX/SHUTTERSTOCK

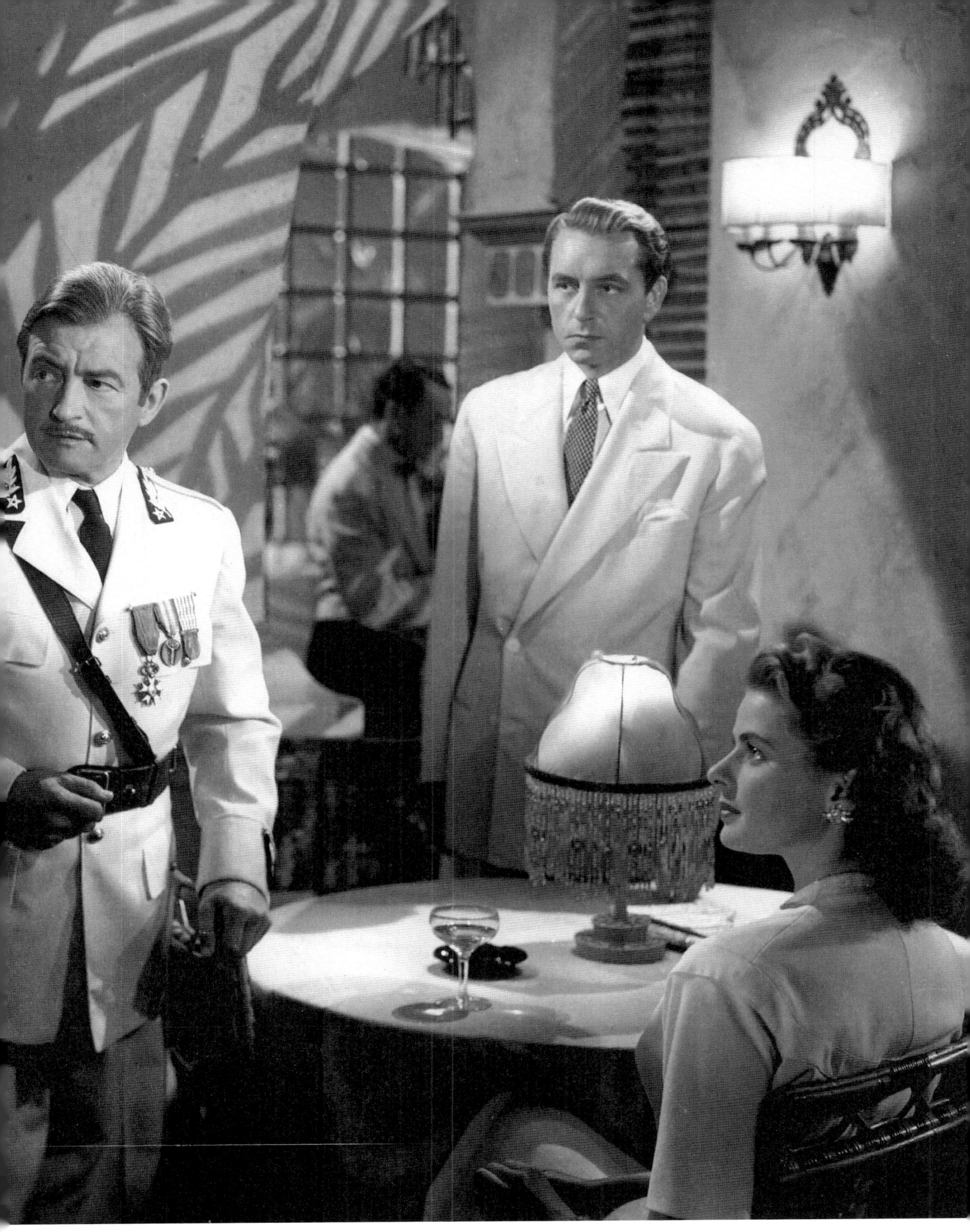

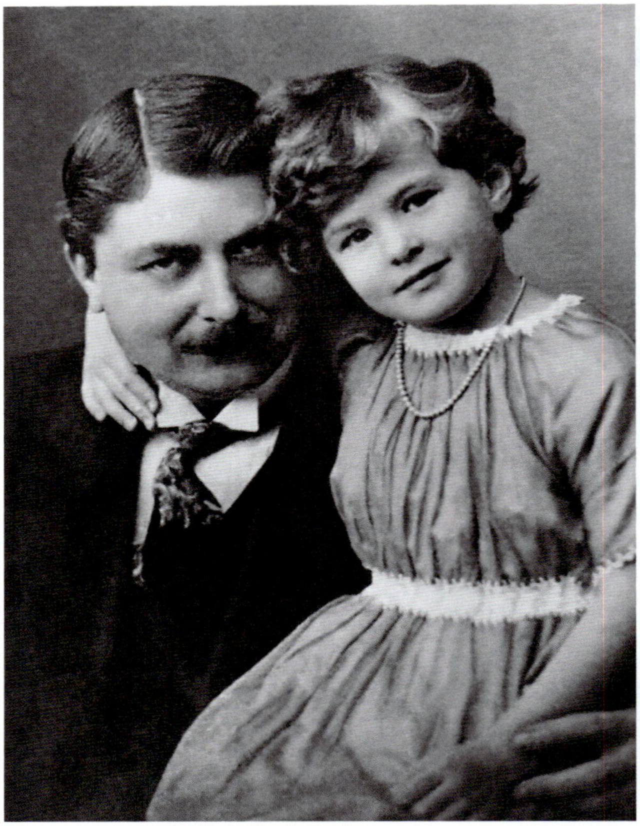

ARCHIVE PHOTOS/GETTY

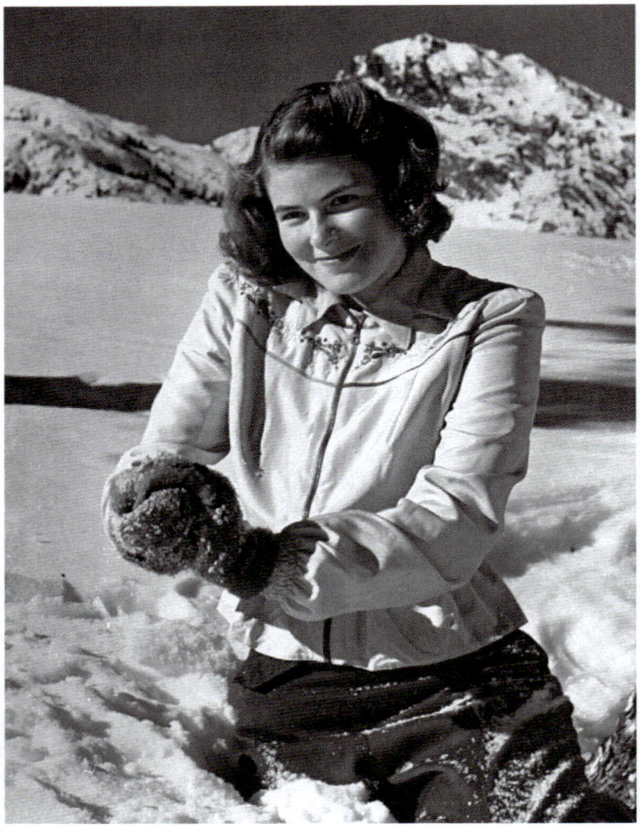

BOB LANDRY/THE LIFE IMAGES COLLECTION/GETTY

improbable as *Casablanca's* success as a film. From its inception to its theatrical release, the movie fell into place in a cascade of accidents. The play that inspired the script, *Everybody Comes to Rick's,* had gone unsold for more than a year but landed on the desk of Warner Bros. head of production Hal Wallis just days after the bombing of Pearl Harbor. The coincidence ensured a deal and propelled the project to the front of the line. The director, Michael Curtiz, and cinematographer, Arthur Edeson, were chosen largely because they were available. Ditto for many of the actors. Seven different writers were brought in to shape the script, and when filming began, they were still at it, unable to justify why and how Ilsa would choose to leave Rick and escape to Lisbon with her husband, Victor Laszlo. In a final stroke of happenstance, just three months after the film wrapped in August 1942, the Allies landed in North Africa, launching the city of Casablanca into the headlines. Warner Bros. rushed a cut into a New York theater to capitalize on the free publicity, and released the movie nationally in January 1943.

Most of the cast and crew involved in making *Casablanca* didn't even think they were working on anything special. The only exception perhaps was producer Hal Wallis, an 18-year veteran with Warner Bros. who had risen from the publicity department to become the studio's head of production. He had such confidence in *Casablanca* that he had paid $20,000 for the rights to *Everybody Comes to Rick's*—one of the highest amounts ever for an untried, unproduced play and more than twice what Dashiell Hammett's *The Maltese Falcon* got just a year earlier. As 1942 began, Wallis was negotiating to exit Warner Bros. and form his own production unit. He would still make four pictures a year for Warner and have his pick of the best contract writers, directors, and actors and of course scripts. At the

NATURAL BEAUTY

Top left: Bergman, circa 1920, with her father, Justus Bergman, who owned a photography shop and captured much of her early life on film. A 1941 LIFE story about the starlet, photographed at June Lake, in California (top right), described her as "Sweden's most promising export to the U.S. since Greta Garbo." Opposite: A publicity photo that illustrates why early reviews of Bergman's films in the United States often contained the word *radiant*.

HERBERT DORFMAN/CORBIS/GETTY

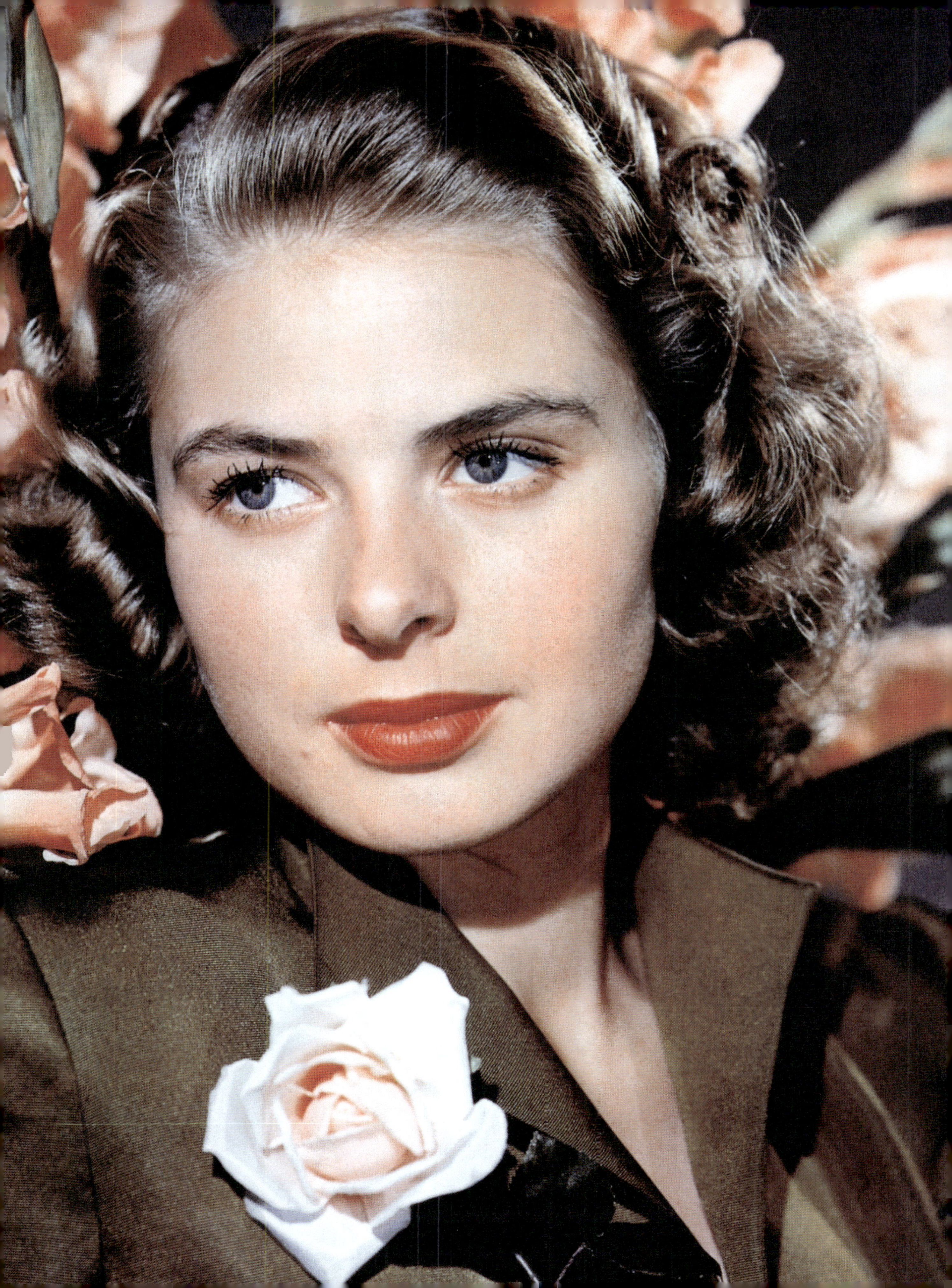

THE COMPETITION

Producer Hal Wallis considered actresses (below, from top) Ann Sheridan, Hedy Lamarr, and Michèle Morgan for the role of Ilsa, but there were problems with each. A fourth contender (not pictured) was French star Edwige Feuillère, but Wallis wondered if she could speak English. At right, Bergman with producer David O. Selznick, who lent her to Warner in exchange for Olivia de Havilland.

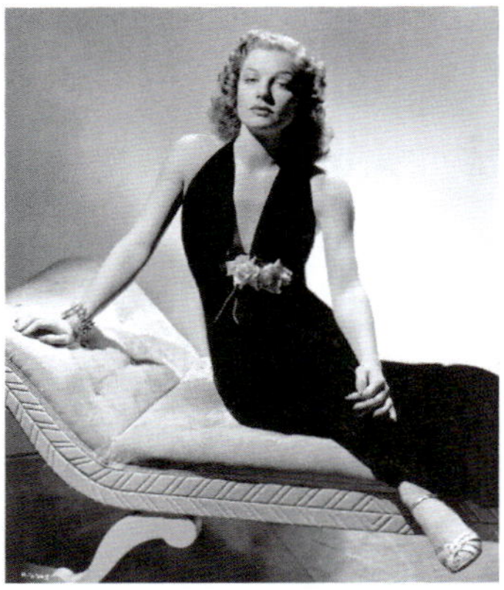

HULTON/GETTY

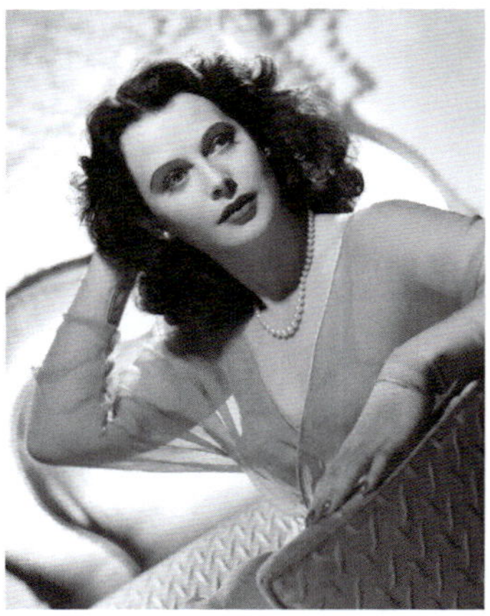

CLARENCE SINCLAIR BULL/ JOHN KOBAL FOUNDATION/HULTON/GETTY

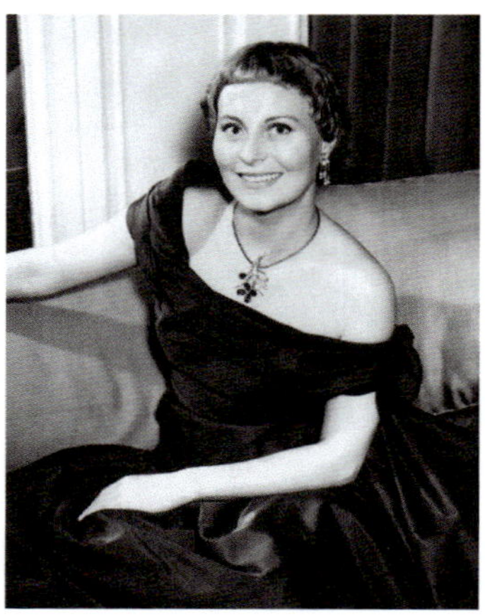

KEYSTONE-FRANCE/GAMMA-RAPHO/GETTY

top of his list: *Casablanca.*

With shooting set for May, casting had to be completed quickly. Wallis was not concerned about the role of Rick, the moral center of the film. Bogart was the only actor he really considered and the script was written with Bogie in mind. Ilsa however was another story. In the play, the lead female was a promiscuous American, Lois Meredith, whose extramarital affair with Rick in Paris is renewed when they meet again in Morocco. For Meredith, Wallis wanted Ann Sheridan, whom Warner Bros. was billing as the "Oomph Girl," after a line in a Walter Winchell column (Sheridan had "an 'umphy' quality," Winchell wrote). The actress had the right mix of rough edges and made-in-the-U.S.A. good looks for the role, but soon Wallis had begun to rethink the character, and Lois became Ilsa, a more opaque and mysterious European. Sheridan wasn't the right fit for that woman at all.

For weeks, Wallis encountered one dead end after another in his search for the right Ilsa. MGM refused to loan out his next choice, the Austrian-born Hedy Lamarr, and Michèle Morgan, a French actress often compared to Greta Garbo, wanted a budget-breaking $55,000. Wallis screen-tested her anyway while briefly considering one of Morgan's contemporaries in France, Edwige Feuillère. He also approached independent producer David O. Selznick of *Gone with the Wind* fame about yet another option, Ingrid Bergman, on the theory that at least one of the women would work out.

Bergman was a wholesome Swedish beauty whom Selznick had signed to a contract in 1939. Raised by relatives in Stockholm after her parents died, Bergman had known from an early age that she wanted to act. She began winning film parts as a teen and by 1936 had become a star in her homeland with *Intermezzo,* about

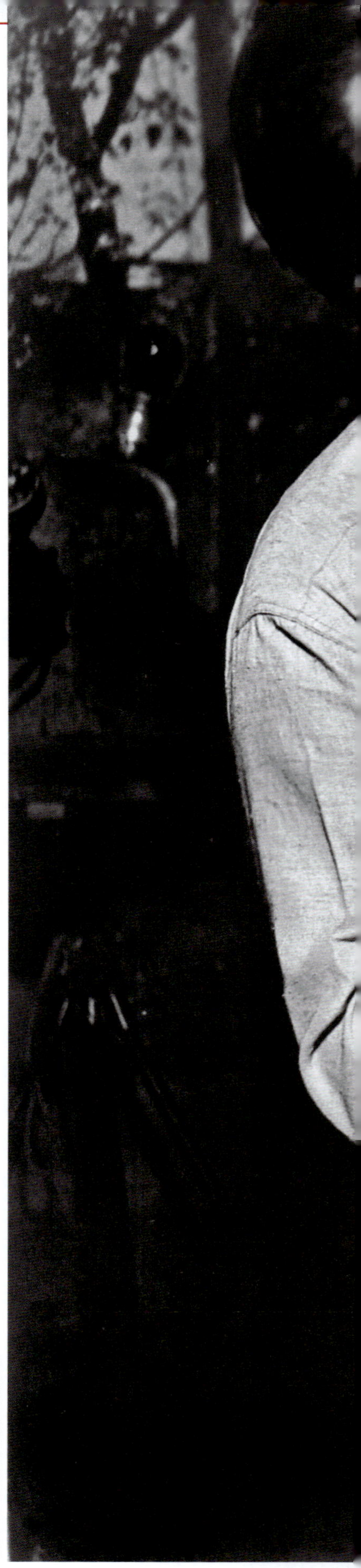

MARC WANAMAKER/BISON ARCHIVES

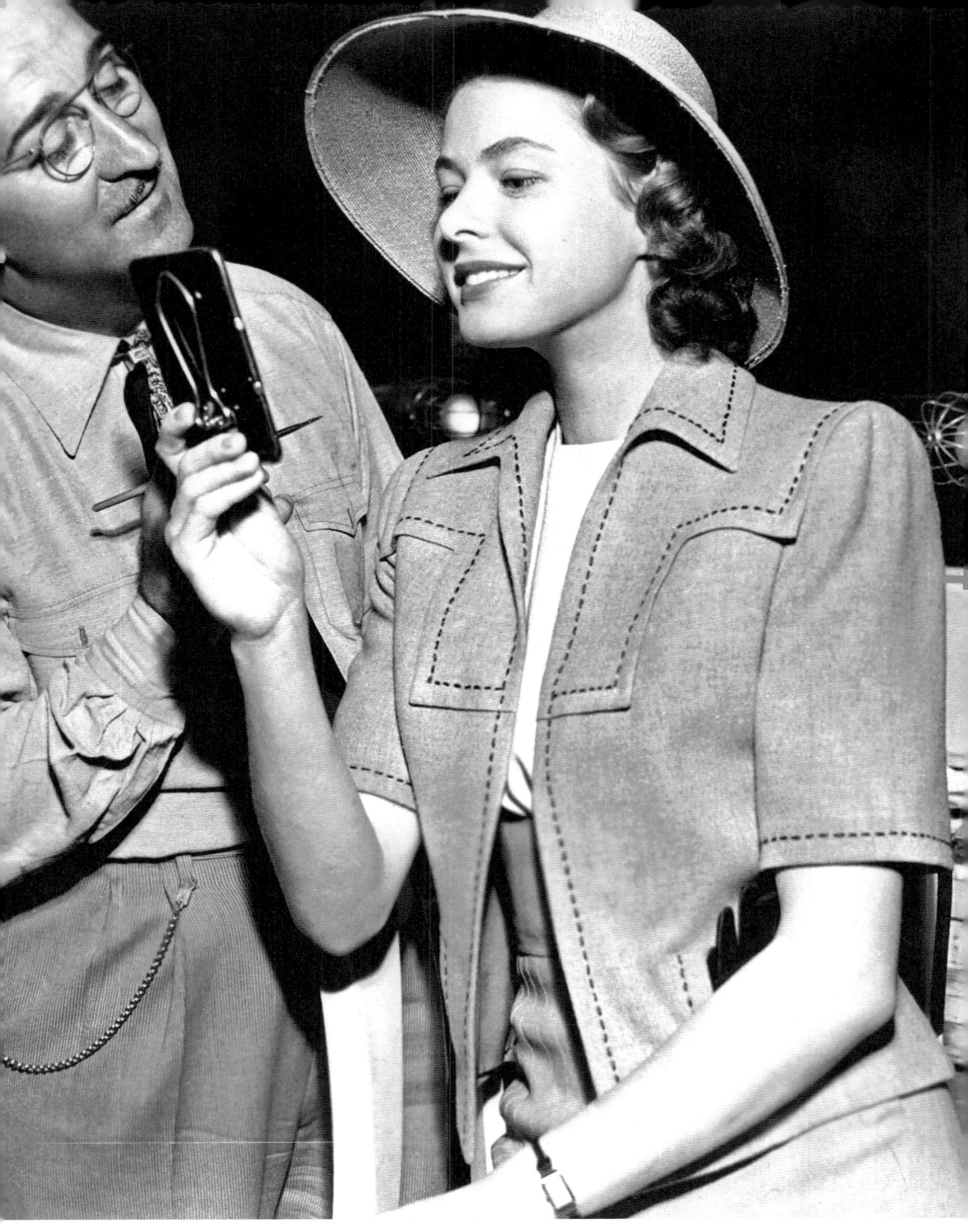

BOGIE AND ME

Below: Some biographies report that Bogart, here at 10 months, was born on Christmas Day, 1899, but others have disputed that as an invention of a studio publicity department. At right, Bogart holds the Scottish terrier Mac, his costar in the 1937 comedy *Stand-In*, about a foundering Hollywood studio.

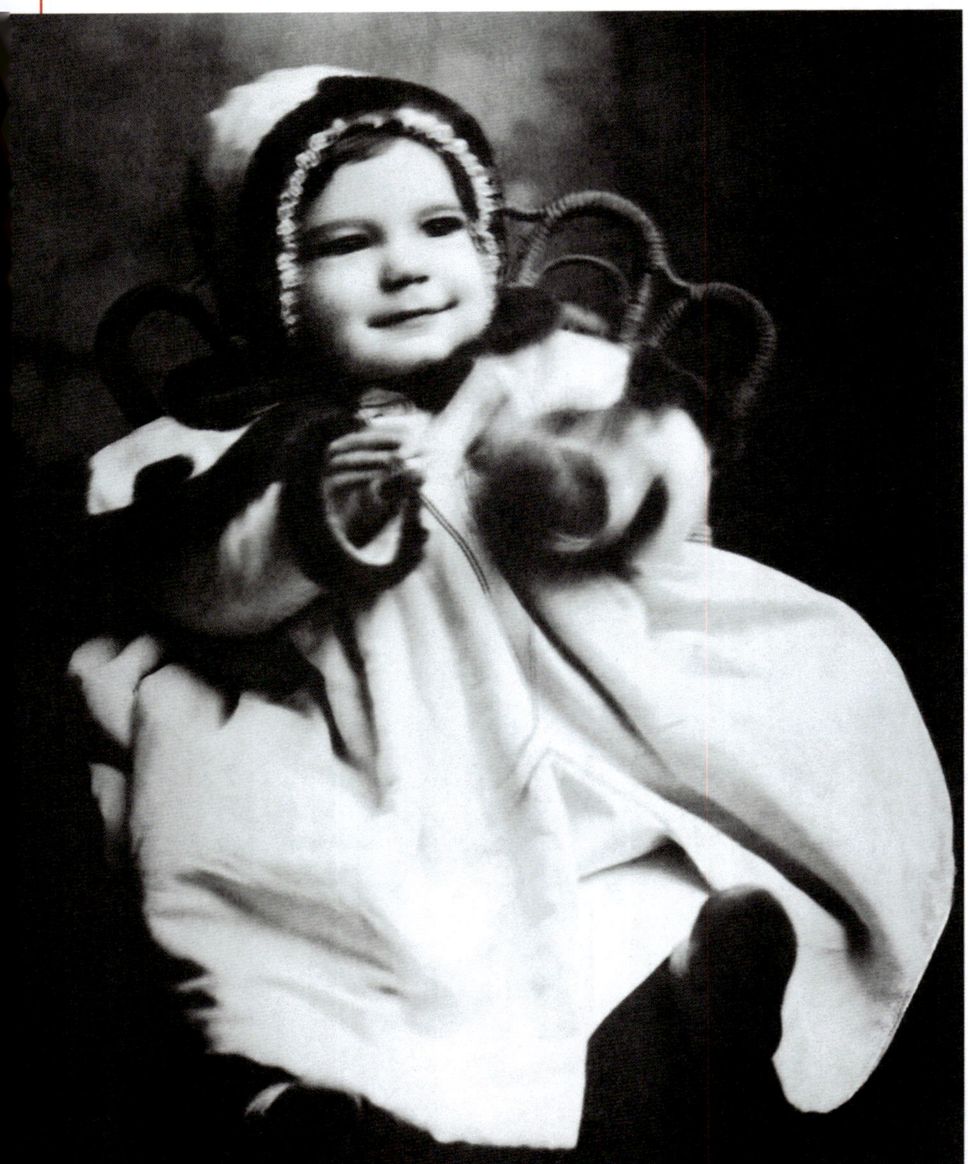

BETTMANN/GETTY

a young piano teacher who falls in love with a violin virtuoso. The following winter, a chance encounter in New York between a Swedish elevator operator and a talent scout brought Bergman to Selznick's attention. The elevator man suggested the scout check out Bergman's performance in *Intermezzo,* and impressed with what she saw, the scout alerted Selznick. He flew the actress to the United States and offered her the standard contract of seven years, a weekly salary, and no choice in scripts. Selznick also recommended that to make it in American films, Bergman cap her teeth, lose weight, shave her eyebrows, and change her name. Then 23 years old and uninterested in conforming to Hollywood standards, Bergman did none of those things and rebuffed the contract offer. Instead, she agreed to a single-film deal, an English-language version of *Intermezzo,* in which she costarred with Leslie Howard.

By 1942, when Wallis was casting around for his Ilsa, that first role in *Intermezzo* had evolved into a longer-term deal with Selznick, and Bergman had been cast in a handful of fairly forgettable films (*Rage in Heaven, Adam Had Four Sons*). She was tired of playing passive, love-torn heroines like Ilsa and was determined to land a meatier role, one with Oscar potential. The part she seized on was Maria, the traumatized young woman in *For Whom the Bell Tolls* who, after being raped, joins the fight against the Nationalists in the Spanish civil war. Selznick encouraged the audition, but Paramount instead chose Vera Zorina, a ballerina married to choreographer George Balanchine. (As it happened, while she was shooting *Casablanca,* Bergman received word that Paramount was dropping Zorina and wanted her as Maria, to begin filming as soon as *Casablanca* wrapped. The role won her her coveted first Oscar nomination.)

Meanwhile, Selznick was making his own set of calculations. He worried that Sweden might enter World War II on the side of the Axis powers, and that Bergman, with a German mother, would become unemployable. Maneuvering to secure the part of Ilsa for her, Selznick played hard to get with Wallis, avoiding meeting him and dodging his phone calls. Finally, Wallis dispatched screenwriters Julius and Philip Epstein to Selznick's office to win the producer over, a sales pitch that must not have taken much effort. In the siblings' telling, Selznick barely looked up

JOHN SPRINGER COLLECTION/CORBIS/GETTY

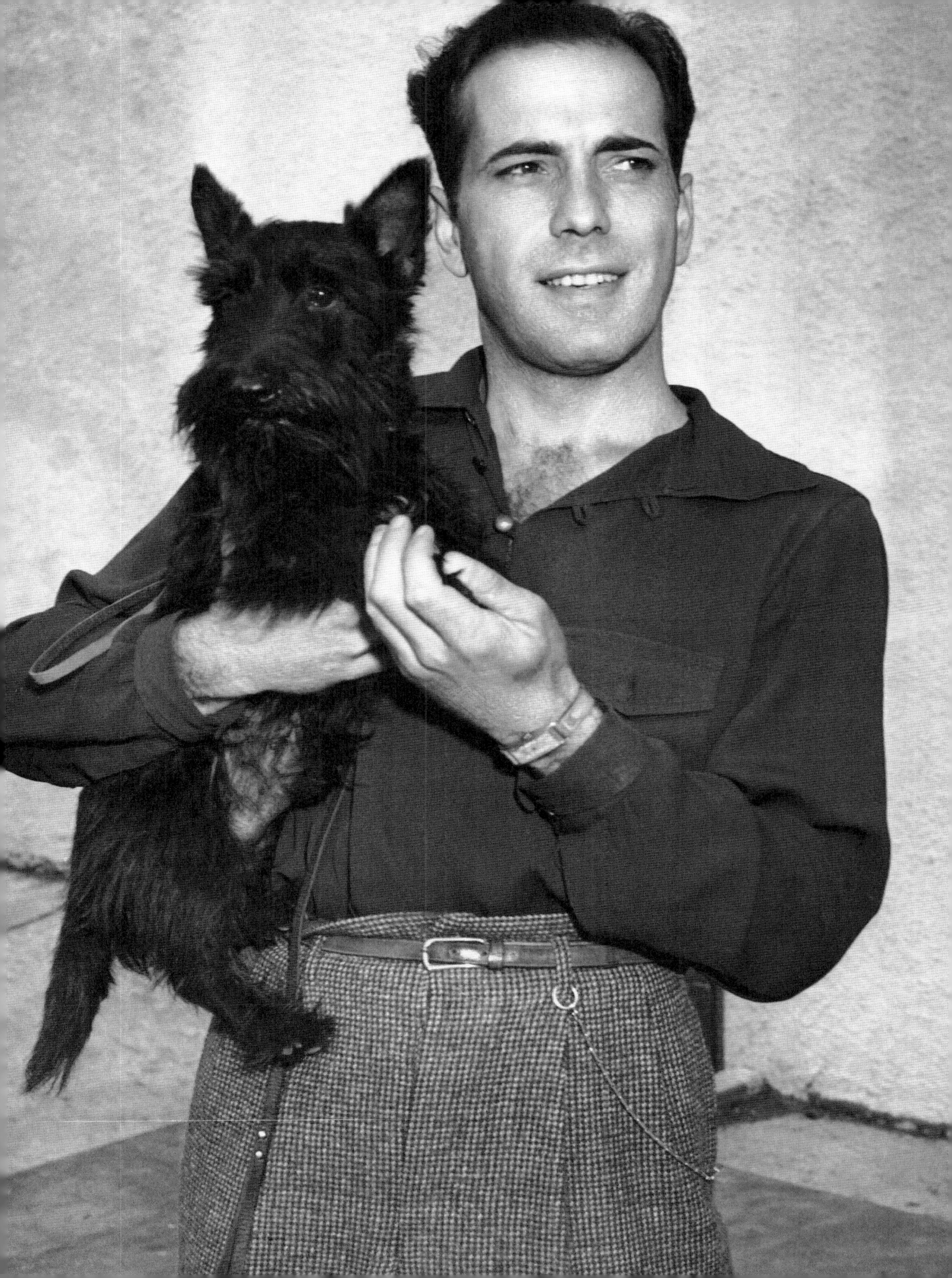

THE QUIET MAN

Below: Bogart, seated, far left, appears in a Skowhegan, Maine, production of *Rain*, about a missionary who tries to reform a prostitute. Bottom: Peter Lorre and Bogart, frequent costars, spar in a scene from 1941's *The Maltese Falcon*. At right: Bogart on a Warner Bros. set. While shooting *Casablanca*, he often retreated to his dressing room between scenes.

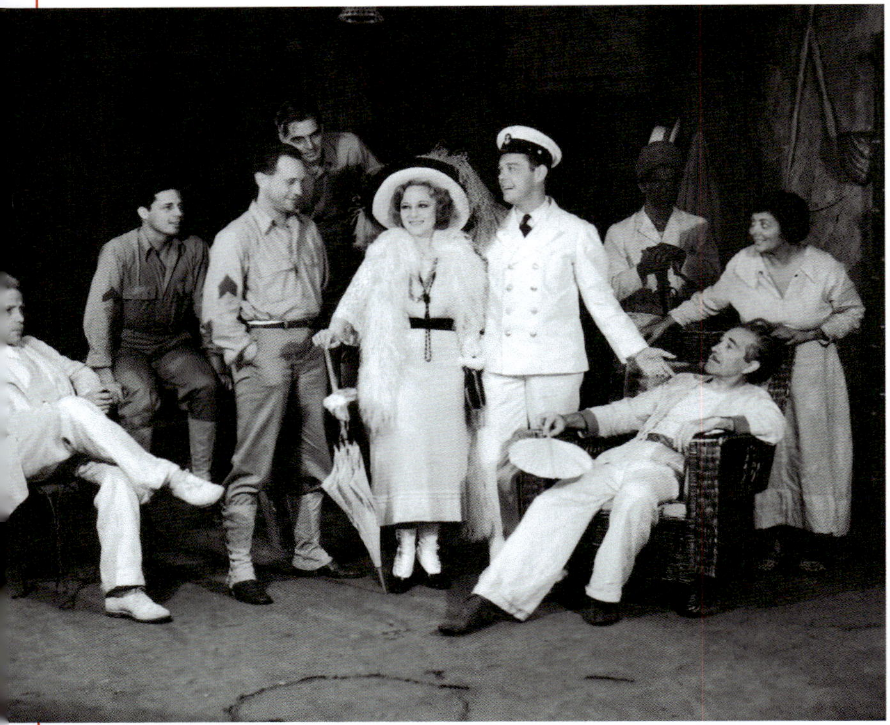

BETTMANN/GETTY

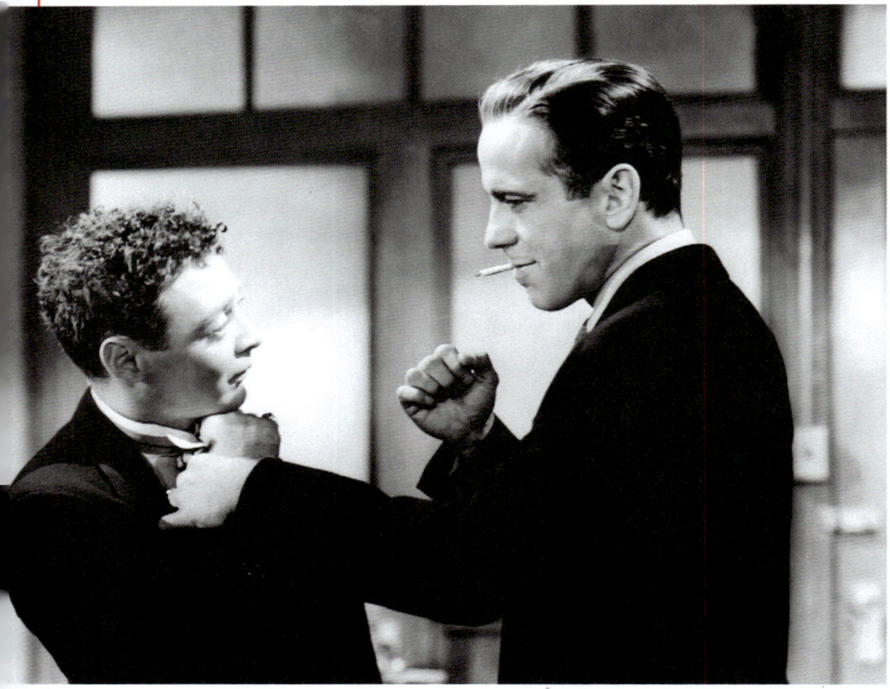

EVERETT

from his lunch, though he did nod his approval at the end of the meeting, signaling that they had Bergman. The actress, who preferred to work rather than not, accepted the offer, writing a friend that she'd been cast in a picture "called *Casablanca* and I really don't know what it's all about." It was April, and Wallis finally had gotten his girl.

Bogart's journey to the set of *Casablanca* was no less circuitous. Growing up in New York City, Bogart, who made a name for himself playing hoodlums and bad actors, was very much the son of privilege. His father, Belmont DeForest Bogart, was a physician and a graduate of Columbia and Yale. His mother, Maud Humphrey, was a suffragette and commercial illustrator (she used a drawing of baby Humphrey in an advertising campaign for Mellin's baby food). The Bogarts were distant as parents and Humphrey, an indifferent student, was enrolled in a series of private schools, including the prestigious Phillips Academy in Andover, Massachusetts. But once the teen was expelled from Phillips, supposedly for some combination of smoking, poor grades, and misbehavior, his formal education came to an end. He enlisted in the U.S. Navy, where he acquired the distinctive scar on his upper lip and its accompanying lisp. Depending on who is telling the story, the injury was sustained in battle, while walking another sailor to jail, or in a bar fight. "Goddamn doctor," Bogart later told his friend actor David Niven, "instead of stitching it up, he screwed it up."

On leaving the service Bogart gravitated to the theater, usually playing rich, pretty boys, and when the stock market crash of 1929 decimated Broadway audiences, he branched out to film. Bogie's big break came in the stage production of *The Petrified Forest*, a crime drama in which he was cast against type as Duke Mantee, a gangster based on

MARC WANAMAKER/BISON ARCHIVES

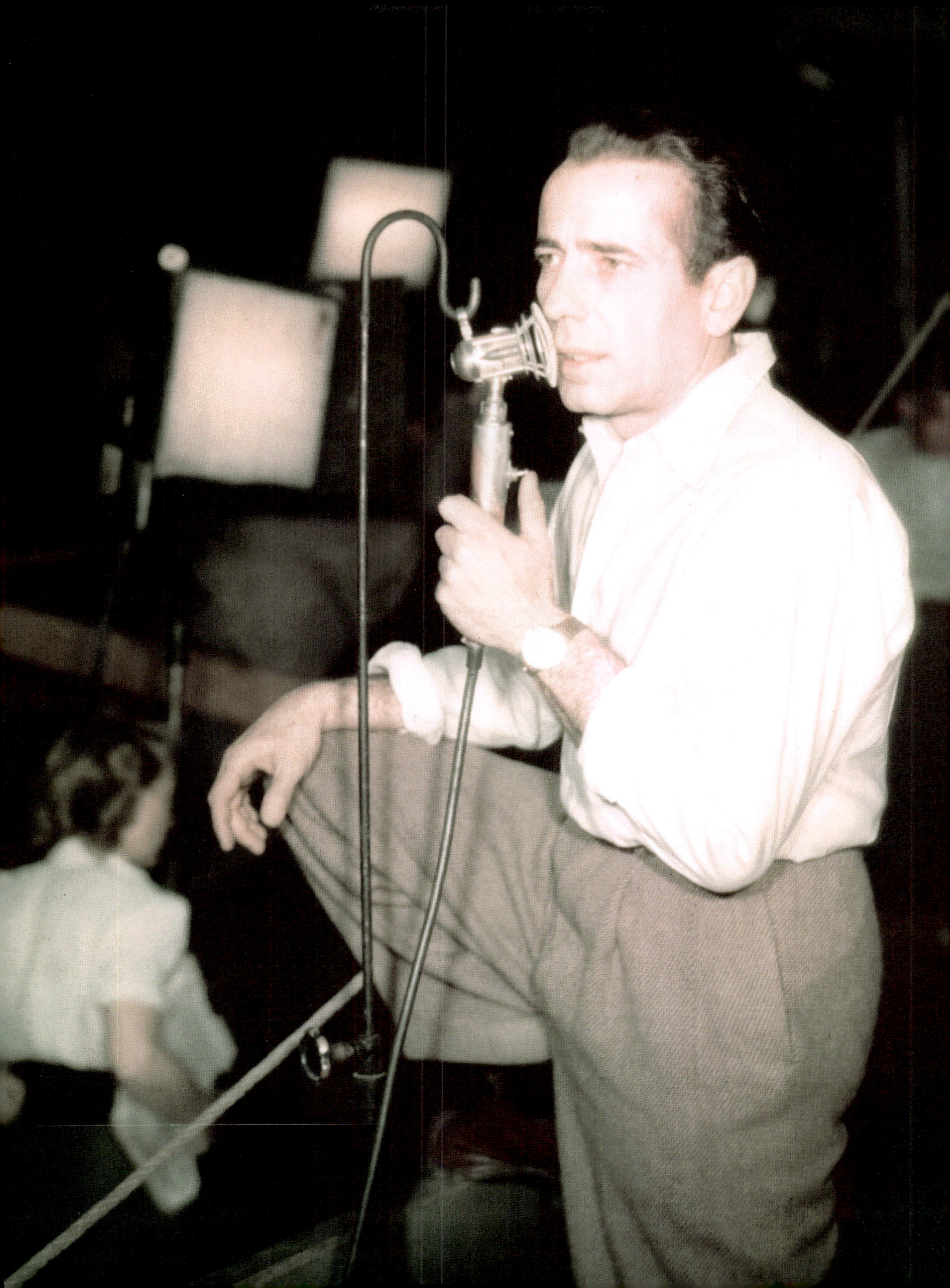

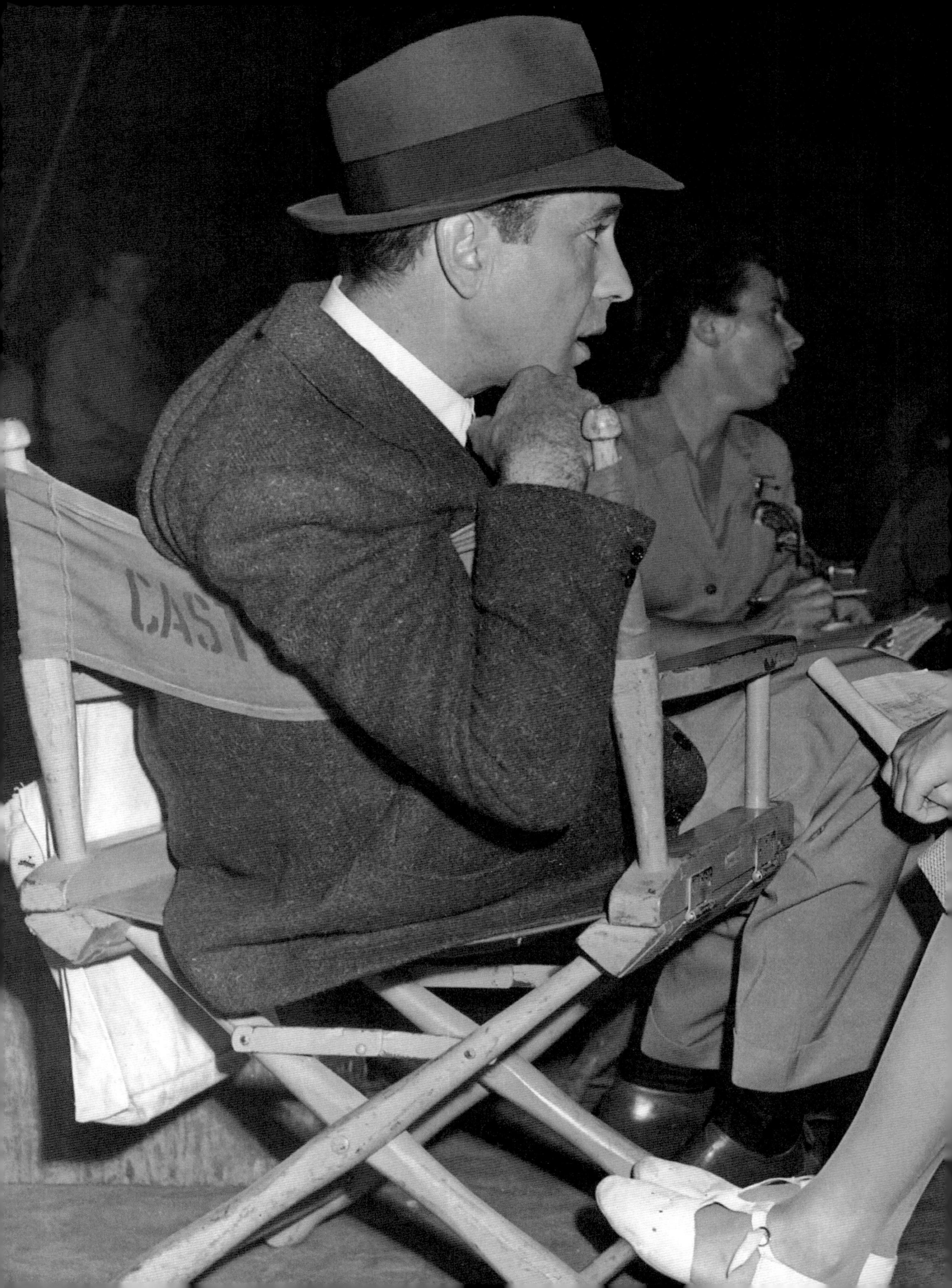
CAST

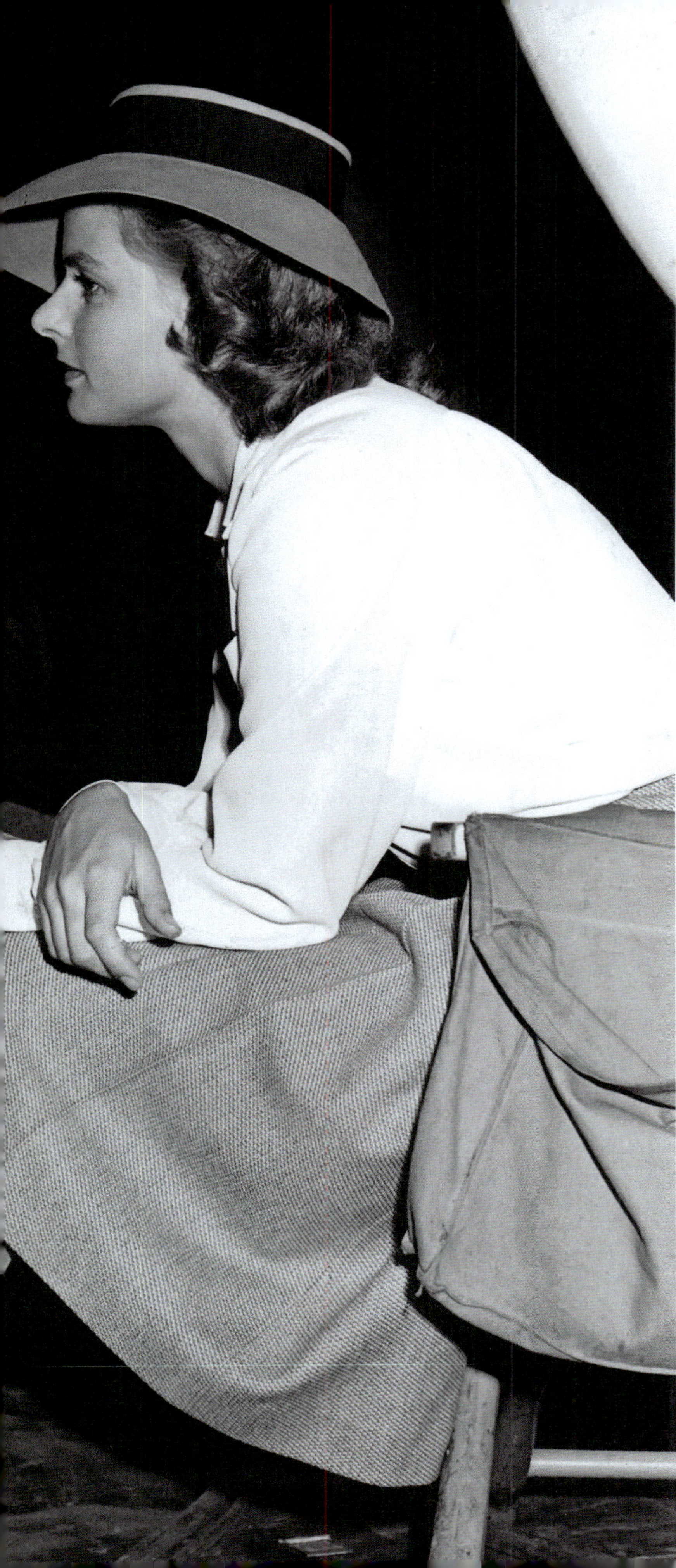

WARNER BROS./KOBAL/REX/SHUTTERSTOCK

John Dillinger. Audiences gasped when a snarling, stubble-faced Bogart sauntered onto the stage, and the play's star, Leslie Howard (who would later costar with Ingrid Bergman in *Intermezzo*), was so impressed with his performance that he insisted Warner Bros. cast Bogie—and not the more bankable Edward G. Robinson—in the film version. The movie was successful and Bogart was forever grateful to Howard, naming his daughter (with Lauren Bacall) after his friend—Leslie Howard Bogart.

The period that followed might be characterized as Bogart's rising, when the young actor morphed from central casting's preferred malcontent to its favorite principled loner. After the success of *High Sierra* and *The Maltese Falcon,* Bogart entered 1942 at the top of his game—a bona fide star with a bona fide star's contract. The only stumbling block when it came to *Casablanca* was that Bogie still saw himself in his gangster persona. He had been in more than 30 films for Warner, and in his mind he was a medium height, balding man known for pulling the trigger, as his son, Stephen, described Bogart's image of himself. Bogie worried the public would not believe that Ingrid Bergman would fall for him and was doubtful he could do the part at all. Even Jack Warner had his misgivings, allegedly commenting "Who would want to kiss Humphrey Bogart?"

As late as 10 days before filming began, Bogart and Bergman both were entertaining second thoughts, according to *Round Up the Usual Suspects* by Aljean Harmetz. A lunch between them with a mutual friend,

MR. CONGENIALITY

With Bergman, Bogart was always polite. That contrasted with his treatment of Lauren Bacall on the set of *To Have and Have Not,* where he teased her from day one, even handcuffing her once to a dressing room.

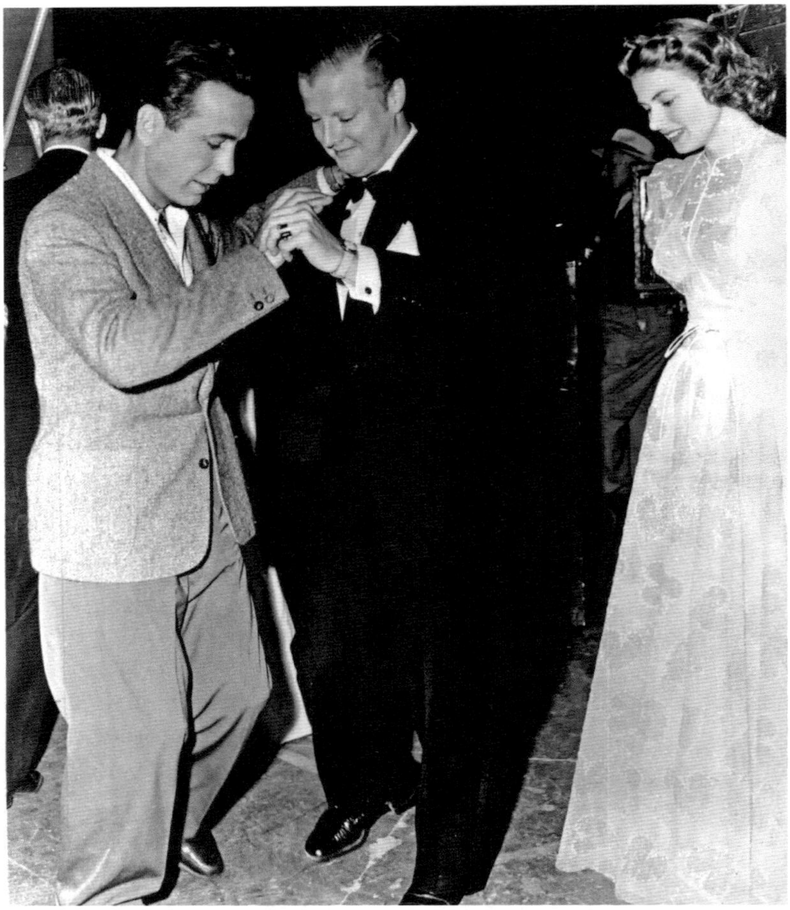

MARC WANAMAKER/BISON ARCHIVES

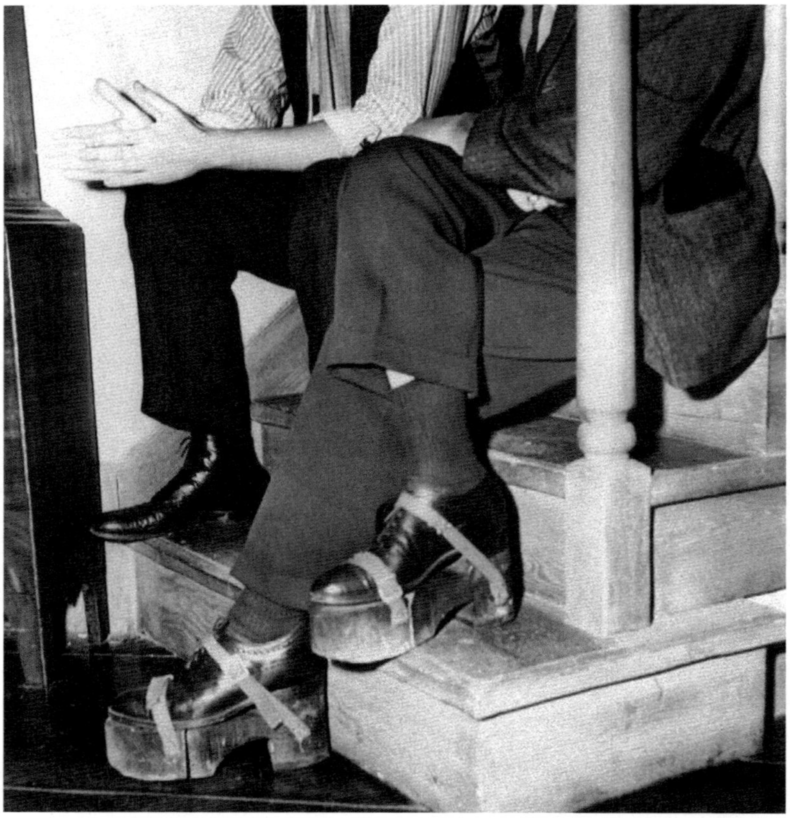

KURT STRUMPF/AP/REX/SHUTTERSTOCK

actress Geraldine Fitzgerald, turned into a beef session. "They thought the dialogue was ridiculous and the situations were unbelievable," Fitzgerald told Harmetz. Bogart thought Rick was self-pitying and didn't like some of his lines. "And Ingrid was terribly upset because she said she had to portray the most beautiful woman in Europe, and no one would ever believe that," said Fitzgerald. Unable to connect emotionally with Bogart, Bergman resorted to studying him on-screen in *The Maltese Falcon,* which was still in theaters.

From the very first scenes shot by director Michael Curtiz—the flashbacks of Rick and Ilsa in Paris—the stars' relationship or lack of one loomed large. In Paris, Rick and Ilsa were supposed to drink champagne, dance, and share confidences to establish their early happiness—all crucial to the plot's credibility. The dance scene went poorly because Bogart had trouble learning to rumba and because Bergman was taller. For her part, Bergman found it difficult to strike the right note, since the script was still not completed and she was unsure if she was supposed to be in love with Rick or her film husband, the resistance fighter Victor Laszlo. Curtiz's advice: "Play it in between."

Adding to Bogart's troubles was his third wife, Mayo Methot, who suspected that her husband was having an affair with Bergman and who would show up on set at unpredictable times to confront him. Bogart had nicknamed Methot "Sluggy" in the early days of their marriage for her drunken rages, and the couple's nightly shouting matches depressed Bogart even more. He spent most of his time in his trailer, playing chess and drinking. On the set, he often argued with Curtiz about his lines, the number of takes, and the way he should romance Ilsa. "He came out of his dressing room, did his scene, then fled away again," Bergman recounted

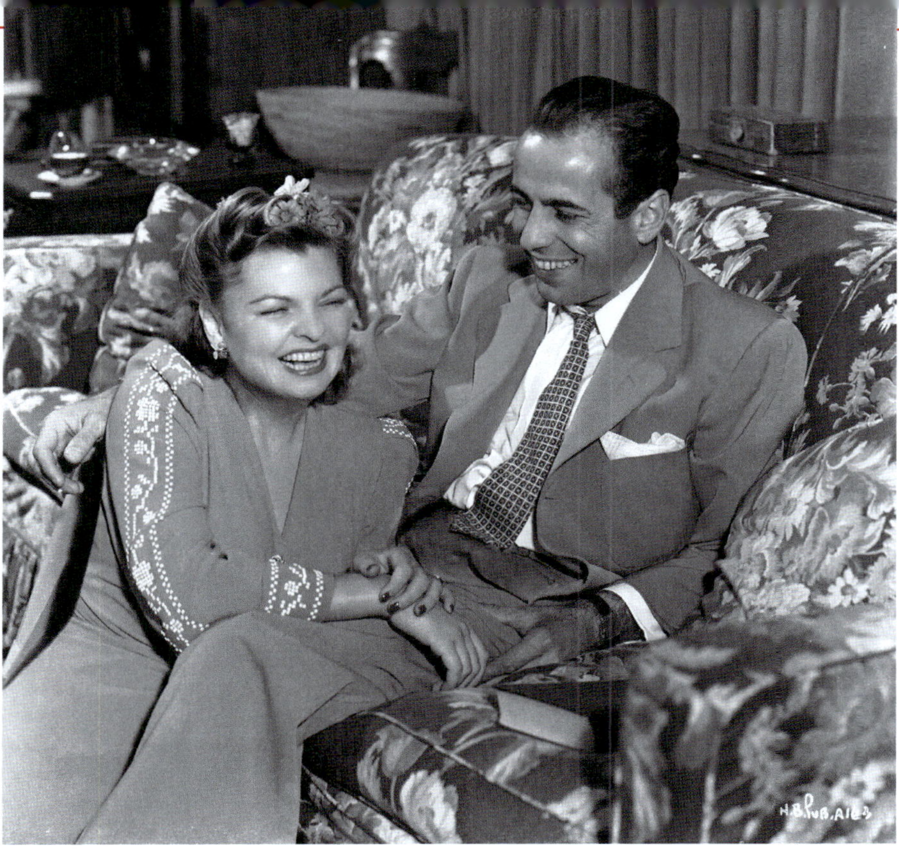

JOHN KOBAL FOUNDATION/GETTY

ALL THE RIGHT MOVES

Opposite: At top, Bogart got rumba lessons to prepare for his scene in a Paris nightclub with Bergman. Supposedly Bogart dreaded the dance because he was shorter than his costar, and was given lifts to wear to make him taller (bottom). At left, Bogart relaxed with his third wife, Mayo Methot, whom he would later divorce to marry Lauren Bacall. In the scene below, Ilsa visits Rick after hours in his café. He asks why she has come to Casablanca.

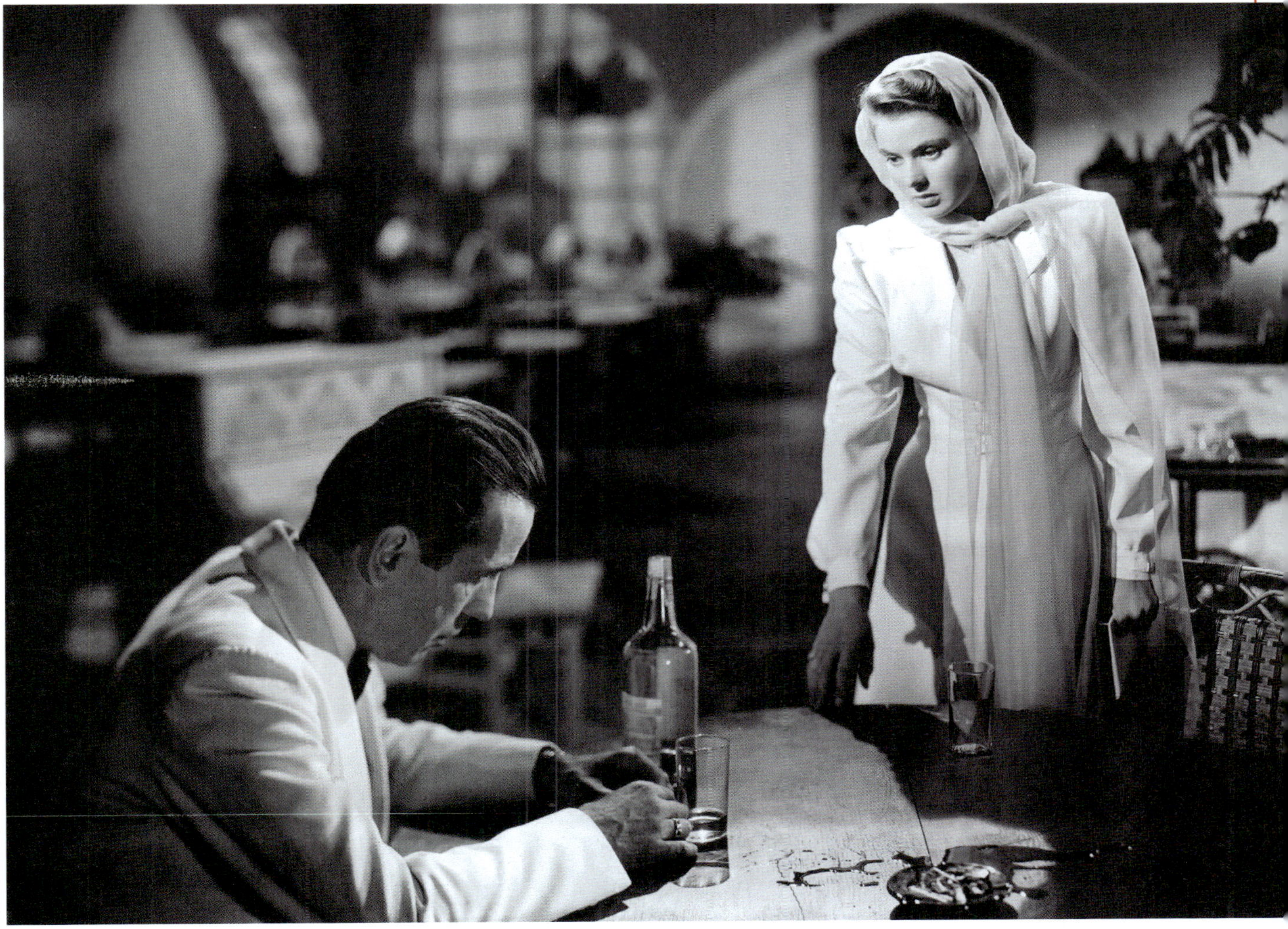

WARNER BROS./KOBAL/REX/SHUTTERSTOCK

later. "It was all very strange and distant."

By some miracle, dailies revealed none of the friction, or if they did, it translated as intentional and part of the film's sexual tension. On celluloid, Bergman and Bogart radiated emotional intensity. Unmistakable pain filled Rick's eyes when he found Ilsa in Rick's Café Américain, with a husband; he exposed naked bitterness when drinking with Sam, pounding the table and grabbing his forehead, uttering one of the film's most famous lines, "Of all the gin joints in all the towns in all the world..." Likewise, Ilsa's passion for Rick was clear even while she threatened him with a gun to obtain the letters of transit—and before she melted in his arms declaring, "I still love you." The closing moments when Rick insisted Ilsa board the plane defined the depth of their love and sealed the inevitability of their parting, as he told her, "We'll always have Paris."

Decades later, Bergman continued to be confounded by *Casablanca*'s success. "I made so many films which were more important, but the only one people ever want to talk about is that one with Bogart," she complained. For his part, Bogart, who earned an Oscar nod for his turn as Rick, was transformed into one of the highest paid actors in the world, and Hollywood's most unconventional leading man. "Of course," he later told his fourth wife, Bacall, "I did nothing in *Casablanca* that I hadn't done in 20 movies before that, and suddenly they discover I'm sexy. Any time that Ingrid Bergman looks at a man, he has sex appeal." ■

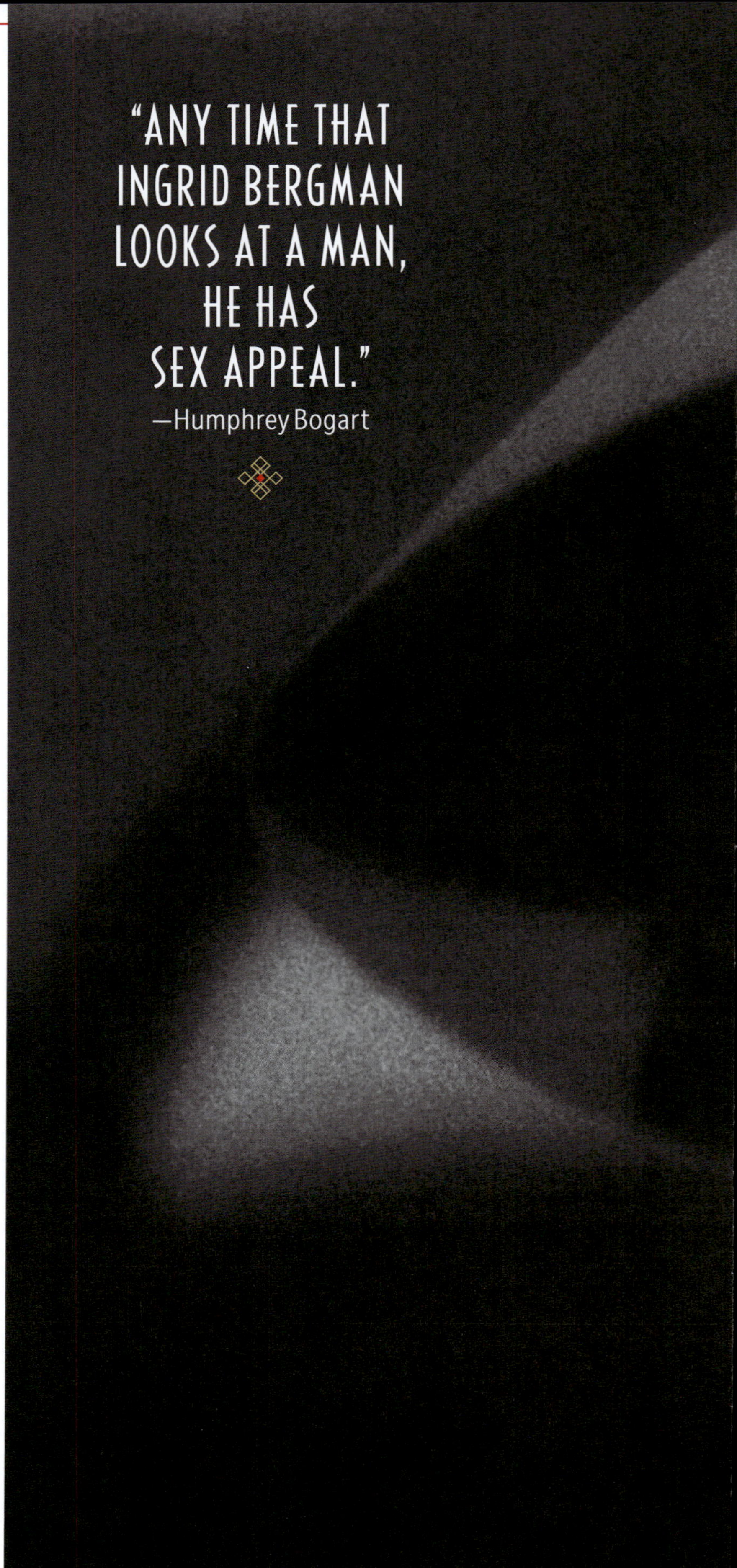

"ANY TIME THAT INGRID BERGMAN LOOKS AT A MAN, HE HAS SEX APPEAL."
—Humphrey Bogart

STICKLER FOR DETAIL
Bergman was not a temperamental star, but when it came to her character, she was quite firm. She even refused to allow the stylist to anchor her hair with bobby pins because she wanted a natural look.

THA/WARNER BROS.

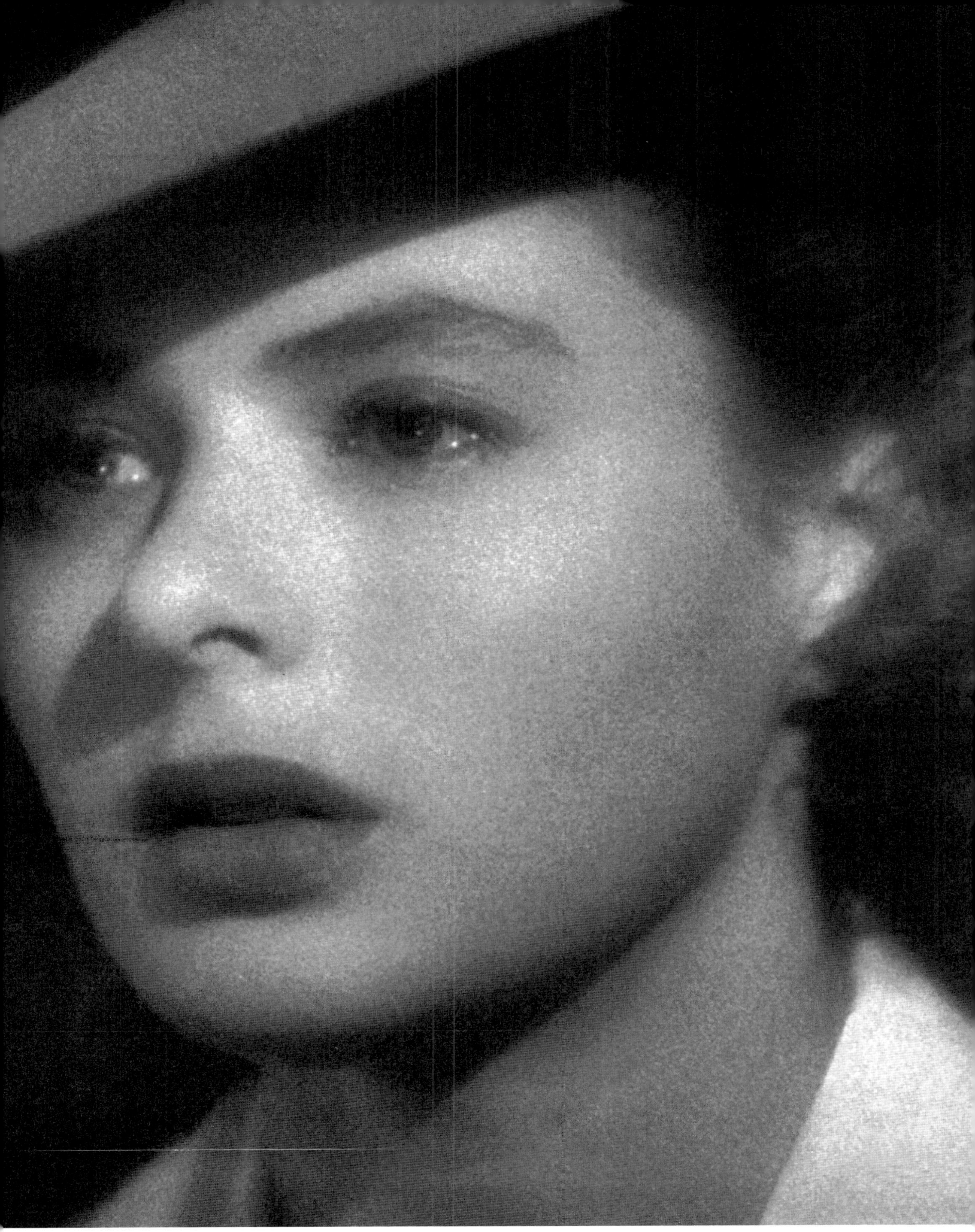

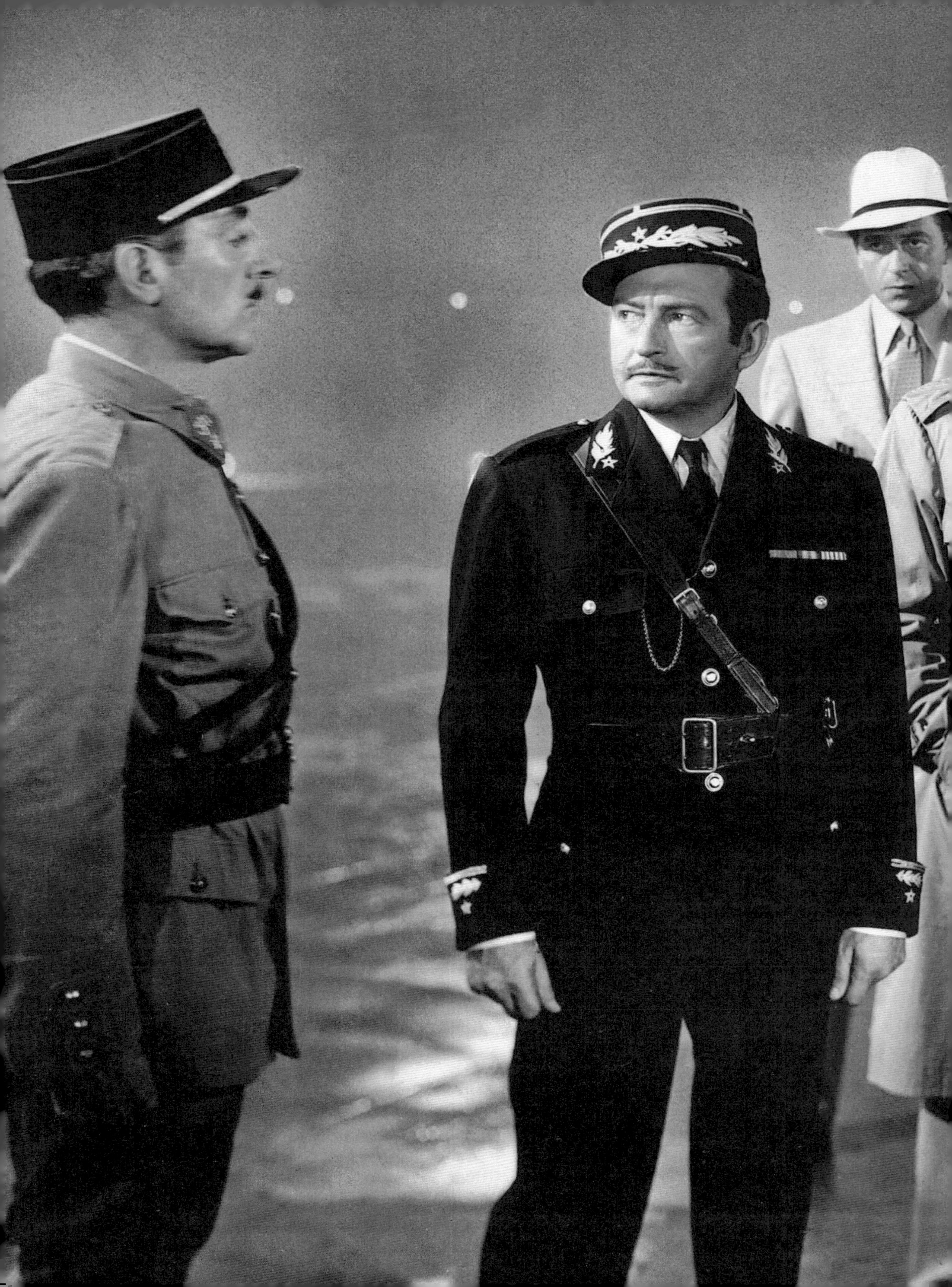

THE USUAL SUSPECTS

Casting *Casablanca* was a protracted affair involving stunt press releases, horse-trading with other studios, scheduling conflicts, and dud screen tests

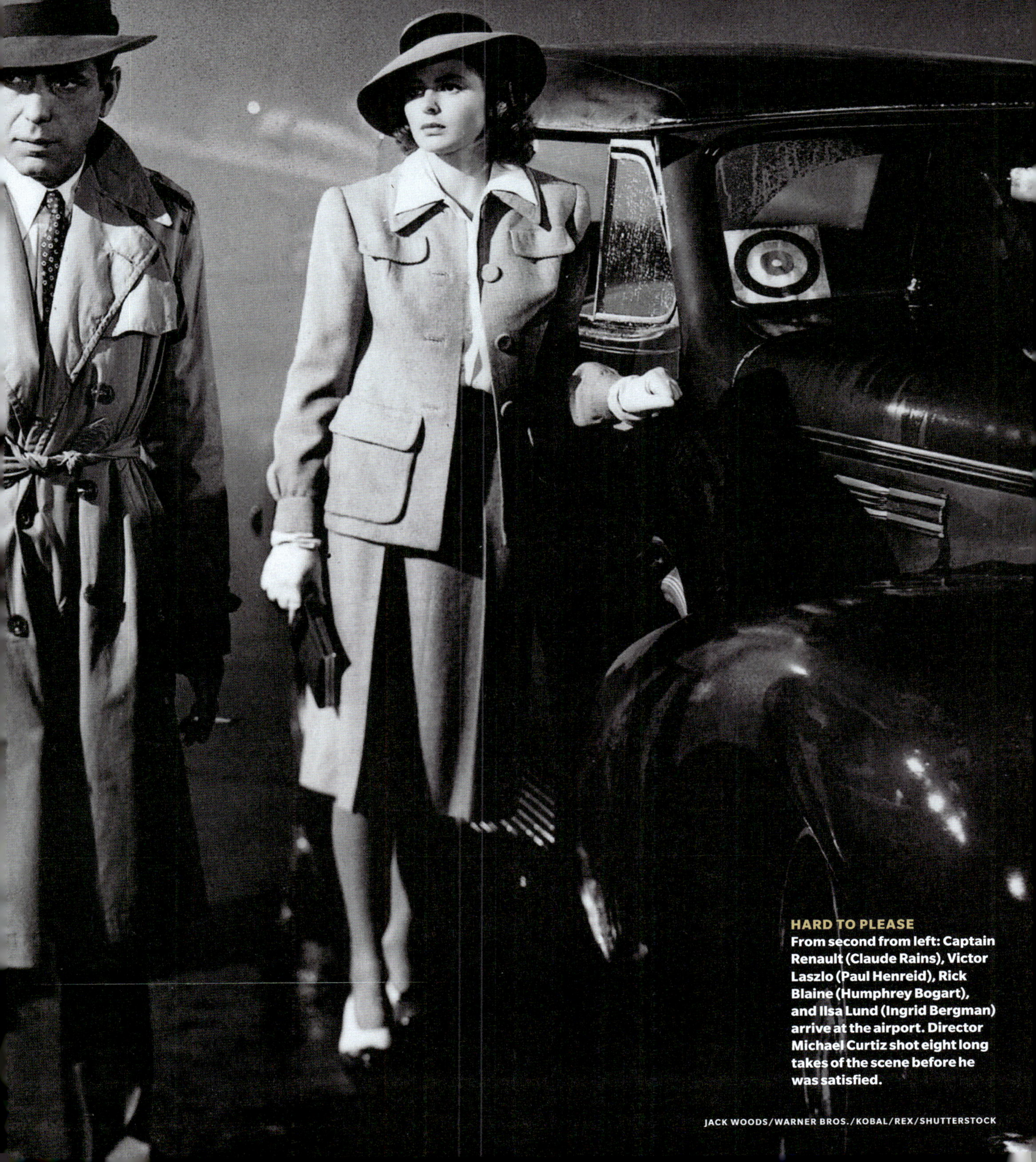

HARD TO PLEASE
From second from left: Captain Renault (Claude Rains), Victor Laszlo (Paul Henreid), Rick Blaine (Humphrey Bogart), and Ilsa Lund (Ingrid Bergman) arrive at the airport. Director Michael Curtiz shot eight long takes of the scene before he was satisfied.

JACK WOODS/WARNER BROS./KOBAL/REX/SHUTTERSTOCK

CLAUDE RAINS

Captain Louis Renault

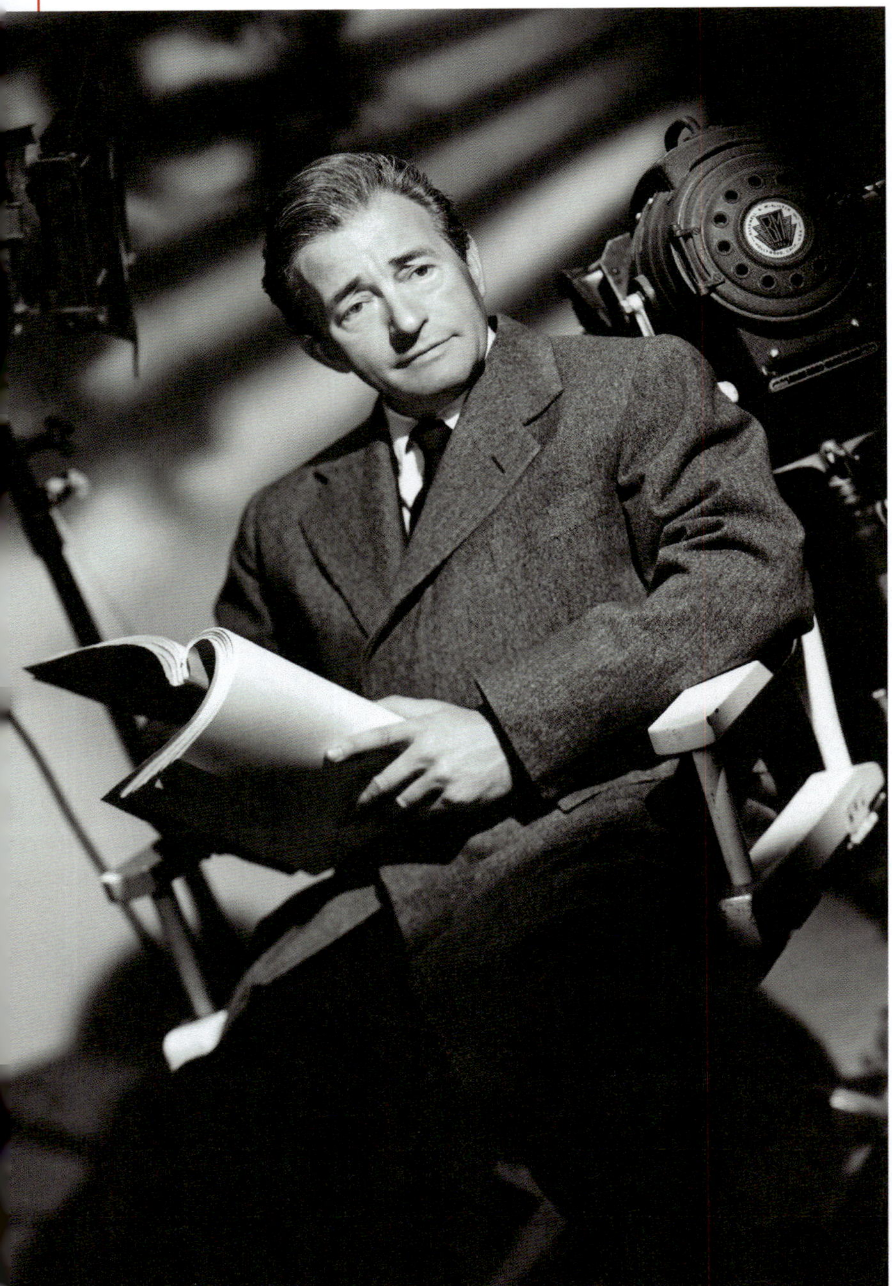

HE'S THE ONE
Rains, who often played mild-mannered English types for Warner Bros., was the obvious choice for Captain Renault. Opposite: In a scene with Conrad Veidt, *Casablanca's* Major Strasser.

Before Frank Sinatra, actor Claude Rains was the Voice. His was urbane, cynical, and wry, and it made him one of Hollywood's great character actors, a staple of such classics as *Lawrence of Arabia, Mr. Smith Goes to Washington,* and *Now, Voyager.* Rains's velvety chords and suave comportment were also completely of his own making. Born poor in London in 1889, the actor was one of 12 children, nine of whom died young. His mother took in borders to support the family, and Rains attended school only through the second grade. He later took elocution lessons to get rid of a thick cockney accent and to correct a speech impediment. At 11, Rains started acting, and he went on to teach at the Royal Academy of Dramatic Art, where he counted John Gielgud and Lawrence Olivier as students.

With the outbreak of World War I, Rains stepped away from the stage and enlisted in the British infantry. Though he was largely blinded in one eye in a gas attack, he rose to the rank of captain before leaving the army and moving to New York, where he became a leading stage actor. He didn't appear in his first film until age 44, when the director of *The Invisible Man,* overheard, but didn't see, the actor's screen test, and reportedly remarked, "I don't care what he looks like, that's the voice I want," according to *Round Up the Usual Suspects* by Aljean Harmetz. By the time *Casablanca* was being cast, Rains had appeared in 31 films and he was the only real contender for the role of Renault, the corrupt Vichy captain who is "shocked—*shocked*—to find that gambling is going on" at Rick's, even as he receives his winnings from the croupier. ■

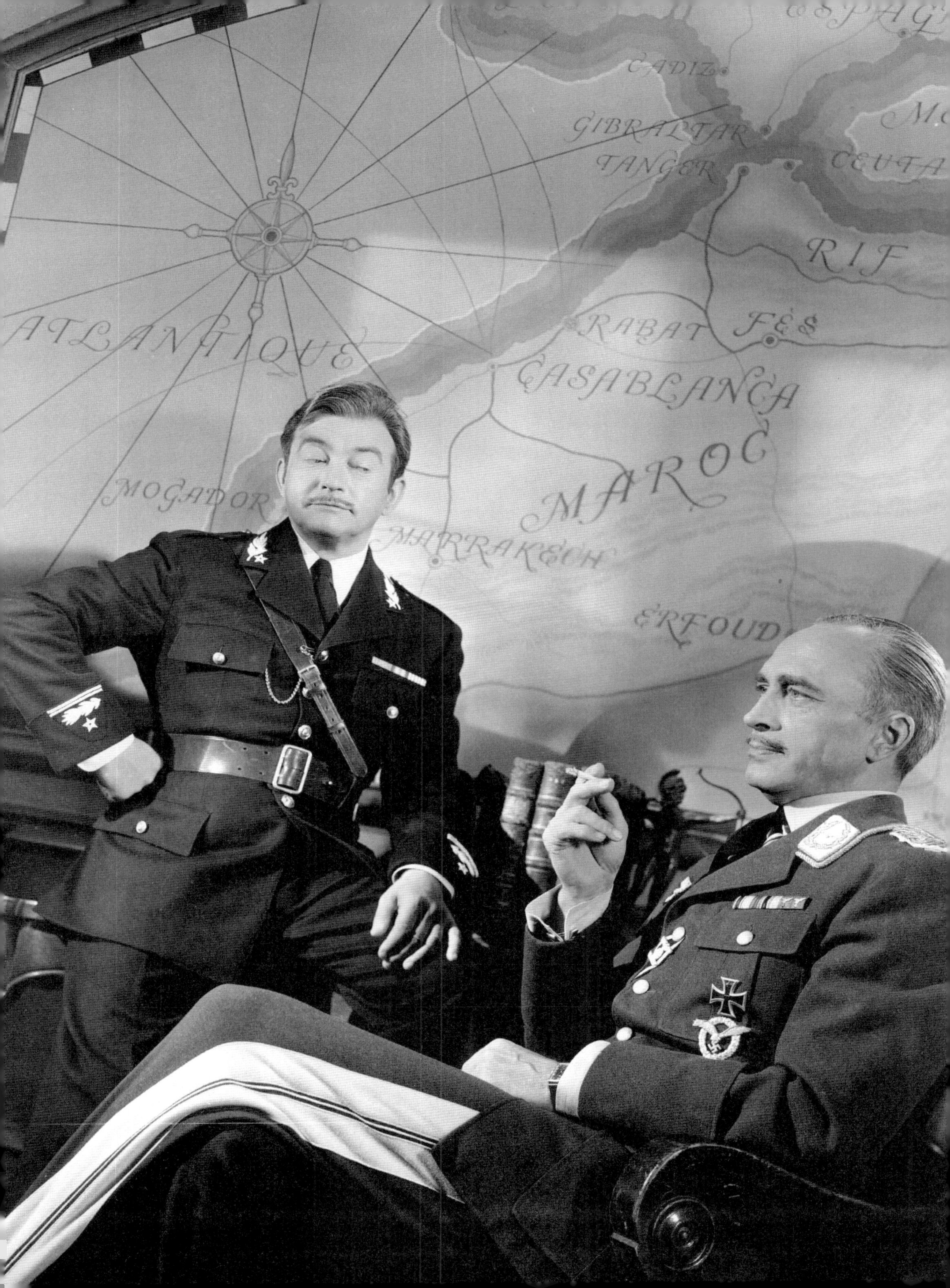
CADIZ
GIBRALTAR
TANGER
CEUTA
RIF
ATLANTIQUE
RABAT
FÈS
CASABLANCA
MAROC
MOGADOR
MARRAKECH
ERFOUD

SYDNEY GREENSTREET

Signor Ferrari

If Sydney Greenstreet had a single defining characteristic, it was his girth, and he used it to discomforting effect in *Casablanca* as club owner Signor Ferrari. On-screen for less than five minutes, the nearly 300-pound Greenstreet is effete and insinuating from his first big scene, where he looms near the piano player, Sam, and seeks to lure him away from Rick.

Ferrari: What do you want for Sam?

Rick: I don't buy or sell human beings.

Ferrari: Too bad. That's Casablanca's leading commodity.

Even if Ferrari is not strictly evil, he becomes an oversize stand-in for corruption and greed, brought home clearly by his declaration that "as leader of all illegal activities in *Casablanca,* I am an influential and respected man." It was a familiar role for Greenstreet, who was often cast as a partner (or rival) in crime with the tiny Peter Lorre, who plays the black-marketeer Ugarte in *Casablanca*. The two did not share any scenes in the film, but their personas were so linked for the public, its almost as if they did.

Greenstreet's success in film was a late-in-life phenomenon. Born in Britain in 1879, he spent decades on the stage, often in Shakespeare and musical comedies, but his original ambition had been to make his fortune as a tea planter. He was just a teenager when he moved to Sri Lanka and discovered a volume of Shakespeare's works that his mother had packed in his suitcase. With nothing else to do in the evenings, he memorized the plays, and when a drought forced him to leave Sri Lanka he returned to England and began studying acting. Greenstreet arrived in the U.S. in 1904 and worked for years in the theater, rebuffing overtures from Hollywood. A chance meeting with *The Maltese Falcon* director John Huston led to his being cast, at 62, in that film as the malevolent Kasper Gutman, who is desperate to track down the jewel-encrusted statuette. Peter Lorre was his foil, playing Joel Cairo, and Humphrey Bogart was the hero, as gumshoe Sam Spade. The trio would make three films together. ■

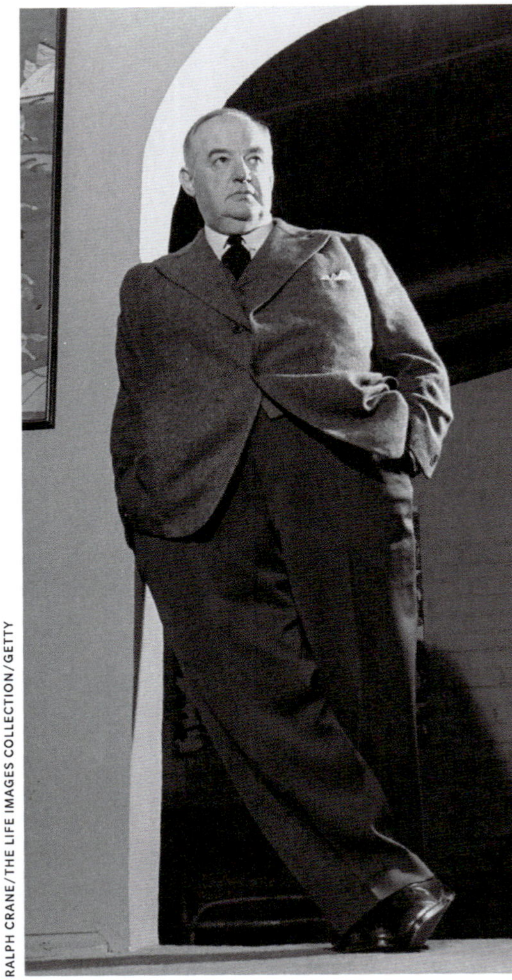

RALPH CRANE/THE LIFE IMAGES COLLECTION/GETTY

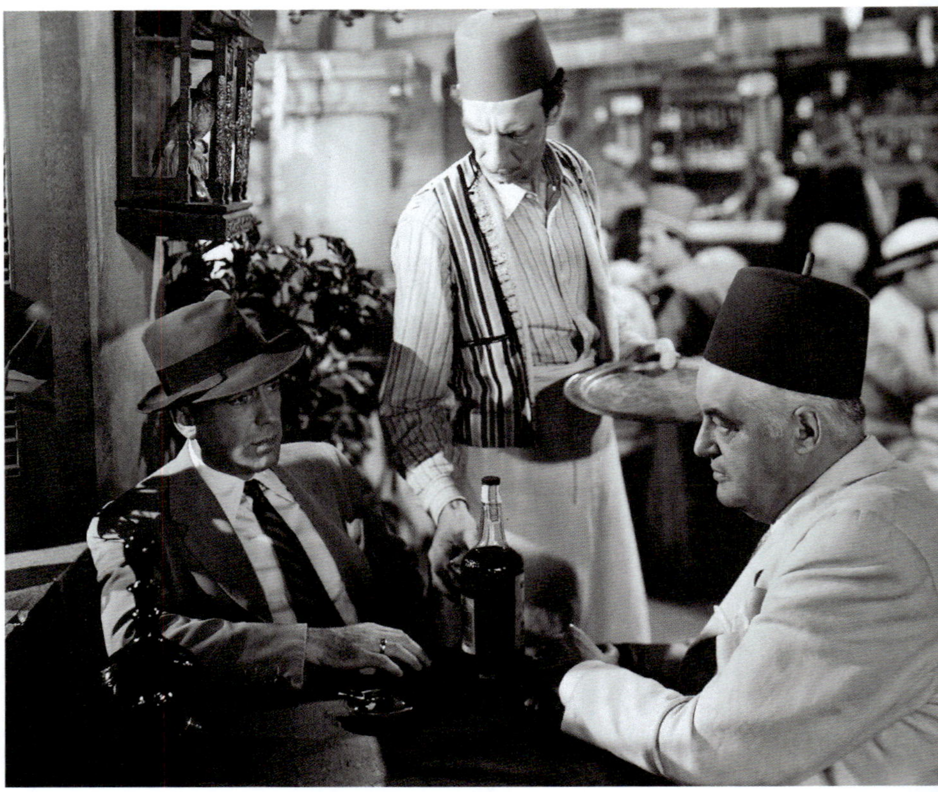

WARNER BROS./KOBAL/REX/SHUTTERSTOCK

NICE PAYDAY

To entice Greenstreet, top, into accepting the small role of Signor Ferrari, Warners offered him $3,750 a week, more than double his usual salary. At right, in conversation with Bogart at the Blue Parrot.

PETER LORRE

Ugarte

Portraying the wheedling black-marketeer Ugarte, Peter Lorre speaks fewer than 400 words and clocks less than four minutes of screen time before he is arrested and disappears from the action. But by killing two German couriers to obtain the valuable letters of transit—and giving them to Rick to hold—he sets the plot in motion.

Invariably described as pasty-faced and saucer-eyed, Lorre began perfecting his villain persona in 1931, when after a career on the stage in Vienna and Berlin, he starred in Fritz Lang's *M* as a sympathetic child murderer. (Yes, you read that correctly.) The role was modeled loosely on a German serial killer who was executed by guillotine just weeks after *M* was released and the attendant publicity turned Lorre into an international celebrity.

By then, the Nazi party was on the rise in Europe and the Jewish Lorre and his fiancée were among the first wave to escape Adolf Hitler, in 1933. The couple eventually landed in England, where Lorre convinced Alfred Hitchcock to cast in him as the assassin Abbott in *The Man Who Knew Too Much,* even though he did not yet speak English.

One fan of his performances was Hitler himself, who, unaware of Lorre's religion, invited him to return to Germany to join the Nazis' nascent film industry. Lorre's rejection letter—"Thank you, but I think Germany has room for only one mass murderer of my ability and yours"—apparently got under Hitler's skin. When a Nazi saboteur was captured by the FBI later in the war, Lorre's name was third on his list of 100 people to be assassinated. ■

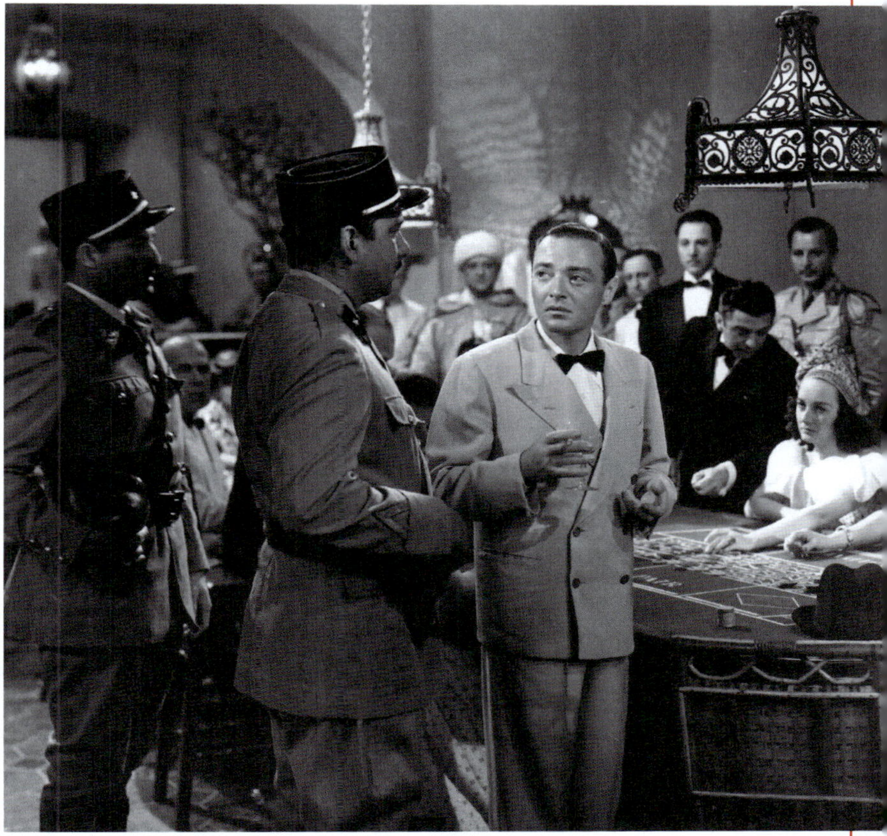

MARC WANAMAKER/BISON ARCHIVES

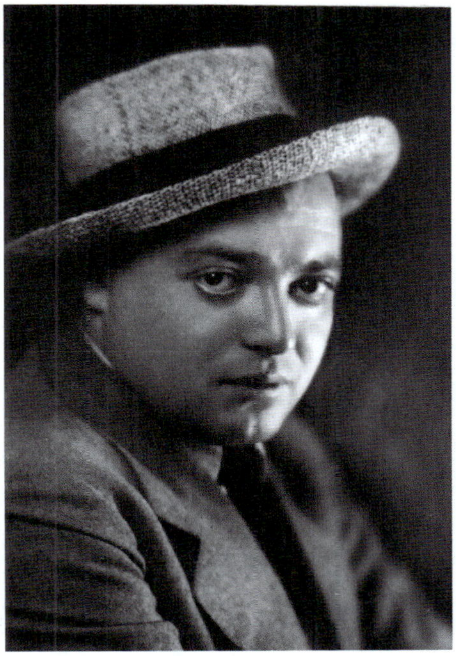

BETTMANN/GETTY

FUNNY MAN
Lorre as Ugarte (above), a character the actor's biographer described as "a blanched weasel." On set, he was known as a prankster, playing practical jokes and extinguishing director Curtiz's cigarettes to fluster him.

PAUL HENREID

Victor Laszlo

An Austrian aristocrat whose father had been knighted by Emperor Franz Josef I, Paul Henreid was known for his imperious behavior on set and off. He initially dismissed the *Casablanca* script as a "ridiculous fairy tale" and balked at playing the second romantic lead to Humphrey Bogart's Rick Blaine. Henreid also claimed, without proof, that he had a clause in his contract guaranteeing that he would win Ilsa back by the final scene. In the end, Henreid took the part of the resistance fighter mainly at the insistence of his agent, Lew Wasserman, who hoped to insulate his client from restrictions on "enemy aliens" working in Hollywood as World War II tensions mounted in the United States.

Henreid's apprehension about playing the part may have been somewhat justified. Before *Casablanca,* he had been built up by his studio, RKO, as a suave ladies' man (once even having to fend off a claque of prostitutes who had been called in as part of a publicity stunt). Henreid had played the romantic lead in *Now, Voyager* with Bette Davis, and sparked a national craze when he slid two cigarettes into his mouth, lit both, and passed one to Davis. But after *Casablanca,* the actor's career lost momentum. Instead of leading roles, he was sidelined as an accented stereotype—a Polish count, a freedom fighter, or some sort of European character. During the anticommunist McCarthy era, Henreid protested the political witch hunt and was blacklisted. He finished his career directing television. ■

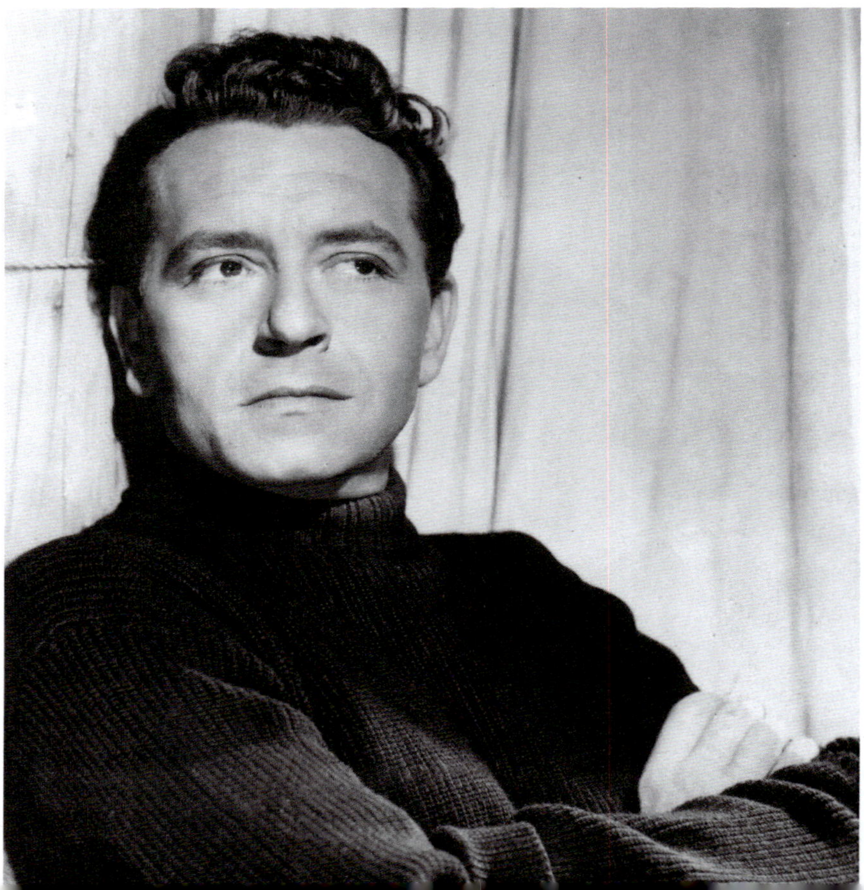

PRINT COLLECTOR/HULTON/GETTY

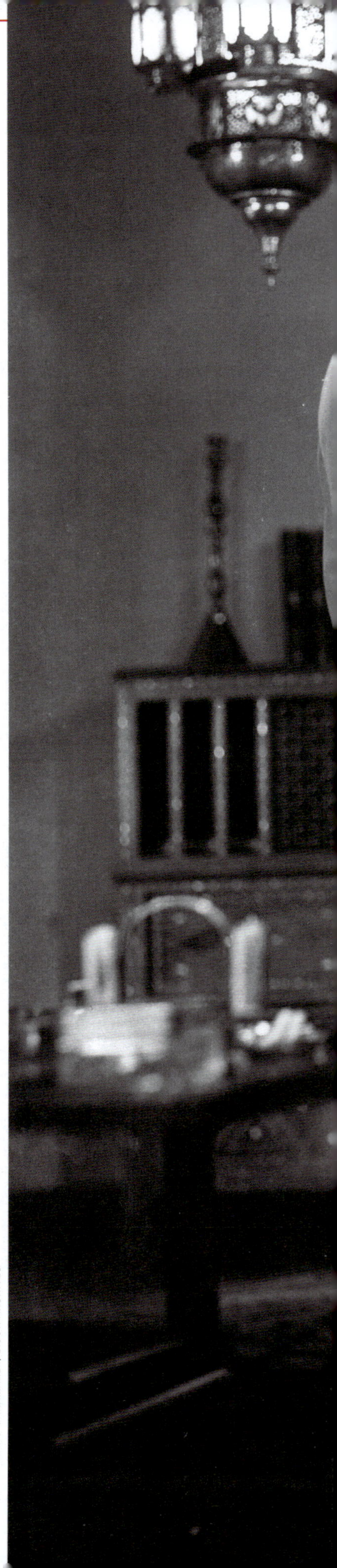

MARC WANAMAKER/BISON ARCHIVES

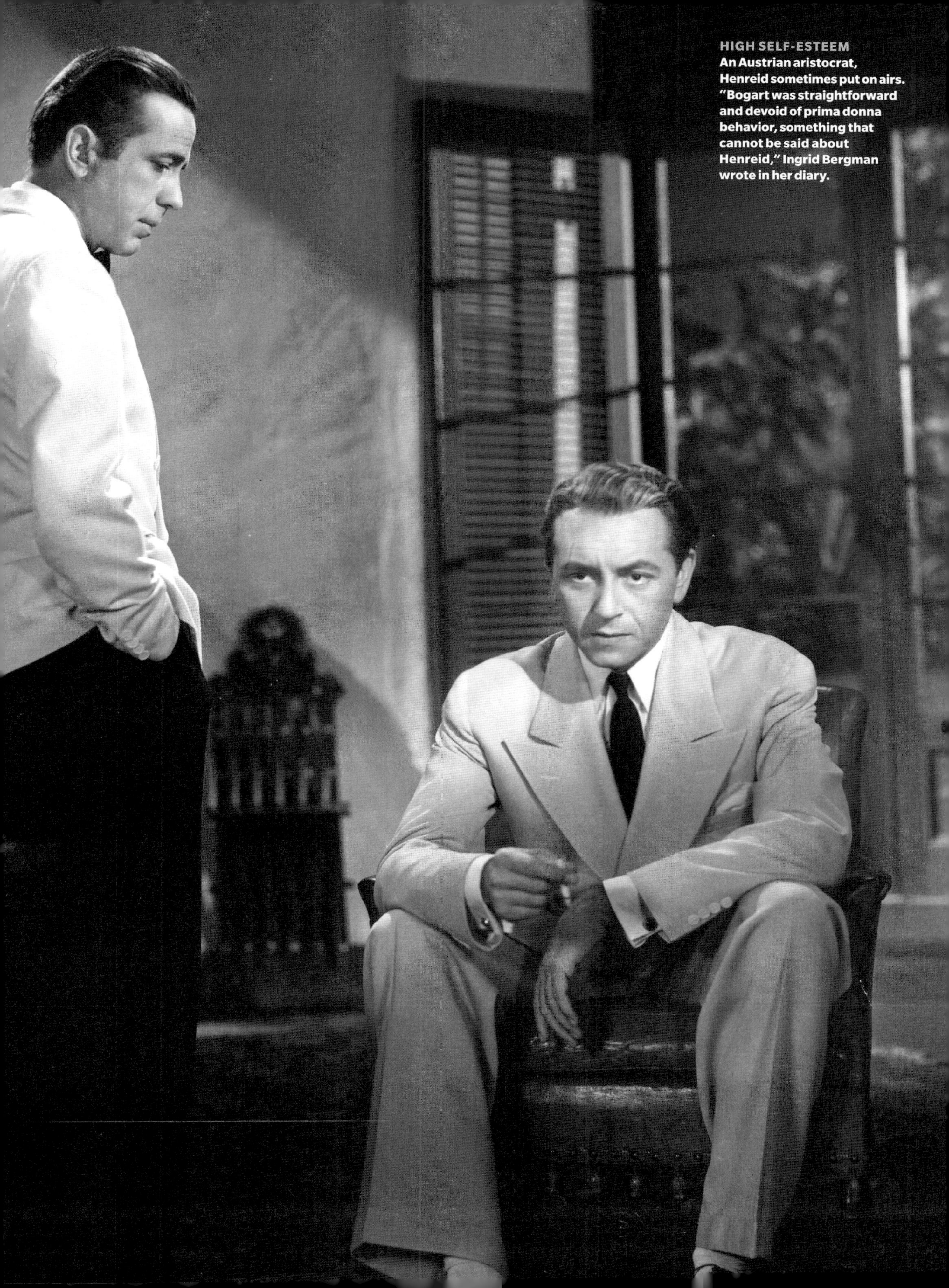

HIGH SELF-ESTEEM
An Austrian aristocrat, Henreid sometimes put on airs. "Bogart was straightforward and devoid of prima donna behavior, something that cannot be said about Henreid," Ingrid Bergman wrote in her diary.

ROLE FATIGUE

German-born Veidt tired of playing Nazis like Strasser. In MGM's *Nazi Agent*, he was both an evil Nazi spy and his loyal twin American brother.

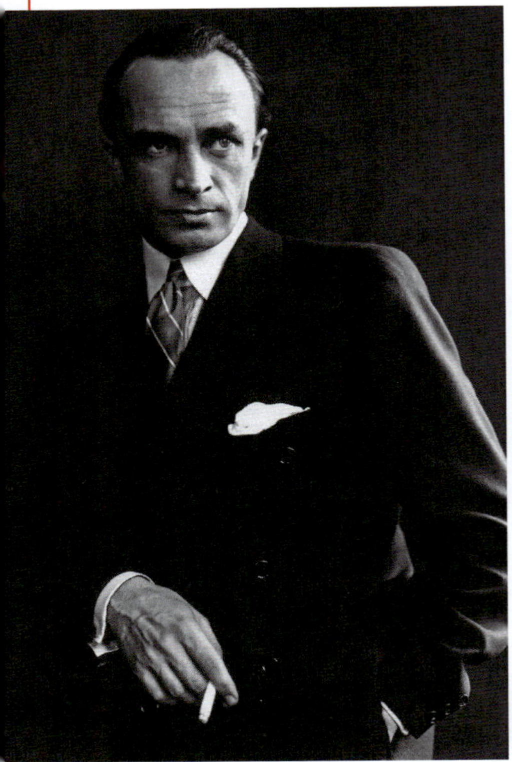

HANS ROBERTSON/ULLSTEIN BILD/GETTY

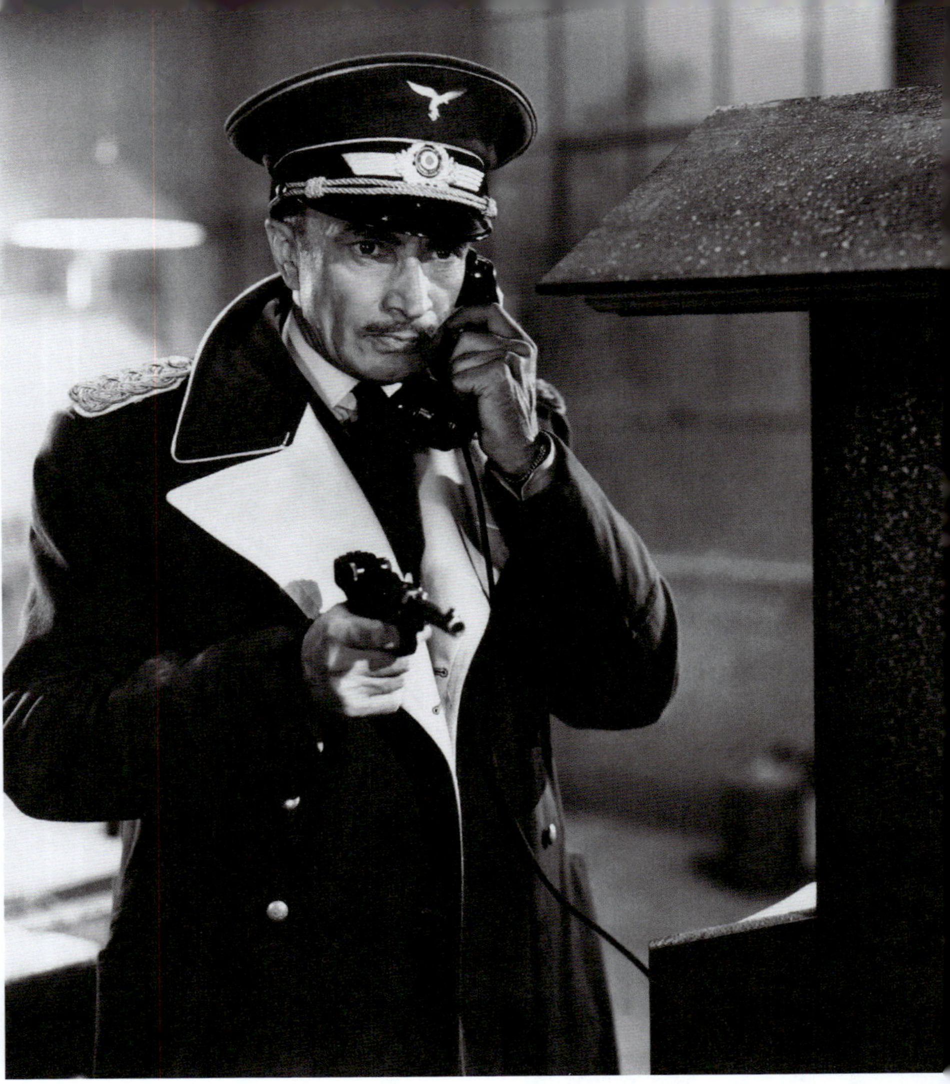

CONRAD VEIDT

Gestapo Major Strasser

The German-born Conrad Veidt was an ardent antifascist who fled the Third Reich and supposedly wrote "*Jude*" when asked to state his ethnic background, even though he was not Jewish. But in Hollywood, his thick accent guaranteed one thing: that he almost always was cast as a Nazi villain. In 1942 alone, Veidt played a Nazi in three films, including the part of Major Strasser in *Casablanca,* beating out director Otto Preminger for the role. He brought gusto to the part, oozing condescension when he uttered lines like "No one could take your place in the event anything unfortunate should occur to you," to Laszlo and (in describing Rick) "You give him credit for too much cleverness. My impression was that he's just another bumbling American."

Veidt first came to prominence in 1920 playing the murderous somnambulist Cesare in *The Cabinet of Dr. Caligari*. The part caught the attention of John Barrymore, who invited Veidt to Hollywood, where he appeared in a number of films, including *The Man Who Laughs* (1928), about a character with a rictus grin that is said to have inspired Batman's adversary the Joker. Veidt returned home, but with the rise of Hitler, Veidt and his wife, Lily, immigrated to England and then, as World War II intensified, back to the United States in 1940. He gave most of the money he earned acting to the British War Relief Society, including the $25,000 fee he earned on the set of *Casablanca*. But his life was cut short. In April 1943, the 50-year-old actor died of a heart attack while playing golf in Los Angeles. ■

MADELEINE LEBEAU

Yvonne

Madeleine Lebeau's character, Rick Blaine's jilted lover Yvonne, is dismissed early in the film, but it was enough screen time to turn the dewy 19-year-old into the face of the French resistance. In a pivotal scene, a group of Nazi officers inside Rick's Café belt out "The Watch on the Rhine," the de facto German anthem, and French patriots respond defiantly with their anthem, "La Marseillaise." The camera zooms in on Lebeau's face, streaming with tears, and captures her passionate cry, *"Vive la France!"*

The emotions were likely quite genuine, as Lebeau and her then husband, Marcel Dalio, who played the croupier Emil, were refugees from France and had made the same treacherous journey from Europe to America that was central to the plot of *Casablanca*.

An image of Dalio, an actor in France, was being used by the Nazis to identify Jewish-looking features, and the couple escaped Paris just hours ahead of the Germans. They made their way to Lisbon, and using forged Chilean visas, booked passage on a Portuguese cargo ship that was carrying some 300 refugees. Most of the passengers were refused admittance to New York and Veracruz, Mexico, but Lebeau and Dalio secured papers that allowed them to enter California legally. Despite the journey the couple had made together, their marriage did not last. Dalio, 20 years older than Lebeau, filed for divorce during the filming of *Casablanca* and Warner Bros. soon terminated Lebeau's contract. After the war, Lebeau returned to Europe, eventually appearing in Federico Fellini's *8½* and marrying one of the movie's writers. ■

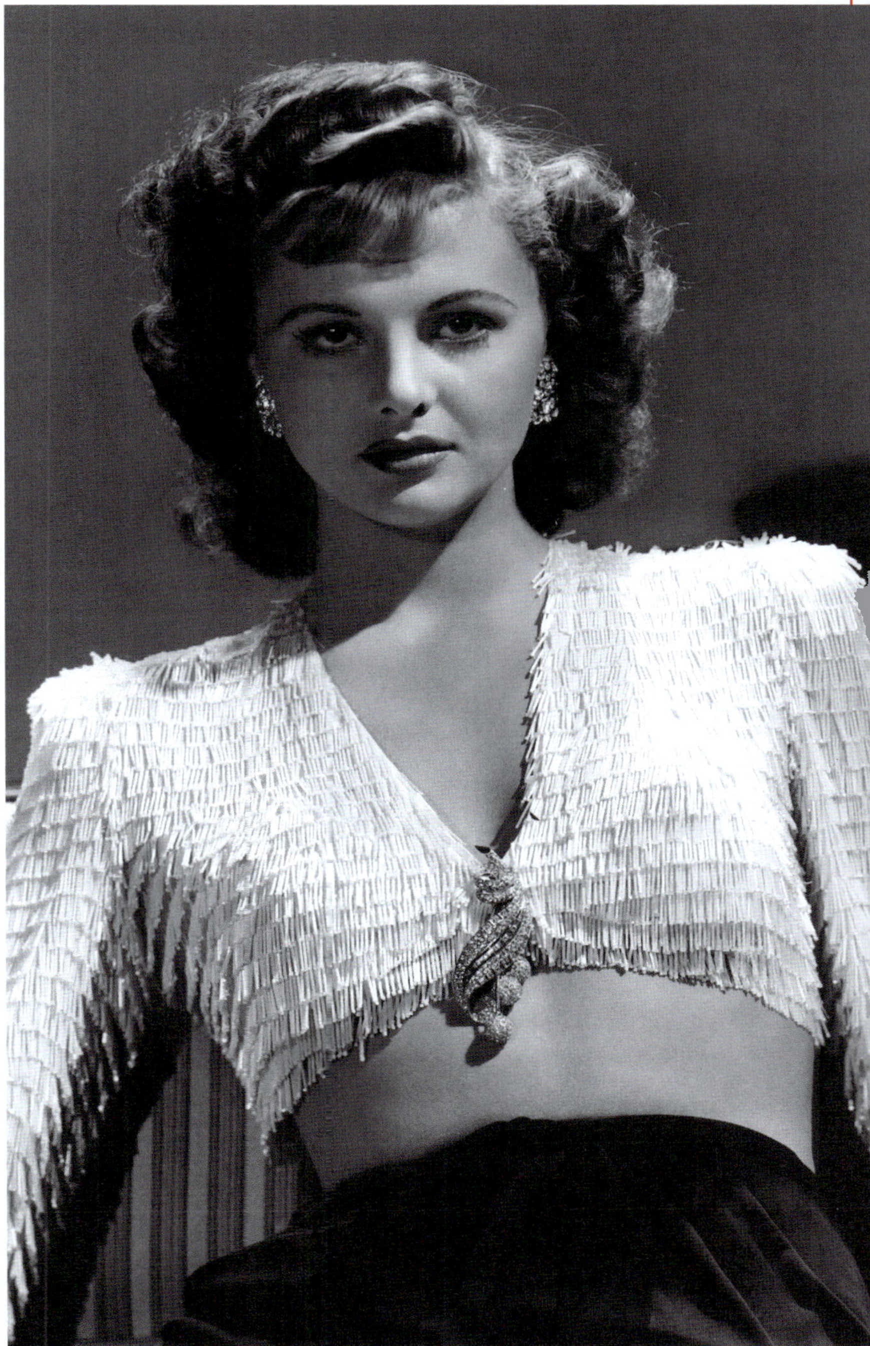

EVERETT (2)

LONG LIFE
When Lebeau died in 2016 at age 92, she was the last surviving credited cast member of *Casablanca*.

ARTHUR "DOOLEY" WILSON

Sam

One of producer Hal Wallis's first casting ideas was to give the part of the black cabaret performer Sam to a woman. He was particularly interested in the jazz singer Hazel Scott, but he also considered Ella Fitzgerald and Lena Horne. It isn't known who talked Wallis out of the idea, or if he decided on his own to revert, but either way, it is difficult to imagine *Casablanca* without Arthur "Dooley" Wilson at the piano.

Wilson's role as Rick's loyal friend, the one who looks out for his best interests, is small but crucial, and at the time it was also one of the few nondemeaning parts in Hollywood for an actor of color. Black men were typically cast as porters, waiters, or house servants—stereotypes Wilson had tried to avoid throughout his career. He wasn't always successful. The nickname Dooley came from the period he worked for a black theater troupe in Chicago playing Irishmen, in whiteface, and singing the song "Mr. Dooley." But the part that brought Wilson to Hollywood in 1940 was "Little Joe" Jackson, a gambler seeking redemption in *Cabin in the Sky,* an all-black Broadway musical that the *Communist Daily Worker* dismissed as demeaning to its cast. Still, Wilson earned good reviews and came to the attention of Paramount, which offered him a $350-a-week contract. The studio then lent Wilson to Warner Bros. for *Casablanca.* Ironically, Wilson was a drummer, not a pianist, yet he sang all his songs in the film, including "As Time Goes By," "It Had to Be You," "Shine," and "Knock on Wood." He would appear in a dozen more films and finished his career on the television sitcom *The Beulah Show.* ■

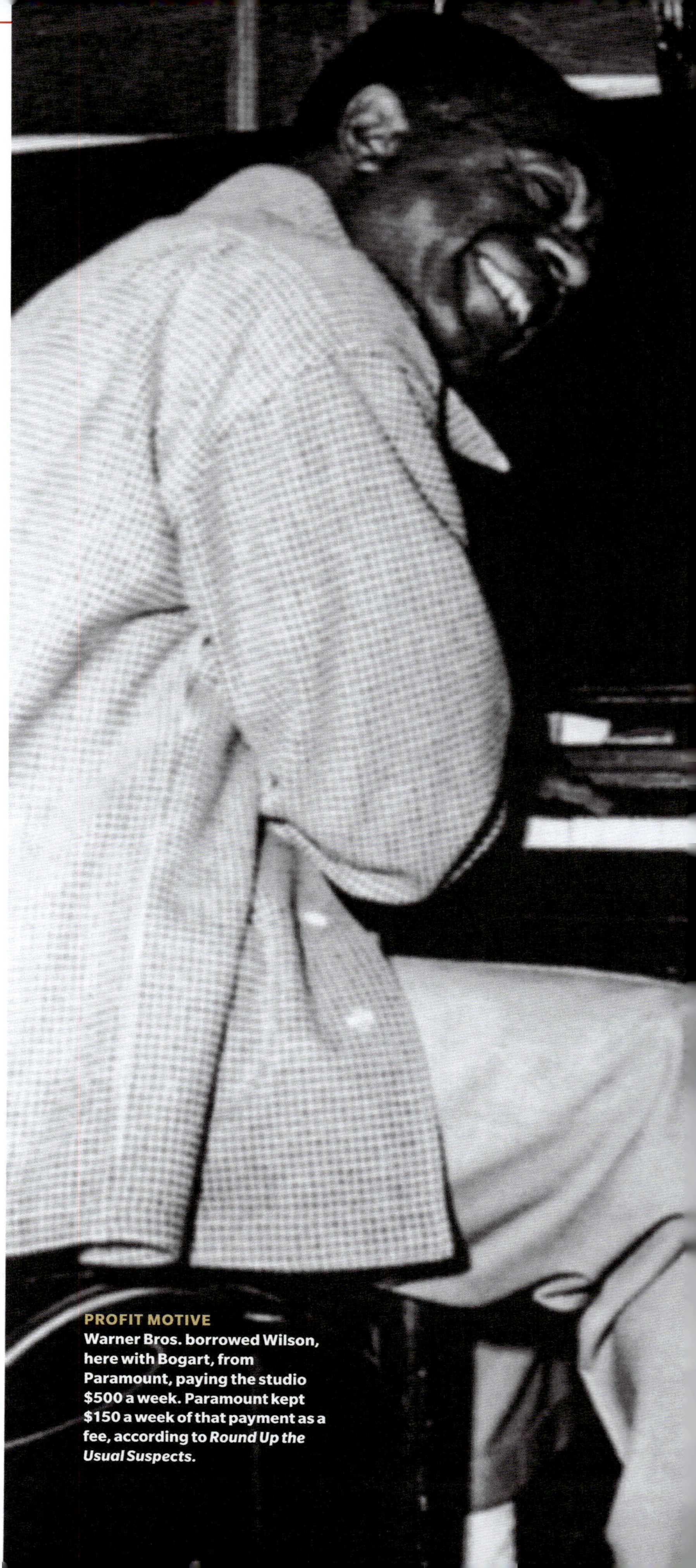

MARC WANAMAKER/BISON ARCHIVES

PROFIT MOTIVE
Warner Bros. borrowed Wilson, here with Bogart, from Paramount, paying the studio $500 a week. Paramount kept $150 a week of that payment as a fee, according to *Round Up the Usual Suspects.*

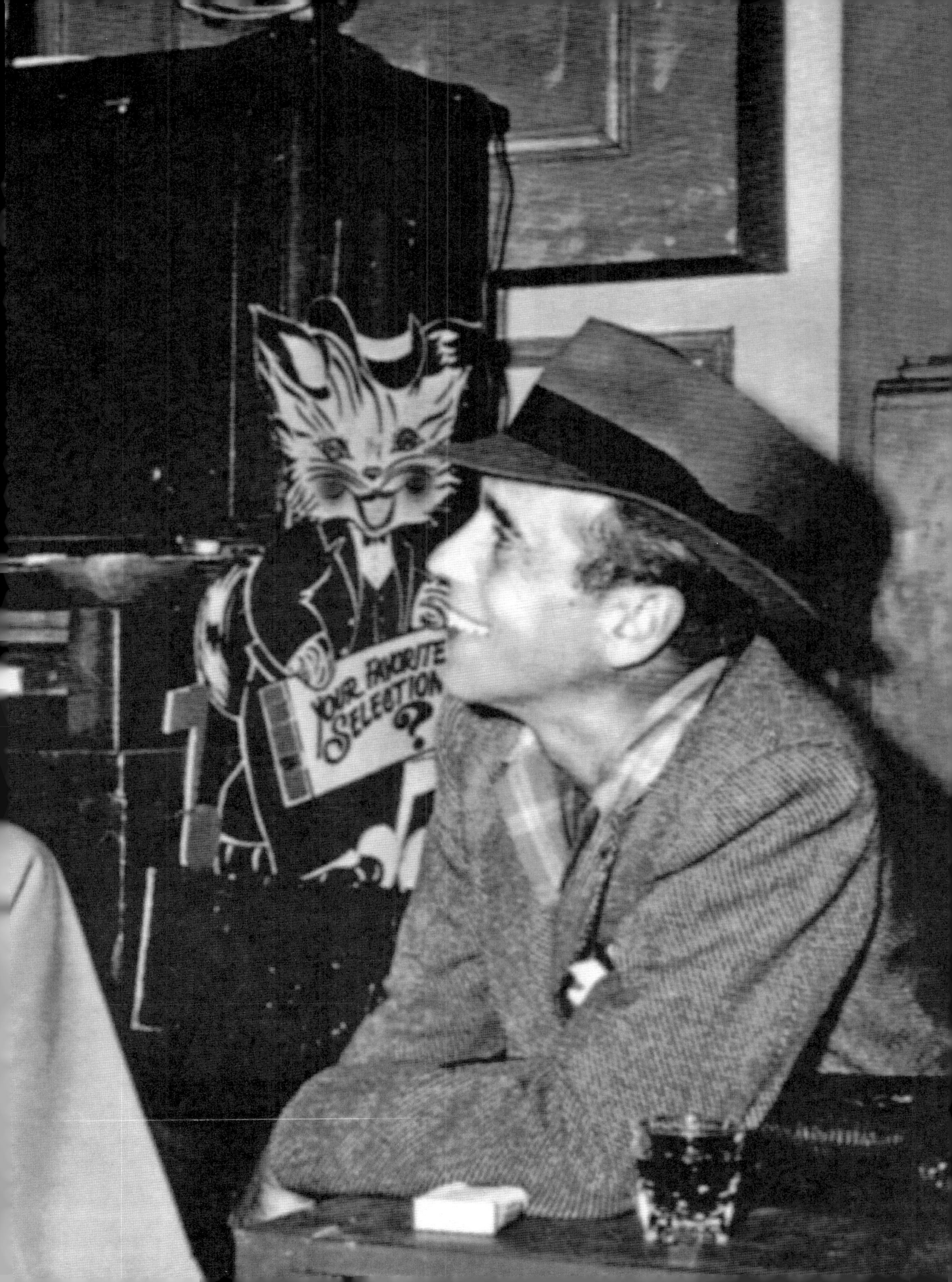
YOUR FAVORITE
SELECTION
?

MICHAEL CURTIZ

Director

In his 28 years at Warner Bros., Michael Curtiz made dozens of films, including golden age classics such as *Mildred Pierce, Life with Father, Yankee Doodle Dandy,* and *The Adventures of Robin Hood.* He auditioned Doris Day and gave the starlet her first role, in *Romance on the High Seas.* He helped popularize the swashbuckler with then little-known extra Errol Flynn. He even directed Elvis Presley to positive reviews in *King Creole.* Yet, oddly, for all of Curtiz's success as a director, he is often classified as a disciplined journeyman rather than an auteur with a vision—a judgment Curtiz might embrace, having once commented that "I put all the art into my pictures that I think the audience can stand."

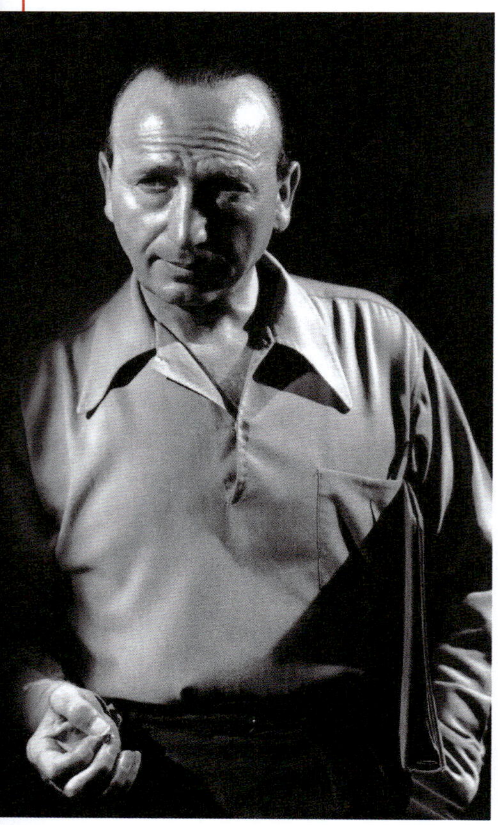

ARCHIVE PHOTOS/GETTY

The Hungarian-born Curtiz had a well-established directorial career in Europe, with more than 60 films to his credit, before moving to Hollywood in 1926 at the behest of Jack and Harry Warner. The Warners started Curtiz slow with some minor films, and he illustrated his command of the moving camera. For his first outing, *The Third Degree,* about a murder and the interrogation of the suspect, Curtiz showed the action in one scene from the perspective of a bullet. For *Yankee Doodle Dandy,* about entertainer George M. Cohan, he went nostalgic and slick. For *Casablanca,* his tactic was to infuse the North African setting with an unforgettable noirish tinge, to softly light the flashbacks, and to reverently embrace Ingrid Bergman's and Humphrey Bogart's every move.

As his career progressed, however, Curtiz alienated many actors and eventually Warner Bros. with his arrogance. To elicit genuine terror in the climactic flooding scene of 1928's *Noah's Ark,* Curtiz never told the extras (including a young John Wayne) they would be deluged with water. He insulted actors standing quietly on the set with comments like "Mr. Bum! Be so kind as to act in our picture, please!" Errol Flynn, who owed his career to Curtiz, fought with the director on the set of *Dive Bomber* and refused to work with him again. Of course, actors who won Oscars under Curtiz's direction were more tolerant. And he could be entertaining with his famous malapropisms. He once barked at a prop man, "Next time I send a damn fool, I go myself," and reprimanded a child actor with "By the time I was your age, I was 15." ■

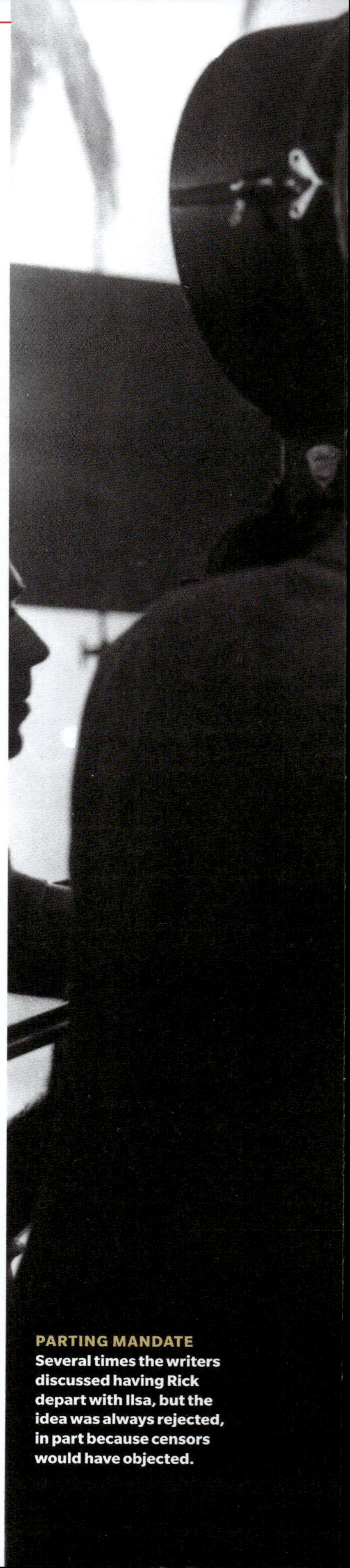

MARC WANAMAKER/BISON ARCHIVES

PARTING MANDATE
Several times the writers discussed having Rick depart with Ilsa, but the idea was always rejected, in part because censors would have objected.

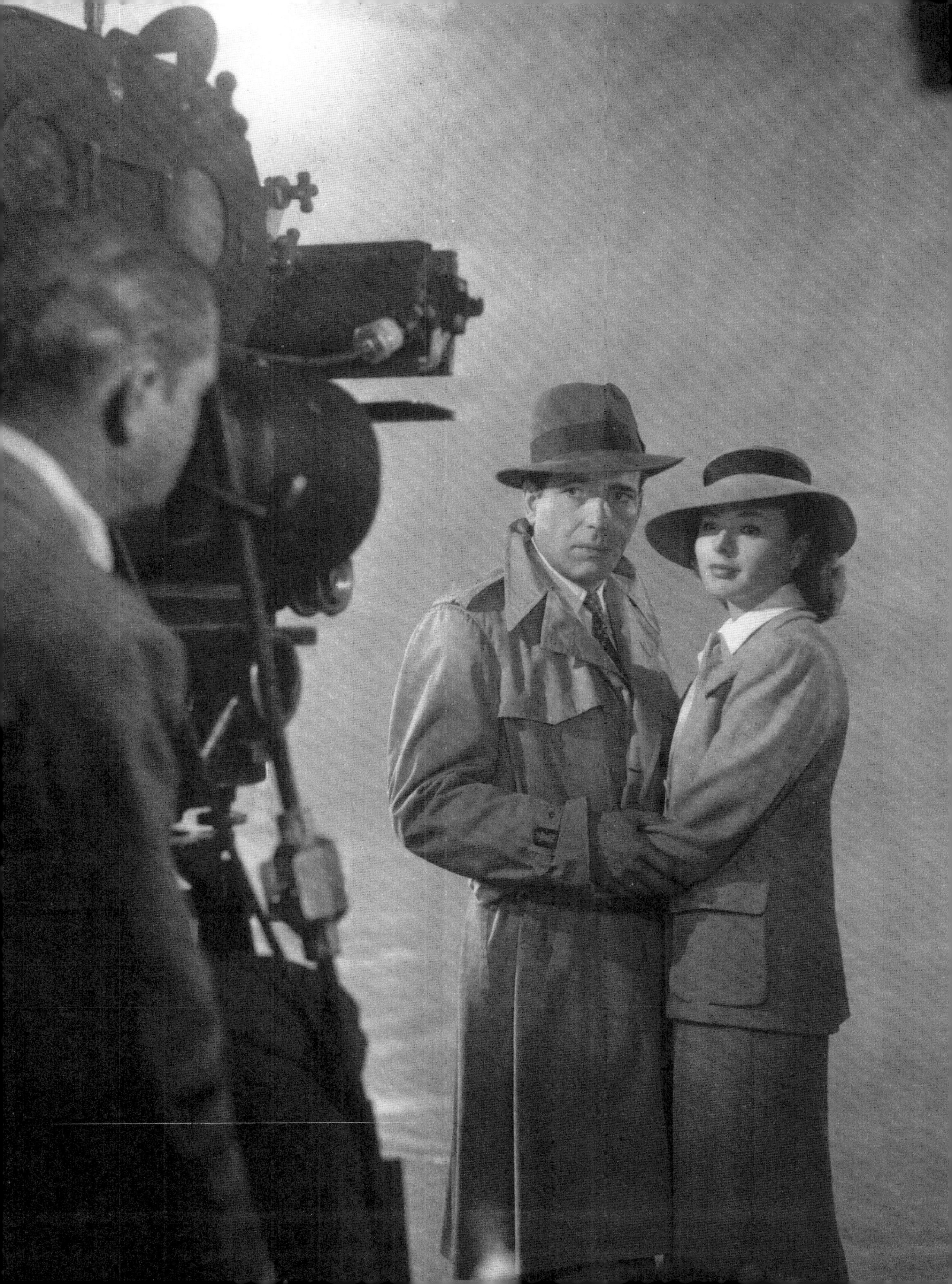

AS TIME GOES BY

Ilsa: Play it once, Sam, for old times' sake.
Sam: I don't know what you mean, Miss Ilsa.
Ilsa (whispered): Play it, Sam. Play "As Time Goes By."

It's often listed as one of the world's greatest songs and is such an essential part of *Casablanca* it could be listed as a cast member, but "As Time Goes By" almost ended up on the cutting room floor.

Composed by Tin Pan Alley songwriter Herman Hupfeld in 1931, "As Time Goes By" was included in a short-lived Broadway show, recorded by crooner Rudy Vallée, and then forgotten—by about everyone except Cornell University student Murray Burnett. The young man played the record so many times his fraternity brothers complained, but it continued to captivate him. In 1938, Burnett heard the song again, this time played by a black piano player in a club on the French Riviera where Burnett, by then a teacher, had traveled with his wife. During the trip, Burnett helped his wife's family smuggle valuables out of Vienna and witnessed firsthand the Nazi threat; alarmed, he wrote a play about the developments to inform and warn Americans. He included the bar, the piano player, and the song in his script, *Everybody Comes to Rick's,* which would be adapted by Warner Bros. into *Casablanca* after the bombing of Pearl Harbor.

The film's composer, Max Steiner, however, was less enthusiastic about "As Time Goes By," and producer Hal Wallis let him write a love theme for the movie. But by that time, filming had been completed—and Ingrid Bergman's hair was cut short for her next project, *For Whom the Bell Tolls*—and Wallis insisted the song remain. Steiner listened to "As Time Goes By" again and, revising his opinion of it, decided to make it a recurring element in the score.

The love song exposes Ilsa and Rick's shifting feelings. Sam plays "As Time Goes By" for Ilsa when she first comes into Rick's café, and the audience sees the shock on Rick's face when he spots her for the first time since she abandoned him in Paris. During one flashback, a jaunty version of the song accompanies shots of Rick and Ilsa happily in love. It plays under the scene at the Paris train station when Ilsa leaves Rick, and under the final goodbye, as Rick convinces Ilsa to board the plane out of Casablanca with her husband. After the movie's release, "As Time Goes By" stayed on the radio hit parade for 21 weeks. ■

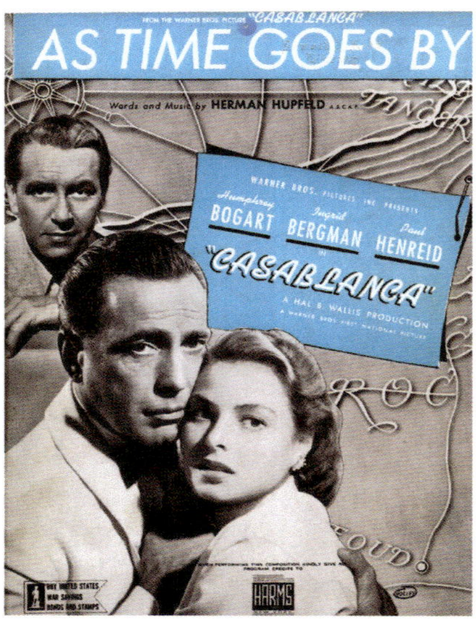

MARC WANAMAKER/BISON ARCHIVES (2)

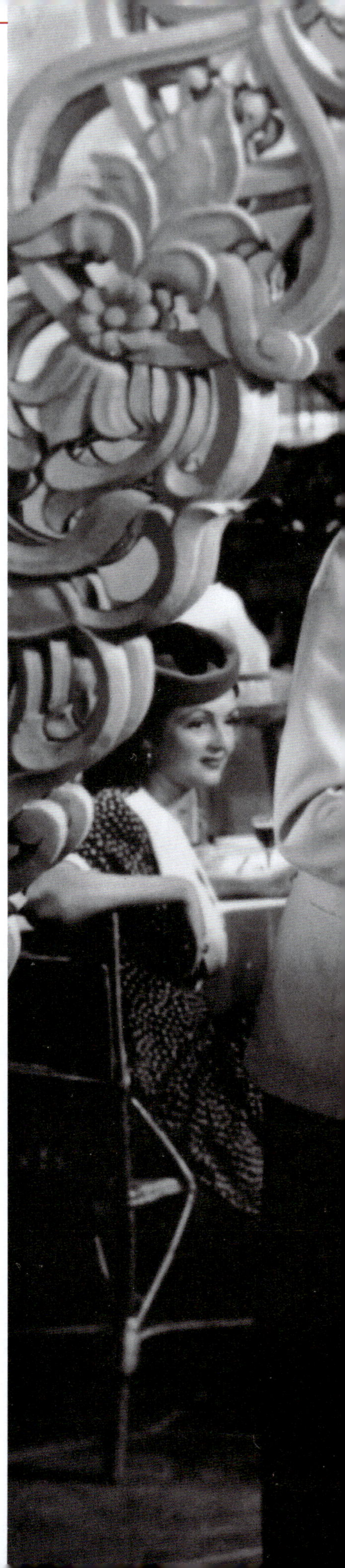

FACTS OF LIFE
"As Time Goes By" debuted in the 1931 musical *Everybody's Welcome* and was also recorded that year by Rudy Vallée.

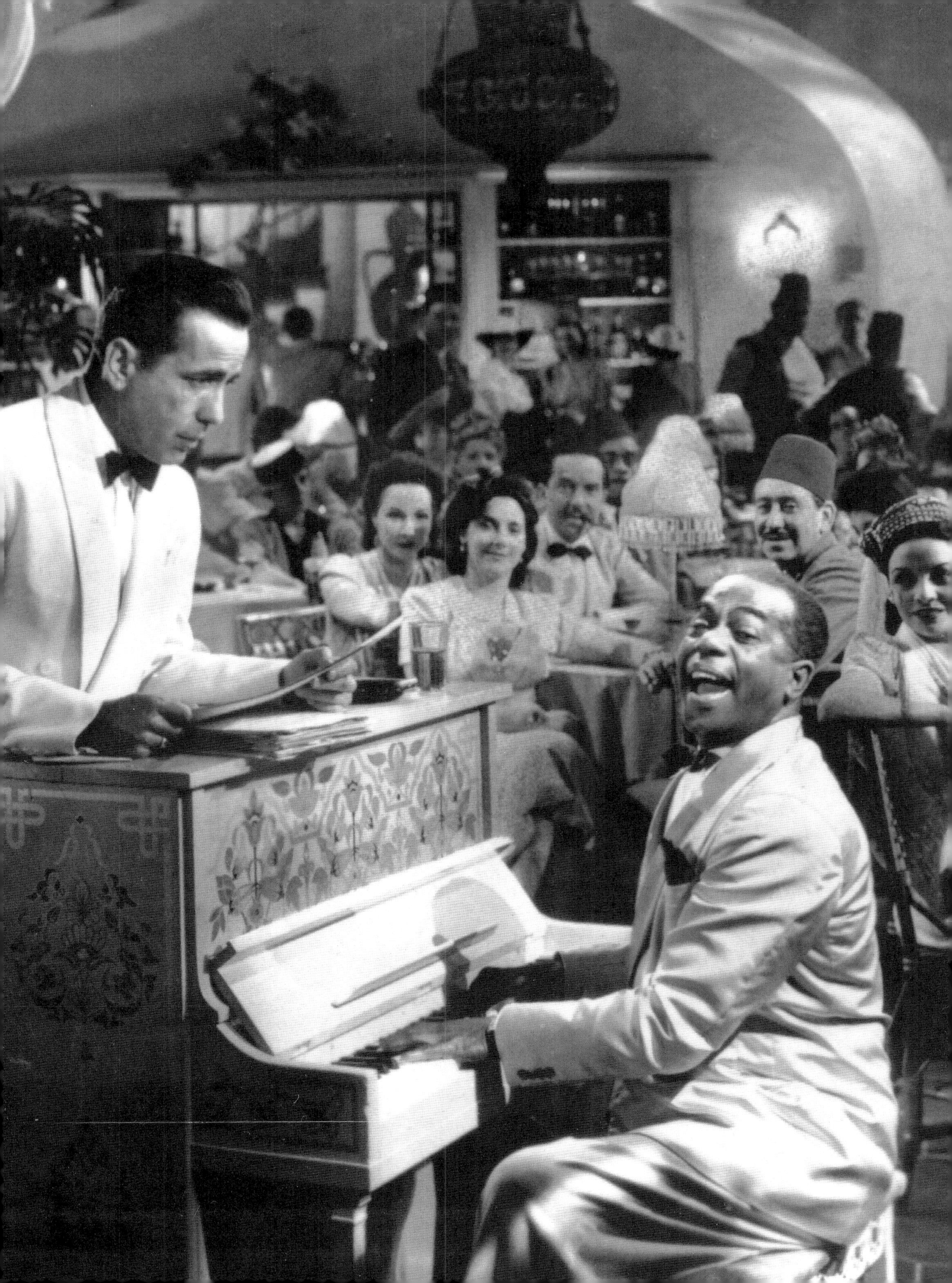

DATELINE CASABLANCA

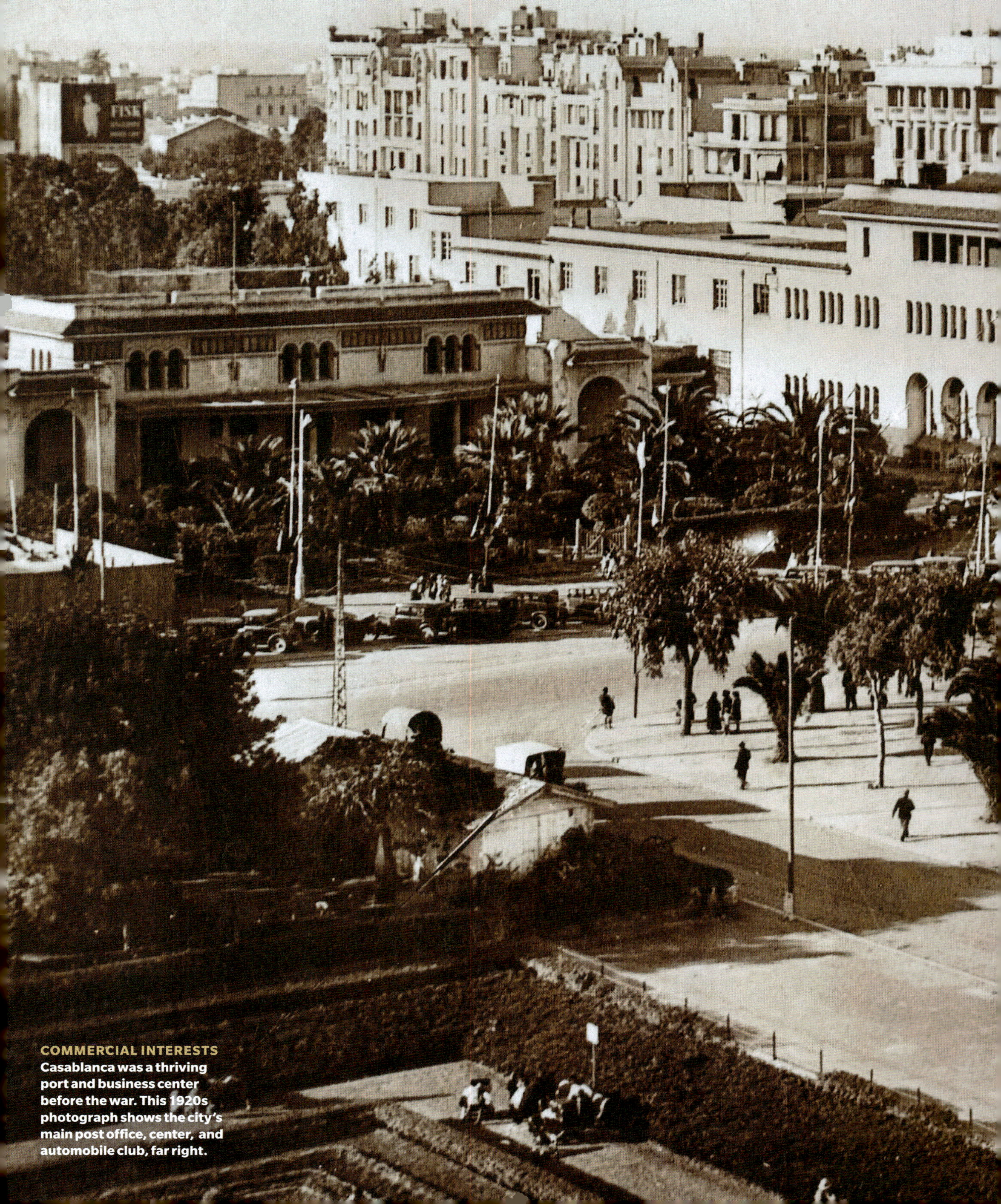

COMMERCIAL INTERESTS
Casablanca was a thriving port and business center before the war. This 1920s photograph shows the city's main post office, center, and automobile club, far right.

The exotic city of the movie, where refugees, spies, and black-marketeers mingle, is an amalgam of Casablanca, Marseille, Lisbon, Oran, and Tangier

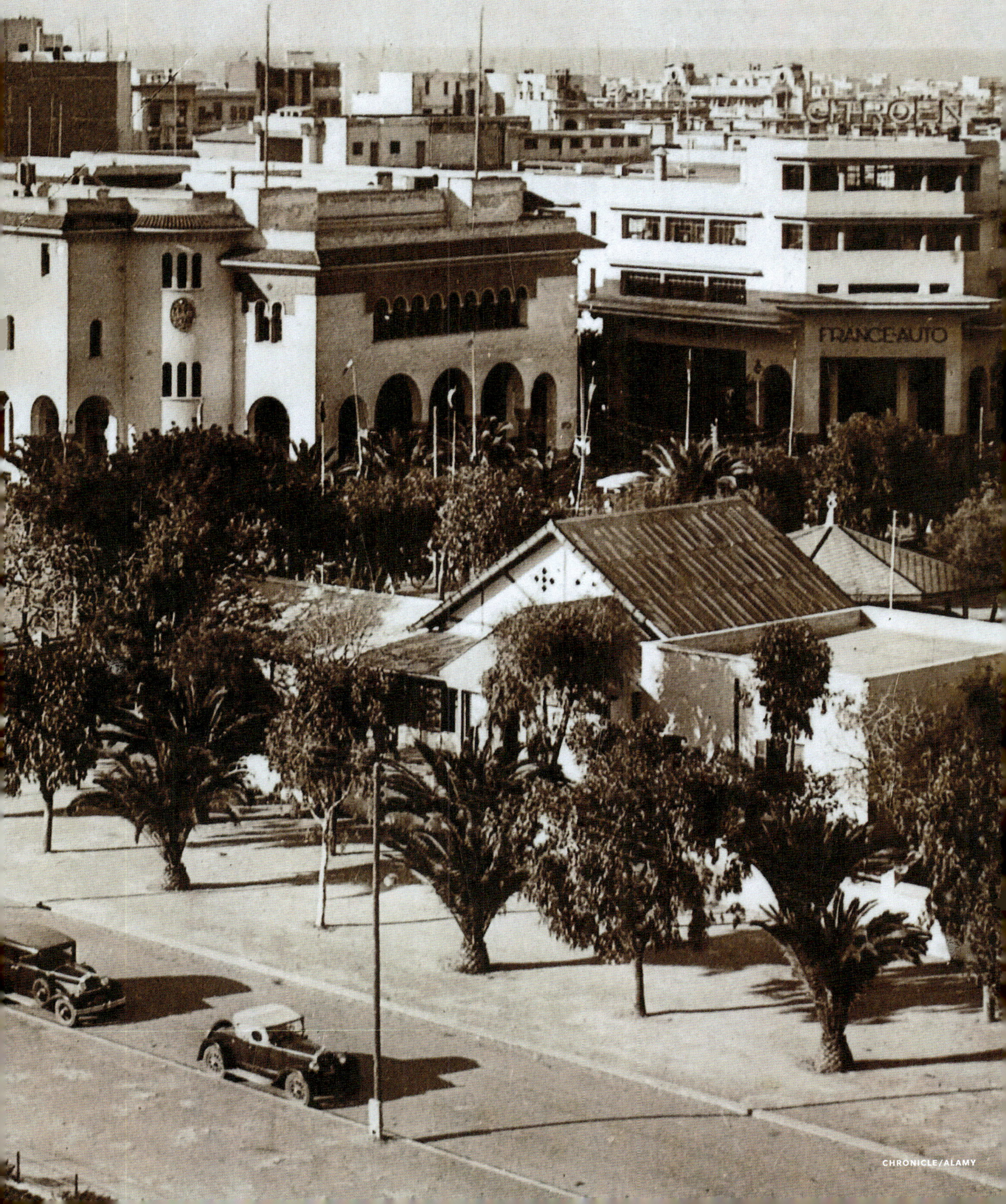

CHRONICLE/ALAMY

The Casablanca of *Casablanca* bears little resemblance to wartime Casablanca.

Yes, in the years leading up to World War II—and after armed conflict broke out in Europe—Casablanca was a haven for refugees. And yes, the Moroccan city was international, with a large European population. But many descriptions of Casablanca then and now include the word *charmless,* or something like it, which is indeed a fair description. It's not a city that makes for a theatrical backdrop. In fact, Murray Burnett and Joan Alison, the authors of *Everybody Comes to Rick's,* which became the basis for *Casablanca,* originally planned to set the play in the much more atmospheric Lisbon. They never visited Casablanca and invented its fictional counterpart out of whole cloth. The setting seems to be based, at least partly, on places Burnett had stayed during a 1938 trip to Europe, as well as ports that catered to refugees, including Marseille, Lisbon, Oran, and Tangier.

There was never a Rick's Café Américain and its real-life inspiration was more than a thousand miles away on the outskirts of Nice, France. Fittingly, the ersatz Rick's Café found today on Casablanca's Boulevard Sour Jdid was built long after the war, to capitalize on the film's popularity. Even some of the movie's oft-quoted dialog gets Casablanca's geography wrong. In grilling Rick on why he came to the city, Captain Renault disputes the expat's assertion it was "for the waters." "The waters? What waters? We're in the desert," Renault tells Rick, prompting the deadpan retort, "I was misinformed." But Casablanca is not in the desert. It's on the Atlantic Ocean, nestled in a wide, fertile area, where it rains about 16 inches a year, about as much as, say, in Salt Lake City or San Jose.

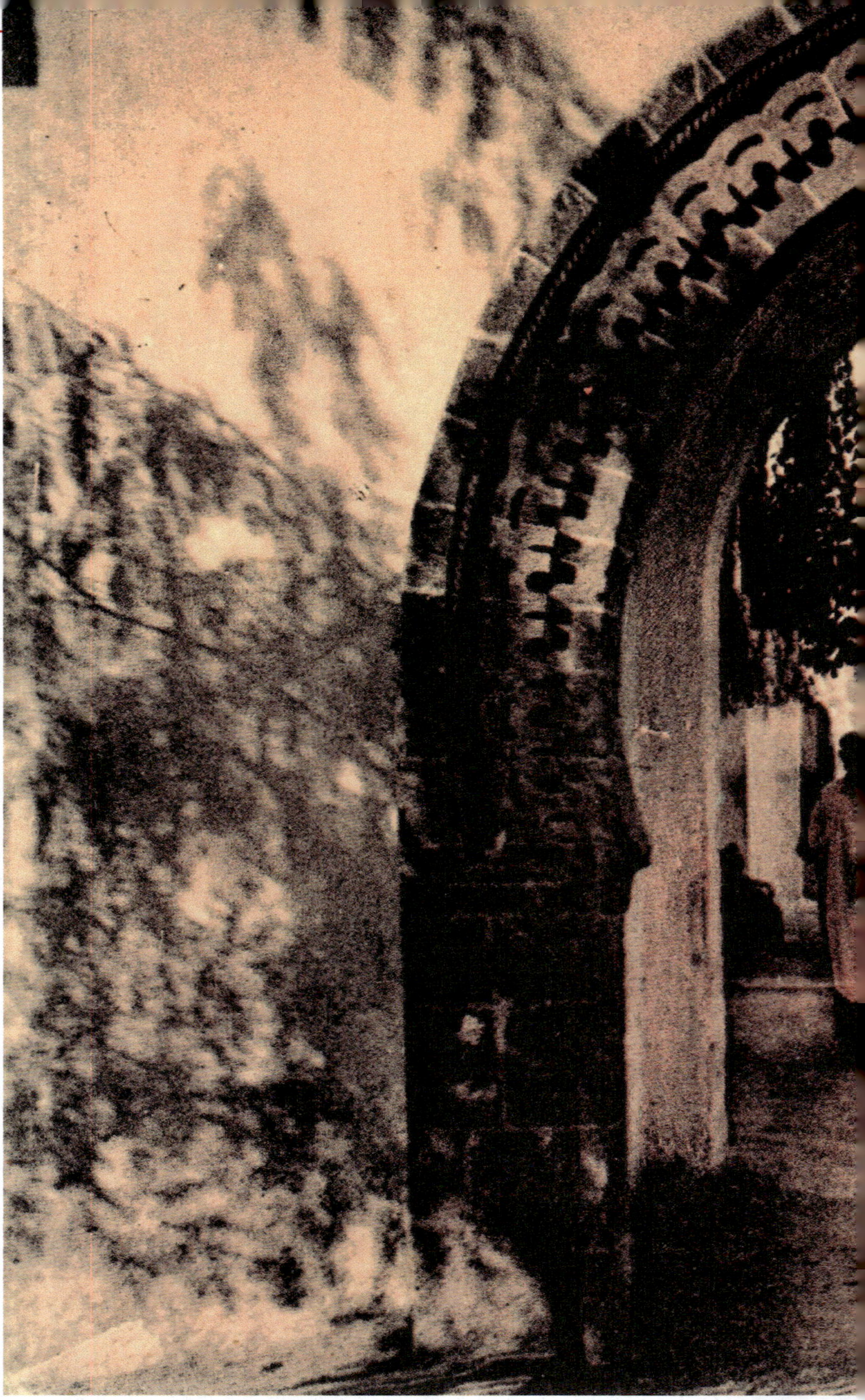

ARKIVI/AKG IMAGES

Yet Hollywood magic paired with an unlikely assist from some real world circumstances produced a Casablanca so emotionally accurate it seemed at times the film broke the fourth wall. Part of the resonance came from the actors—not the headliners but the supporting cast and extras, many of whom were themselves refugees from Europe and had escaped via routes similar to those referenced in the film's opening montage. During filming, Hitler still seemed unbeatable and emotions on set were close to the surface. *Casablanca* was made even more real to audiences after the Allies invaded North Africa in 1942, via Casablanca and other ports.

"If you think of *Casablanca* and think of all those small roles being played by Hollywood actors faking the accents, the picture wouldn't have had anything like the color and tone it had," observed *New Yorker* critic Pauline Kael.

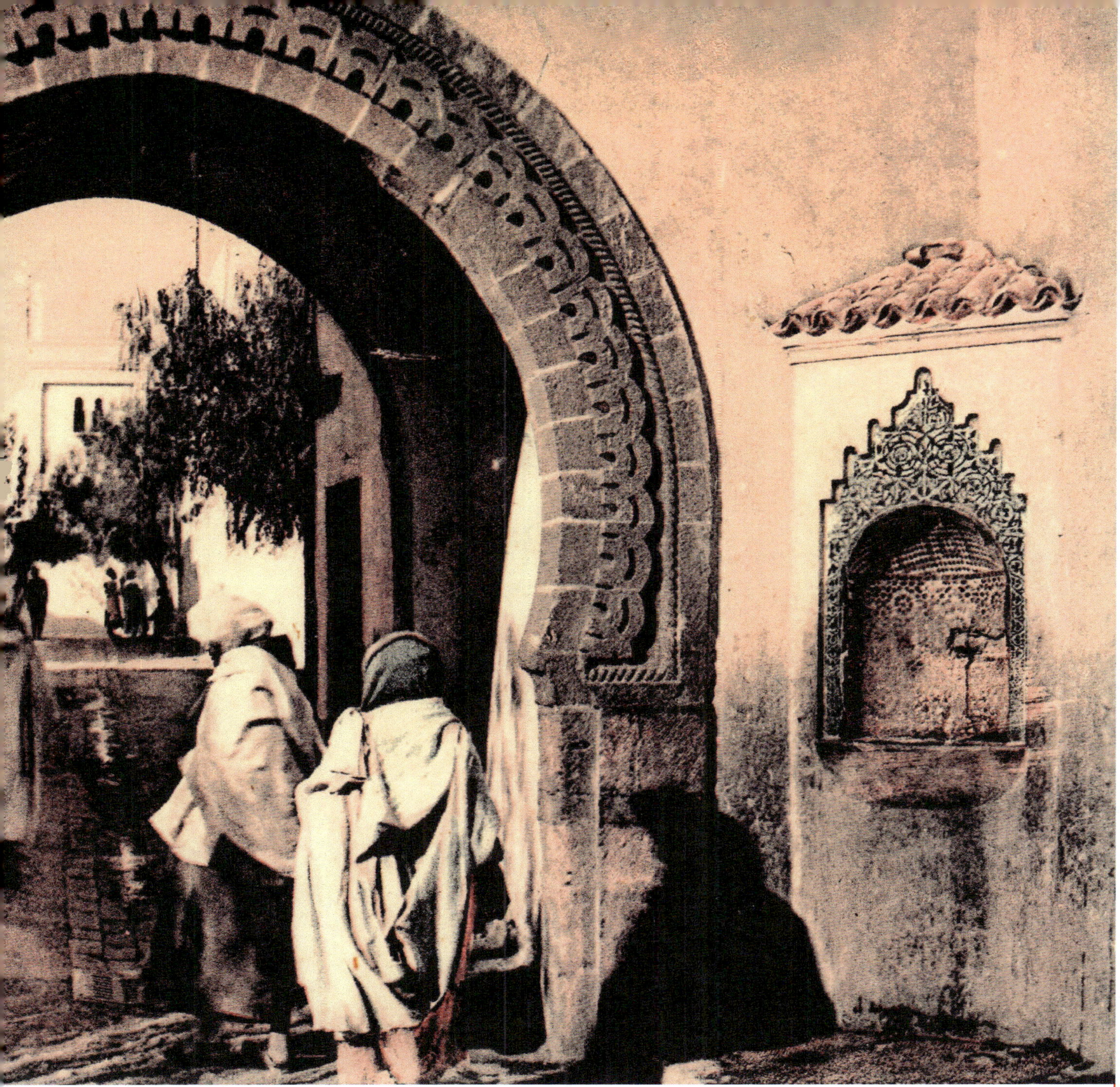

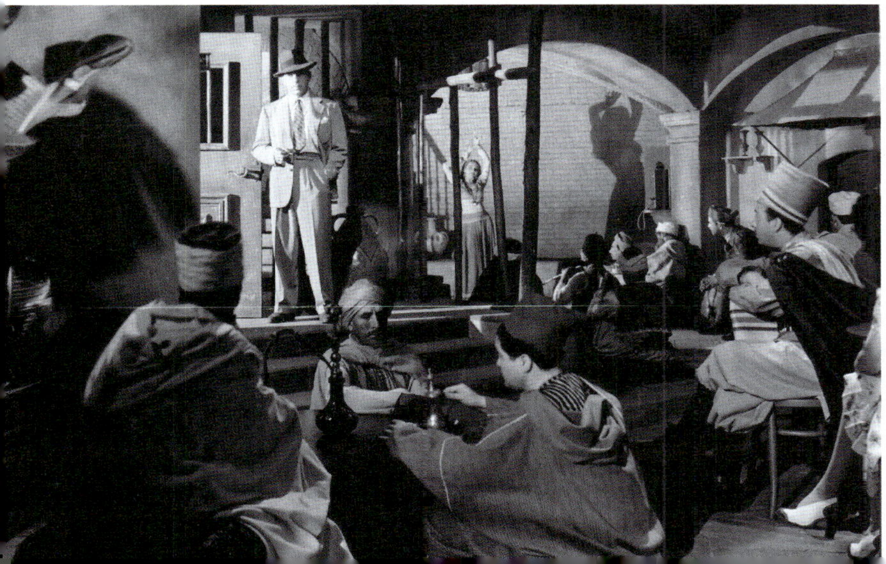

EVERETT

MODEL MAGIC
Casablanca's new medina, shown above in an undated photograph, was an inspiration for Warner Bros. designers constructing a set of the mazelike quarter. Bogart, left, enters the Blue Parrot.

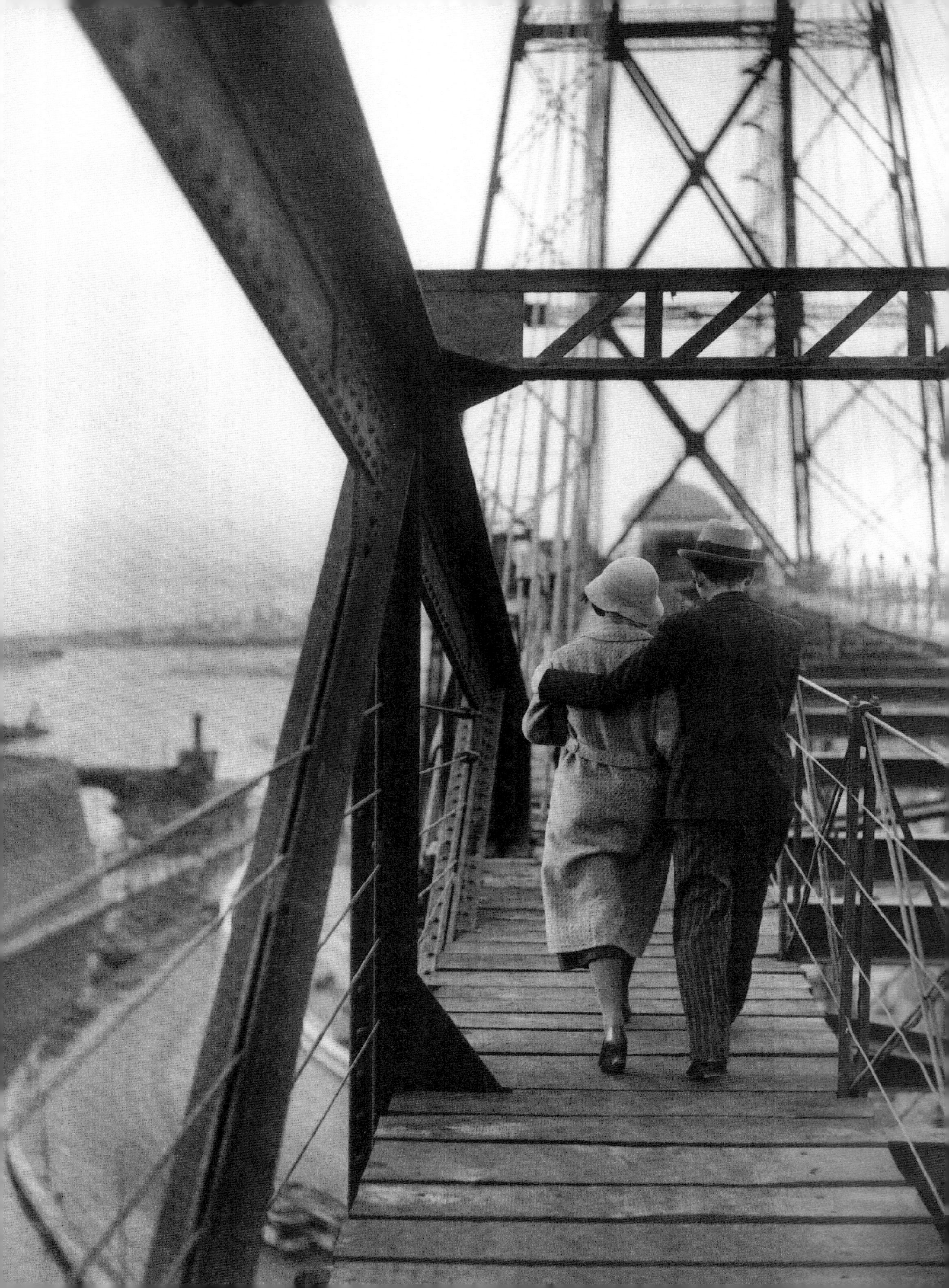

It was only natural that Burnett and Alison would decide to set their play in Casablanca, its cinematic shortcomings aside. At the outbreak of the war Morocco was a French colony, and Casablanca its main port and economic center. When Germany invaded France in 1940, Morocco, like southern France, fell under Vichy rule. That was the "free" zone, with a puppet regime installed by the Nazis, versus the occupied zone of northern France, which was a de facto Nazi dictatorship. Casablanca, in the free zone, teemed with German soldiers and Nazi officials like the film's villain, Major Heinrich Strasser, and Vichy functionaries, like Renault. Personifying morally corrupt Vichy collaborationists, Renault berates Rick for operating a casino—"I am shocked—*shocked*—to find that gambling is going on in here!"—while pocketing his earnings. (To give Renault his due, he does commit himself to the Allied cause in the end, just as the Allies embraced the government in exile of France's Charles de Gaulle).

Refugees flocked to Casablanca because in spite of the abuse of political prisoners and Jewish refugees, life was better there than in Poland, Czechoslovakia, or Germany. There was no Nazi-imposed terror equivalent to the horror unfolding on the continent. Morocco boasted a young, progressive ruler, King Mohammed V, who remained the ceremonial head of state throughout the war. While he could, Mohammed sought to protect all of his subjects. When the Vichy government

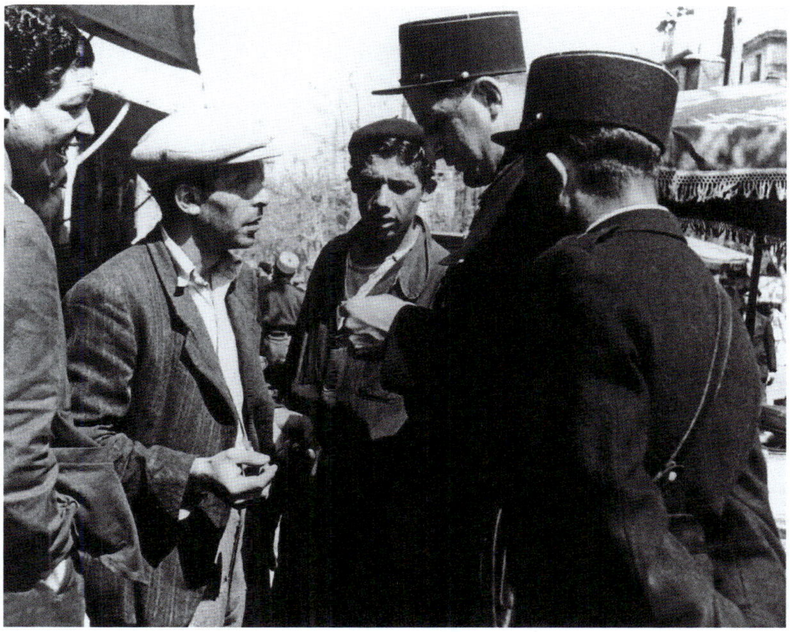

KEYSTONE-FRANCE/GAMMA-KEYSTONE/GETTY (2)

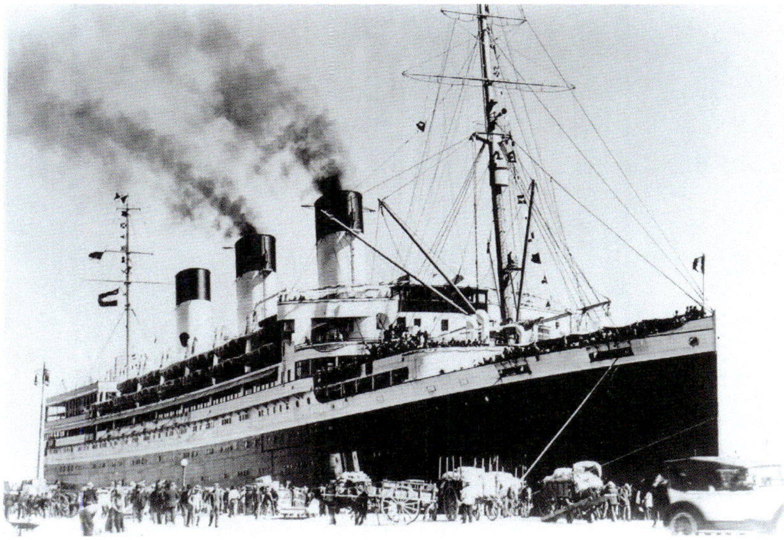

ULLSTEIN BILD/AKG IMAGES

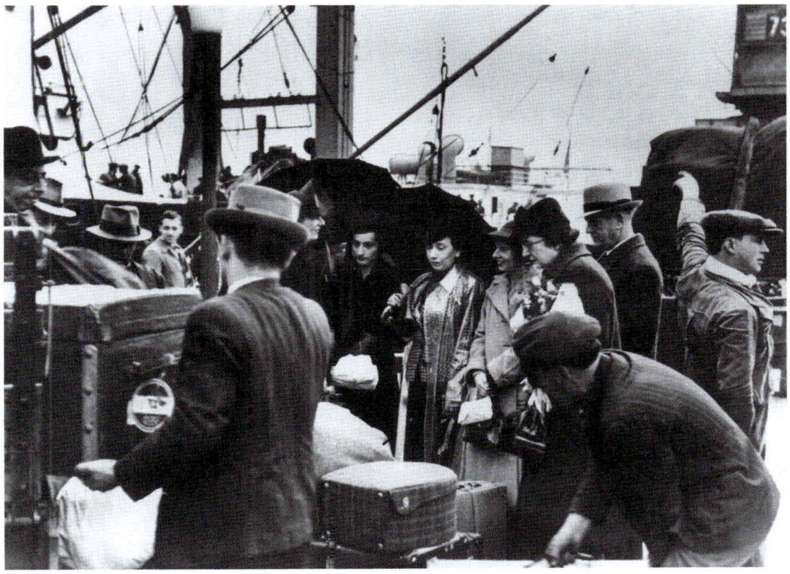

ULLSTEIN BILD/GETTY

STREET SCENES

Opposite: Marseille in 1935, already a center for the French resistance. This page, from top: Marseille police question black market suspects in the late 1930s; the German liner *Cap Arcona* in Casablanca, 1936; Jewish emigrants in Lisbon wait to ship out of Europe during World War II.

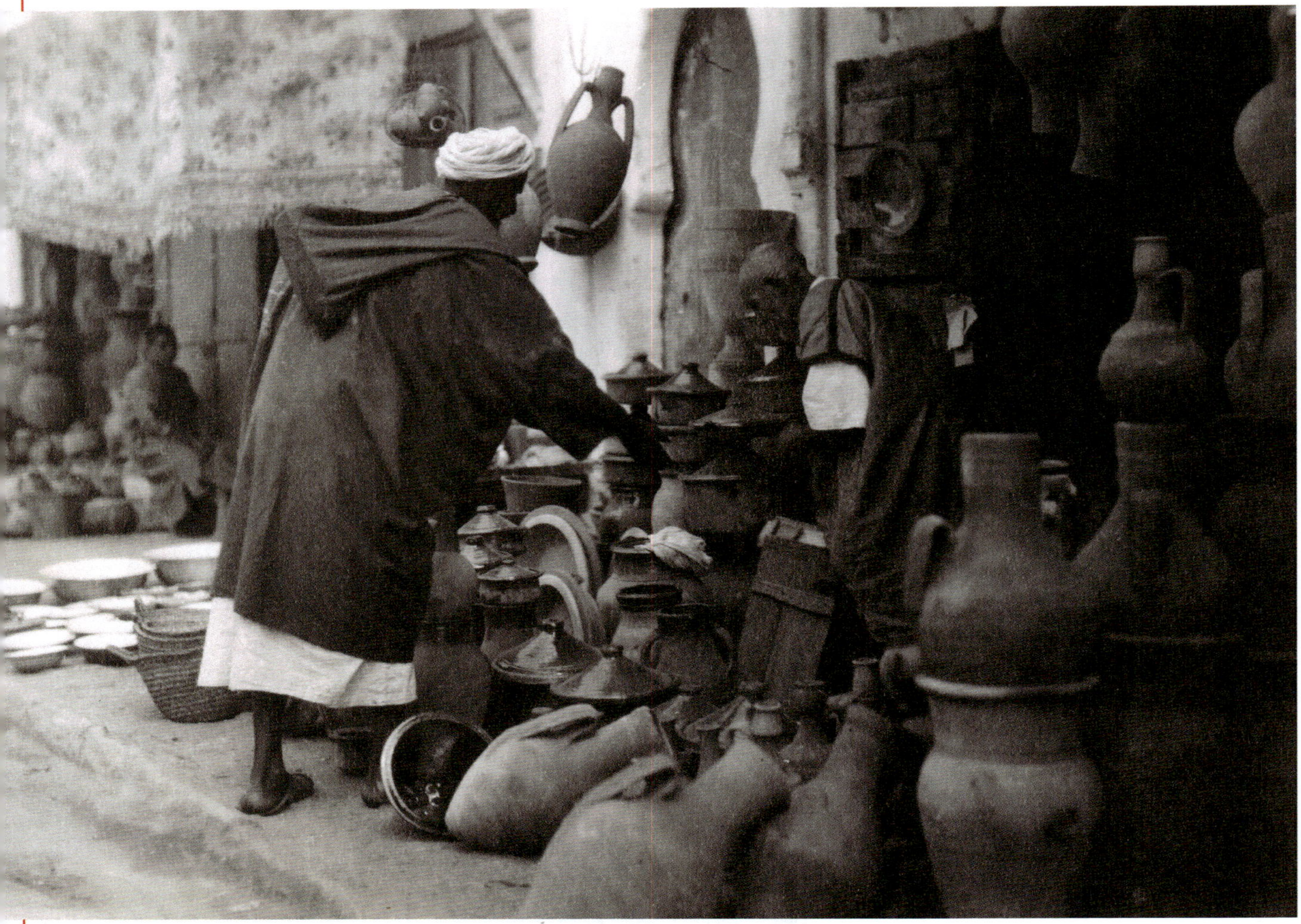

CHRONICLE/ALAMY

demanded Mohammed enact legislation against the Jews in the country (there were some 250,000), he refused, declaring, "There are no Jews in Morocco, only Moroccans."

Lisbon, meanwhile—another inspiration for Burnett and Alison—was a true noir vision. Filled with river mist and fog, Lisbon is the city Ilsa and Victor want to escape to. In 1941, it was shabby but beautiful, with trams rattling through the streets. It was also rife with soldiers and spies. Among other wartime visitors, the Portuguese capital hosted James Bond creator Ian Fleming (who based his Casino Royale on the chic seaside casino in Estoril, west of Lisbon), novelist Graham Greene, Soviet spy Kim Philby, and British journalist Malcolm Muggeridge. Portugal was neutral throughout the war, so at a time when electricity was short around Europe, Lisbon was still brightly lit and became a hub for refugees. Early on there was food, shopping, and parties. The moneyed elite flocked to the Hotel Aviz or were invited as guests to the private homes of the city's upper classes. Historian Neill Lochery, in his book *Lisbon: War in the Shadows of the City of Light, 1939–1945,* mentions an operations officer in 1944 describing the daily scene at the Lisbon airport, overrun by smugglers, refugees, and black-marketeers, as *Casablanca* magnified twentyfold.

The Casablanca of *Casablanca* also included a touch of Marseille, the picturesque port in the south of France. Marseille was an early center for the resistance and the only

TO MARKET, TO MARKET

Above: The wares sold in the souks of Casablanca have not changed much from the 1950s, when this photograph was taken. Opposite: The street bazaar scenes for the movie were filmed on the same studio back lot as *The Desert Song* (1943), which earned an Oscar nomination for Best Art Direction. Ingrid Bergman poses on the market set.

MARC WANAMAKER/BISON ARCHIVES

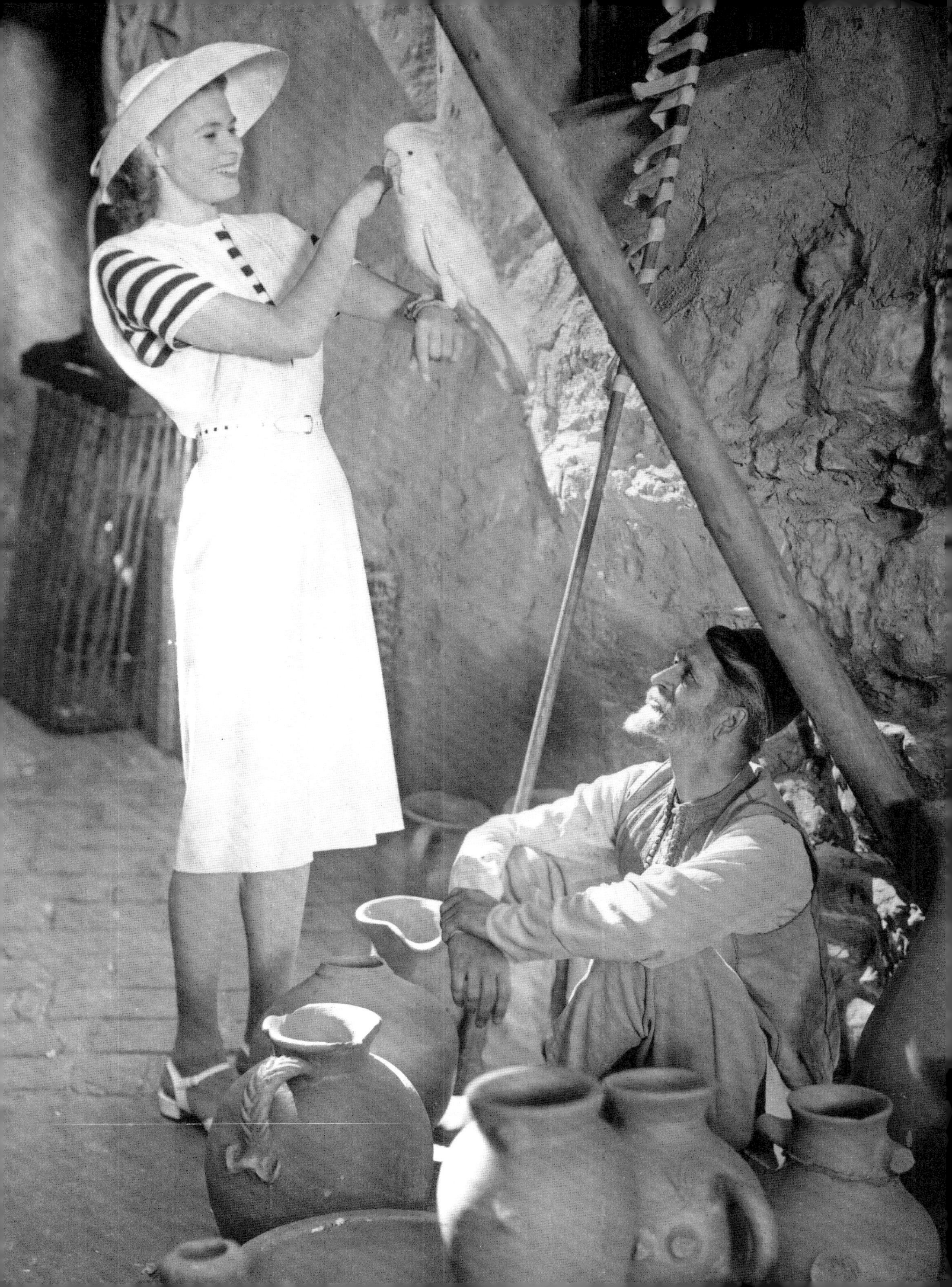

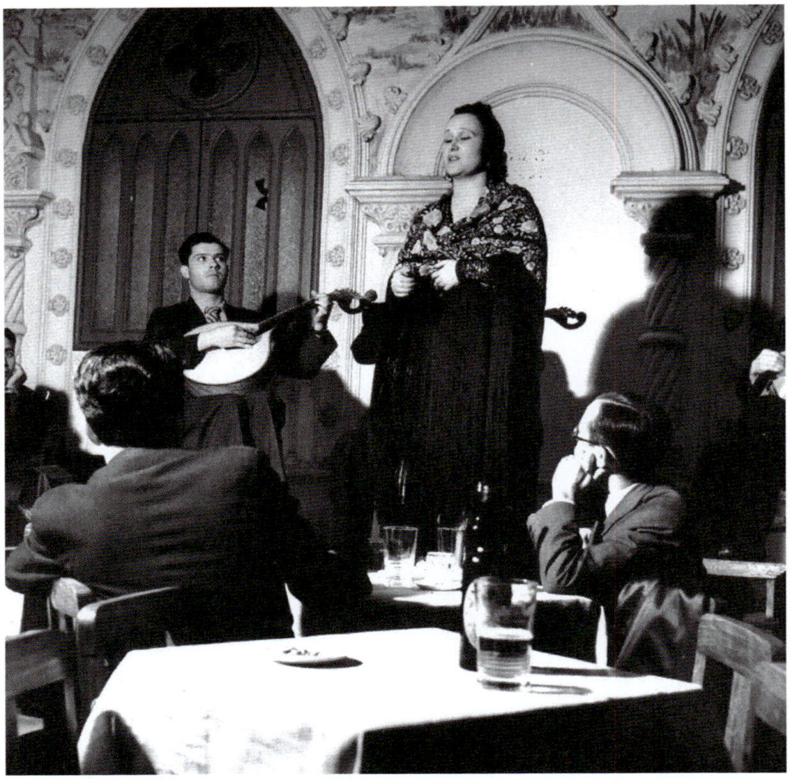

BERNARD HOFFMAN/LIFE/THE PICTURE COLLECTION

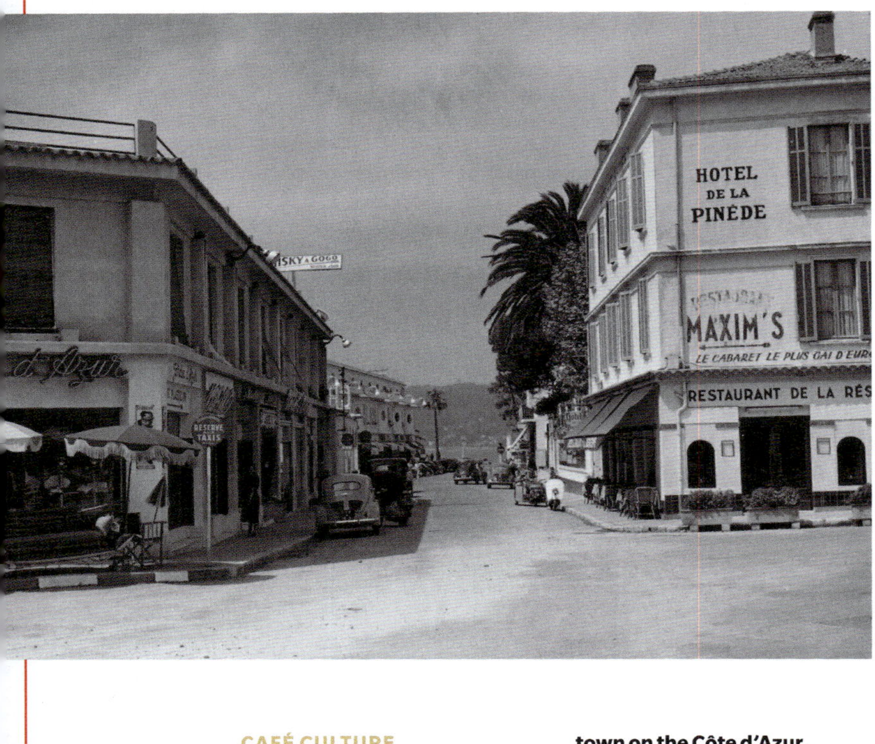

GEORGE W. HALES/FOX PHOTOS/GETTY

functioning port in the free zone after France was partitioned in 1940. Belgians, Czechoslovaks, Poles, anti-fascist Italians, communist and anarchist Spaniards, and anti-Nazi Germans stopped in Marseille en route to safety. Artists denounced by the Third Reich, including Max Ernst, Marc Chagall, and Consuelo de Saint-Exupéry, took refuge in places such as Villa Air-Bel, a chateau on the outskirts of town financed by an emergency rescue committee. Exiles flocked to bars on the old port, where they heard news of ship traffic and police movements, checked the expiration dates on their transit papers, and played cards.

Casablanca director Michael Curtiz was helped in capturing this anxious mood by a cast that knew it well, according to author Aljean Harmetz in *Round Up the Usual Suspects.* Curt Bois, who played the pickpocket, had left Vienna, and Peter Lorre, the black-marketeer Ugarte, had left Germany. Conrad Veidt, who played Strasser, fled Germany with his Jewish wife. Trude Berliner, the woman at the baccarat table who asks if Rick will have a drink with her, was a German Jew from Berlin. Marcel Dalio, who played Rick's croupier, and his wife, Madeleine Lebeau, who played Yvonne, Rick's jilted girlfriend, were refugees from occupied France.

"Acting is what actors do. It is not necessary to be a murderer to portray one," notes Harmetz. "But a dozen good actors, cast adrift, brought to a dozen small roles in *Casablanca* an understanding and a desperation that could never have come from central casting."

Even after filming and postproduction were completed, *Casablanca* continued to be shaped by external forces. In the late summer of 1942, Warner Bros. executives had the final cut in the can and scheduled the movie for release in the summer of 1943. But on November 8, 1942,

CONTINUED ON PAGE 71

CAFÉ CULTURE

Top: A fado singer and guitarist entertain in Lisbon, a stopping point for many war refugees. Above: Avenue Georges Gallice in Juan-les-Pins, France, in 1955; the nightclub that inspired Rick's Café was located northeast of this resort town on the Côte d'Azur. Opposite: Bogart in front of the studio Rick's. Sets for the film were designed by art director Carl Jules Weyl and decorated by set dresser George James Hopkins. They were remarkably well executed, given wartime restrictions.

WARNER BROS./KOBAL/REX/SHUTTERSTOCK

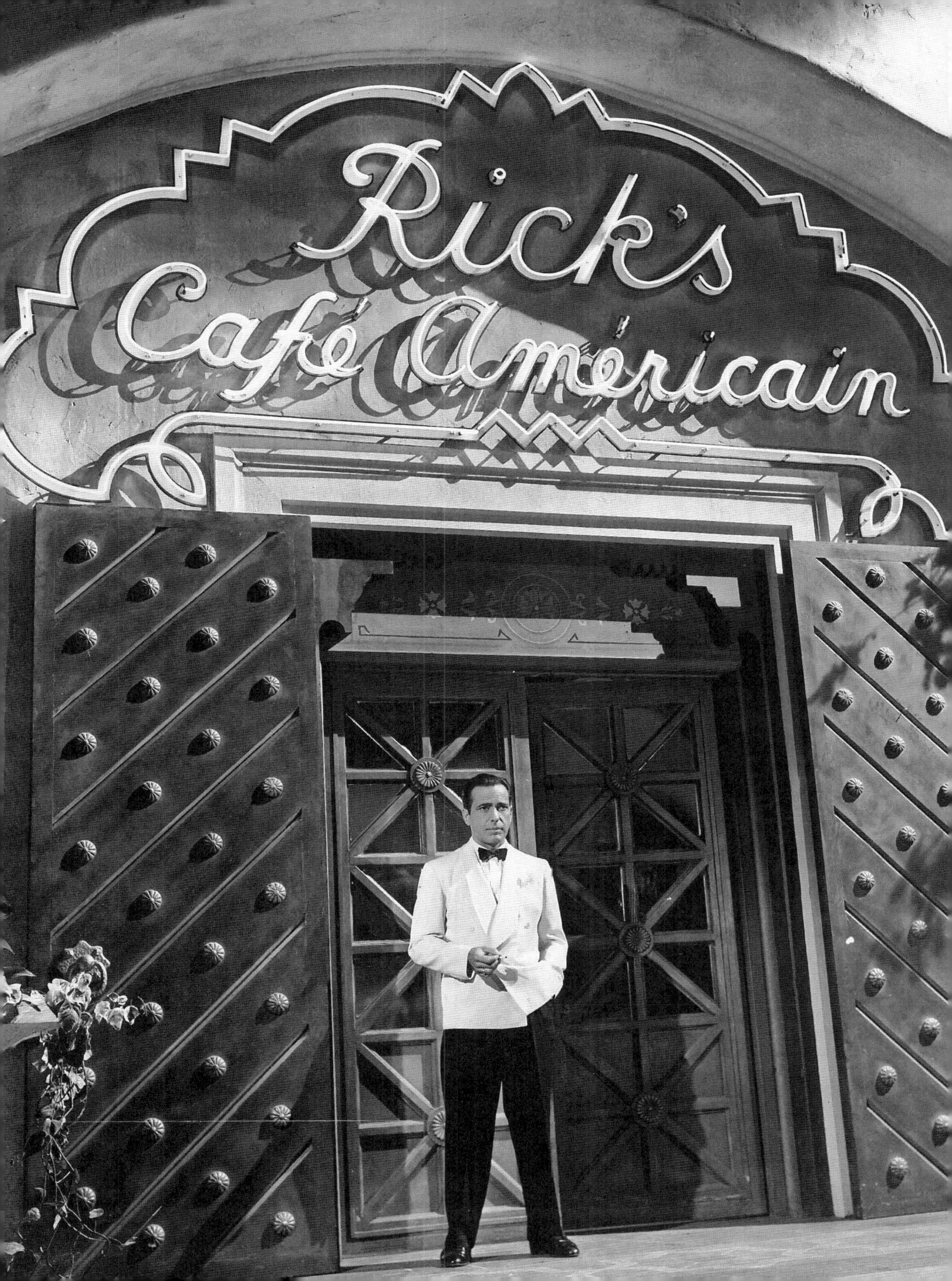
Rick's
Café Américain

SHOW OF FORCE
In the wake of the Allied landing in North Africa, known as Operation Torch, American and French troops marched through Casablanca on December 30, 1942.

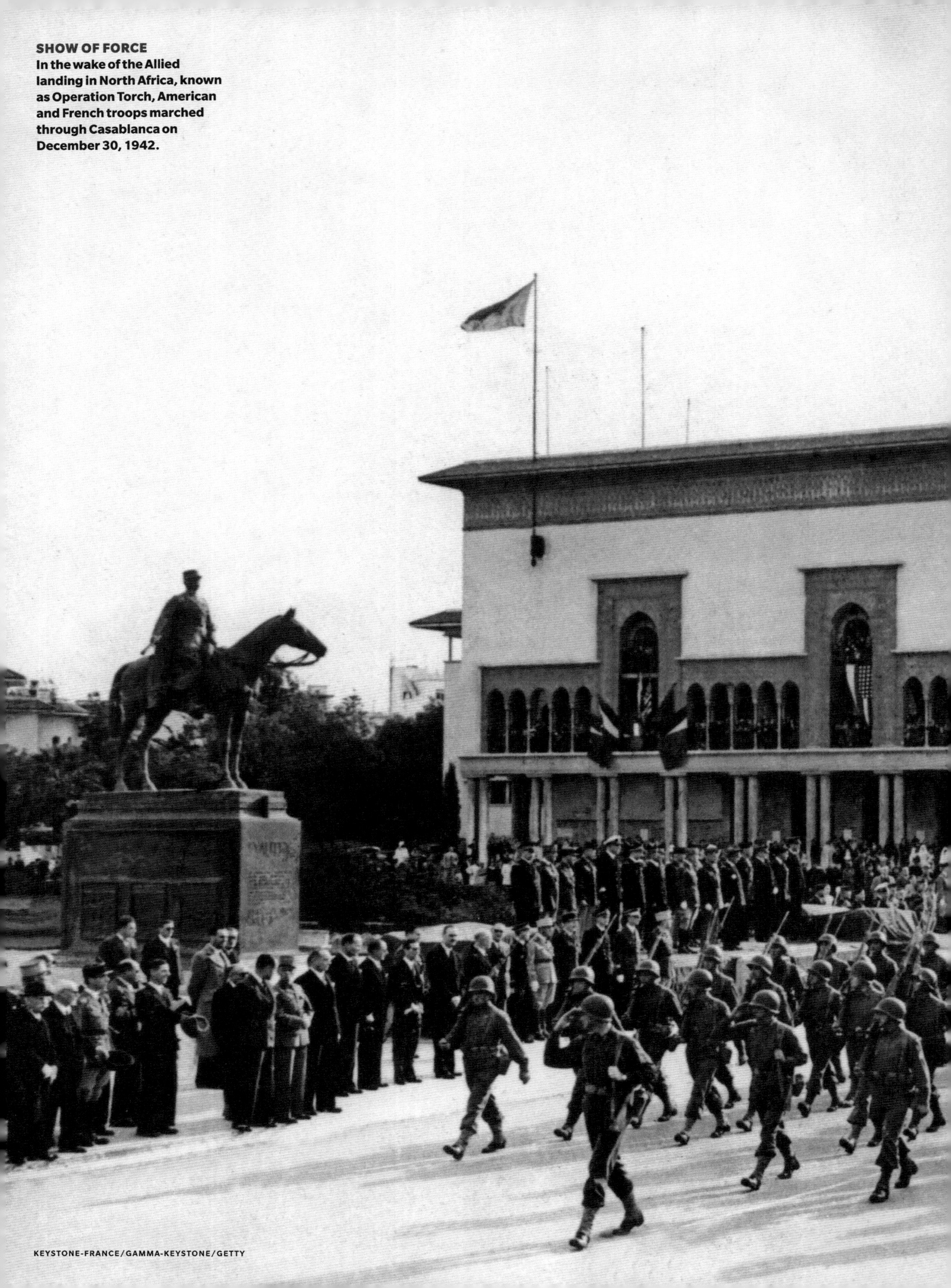

KEYSTONE-FRANCE/GAMMA-KEYSTONE/GETTY

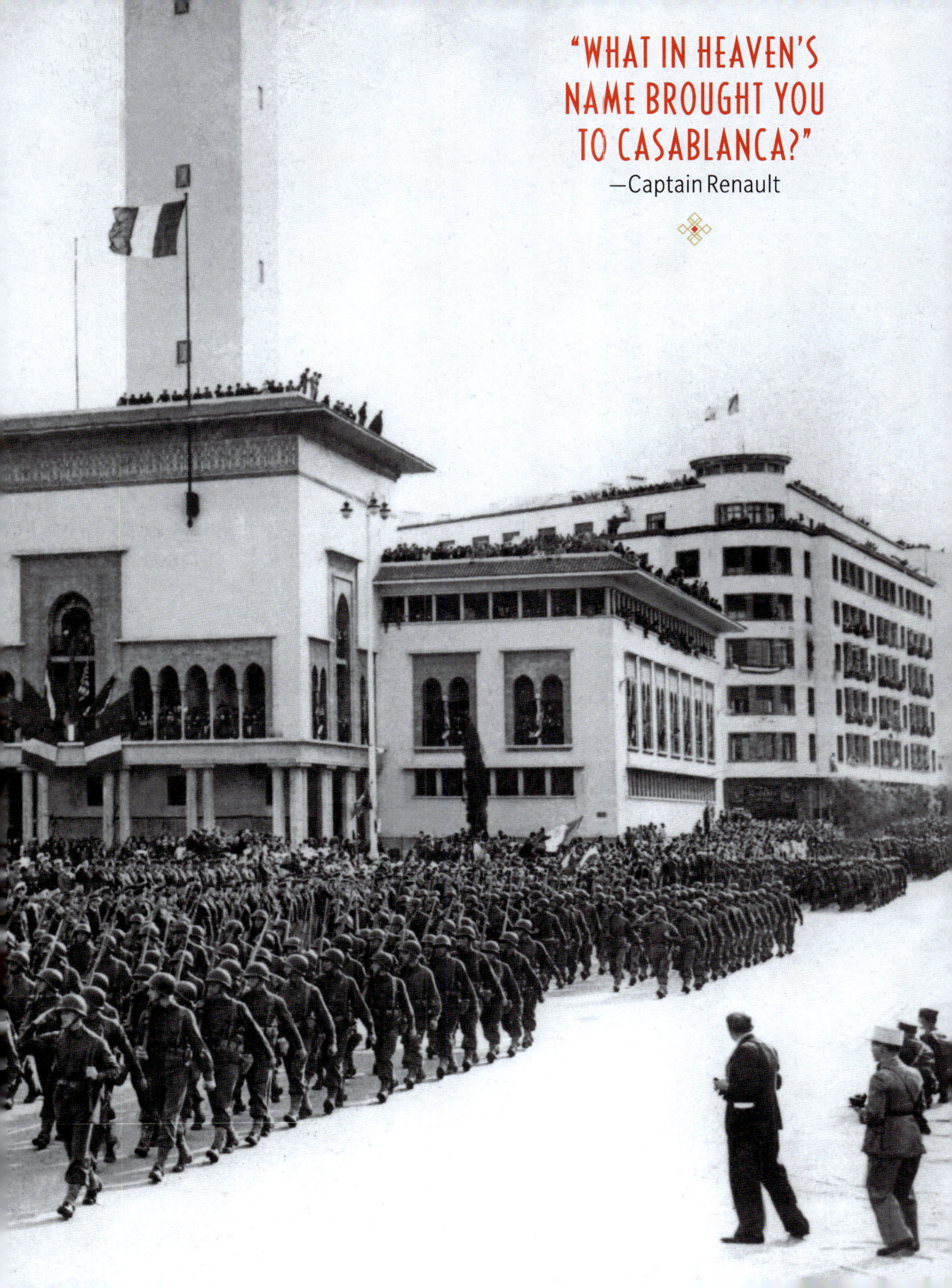

"WHAT IN HEAVEN'S NAME BROUGHT YOU TO CASABLANCA?"

—Captain Renault

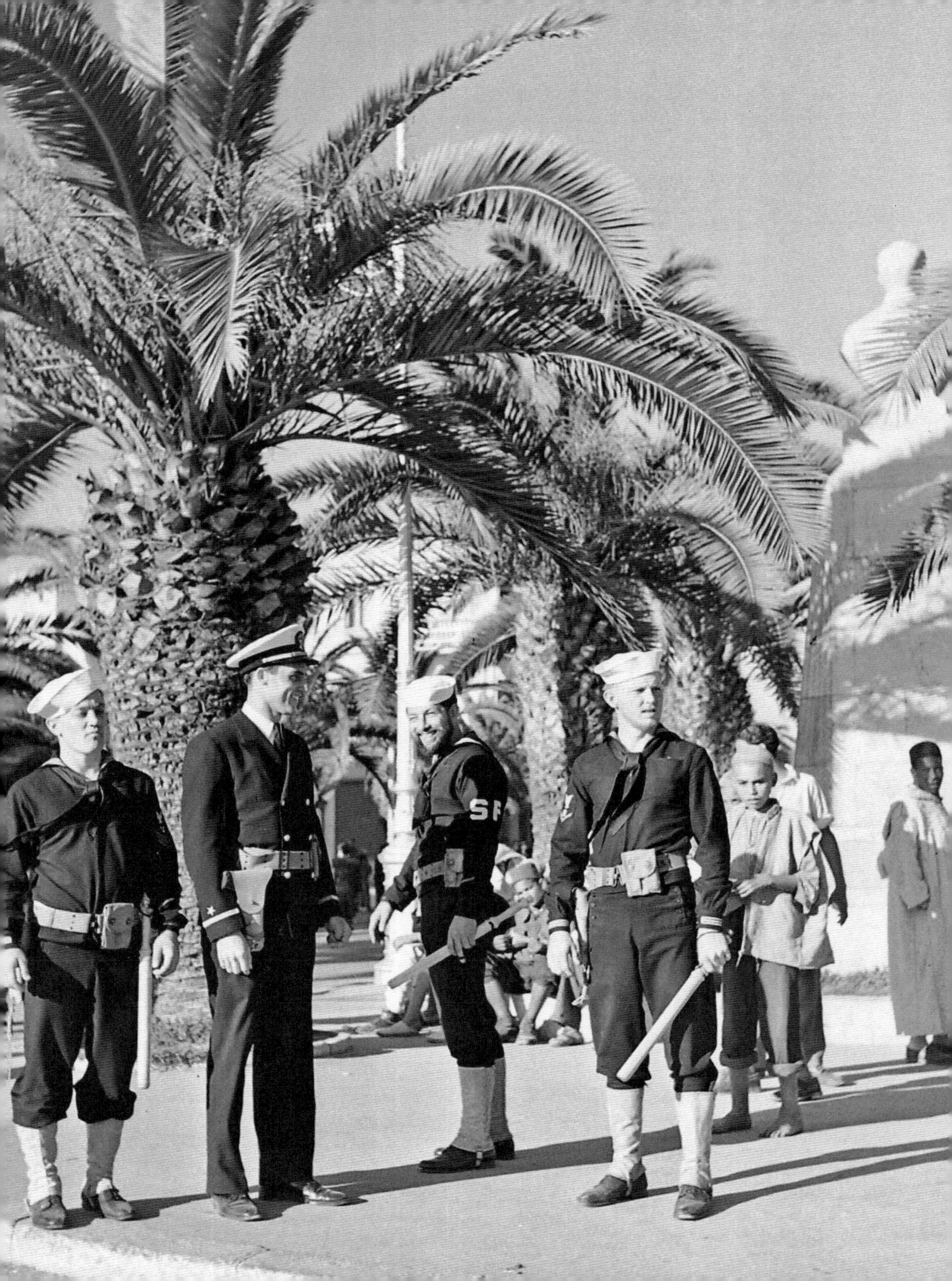
SP

CONTINUED FROM PAGE 66

the Allies invaded North Africa, with three amphibious task forces seizing ports and airports in Casablanca, Oran, and Algiers. It was an early German loss in the war and inserted Casablanca into headlines across the globe. "The entire industry envies us with a picture having the title *Casablanca* ready to release," Jack Warner said to his staff. "We should take advantage of this great scoop."

In a final stroke of marketing luck for the studio, from January 14 to 24, 1943, President Franklin Roosevelt and British prime minister Winston Churchill convened the Casablanca Conference to strategize about the end of the war. The meeting, also attended by generals Charles de Gaulle and Henri Giraud of the Free French forces, had been a closely guarded secret, writes Harlan Lebo in *Casablanca: Behind the Scenes*. But when the conference was announced, "all at Warner Bros. were as surprised as everyone else, but a great deal happier—*Casablanca* had opened nationwide the day before." ■

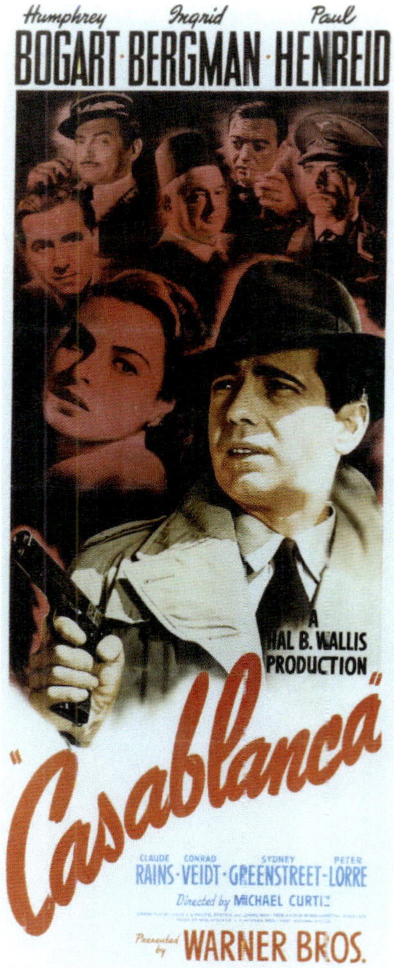

MARC WANAMAKER/BISON ARCHIVES

SURVEYING THE FIELD

Opposite: After Operation Torch, Casablanca became a key base for the Allied Forces for the remainder of the war. Left: Even 75 years after *Casablanca's* release, there is a thriving market in the film's original posters. Below: President Franklin D. Roosevelt and British prime minister Winston Churchill met in Casablanca to plan operations.

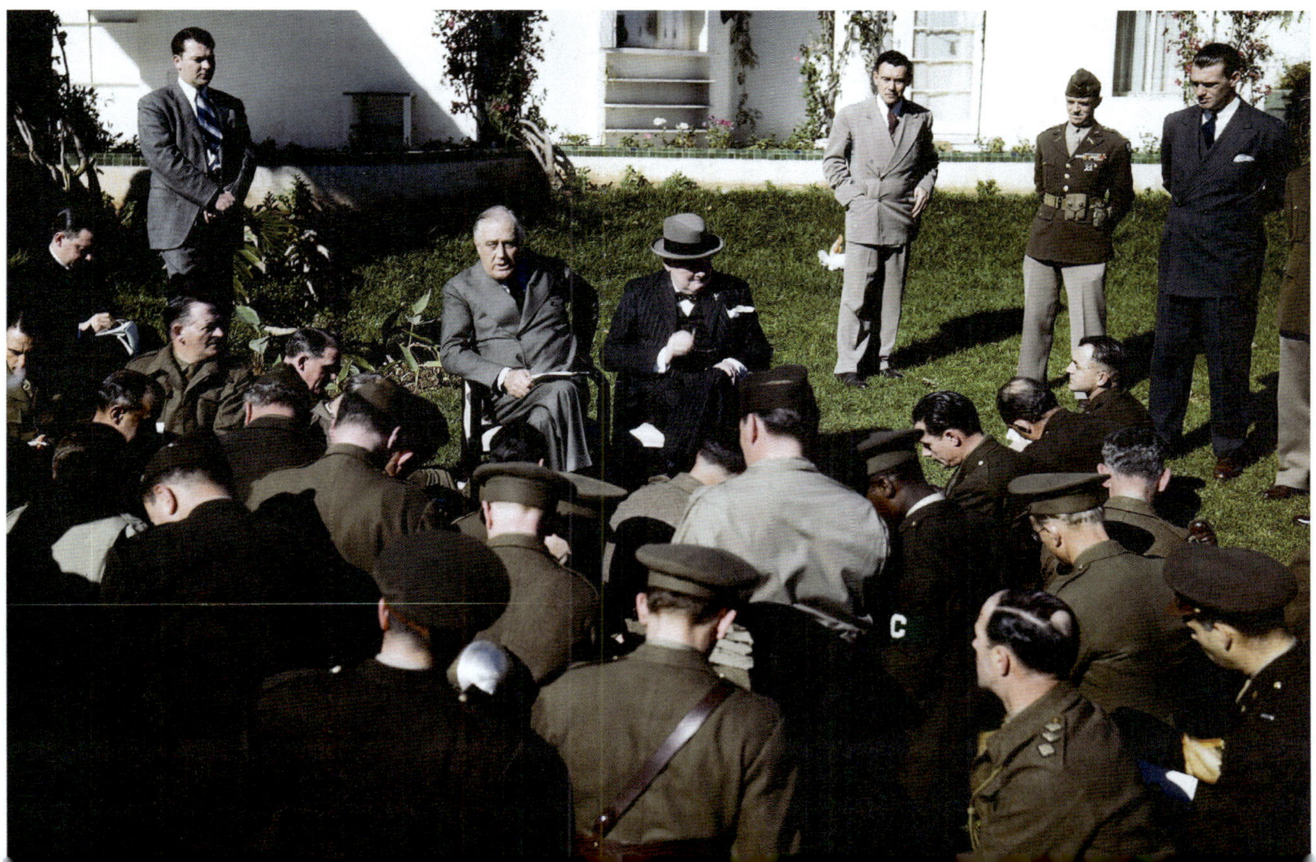

J.R. EYERMAN/LIFE/THE PICTURE COLLECTION

AP/REX/SHUTTERSTOCK

CASABLANCA WORSHIP

First came the copy cats. Then the nods, winks, and homages. The more that time goes by, the more *Casablanca* becomes ingrained in the pop culture fabric

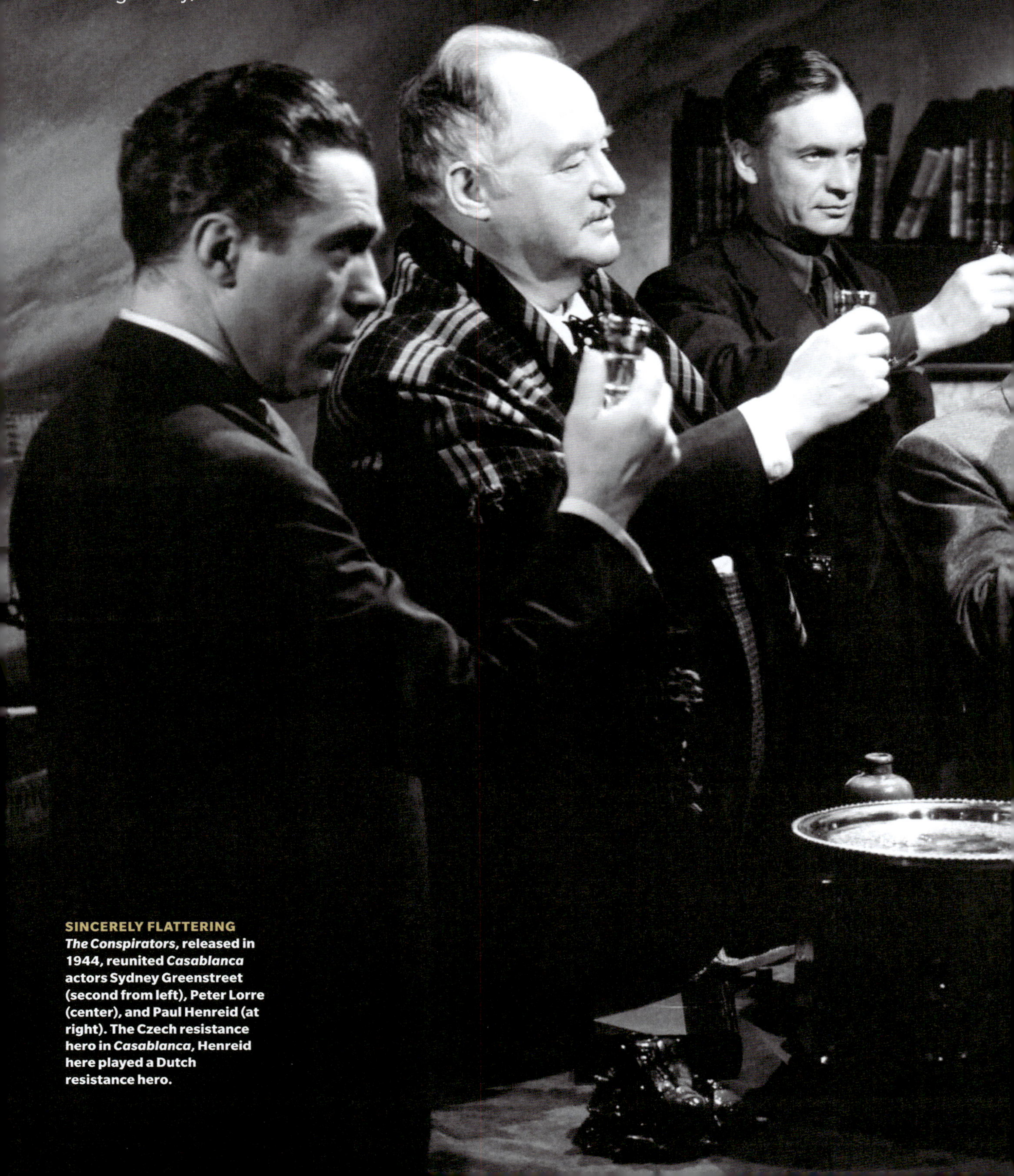

SINCERELY FLATTERING
***The Conspirators*, released in 1944, reunited *Casablanca* actors Sydney Greenstreet (second from left), Peter Lorre (center), and Paul Henreid (at right). The Czech resistance hero in *Casablanca*, Henreid here played a Dutch resistance hero.**

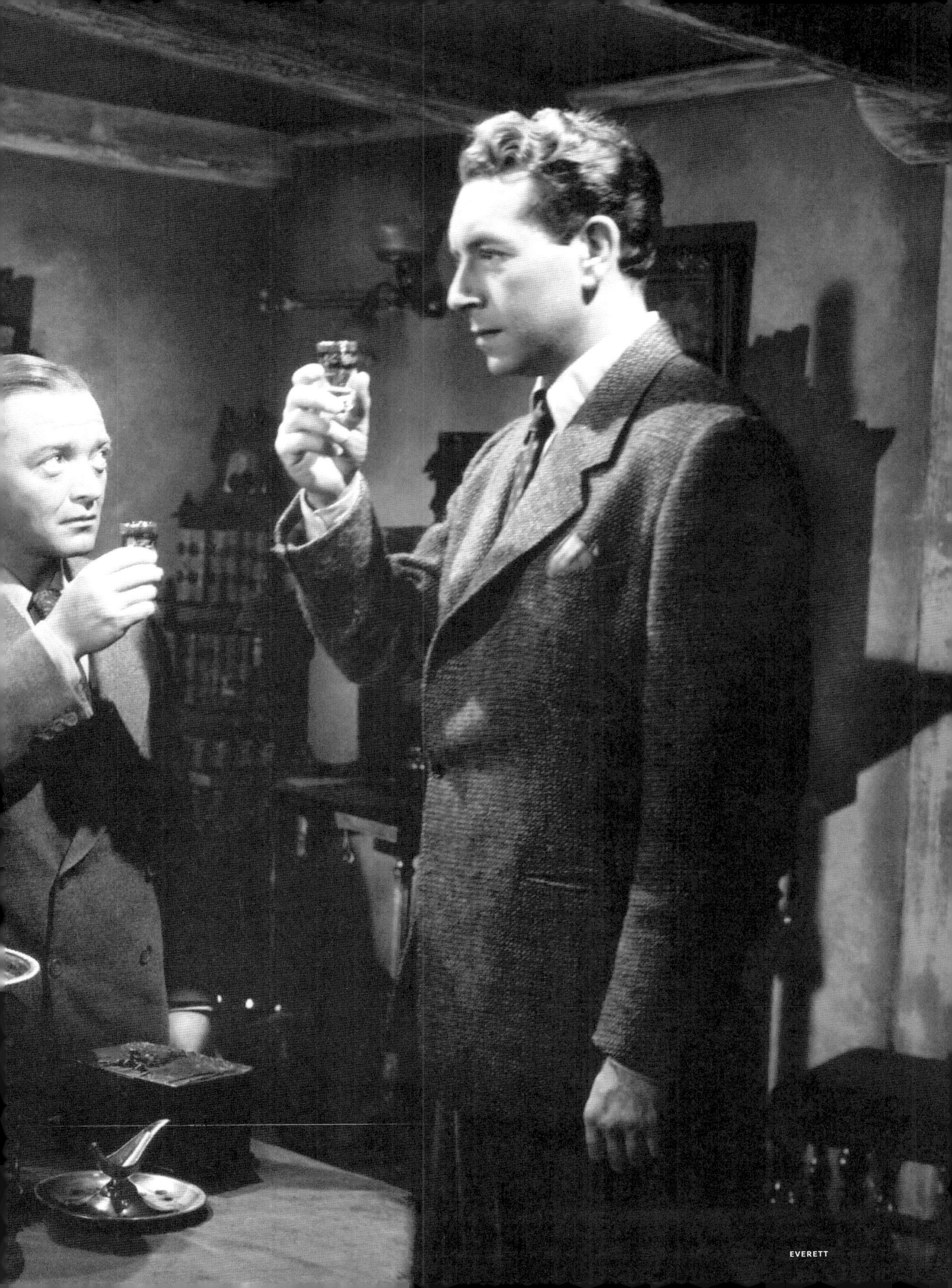

EVERETT

In the 2017 Academy Award–winning film *La La Land,* the bedroom of the actress Mia (Emma Stone) is, like the rest of the film, a quirky homage to Hollywood. Mia's walls are hung with posters from *Lilies of the Field,* a 1924 movie about love and infidelity; *The Black Cat,* which came out in 1941 and was inspired by an Edgar Allan Poe short story; and *The Dove,* a 1927 film about a dance hall girl in love with a gambler. But the film that looms largest for Mia—quite literally, in a floor-to-ceiling painting—is *Casablanca.*

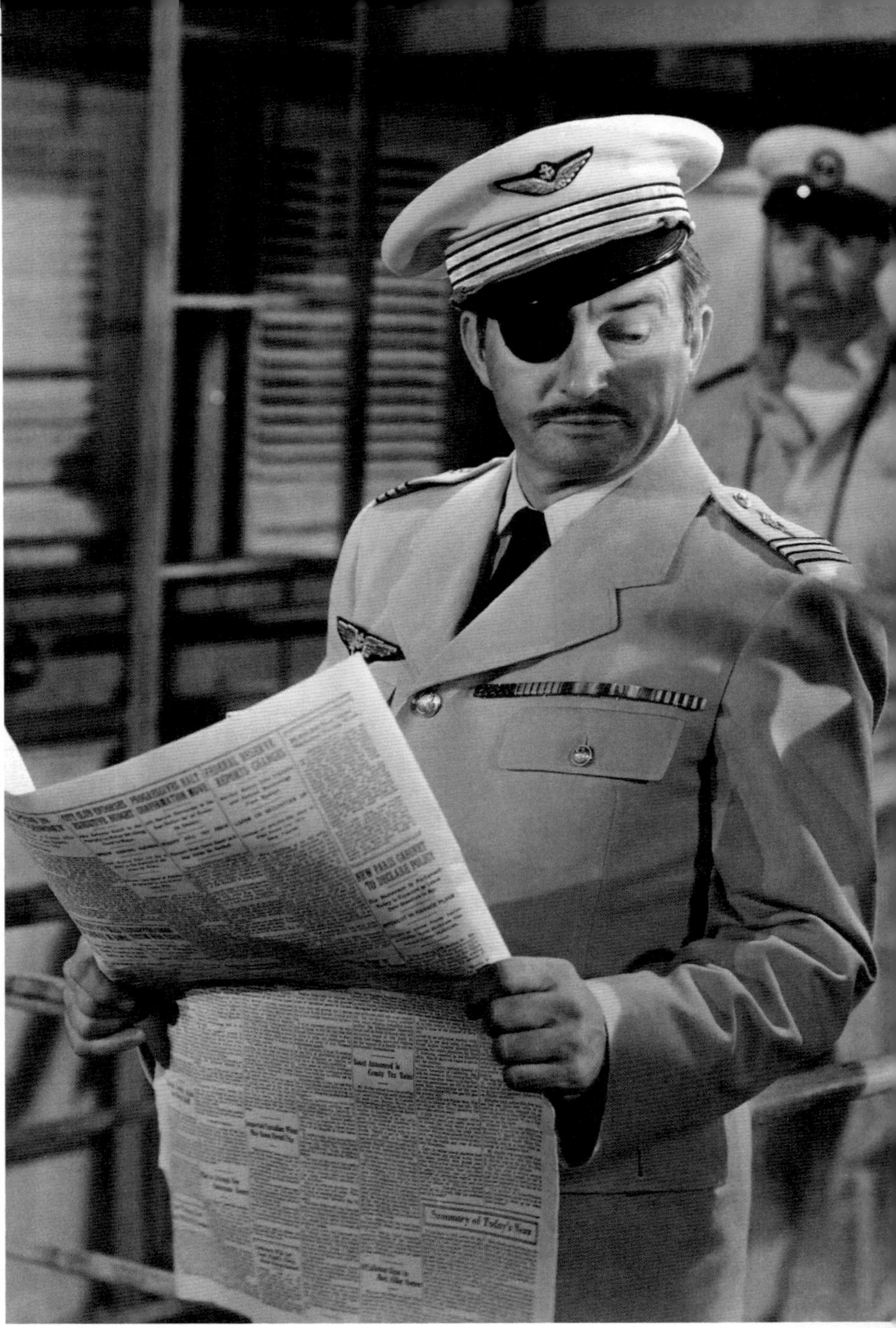

The same could be said of *La La Land* director Damien Chazelle, who packed his Oscar-winning musical with *Casablanca* nods and winks: Audiences catch a glimpse of Ingrid Bergman on a billboard next to the Chateau Marmont; Mia works at a café on the Warner Bros. lot, the studio that produced *Casablanca,* across from a window set used for a key Paris flashback scene between Humphrey Bogart and Bergman. Five years later, in *La La Land's* final moments, Mia and her husband of five years wander into a piano bar owned by Sebastian (Ryan Gosling), the former flame she's left behind.

"You could almost hear Gosling ruefully say to himself: 'Of all the gin joints in all the towns in all the world, she walks into mine,'" observed the film site IndieWire.

Casablanca was not the favorite for Best Picture going into the Academy Awards ceremony in 1944. That was the drama *The Song of Bernadette.* Nor was it the biggest box office draw of '43. That honor went to *For Whom the Bell Tolls,* which also starred Bergman. Some attribute *Casablanca's* surprise win to mishandled Oscar campaigns. At the time, extras—the actors who are the nameless faces in a crowd—were a powerful voting bloc with the Academy of Motion Picture Arts and Sciences, according to the *Los Angeles Times.* To create support for *Bernadette* and *Bell,* the studios focused on Hollywood elite, pricing tickets for the films quite high. As a result, some three quarters of the extras did not see those two movies. On the other hand, many more saw *Casablanca,* giving it a substantial leg up.

There were no films from that year, or any in Hollywood's history, that can rival *Casablanca* for its pop culture afterlife. Over the past seven and a half decades, the film has been much laureled, imitated, and parodied. Some dozen lines of dialog have become embedded in the world's lexicon. *Casablanca* has been a plot point in many other movies, a springboard for two television series, and the source of the title of Fall Out Boy's single "Of All the Gin Joints in All the World." In 2014, the piano from Rick's Café sold at auction for $3.4 million. The centerpiece of Hugh Hefner's 86th birthday party at the Playboy Mansion in 2012: a large cake with Hef's face superimposed on Bogie's body on a *Casablanca* poster.

Even some *Casablanca* haters

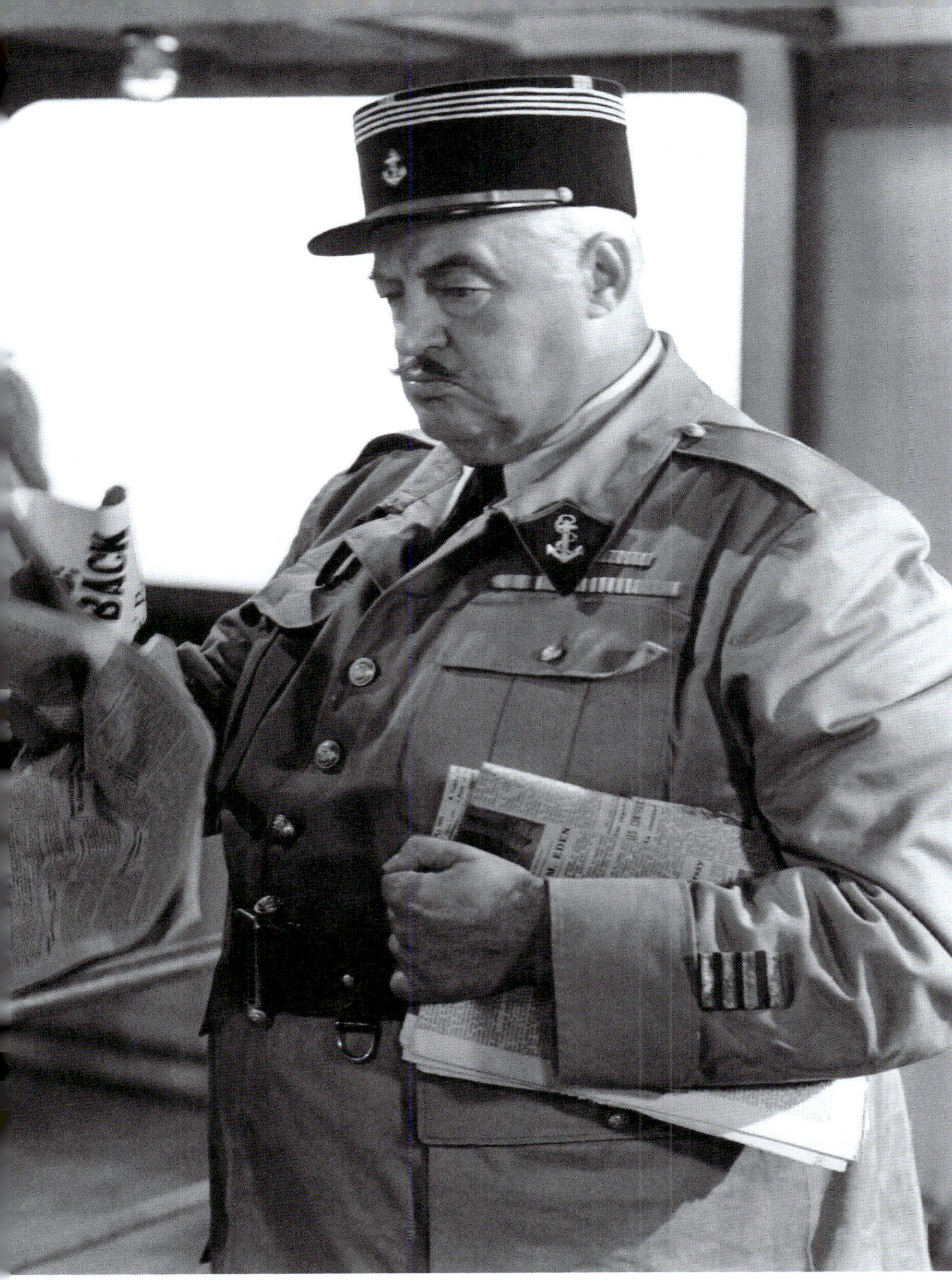

EVERETT

SOUND FAMILIAR?
1944's *Passage to Marseille* (left) not only used many of the same stars as *Casablanca*—Humphrey Bogart, Claude Rains, Sydney Greenstreet, and Peter Lorre—it shared the same director and producer. The trailer further clarified: "Last year, Warner Bros. electrified the world with *Casablanca*. This year, Warner Bros. announce *Passage to Marseille . . .*" Below, *To Have and Have Not*, also from 1944, mimicked *Casablanca's* plot and starred Bogart with his future wife, Lauren Bacall.

marvel at the film's staying power. In his famous 1994 essay, "*Casablanca*, or, the Clichés are Having a Ball," Italian semiotics professor Umberto Eco labeled the movie "mediocre" and compared it to a comic strip.

Yet, in discussing how the film hoodwinked audiences through familiar archetypes, Eco had praise. Good stories, he pointed out, usually employ merely one archetypal plot or character device, say, "Civilization Against Barbarism" or "Flight." But *Casablanca* loaded in dozens. It opened with a magical place,

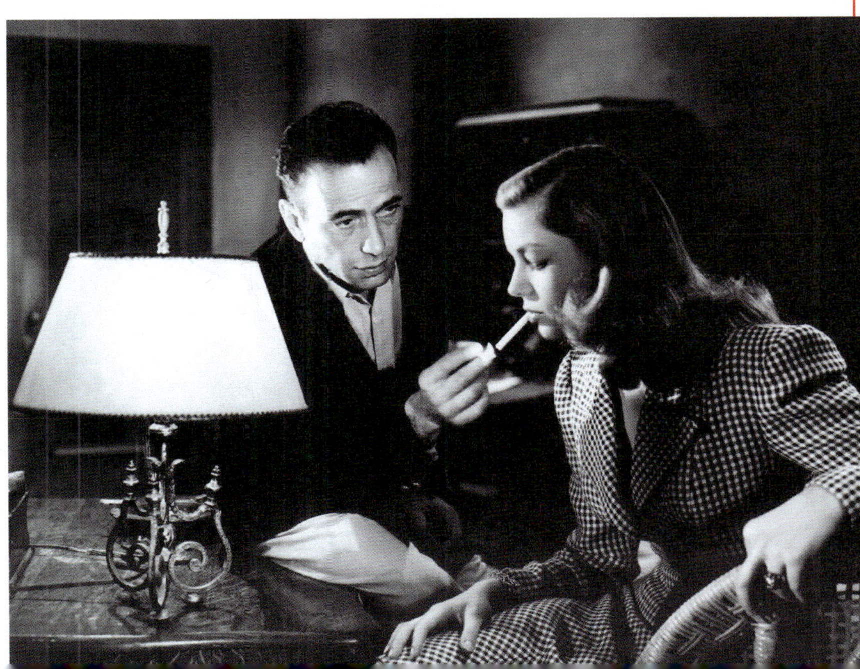

© WARNER BROS., COURTESY PHOTOFEST

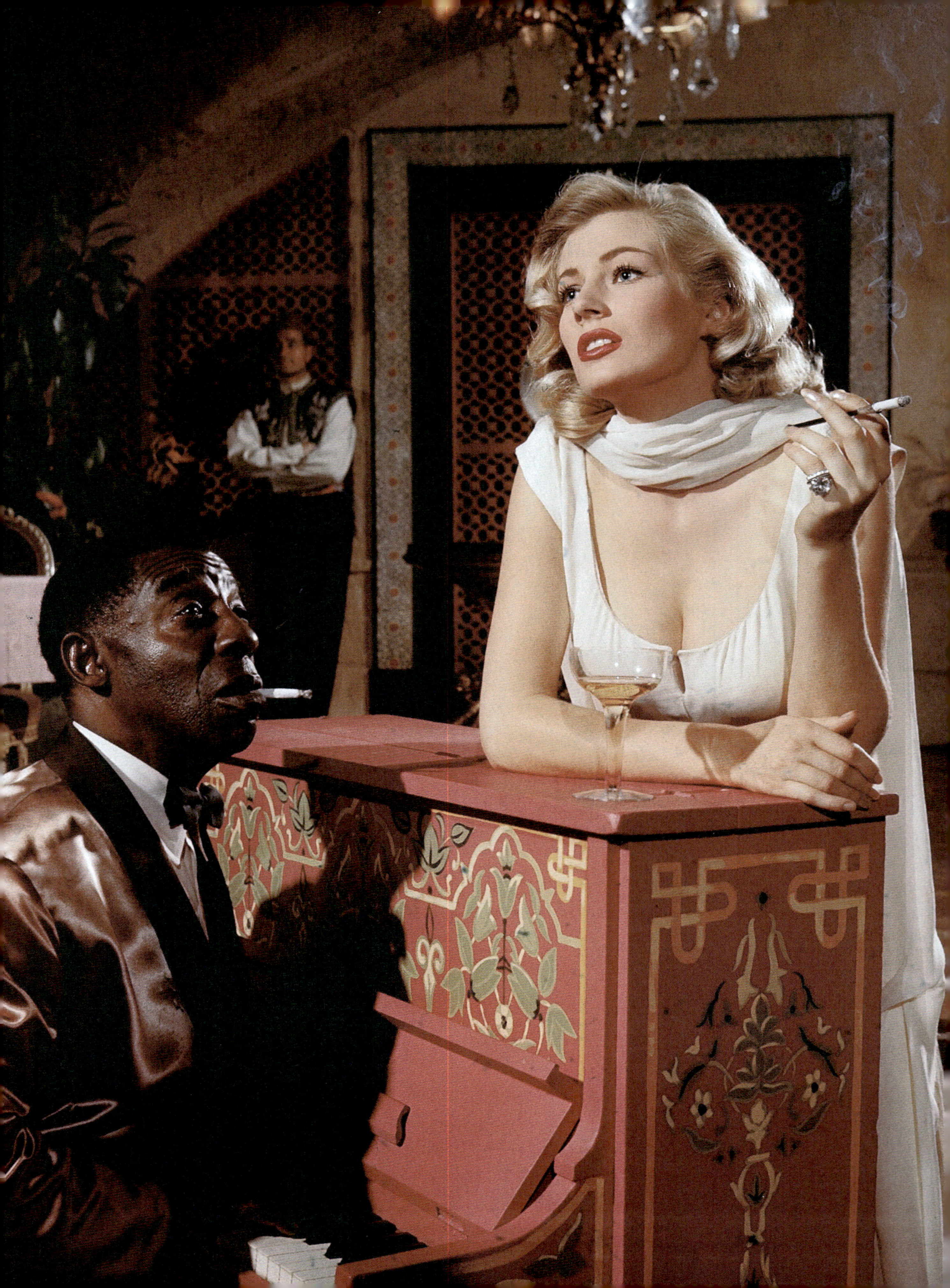

Morocco, "the Exotic." There was "Passage to the Promised Land" (out of Morocco), which required a "Magic Key" (the letters of transit). Rick was both the "Ambiguous Adventurer" and the "Redeemed Drunkard." All of this was squeezed into the conceit of "Sacrifice" and "Unhappy Love." Eco ticked off multiple other examples before summing it all up: "Two clichés make us laugh. A hundred clichés move us." *Casablanca's* ability to manipulate moviegoers, he wrote, was a "phenomenon worthy of awe."

Why has *Casablanca* endured so powerfully while dozens of other World War II dramas have not? Aside from an almost perfect blend of star power, romance, and snappy dialog, the most oft-cited explanation is that in *Casablanca,* and especially in Bogart, American audiences recognize themselves, or at least the selves they want to be. Rick is a cynic and loner. Like isolationist America in 1939, 1940, and most of 1941, he declares his policy to "stick my neck out for nobody." For moviegoers having doubts about the U.S. entrance into World War II, Rick's decision to give up his love in order to help defeat the Nazis was an affirmation: The country had made the right choice. The move also transformed Bogart's career. Before *Casablanca,* he was a popular tough-guy movie star; after, he was an international sex symbol and one of Hollywood's highest paid actors.

Still, *Casablanca's* evolution from period piece to cultural touchstone was hardly preordained. The film won the Best Picture Oscar and did well enough at the box office, grossing $3.7 million on an $878,000 budget. Encouraged, Warner Bros. tried to repeat the formula, with varying degrees of success. In 1944, the studio released *Passage to Marseille,* a World War II drama directed by *Casablanca's* Michael Curtiz and

LOOMIS DEAN/LIFE/THE PICTURE COLLECTION

INSPIRATION POINT

A 1955 television series based on *Casablanca*, with, opposite, Clarence Muse as Sam and Anita Ekberg in an Ilsa-like part, was short-lived (Charles McGraw starred in the Rick role). Bogie never said, "Play it again, Sam," but that was the title Woody Allen (below, with Diane Keaton) gave his 1972 film, about a divorcé who gets dating advice from his hero, Humphrey Bogart.

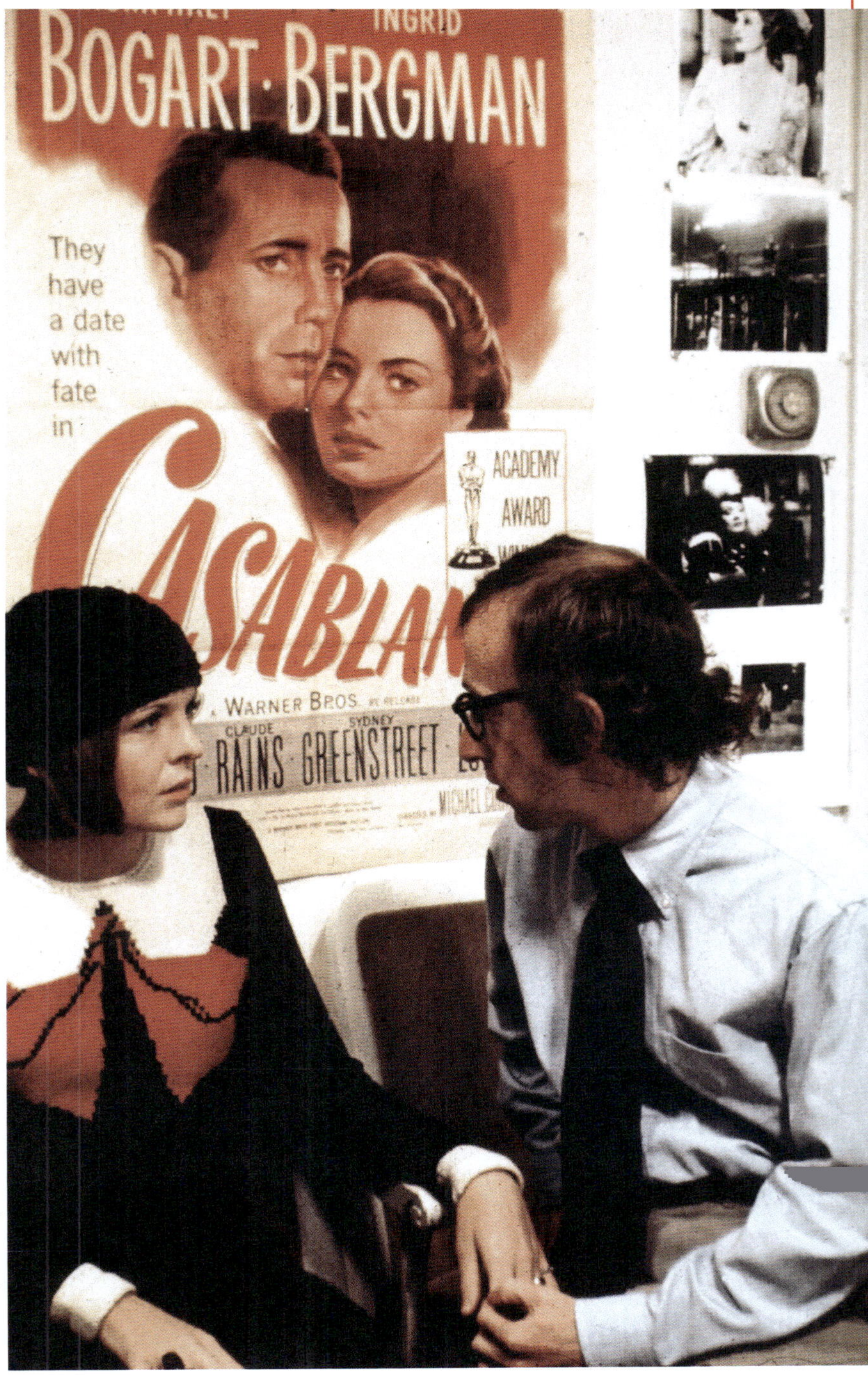

MARY EVANS/ROLLINS-JOFFE PRODUCTIONS/RONALD GRANT/EVERETT

starring much of *Casablanca's* cast. But *Passage* was critically panned, and domestically it took in less than it cost to make. It only recouped Warner's investment with overseas distribution and a helping hand from the U.S. government, which flew reels of American films with French subtitles to theaters in Algeria and Morocco, attempting to counteract Axis propaganda.

As the war raged on in Europe and the Pacific, the studio tried again in October 1944, releasing two more *Casablanca* clones, *The Conspirators* and *To Have and Have Not.* With Paul Henreid as a freedom fighter and Sydney Greenstreet as head of a resistance group, *The Conspirators* was a misfire and panned by critics.

To Have and Have Not, based on the Ernest Hemingway novel, was a different story. Rewritten extensively to mimic *Casablanca,* the film was the beginning of one of Hollywood's most beautiful love stories. Bogie played an expatriate fishing boat captain named Harry who reluctantly helps transport a Free French resistance leader and his beautiful wife, while hanging out with a nightclub singer. *To Have and Have Not* was a hit, grossing about the same as *Casablanca,* and garnering raves for the chemistry between Bogart and a 19-year-old actress, Lauren Bacall. Bogart and Bacall would marry in 1945 and go on to do three more films together.

With the end of the war and the arrival of peace, Warner Bros. set *Casablanca* themes aside and the movie quickly faded from public memory. The studio attempted, unsuccessfully, to resurrect it in 1955 as a television show starring Charles McGraw as Rick and Marcel Dalio (the croupier in the original film) as the police chief; a much discussed musical version never came together.

It was the death of Humphrey Bogart in 1957 that helped put *Casablanca* back on the culturati map. To honor Bogie's career, the owners of the Brattle, a small art cinema in Cambridge that catered to Harvard students, decided to show *Casablanca* for a week. The screening went over so well, the Brattle extended the engagement to a second week. The second turned into a third, then a fourth and a fifth. The audience began to recite lines, the way college students would two decades later with *The Rocky Horror Picture Show.* "It was more than just going to the movies," Cyrus Harvey Jr., one of the Brattle owners, told the *New York Times* in 1992. "It was sort of partaking in a ritual."

Bogie fever boomeranged around the country, from campus to campus and town to town. In 1969, it lit notably on Broadway, in a play by Woody

MISE-EN-SCÈNE

Below: Giuseppe Tornatore's 1988 film, *Cinema Paradiso*, is full of Hollywood references, including ones to *Casablanca*. Opposite: The film is an early theme in 1989's *When Harry Met Sally . . .*, with Harry (Billy Crystal) and Sally (Meg Ryan) disagreeing on why Rick puts Ilsa on a plane. Later, while they watch the movie in their own apartments, Harry tells Sally that she is high maintenance and Ingrid Bergman is low maintenance.

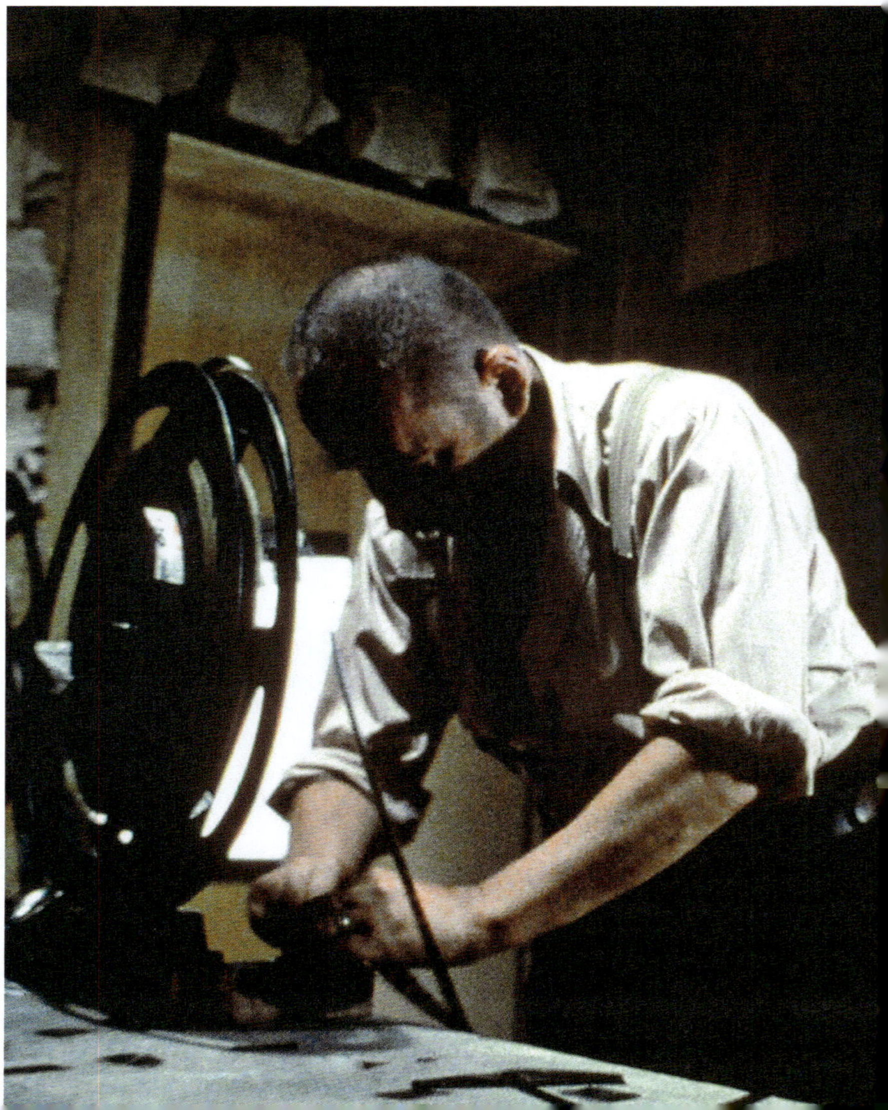

MIRAMAX/EVERETT

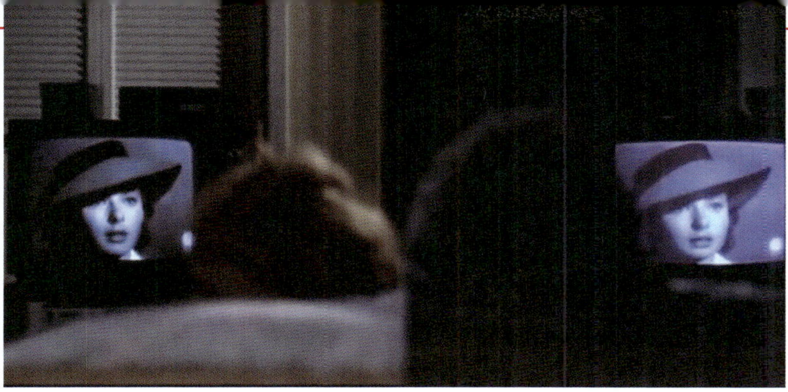

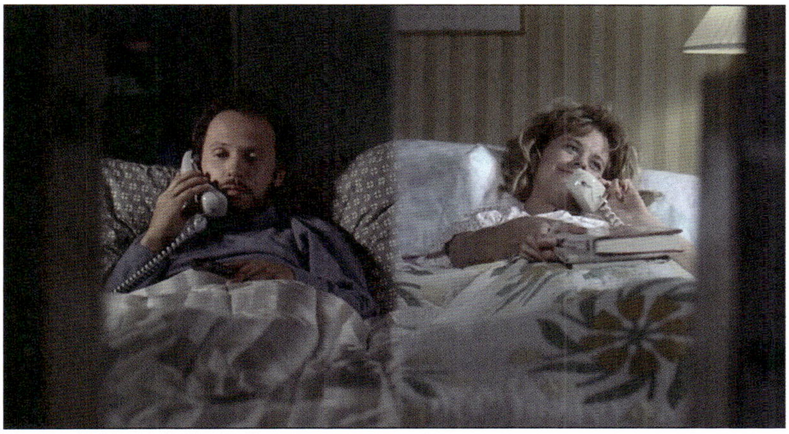

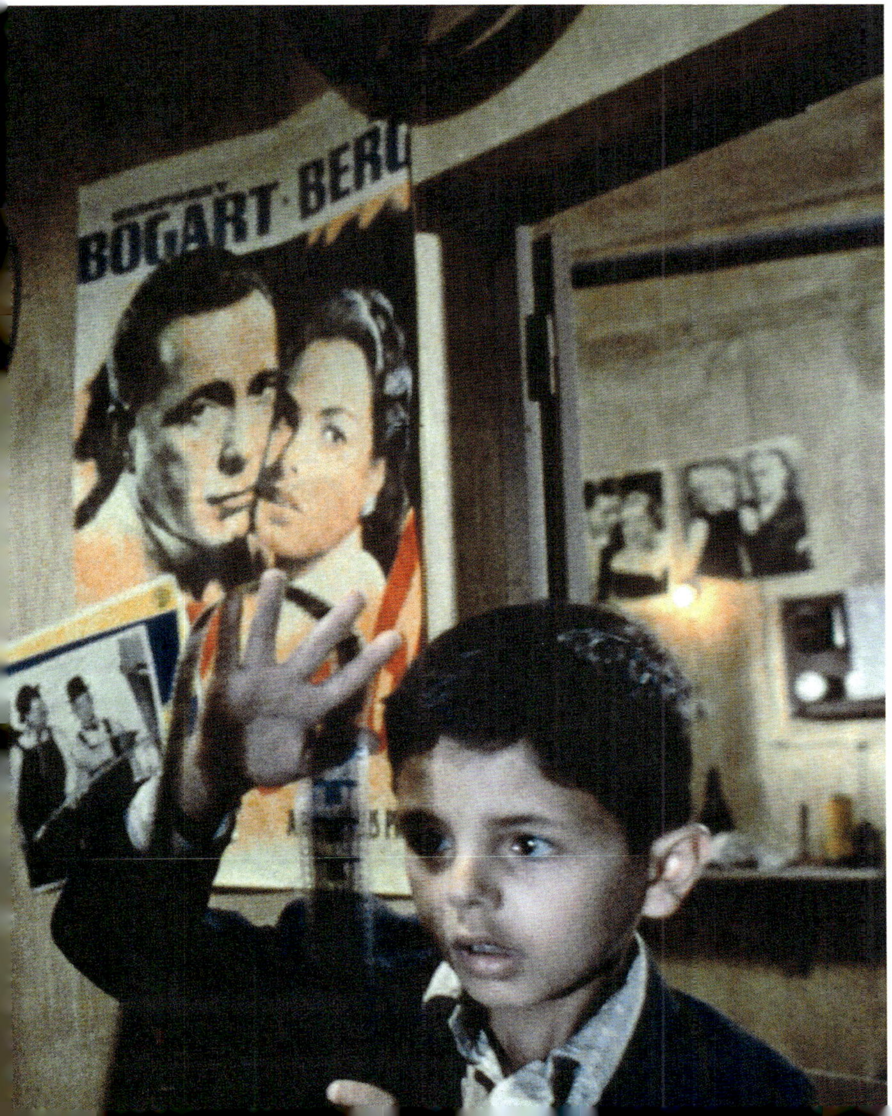

Allen. A neurotic, nebbishy New Yorker, Allen—who could be described as Bogart's polar opposite—wrote *Play It Again, Sam,* about a neurotic, nebbishy New Yorker named Allan Felix who idolizes Bogie. In the story, Allan has just come through a nasty divorce, and as he begins dating, Bogart's ghost appears to offer words of wisdom. Bogie is at his hard-boiled best counseling Allan through an affair with Linda, his best friend's wife, and helping him overcome myriad insecurities.

Bogart: What's that stuff you were putting on your face?

Allan: Canoe. It's an aftershave lotion.

Bogart: And the other stuff?

Allan: That was Mennen spray deodorant, Lavoris, and Johnson and Johnson baby powder.

Bogart: For Christ's sake, you're going to smell like a French cathouse.

For the finale, played out on a tarmac like in *Casablanca,* Allan tells Linda to return to her husband, delivering Bogie's on-screen breakup with Bergman verbatim. When the play was made into a movie, it returned *Casablanca* to the country's conversation and introduced the film to a new generation.

Casablanca was back. By 1977, it was the most shown film on television, according to *Round Up the Usual Suspects,* and references snowballed. They were highbrow and low, from *Cinema Paradiso* to *The Simpsons.* Typically, the allusions were just a line of dialog. But occasionally, a *Casablanca*-loving screenwriter like Nora Ephron went deeper. In Ephron's 1989 romantic comedy, *When Harry Met Sally…, Casablanca* becomes a metaphor for the state of relations between Harry, played by Billy Crystal, and Sally, played by Meg Ryan.

The two start off as strangers whose every habit irritates the other. In an early scene, they discuss *Casablanca*'s ending. Harry argues that Bogart wanted Bergman to leave, which is why he put her on the plane, and that any woman, including Sally, would choose Humphrey Bogart over Paul Henreid, whose name he can't even recall. Sally maintains that Bergman didn't want to stay because she wouldn't want to spend her life with a barkeep. As for what she would do personally, it was obvious, and didn't involve marriage to a man who runs a bar.

Harry: You'd rather be in a passionless marriage.

Sally: And be the first lady of Czechoslovakia.

Harry: Than live with the man you've had the greatest sex of your life with, and just because he owns a bar, and that is all he does.

Sally: Yes. And so would any woman in her right mind. Women are very practical, even Ingrid Bergman, which is why she gets on the plane at the end of the movie.

Irritation soon gives way to friendship and when Harry and Sally take up *Casablanca* again, a few years later, their relationship clearly has evolved. On a split screen, the two watch *Casablanca* in their respective apartments while commiserating on the phone about their lives. When Harry comments that the ending quote, "I think this is the beginning of a beautiful friendship," is the best last line of a movie, she appears to murmur in dreamy agreement.

Plenty of others agree with Harry. A decade ago, the American Film Institute voted the line the 20th best in film history. It was one of six from *Casablanca* that made the 100-entry list. The movie was also voted the third greatest in the past 100 years, behind only *Citizen Kane* and *The Godfather*. As for Rick Blaine, facing stiff competition, he was chosen the AFI's No. 4 Hero, bested by James Bond, Indiana Jones, and *To Kill a Mockingbird*'s Atticus Finch.

Not to worry. We'll always have Rick, and he'll always have Ilsa. ■

"I ADVISE THAT THIS PLACE BE SHUT UP AT ONCE!"

—Major Strasser

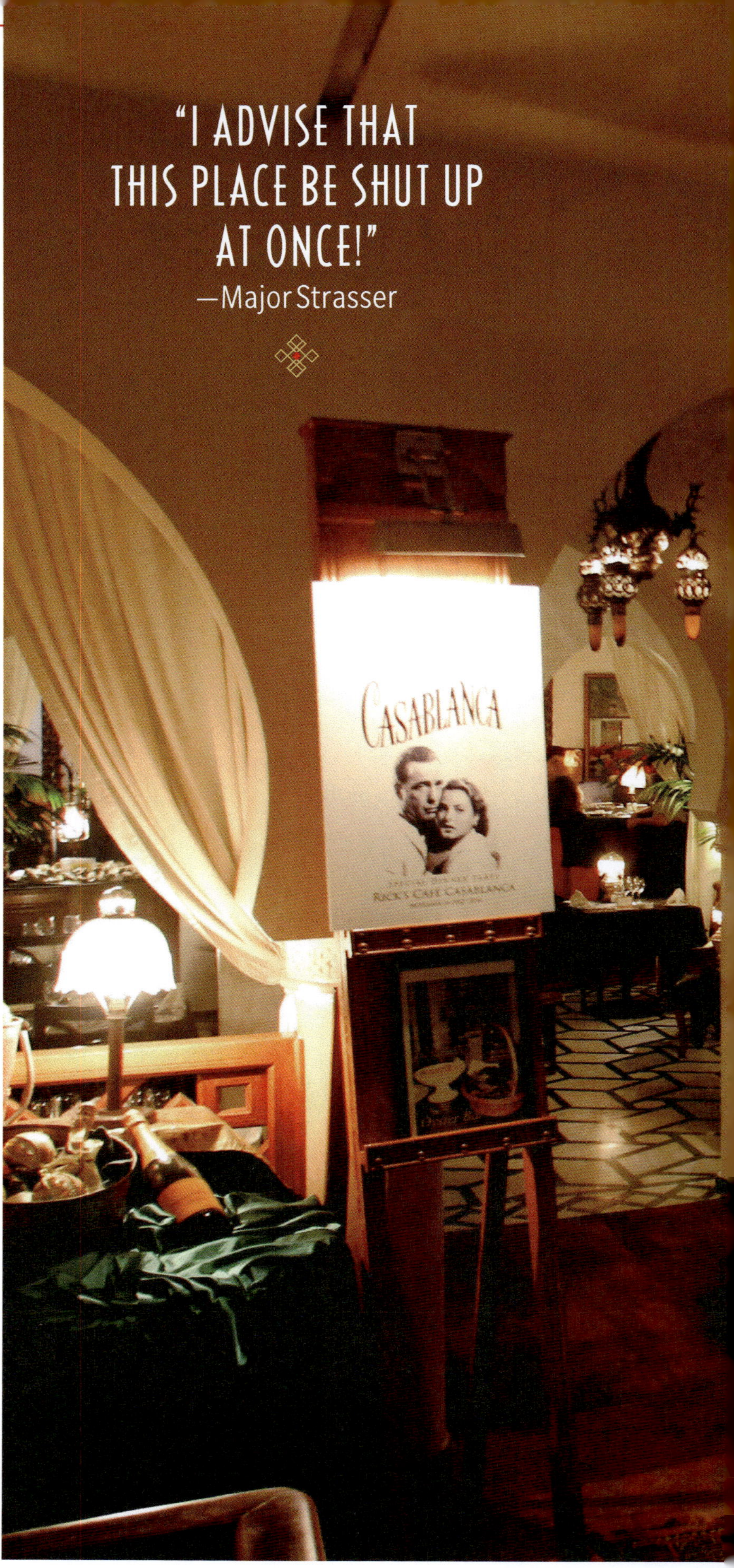

ABDELJALIL BOUNHAR/AP/REX/SHUTTERSTOCK

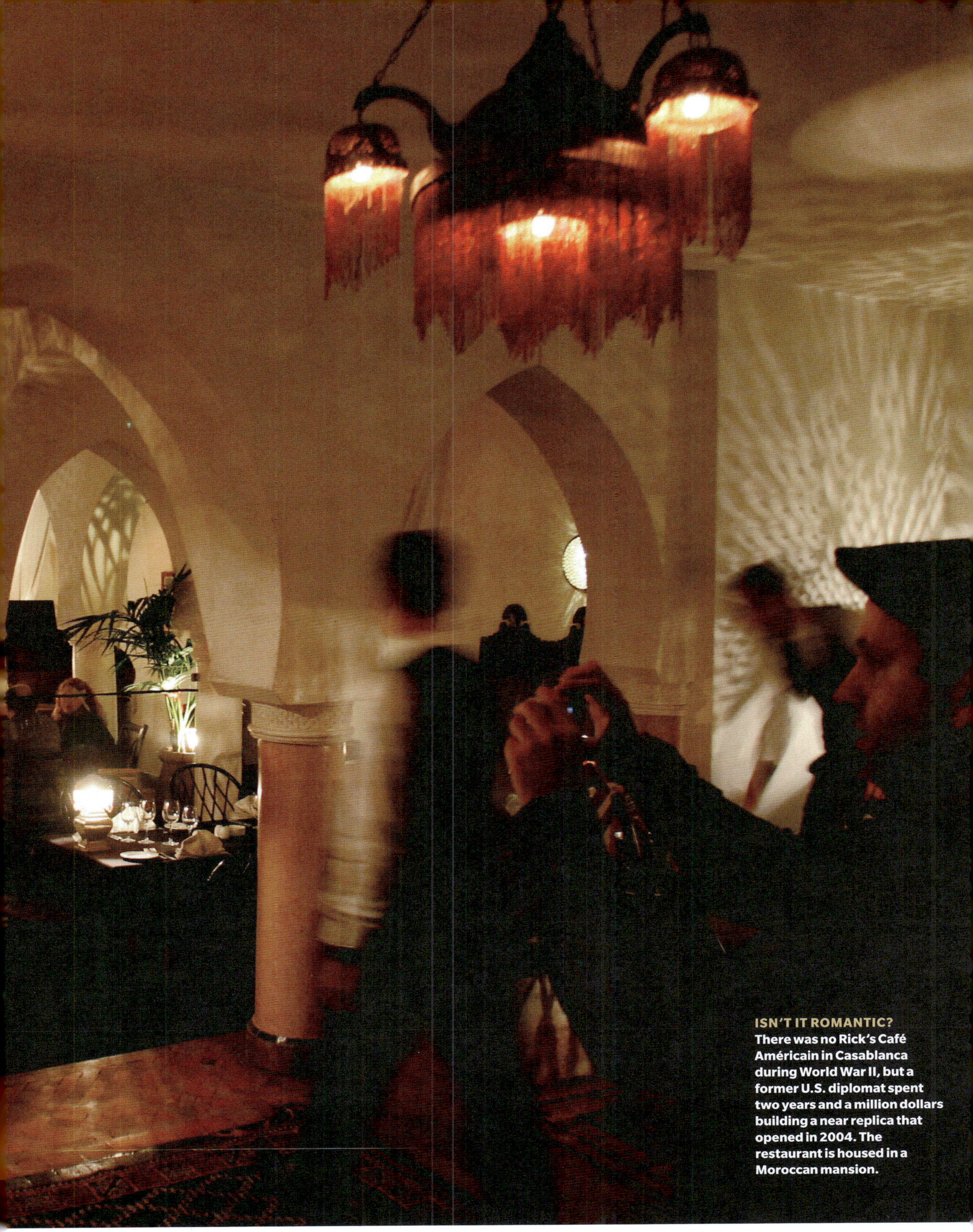

ISN'T IT ROMANTIC? There was no Rick's Café Américain in Casablanca during World War II, but a former U.S. diplomat spent two years and a million dollars building a near replica that opened in 2004. The restaurant is housed in a Moroccan mansion.

YOU MUST REMEMBER THIS

Seven classic images, six unforgettable quotes, and all the crucial plot twists—down to that climactic farewell on the tarmac

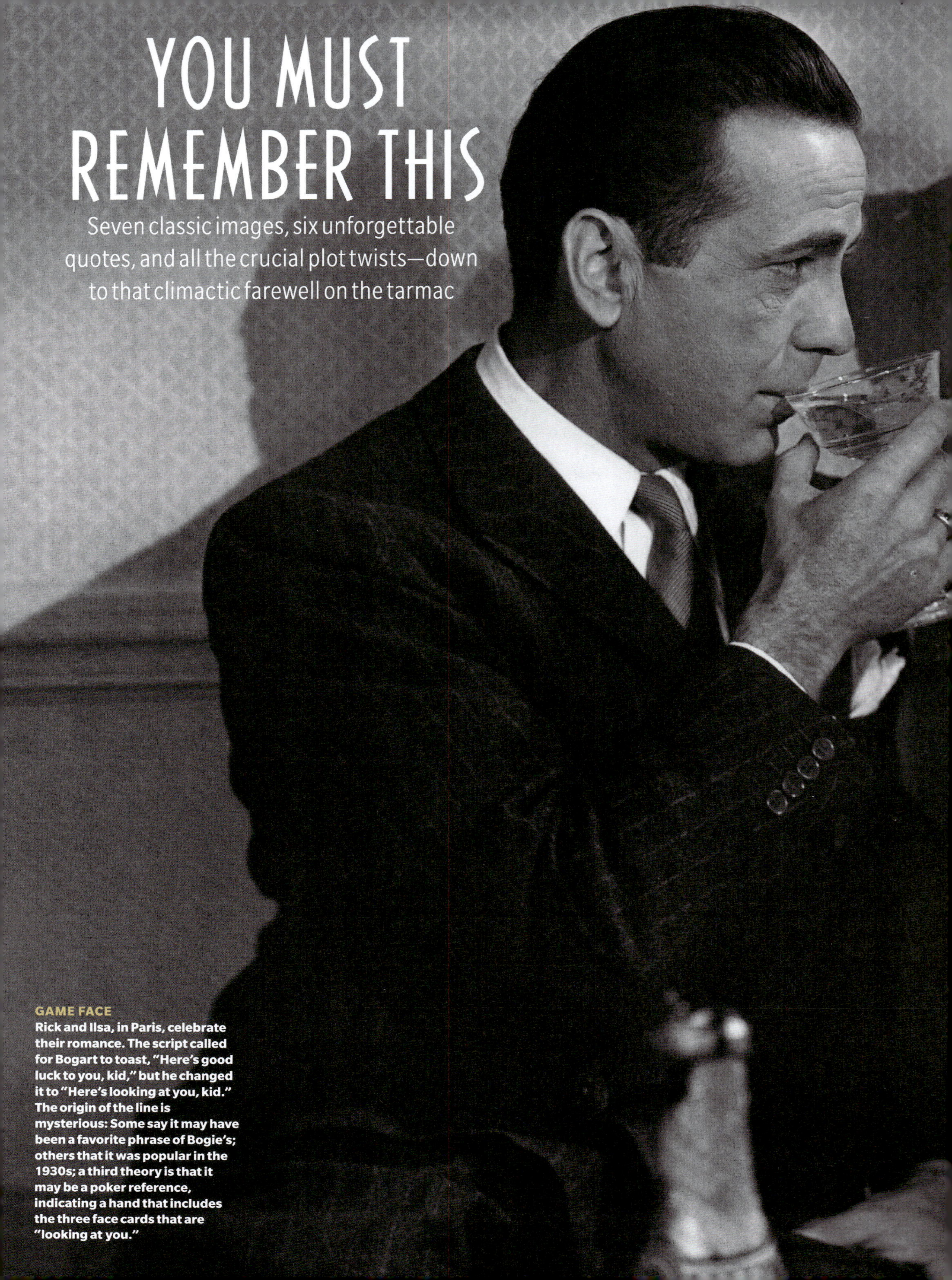

GAME FACE
Rick and Ilsa, in Paris, celebrate their romance. The script called for Bogart to toast, "Here's good luck to you, kid," but he changed it to "Here's looking at you, kid." The origin of the line is mysterious: Some say it may have been a favorite phrase of Bogie's; others that it was popular in the 1930s; a third theory is that it may be a poker reference, indicating a hand that includes the three face cards that are "looking at you."

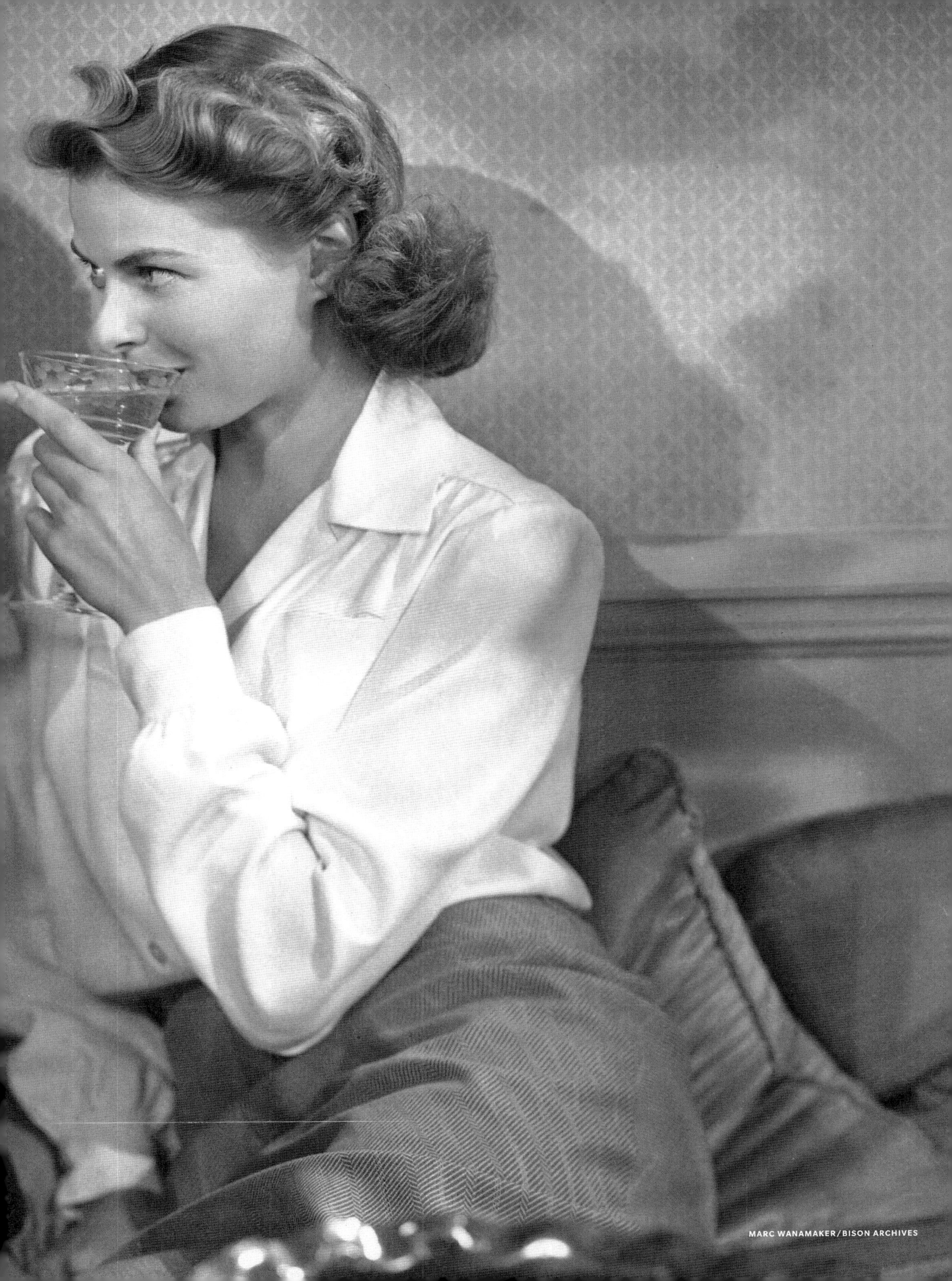

MARC WANAMAKER/BISON ARCHIVES

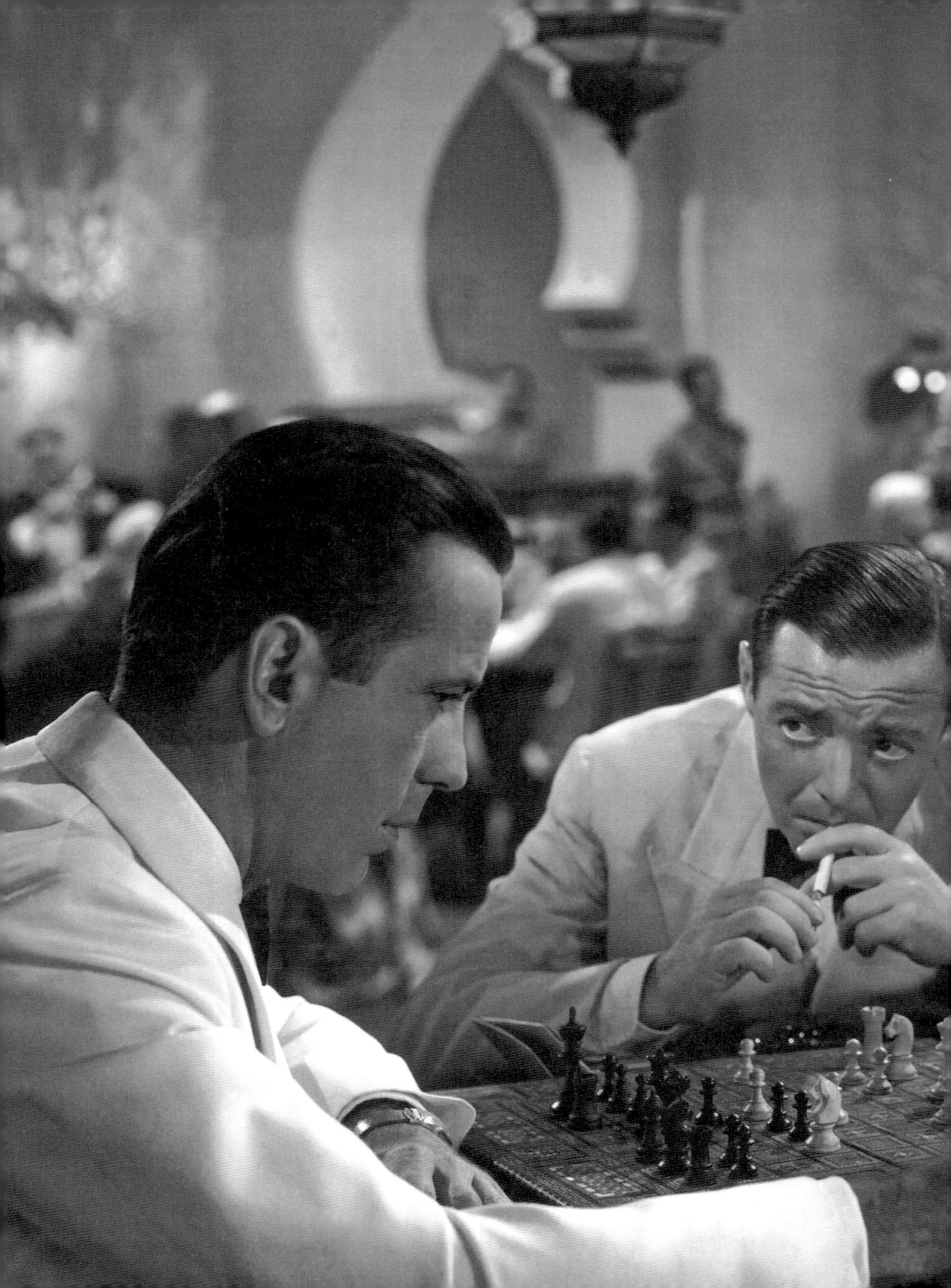

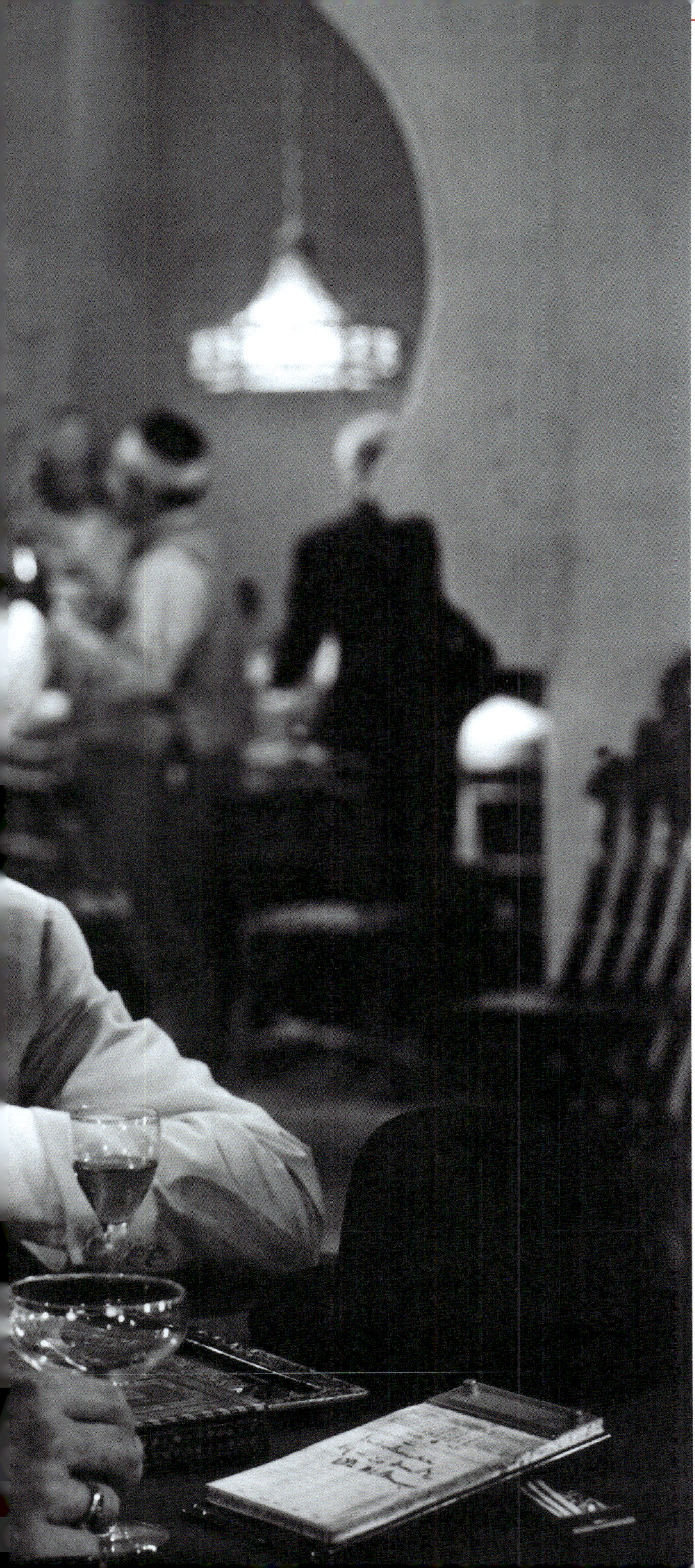

WARNER BROS./KOBAL/REX/SHUTTERSTOCK

"YOU DESPISE ME DON'T YOU?"

—Ugarte

"WELL, IF I GAVE YOU ANY THOUGHT I PROBABLY WOULD."

—Rick

GRANDMASTER BOGIE
Rick contemplates a solitary game of chess as he listens to Ugarte discuss the German couriers whose deaths set the plot in motion. Bogart, a chess fiend, played almost daily, and it was his idea to make Rick a devotee of the game. The match on the board in this scene was real—one Bogie had been playing against the brother of a Warner employee via the U.S. Postal Service. The two men sent letters and postcards to indicate their moves.

"PLAY 'LA MARSEILLAISE.' PLAY IT."

—Victor

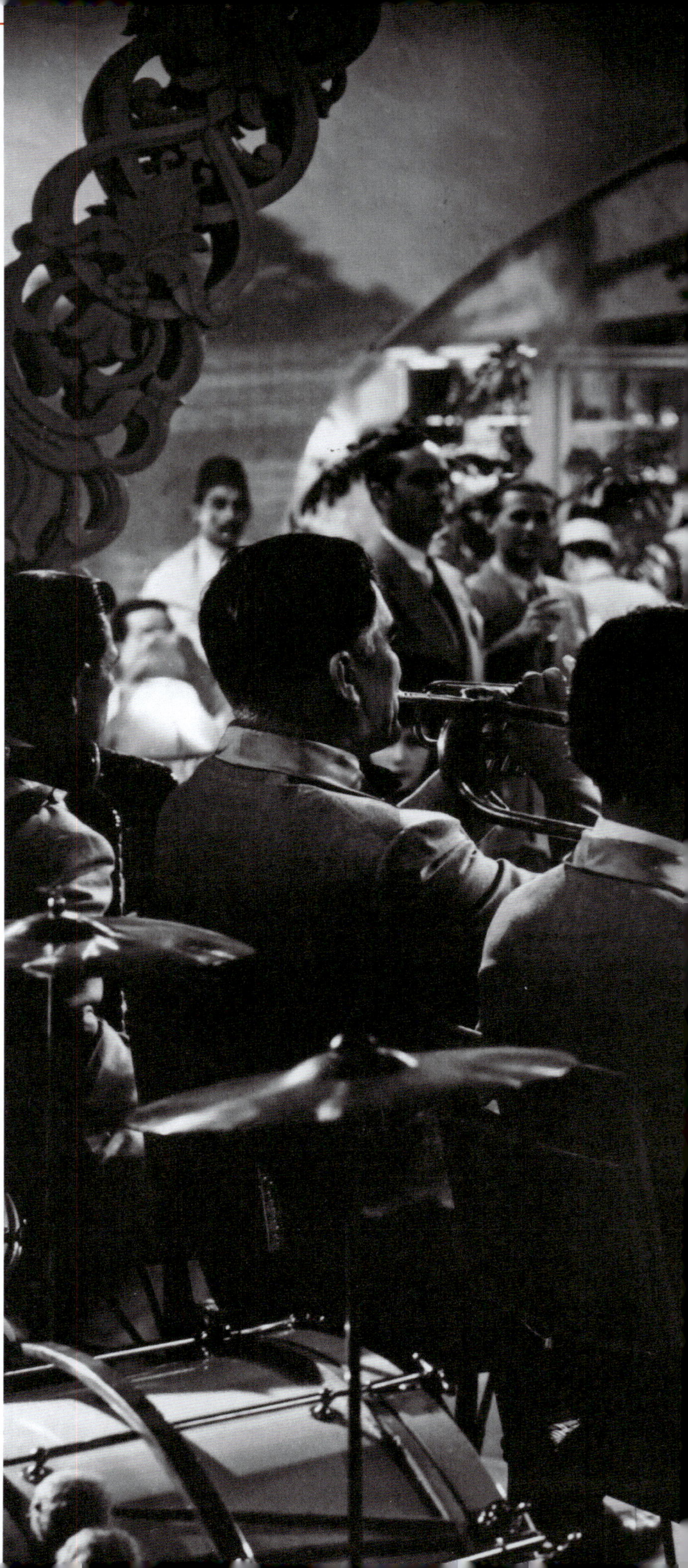

MPTVIMAGES

TAKING SIDES
Resistance fighter Victor Laszlo commands the café band to play "La Marseillaise" in response to Nazi patrons who are singing a patriotic German anthem. The musicians will proceed only with a signal from Rick, who until now has been neutral in the war. In a turning point for Bogart's character, he nods yes, suggesting his sympathies lie with the Allies. During the shoot, Bogart was called to the set and told to nod, but was not told what the gesture meant for the plot. The French anthem drowns out and silences the German song.

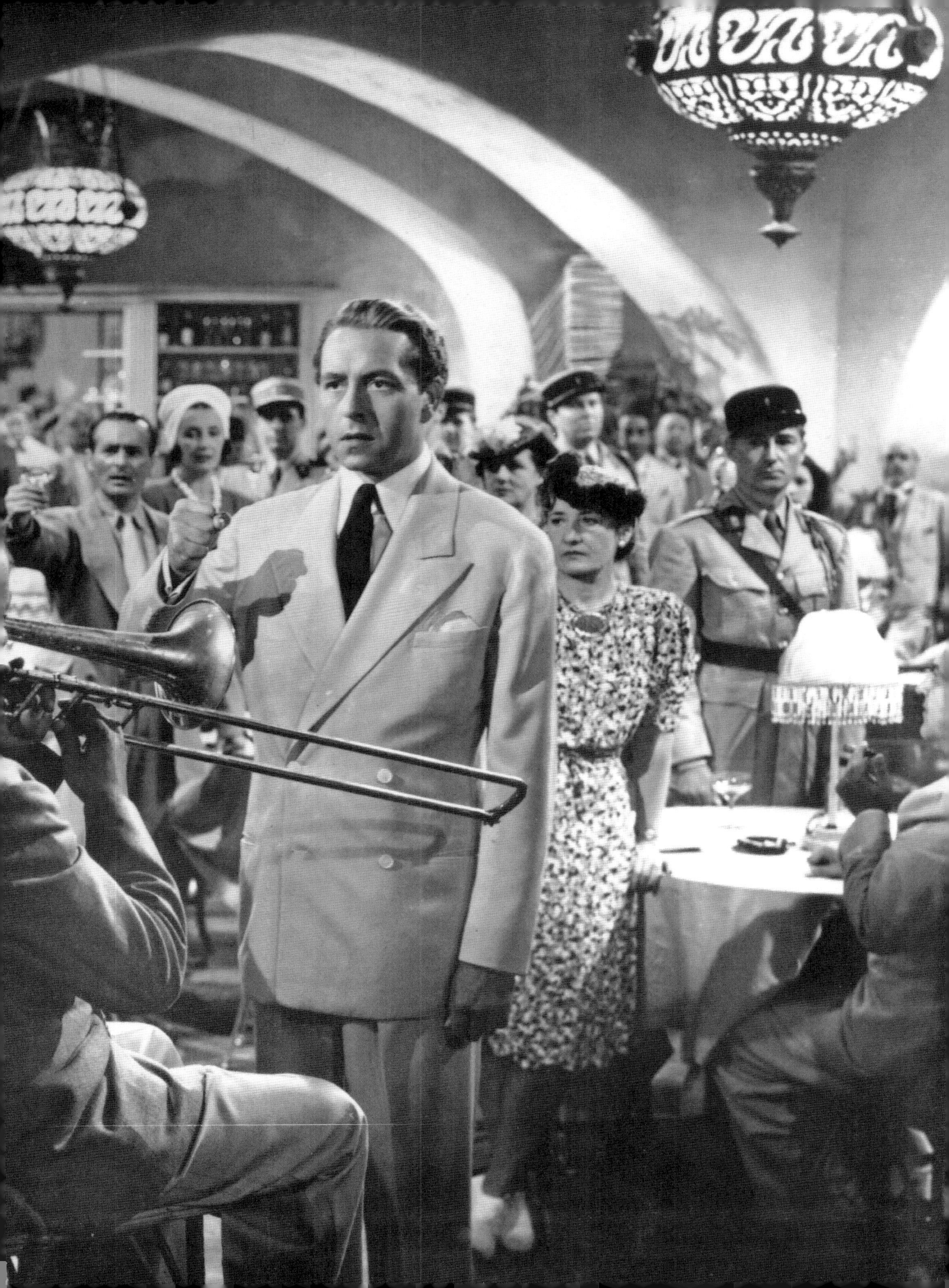

"OF ALL THE GIN JOINTS IN ALL THE TOWNS IN ALL THE WORLD, SHE WALKS INTO MINE."

—Rick

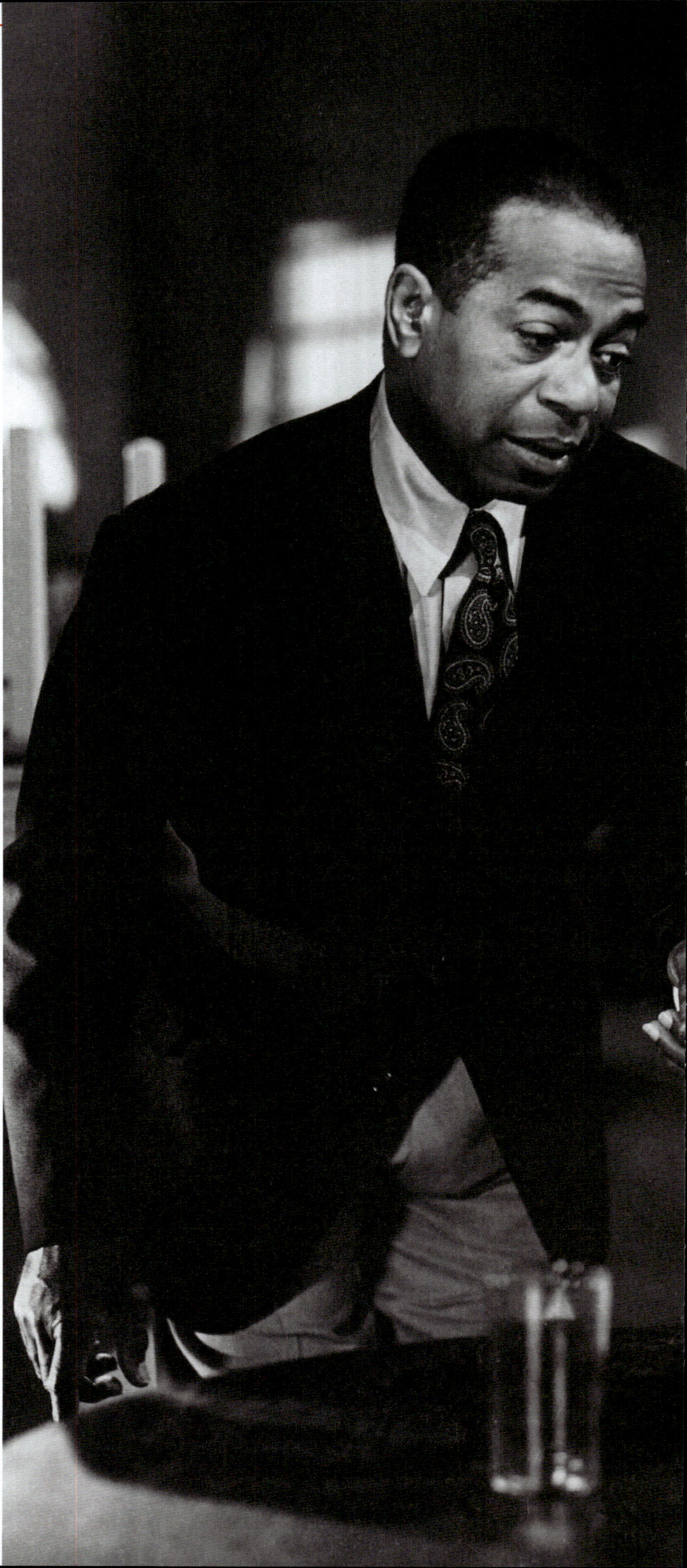

JACK WOODS/WARNER BROS./KOBAL/REX/SHUTTERSTOCK

NOTES ON SAM

Dooley Wilson, who plays Sam, here counsels a drunken Rick, who is distraught that Ilsa, who abandoned him in Paris, has shown up in Casablanca. Wilson was reportedly the only cast member who had visited the Moroccan city, but he may not have been the most qualified Sam. Wilson could drum and sing, but did not know how to play the piano. Another musician, Elliot Carpenter, was brought onto the set and placed just off camera so that Wilson could convincingly imitate his moves.

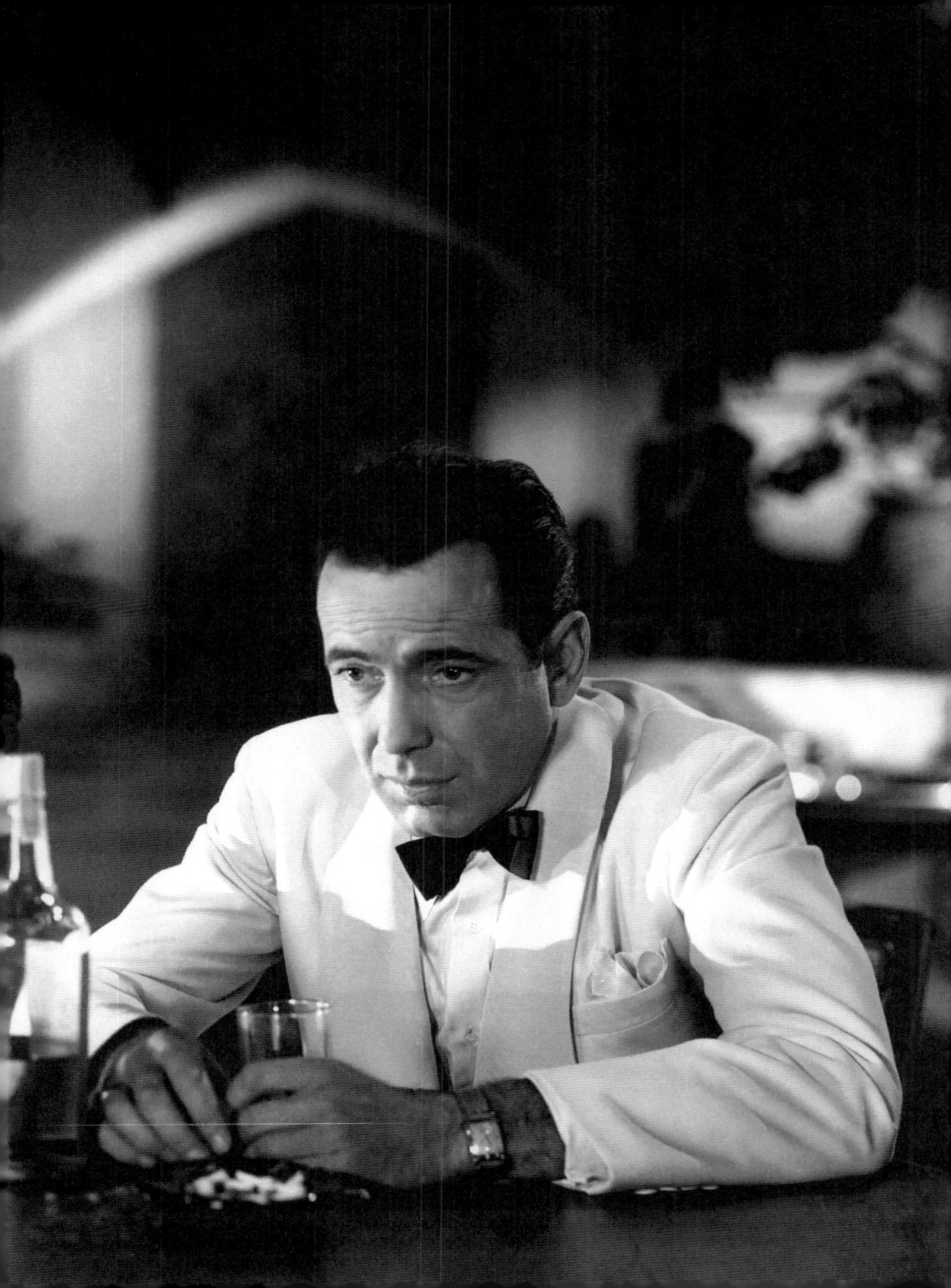

"AND REMEMBER, THIS GUN IS POINTED RIGHT AT YOUR HEART."
—Rick

"THAT IS MY LEAST VULNERABLE SPOT."
—Renault

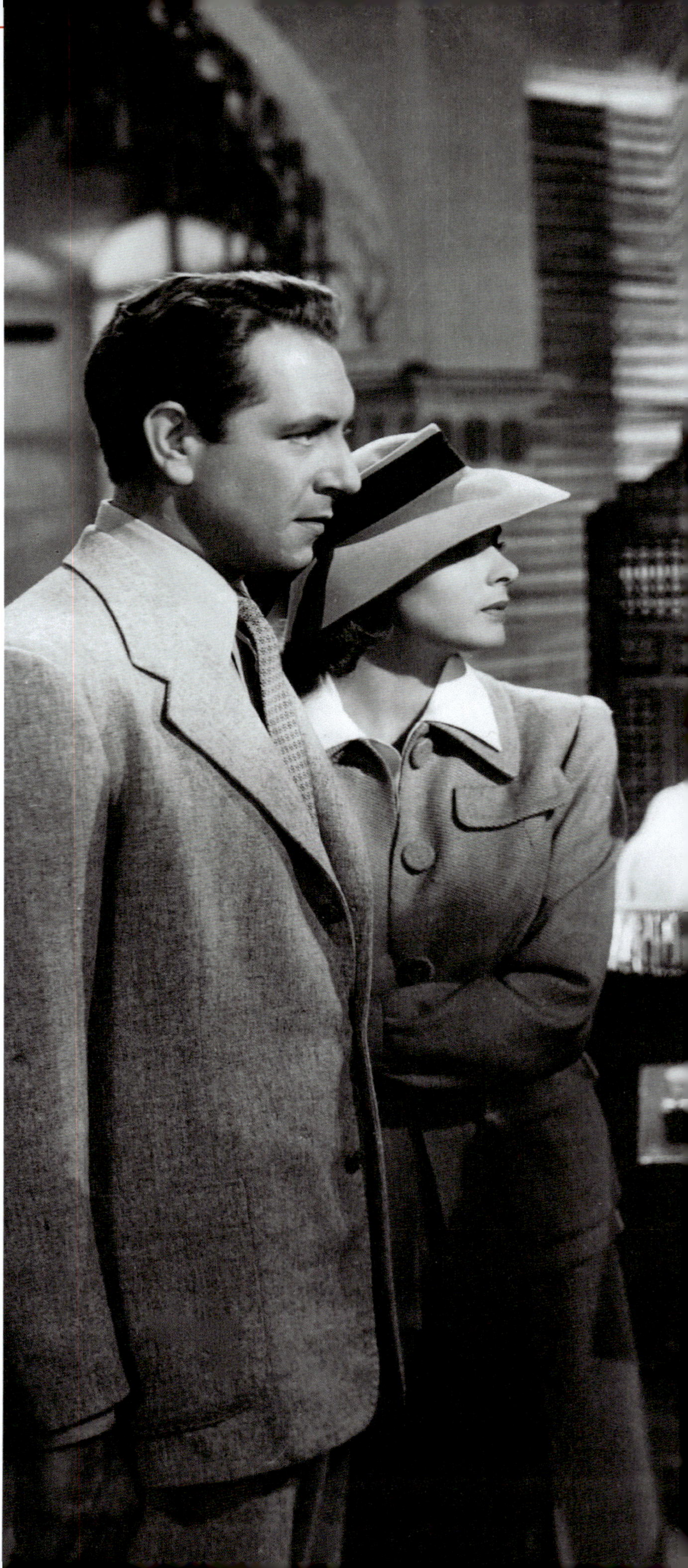

JACK WOODS/WARNER BROS./KOBAL/REX/SHUTTERSTOCK

PAPER CHASE
When Renault tries to arrest Victor and Ilsa for the death of two couriers whose letters of transit have mysteriously disappeared, Rick intervenes with a gun to save the couple. In real life, no such documents would have been necessary for safe passage out of Casablanca. The writers of *Everybody Comes to Rick's* invented the letters as a plot device to move the action along without distracting the audience.

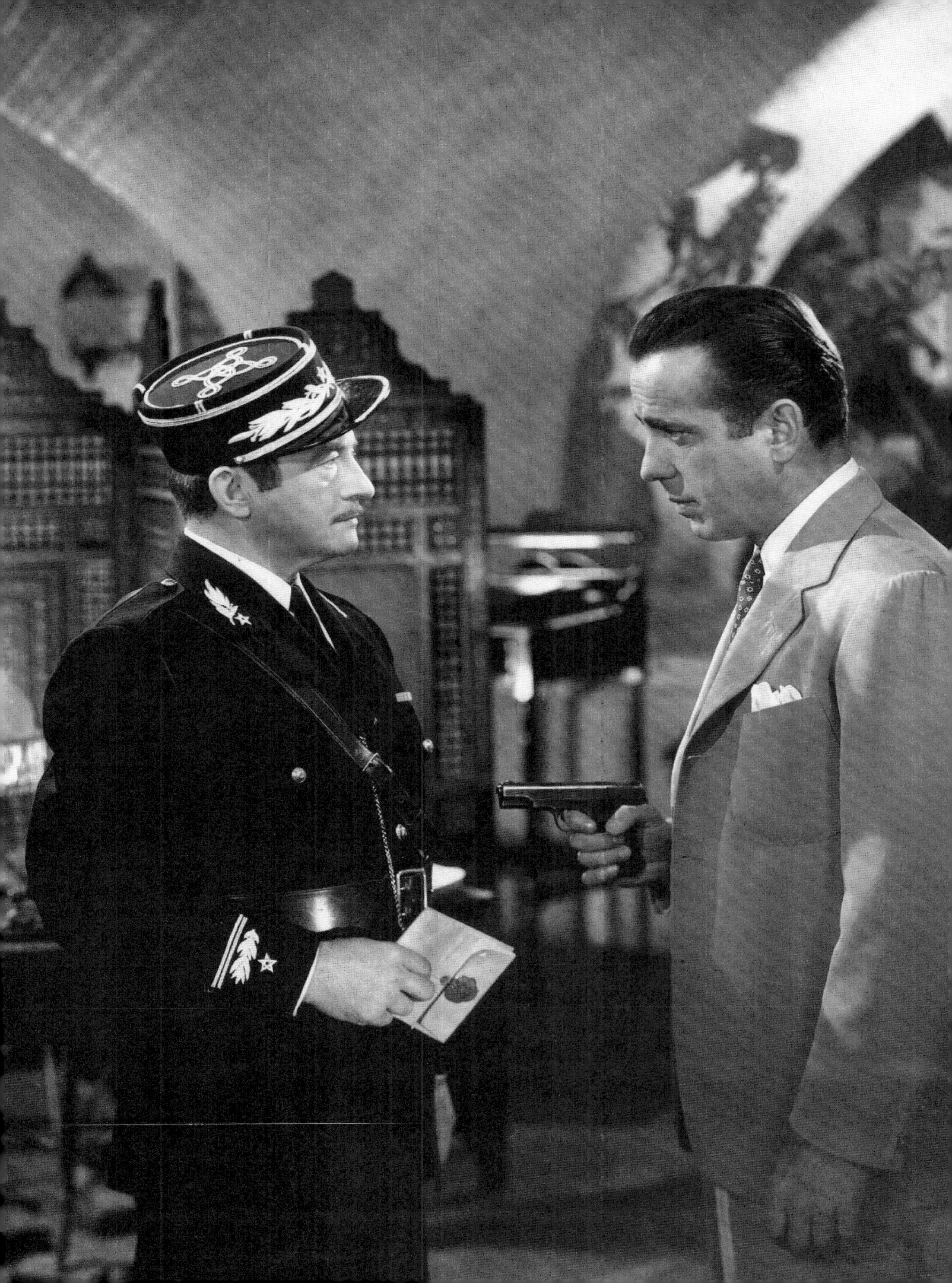

“WE’LL ALWAYS HAVE PARIS.”
—Rick

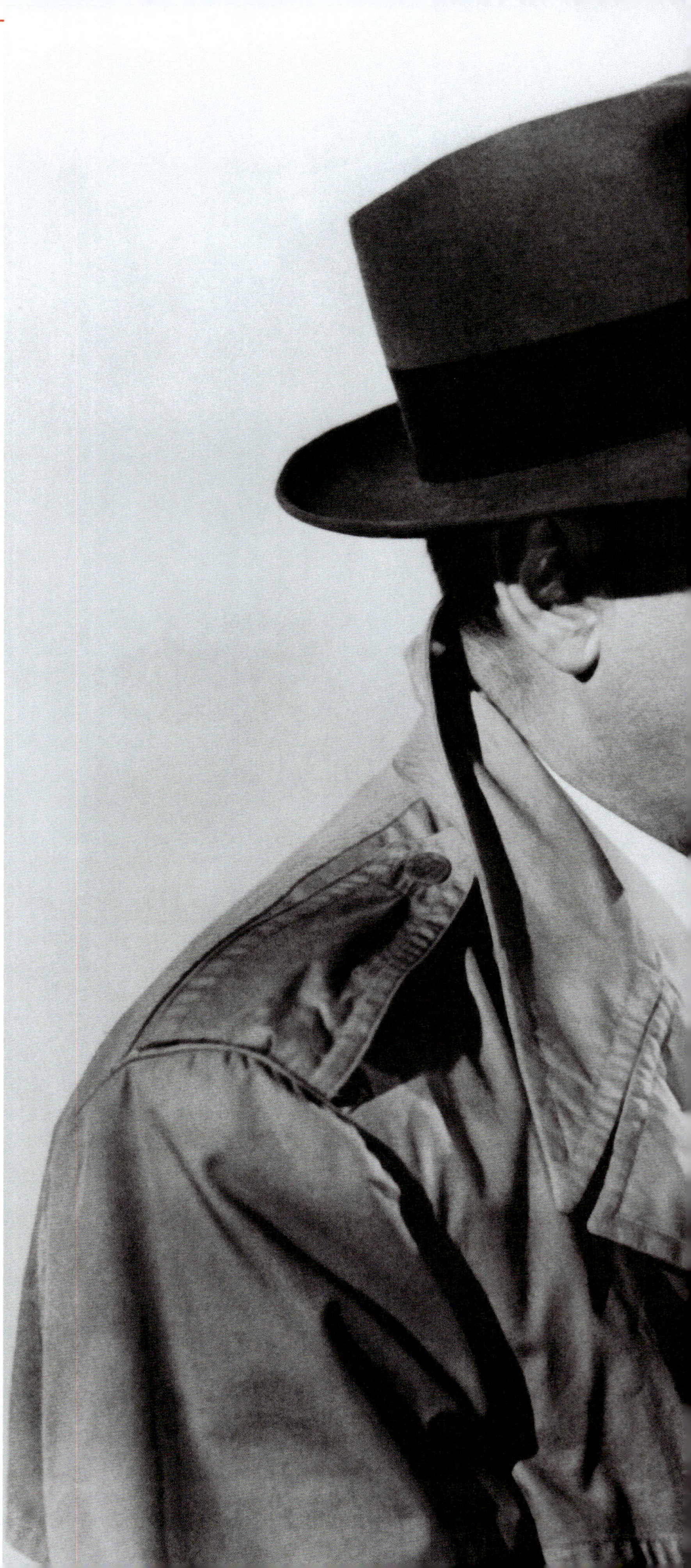

JACK WOODS/WARNER BROS./KOBAL/REX/SHUTTERSTOCK

GRAND ILLUSION
Having decided to let go of his love to further the Allied cause, Rick says his last goodbye to Ilsa on the tarmac as the plane for Lisbon waits to depart. The soundstage was too small to accommodate a real aircraft, so half- and quarter-size models of a Lockheed Electra 12A were built from plywood and balsa. To fudge the proportions, little people were hired to wear jumpsuits and move around the faux plane while a fog machine shrouded the set in mist.

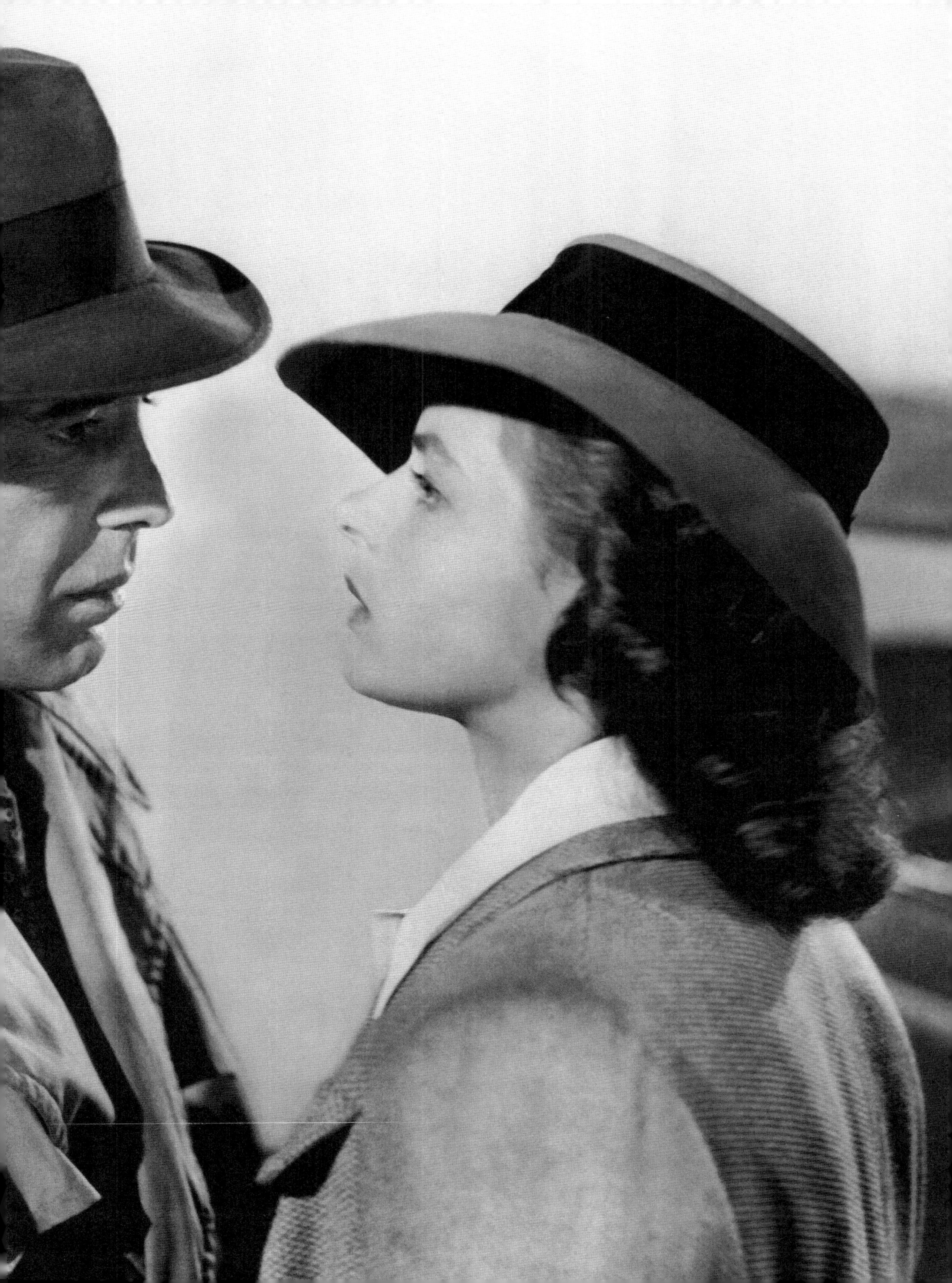

“MAJOR STRASSER HAS BEEN SHOT. ROUND UP THE USUAL SUSPECTS.”

—Renault

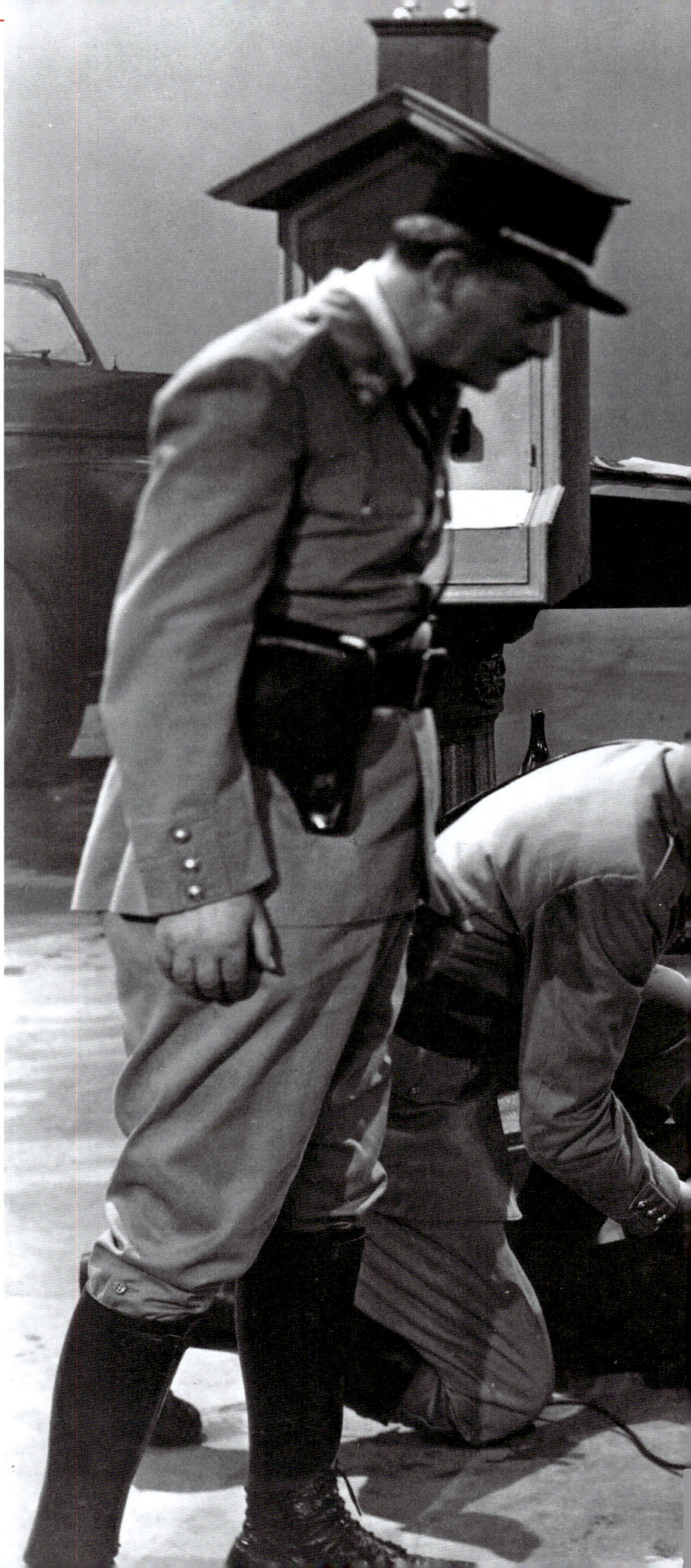
MARC WANAMAKER/BISON ARCHIVES

QUICK THINKING

In this penultimate and pivotal scene, Captain Renault sees Rick shoot Major Strasser, but Renault saves his friend by instructing police to "round up the usual suspects." Twin screenwriters Julius and Philip Epstein claimed they came up with the phrase simultaneously while stopped at a red light. *New Yorker* film critic David Denby called Renault's line "Major Strasser has been shot" the "single best use of the passive voice in movie history."

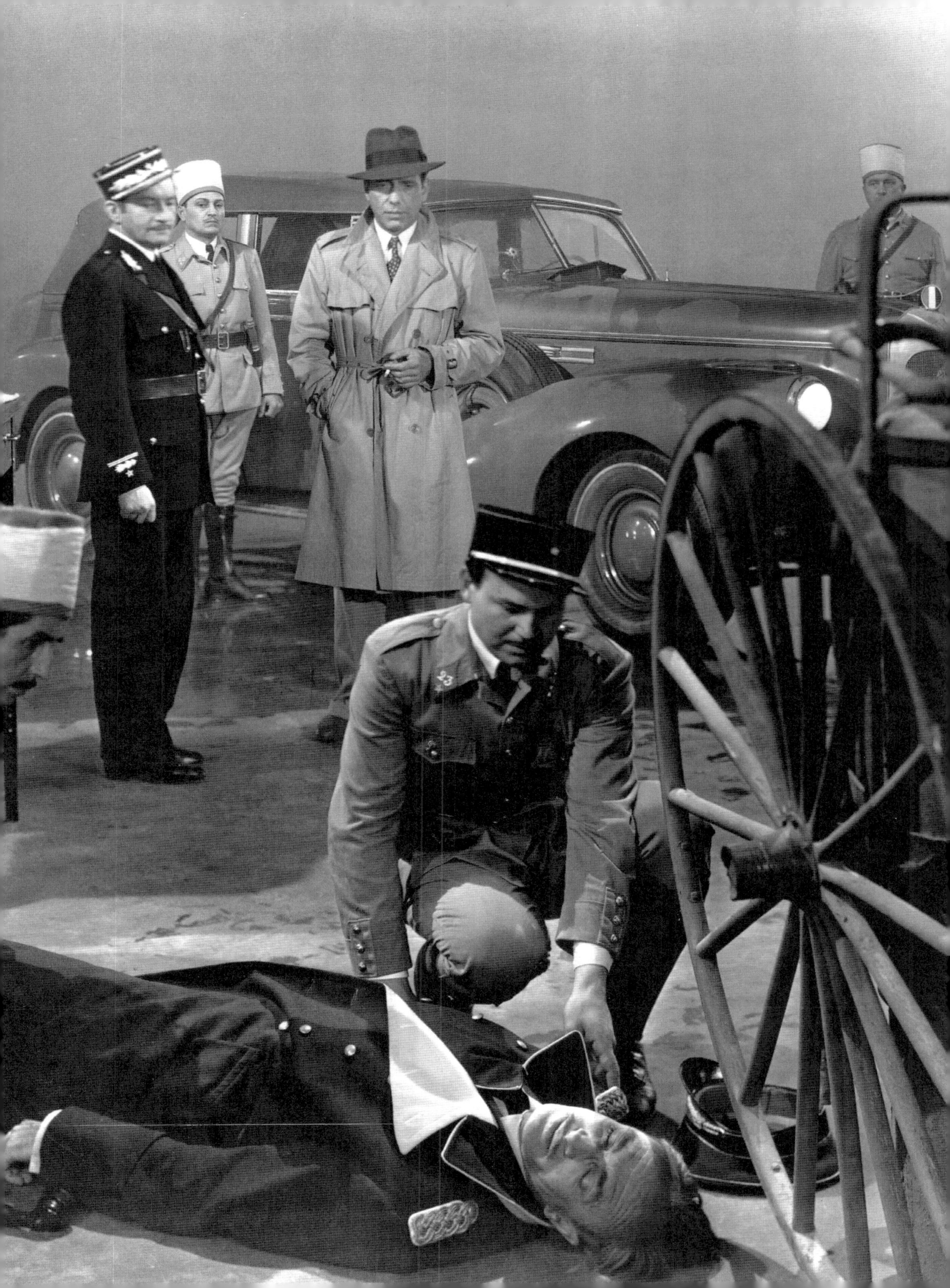

"LOUIE, I THINK THIS IS THE BEGINNING OF A BEAUTIFUL FRIENDSHIP."

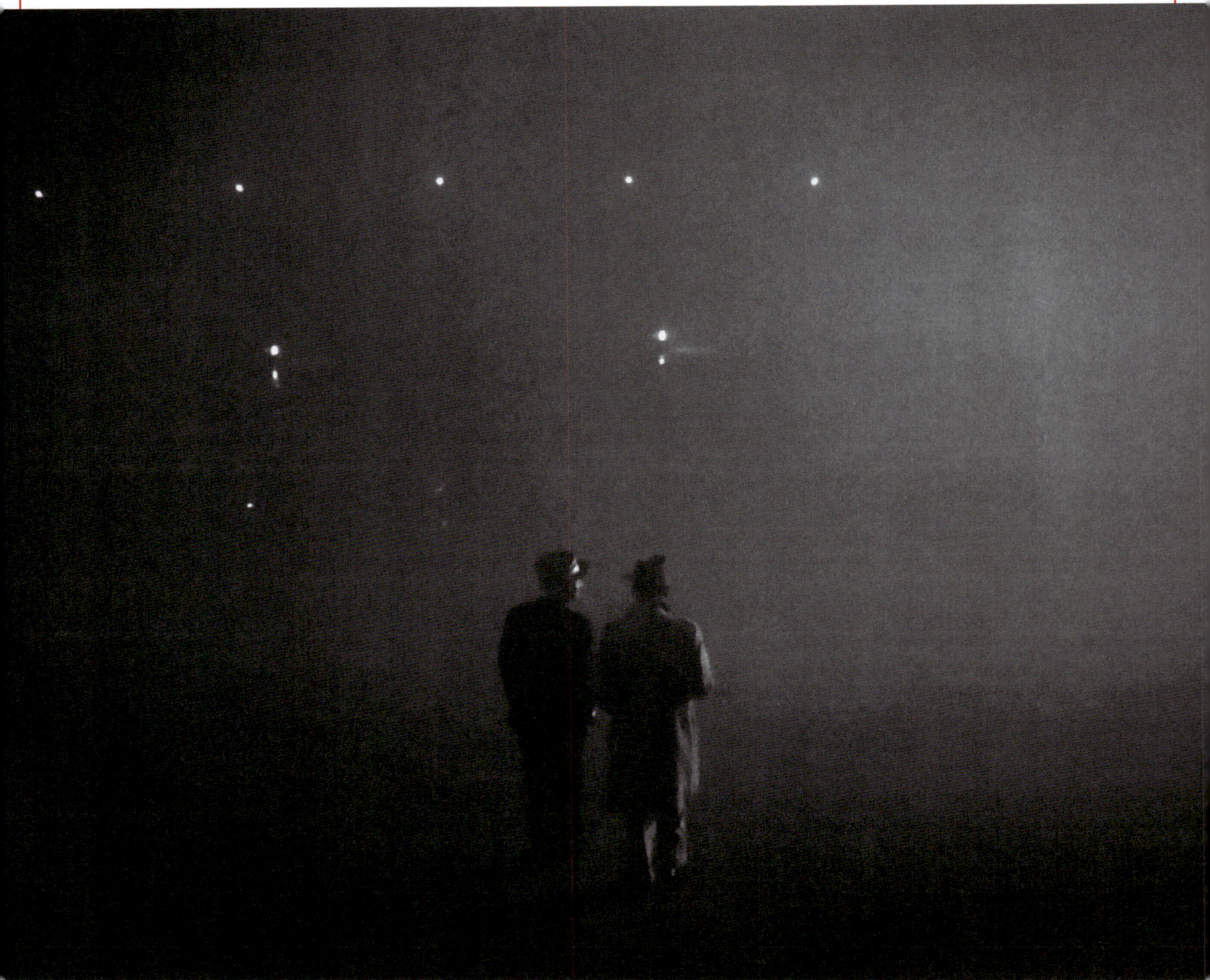

© WARNER BROS., COURTESY PHOTOFEST

A WALK IN THE DARK

Rick has lost everything. Ilsa and Victor have departed for Lisbon. Strasser is dead. Renault has come over to the good guys' side. And in his final bit of dialog, Rick declares that it is just the beginning—a line that came to producer Hal Wallis nearly three weeks after shooting finished. Bogart was called back to dub it in.

Printed in Great Britain
by Amazon

13789285R00056